Woolf Across Cultures

Woolf Across Cultures

Edited by Natalya Reinhold

2004

Pace University Press
New York

Copyright © 2004 by
Pace University Press
41 Park Row, Rm. 1510
New York, NY 10038

All rights reserved
Printed in the United States of America

ISBN: 0-944473-69-5

Contents

Abbreviations   viii

Preface
Natalya Reinhold   ix

Introduction
Natalya Reinhold
Virginia Woolf's Work in Russia: A Success Story of
2.5 Million Copies   1

I Home Thoughts from Abroad

Maria DiBattista
An Improper Englishwoman: Woolf as a World Writer   17

Peter Faulkner
Virginia Woolf and Modernism: New Approaches   33

Mark Hussey
Virginia Woolf in the U. S. A.   47

Marilyn Schwinn Smith
The Activist Pens of Virginia Woolf and Betty Friedan   63

II Translation

Makiko Minow-Pinkney
"The meaning on the far side of language":
Walter Benjamin's Translation Theory and
Virginia Woolf's Modernism   79

Myunhgee Chung
Mediating Virginia Woolf for Korean Readers   95

Hee Jin Park
Translation of Virginia Woolf in Korea   **111**

Galina Yanovskaya
Hermeneutic Lacunae and Ways of Dealing with them in
Translating *Mrs. Dalloway*   **121**

AnnMarie Bantzinger
Holland and Virginia Woolf: The Reception of Woolf's
Translated Work in the Netherlands   **131**

Hogara Matsumoto
Miyeko Kamiya's Reproduction of Modernist Writing Style:
Kamiya, Virginia Woolf, and The Problem of the
"Monstrous" Voice   **149**

III *Orlando* on an International Stage

Noriko Kubota
Orlando and Literary Tradition in Japan: Sex Change,
Dressing and Gender in *Torikaebaya Monogatari*   **167**

Julia Briggs
Constantinople: Virginia Woolf at the Crossroads of the
Imagination   **179**

Maria Cândida Zamith Silva
If Orlando Came to Portugal: Some Fantasies and
Considerations   **191**

Bilge Nihal Zileli
A Study of the Concept of Androgyny in Virginia Woolf's
Orlando   **203**

Natalya Solovyova
The National and "the Other" in the Biography of the
Creative Mind: *Orlando*   **215**

Deborah Epstein Nord
Androgyny, Writing, and Place in Woolf's *Orlando*, and
A Room of One's Own 227

IV Reading Russian—Russian Readings

Natalya Reinhold
"A railway accident": Virginia Woolf Translates Tolstoy 237

Galina Alekseeva
Tolstoy and the World of English Literature: A Survey of
Leo Tolstoy's Book Collection in Foreign Languages
in the Estate Museum, Yasnaya Polyana 249

Natalya Morzhenkova
The Cultural and Poetic Synthesis in Virginia Woolf's Texts 261

Natalia Povalyaeva
The Issue of Self-Identification in Woolf's
Mrs. Dalloway and Cunningham's *The Hours* 269

Christine Froula
The Play in the Sky of the Mind: Dialogue,
"the Tchekov method," and *Between the Acts* 277

Notes on Contributors 291

Index 297

Abbreviations

AROO	*A Room of One's Own*
BP	*Books and Portraits*
BTA	*Between the Acts*
CDB	*The Captain's Death Bed and Other Essays*
CE	*Collected Essays (4 vols.)*
CR1	*The Common Reader*
CR2	*The Common Reader, Second Series*
CSF	*The Complete Shorter Fiction*
D	*The Diary of Virginia Woolf (5 vols.)*
DM	*The Death of the Moth and Other Essays*
E	*The Essays of Virginia Woolf (4 Vols.)*
GR	*Granite & Rainbow: Essays*
JR	*Jacob's Room*
L	*The Letters of Virginia Woolf (6 Vols.)*
M	*The Moment and Other Essays*
MOB	*Moments of Being*
MD	*Mrs. Dalloway*
O	*Orlando*
PA	*A Passionate Apprentice*
TG	*Three Guineas*
TTL	*To the Lighthouse*
TW	*The Waves*
TY	*The Years*
TVO	*The Voyage Out*

Preface
Natalya Reinhold

This volume is based on the Virginia Woolf Across Cultures symposium which was held at the Russian State University for the Humanities (Moscow) and Leo Tolstoy Estate Museum Yasnaya Polyana (Tula Region) on 27 – 29 June 2003. The Woolf symposium shaped itself in the wake of a suggestion made by Jeanne Dubino, Secretary of the International Virginia Woolf Society, in Sonoma, CA during the Twelfth Annual Conference on Virginia Woolf.

From the very start the idea was to consider Woolf's work from a cross-cultural perspective (its Russian chapter has long been in need of scholarly investigation). Maria DiBattista and Peter Faulkner contributed to the embryonic idea of the symposium by suggesting the view of Virginia Woolf as a world writer, and by showing their interest in the reception, comparative and cross-cultural approaches to her work.

The symposium "Call for Papers," both mailed and e-mailed, invited Woolf scholars from different cultural and language contexts to contribute to the discussion of the cross-cultural dimension in lupine studies. The journey to Yasnaya Polyana and the symposium's closing panel on the estate grounds, highlighted in the program, promised a great chance to discuss the Russian chapter and the Tolstoy theme in Woolf's work in the special setting of Yasnaya Polyana.

During five days, from 26 to 30 June 2003, the Russian State University for the Humanities, and Leo Tolstoy Estate Museum Yasnaya Polyana hosted thirty scholars who came from all over the world, from Britain, Canada, Japan, Korea, the Netherlands, Portugal, Russia, and the United States. There were six panels and four plenary sessions on the symposium program. Maria DiBattista (Princeton University), Peter Faulkner (Exeter University, UK), Mark Hussey (Pace University, New York), and Julia Briggs (De Montfort University, UK) were featured speakers.

The three-day symposium program was densely packed with panel work, as well as cultural events. Two student-guided tours of the central part of Moscow on the day before the opening of the symposium and on the day after the event, gave the participants a chance not only to see St. Basil's and the Kremlin Cathedrals, but also to experience Moscow streets vibrant with young people's life. They visited the Moscow Arts Theatre, where a hundred years ago Chekhov saw his plays staged and which now bears his name. They studied the Rare Book exhibition arranged by the University librarians, which featured about seventy volumes of Russian poetry and literary criticism of the

Reinhold

1910s to 1930s, to provide a vivid cross-cultural parallel to the symposium agenda. They rushed to the Moscow house of Leo Tolstoy in Khamovniki on an excursion that made us laugh heartily at one point, and brought tears to our eyes at another, thanks to the talented and enlightened guidance of the English-speaking museum assistant. This excursion came as a useful introduction to the pivotal point of visiting Leo Tolstoy Estate Museum Yasnaya Polyana on the closing day. A train journey 200 km to the south of Moscow, a look and walk around Kozlova Zaseka, the railway station which still remembers Leo Tolstoy's departures and arrivals, the symposium panel arranged in the Volkonsky House and the excursion around the Tolstoys' house and the large estate grounds certainly made for a memorable day.

The articles collected here can hardly give the full flavor of the event. How can they possibly convey the idea of a hushed international audience of speakers under the stern look of classical statues and the busts of Greek philosophers in the University lecture room on the opening day? How can they communicate the feel of Christine Froula's paper read in the conference hall of the two hundred-year-old Volkonsky House in Yasnaya Polyana? How can they infect the reader with the everyday fun and despair at finding yourself at a loss in a foreign culture, which lacks those dear, nice little things that meet your eye at every corner in New York, London or Tokyo? Yet these articles nonetheless not only do credit to the symposium's many-faceted activities, both scholarly and cultural, but they convey something that is perhaps the most significant feature of the forum in question. Unlike a regular international conference which draws tens and hundreds of speakers, a symposium attracts a group of scholars who come together to discuss a certain issue or theme. What is good about symposia is that they allow you to listen to papers and then discuss them at leisure during the two or three days you spend together as a committed group. You become aware of the benefits of this arrangement later when preparing your paper for publication. Then the questions this or that particular speaker asked about your presentation over an unhurried cup of coffee or while walking around come back to you, putting a new light on your train of thought. At least, this is what happened at the Woolf Across Cultures symposium, and afterwards. The prospective authors made a special point of building on and updating their papers with a view to the questions put, and suggestions made. So the articles here differ substantially from the original papers. Yet another difference lies in the volume's much tighter grip on the reception and cross-cultural approaches to the work of Virginia Woolf. The latter became the major principle in selecting the articles for publication.

The reception and comparative strategies are by no means a novelty in Woolf studies. To limit myself to two examples, I would refer to *Virginia Woolf*

Preface

Out of Bounds: Selected Papers from the Tenth Annual Conference on Virginia Woolf (2001), with its section on "Intertexts and Contexts," and the recent *Reception of Virginia Woolf in Europe* (2002). Nonetheless, this volume of articles has a theoretical focus of its own. It combines cultural criticism with Translation Studies in its functional dimension. It addresses translation critically as part of the literature of a given period of time. It treats translation as a special type of activity that bears the imprint of the ideology of a certain society or social group. It considers translation from the point of view of parameters of translators' work in a certain country at a certain moment in the past or present. In short, a target or translated text is researched as an artifact produced by a certain social-cultural practice typical of a target culture and language. We assume that the study of target texts, that is, translations of Virginia Woolf's works, across cultures, can tell us something about the current state of minds. It can help us reveal the latent developments in a culture which otherwise have little chance to be spotted and analyzed. Of course, one should be very careful about making generalizations or drawing far-reaching conclusions. But if we are right in saying that translation is special, due to its close links with social-cultural practice, and indeed a translated text depends on the language and ideological codes typical of its time much more than the original, and this alone explains why translations are many, whereas the original is always in the singular, then the reverse holds: by studying translations we can judge of certain aspects of a culture of a given period.

To return to the *Woolf Across Cultures* volume, as much as the translation studies approach to translated works of Woolf's reveals in cultural contexts, no less does the cross-cultural and comparative perspective come up in Woolf's texts themselves. Woolf as a world writer, Woolf as a translator, Woolf as a social activist, Woolf as a contributor to the world literary tradition of sex and gender change—these are some of the discoveries made by our international authors. The major principle of selection thus was the correspondence of the article proposed to the key comparative-cum-translation studies, reception-cum-cultural criticism perspectives. This also accounts for the obvious regrouping of the papers compared to how they were listed in the symposium program. As for the key text, it turned out to be, for obvious reasons, *Orlando*, with its rich cross-cultural content.

The volume opens with Natalya Reinhold's introduction on "Woolf's Work in Russia: A Success Story of 2.5 Million Copies." Specifically on the Russian reception of Virginia Woolf's work, it nonetheless accentuates the symposium cultural space as foreign to most authors and thus provides a good ground for comparison. It also outlines, in a sketchy way, the issues of an open democratic society and the plurality of writing and reading modes: the issue

Reinhold

which the articles in the opening section on "Home Thoughts from Abroad" address in their provocative and rewarding ways. Maria DiBattista's article on "An Improper Englishwoman: Woolf as a World Writer" advocates the case for Woolf as belonging to the realm of world literature, not just to parochial waters. Peter Faulkner rounds up his survey of recent publications on Virginia Woolf and modernism by observing that "perhaps too we should be pressing ourselves ... to pay more attention to social and political history." As if in response to Faulkner's expectations that academics should make more of *A Room of One's Own* and *Three Guineas*, Marilyn Schwinn Smith offers a comparative study of the social-political agenda in the work of Virginia Woolf and Betty Friedan. In his powerful contribution on "Virginia Woolf in the U. S. A.," Mark Hussey emphasizes Woolf's "profoundly ethical stance toward democracy" as Leslie Stephen's moral legacy, and goes on to ponder "an open question [of] which Woolf will be received in new geographies."

The second section, with its umbrella-like heading "Translation," features six international authors, from Japan and Korea to the Netherlands and Russia, in pursuit of comparative and reception strategies in the study of Woolf's translated works. Makiko Minow-Pinkney embarks on a challenging project of identifying common points in the attitudes to language and meaning of Walter Benjamin and Virginia Woolf. Myunghee Chung and AnneMarie Bantzinger focus on the reception of Woolf's work in Korea and the Netherlands, providing invaluable information of the academics', critics' and common readers' responses to Woolf's work in translated form. Hee Jin Park tackles cultural and language difficulties a Korean translator of Woolf's prose faces. By pointing at the difference that exists between the hermeneutical mode of Woolf's novelistic discourse, and linear translations of her works, Galina Yanovskaia argues in favor of reading (and, for that matter, translating) Woolf's texts both at the narrative and meta-narrative levels. If Yanovskaia's approach requires a microscope, then Hogara Matsumoto's critical-comparative study of the fictional *Virginia Woolf's Autobiography* written by a renowned Japanese psychiatrist, Miyeko Kamiya, asks for cross-cultural bifocals that would allow the reader to find parallels between Kamiya's "oscillating" voice as a product of cultural ambivalence, and modernist subjectivity.

Section III invites us to consider "*Orlando* on an International Stage," and a truly international assembly of scholars it turns out to be. Every author brings a cultural dimension of her own to the discussion of *Orlando*, thus confirming its inexhaustibility, and proving cultures to respond differently to one and the same source text. Noriko Kubota argues in favor of *Orlando* as the first among Virginia Woolf's novels to be translated into Japanese, as early as 1931 thanks to the nine hundred year-old literary tradition in Japan of describing sex

Preface

change. Julia Briggs enhances her argument about imagination and genre in *Orlando* and *To the Lighthouse* by reminding the reader of Constantinople as standing on an East-West and North-South axis, thus dramatizing her scholarly piece through historical and political reminiscences. As if taking up the line of discussion on imagination, Maria Cândida Zamith Silva invites the reader to imagine what would happen if Orlando had come to Portugal on her/his way from Turkey to England, and this imaginary journey serves the author to highlight the specificity of the Portuguese response to the work of Virginia Woolf. Bilge Nihal Zileli's "Study of the Concept of Androgyny in Virginia Woolf's *Orlando*" accentuates the constraints the Turkish language imposes on the notion of gender. The Russian theme in *Orlando*, which is difficult to ignore, finds its interpretation in terms of "the national" and "the Other" in Natalia Solovyova's article on *Orlando* as a biography of the creative mind. "The moment when writing fiction takes over" comes as the pivotal point in Deborah Epstein Nord's article, which addresses the much-debated androgyny issue from the perspective of writing *per se*. Thus the section that first takes readers back to the twelfth-century Japanese literary tradition, finally lands us on the thorny path of current creative writing.

The closing section on "Reading Russian/Russian Readings" provides a groundbreaking, open ending to this volume. For the first time the Russian theme, so indisputably and vividly alive in Virginia Woolf's work, features adequately. Opening with Natalya Reinhold's article on Virginia Woolf's translations from the Russian, the section ramifies, in Galina Alekseeva's survey, to Leo Tolstoy's book collection in Yasnaya Polyana. It extends in Natalia Morzhenkova's article to a vast cultural milieu of allusions to myths and artifacts as found in Woolf's texts. It shrinks to a comparative study of self-identification in Woolf's *Mrs. Dalloway* and Cunningham's *The Hours* in Natalia Povalyaeva's contribution. Breathless and amazed at the rash flight across facts and artifacts, the reader is left looking up at "The Play in the Sky of the Mind," which Christine Froula expertly performs by bringing together "the Tchekov method" and *Between the Acts*.

Obviously, the editing of such an internationally-bound volume could not have been possible without the Internet, and almost every author glued to his or her computer screen for several days at a time. Yet the crucial condition for the successful shaping and editing of this volume was a great sense of goodwill and cooperation among the participants. Pipe-line paperwork went from Japan to Russia to the States, and back to Korea via Holland. Messages flew from Lancashire to Moscow, from Minsk to Portugal, from Nizhny Novgorod to the States and back to Kaliningrad via Turkey. The person on the other side of the Atlantic who bore the brunt of editing, and whom I have found to be one hun-

Reinhold

dred per cent reliable, tolerant and patient, with his sharp critical eye always open, is Mark Hussey. To him go my deepest thanks and admiration.

As for the event that lies at the core of this volume, the Woolf Across Cultures symposium, it became possible thanks to the help and generous financial assistance of individuals and organizations. Cordial thanks to Maria DiBattista and Andrew McNeillie for their letters of support. Special thanks to Yurii Afanasyev, President of the Russian State University for the Humanities, and to Natalia Bassovskaia, a University Vice-Rector. Great thanks to the Open Society Institute (Soros Foundation, Russia), and its President, General Director of the Russian State Library for Foreign Literature, Ekaterina Genieva. Deepest thanks to Vneshtorgbank (Bank for Foreign Trade, Russia), and its Chairman and CEO Andrei Kostin.

Great thanks to Vladimir Ilyich Tolstoy, Director of the Leo Tolstoy Estate Museum Yasnaya Polyana, to Galina Alekseeva, Museum Research Department senior assistant, and to Alla Polosina, Research Department assistant, for their collaboration and help in co-organizing the symposium.

Many thanks to Galina Belaya, Director of the Institute of Philology and History, RSUH, Nikolai Anastasyev, Director of the Publishing House *Kultura*, and Igor Shaitanov, the Literary Secretary of the Booker Prize Committee (Russia), for their professional assistance and help.

Special thanks go to the Steering Committee members, and my dear colleagues Galina Serebriakova, Maria Smirnova, Grigorii Kruzhkov, Aleksei Bagrintsev, and Olga Sudakova. Great thanks to the organizers of the Rare Book Exhibition in the RSUH Reading Rooom, Tatyana Rybina and Yevgeniia Gorbunova. My hearty thanks to Irina Zubanova, for her immaculate work as the conference interpreter.

Millions of thanks to the students of the Translation Studies Department, who went out of their way preparing the symposium materials and hosting the international community of guests and speakers: Olga Adamova, Katya Adamovich, Natasha Kholnova, Anya Bakanina, Tanya Kuzmenko, Olga Markina, Karina Sigalova, Alisa Averchenko, Natasha Issaeva, Yurii Morozkin, and many more whose names would run into pages.

Personal thanks go to Sergey Anton Reinhold, without whose everyday care and support this project would have never been conceived and realized.

Introduction

Virginia Woolf's Work in Russia: A Success Story of 2.5 Million Copies
Natalya Reinhold

On a murky November afternoon in 2002, amidst the turmoil of arranging the Woolf Across Cultures symposium, I started making up a list of Russian translations of Woolf's works published over the last twenty years or so. Taking down the books from the shelves and thumbing through them, I could not help spotting the numbers of copies issued (they are normally recorded, against most countries' publishing practice, on the covers of Russian books). Some numbers surprised me, others made me suspicious—so incredible they looked. Hurriedly I began jotting down the figures on a scrap of paper and summing them up. Simple counting produced the total number of 2.5 million copies of Russian translations of Woolf's works issued from 1978 to 2002, with about two million copies published under *perestroika*, between 1988 and 1993. Unbelievable! How could a success story of 2.5 million Russian copies become possible? I asked myself. For a success story it seemed to be.

A mere flashback, however, will tell us that this is not exactly the case. The story is far from being a blissful chronicle of the steady growth of Russian publishers' and readers' interest in the work of Virginia Woolf over a certain period of time. Its beginning will take us back, to the early 1930s, and make us work through some specifically Russian circumstances of the reception of Woolf first in the former Soviet Union, and then in Russia in the 1990s. It is the dramatic change from complete silence to the explosion in the form of 2.5 million copies that I am going to describe and analyze here.

It is logical to consider the reception of Virginia Woolf in Russia (the former Soviet Union) in a broader comparative perspective. Was her case the same as the case of D. H. Lawrence? Joyce? E. M. Forster (to limit ourselves to novelists alone)? When we turn to facts, we discover several translations of D. H. Lawrence's works published in the mid-twenties.[1] Extended fragments from *Ulysses* had appeared in Soviet periodicals in 1925 and 1935-1936 before the ban was lifted in England in 1936.[2] *Dubliners* was translated and published in book form in 1927.[3] Two different translations of *A Passage to India* by E. M. Forster came out in 1927 and 1937.[4] If we throw our net a bit wider, we shall even catch such queer fish as the Soviet translations of *Lady into Fox* and *A Man in the Zoo* by David Garnett,[5] to say nothing of Aldous Huxley.[6] Obviously, English modernist fiction did not go untranslated[7] and uncommented on[8] in the 1920s and 1930s. Yet there is no trace of work by Virginia Woolf.

The absence of her name from the translators' and publishers' lists of the mid-twenties looks surprising, for the years from 1923 till 1927, between the end of the civil war and the beginning of the Stalinist regime, saw the revival of translation and publishing in Moscow and Leningrad. A combination of three circumstances seemed to work against the possibility of having Virginia Woolf's work translated into Russian in the mid-twenties, alongside the novels by D. H. Lawrence and short stories of Joyce. Apart from the obvious complications caused by the October revolution of 1917 and the civil war of 1918-1921, there was one cultural difference in the reception of Woolf's writing as compared to that of Joyce or D. H. Lawrence. The Russian literary avant-garde was prominently strong in the 1910s, and it is against its background that Joyce and Lawrence had established their reputations as European experimental writers of merit long before any of Virginia Woolf's pieces of new writing of the 1920s could have become known to the Russian public.

The complete silence with which Woolf's name was surrounded in the 1920s and 1930s looks particularly striking when viewed against the background story of translation in Russia. Historically, translated works have always been highly acceptable among Russian readers. The European norm of reading foreign texts in the original has not taken root in Russia, and the scale on which works in foreign languages are translated into Russian is amazing.[9] The fact that there had not been published a single translation of Woolf's work until 1978 testifies to some indirect kinds of limitations on her reception in the former Soviet Union. General observations on the ideological constraints, which allegedly worked against publishing modernists, will not do in this special case.

A closer look into the circumstances of the reception of Virginia Woolf in the USSR in the 1920s and 1930s highlights one particular work of criticism which, I claim, proved to be instrumental in establishing the writer's reputation in Soviet arts and literary criticism. This is the well-known *Intelligentsia* by Dmitri Mirsky. Originally written in Russian and published in 1934 soon after his coming back to the Soviet Union, the book was quickly translated into English.[10] It is a clear exposition of Mirsky's critical view of intellectual life in Britain interpreted in terms of a specifically Russian phenomenon of "intelligentsia" as the response of the educated classes to social developments of the early twentieth century. Mirsky also made a detailed survey of contemporary English arts, including the Bloomsbury Group and Virginia Woolf. Mirsky's book, I argue, played a crucial role in the reception of Woolf in the Soviet

Introduction

Union for decades to come. We shall better understand why it so happened if we analyze Mirsky's text from the point of view of its "voice."

The source text accurately rendered into English leaves the impression of a purged one. The discourse splits into three voices. The observer gives us facts of social and literary life in Britain in the 1920s and early 1930s, allowing the reader a short cut to Mirsky's special experience as a Russian scholar and literary critic who had been active on the English literary stage for twelve years. We also hear the voice of a sharp critic, and his unbiased judgments of English writers. And there rises the shrill foreign voice of a censor who finds it necessary to insert into every paragraph a trite set of communist ideological clichés like, "The beginning of the world crisis and a decisive intensification of the crisis of British capitalism" (Mirsky 108), "a thin-skinned humanism for enlightened and sensitive members of the capitalist class" (Mirsky 113), "the parasitic cream of the bourgeoisie" (Mirsky 118) and "all those decadent individualistic and introspective currents of thought" (Mirsky 108). Let us not forget about the high reputation D. S. Sviatopolk-Mirsky had enjoyed (and still rightly enjoys) among Western scholars and critics.[11] It explains why the Stalinist censors would have never missed a chance to use Mirsky's book for their own political purposes. But it also accounts for the fact that his evaluation of Virginia Woolf and the Bloomsbury Group, thus censured and ideologically spun, stuck for the next forty years.

Mirsky would have hardly figured that his neat description of Bloomsbury and its "principal figures," with their "basic trait" of "a mixture of philosophic rationalism, political rationalism, estheticism, and a cult of individuality" (Mirsky 112) would last till the year 2003 when Russian graduate students would use his critical judgment in their dissertations without acknowledgement (its origin having been long lost in the KGB files and its author forgotten by their senior colleagues). But what Mirsky probably would never have envisaged and put up with are the gross ideological aberrations to which his comments on the Bloomsbury Group and Virginia Woolf, in particular, had been subjected both at the time of their publication, and afterwards. They concerned aesthetics, the Russian influence, and feminism.

Mirsky stressed "minutest inner experiences" (Mirsky 113) and "psychological hair-splitting" (Mirsky 117) as the major aesthetic priorities of the Bloomsbury Group. He was indeed the first among English-speaking critics to mention and expand on the influence Dostoevsky and Chekhov had on Virginia Woolf: "[she] created her own method, a lyrical exposition of her leading characters—what might be described as an esthetisation of the method used by Chekhov in *The Three Sisters*" (Mirsky 117).[12] And he was sharp enough to highlight the gender theme in Woolf's work: "Having 'one's own room'... is,

3

so we are informed by a book written by Virginia Woolf on the emancipation of women, the first condition of civilized creative work" (Mirsky 114). Each of the three above quoted judgments was given an ideological spin by Soviet censorship.

The Bloomsbury interest in "minutest inner experiences" and "psychological hair-splitting" in Woolf's work turned out to be "the suffering" "wrapped up in self-contained rhythms and sublimated from the world of reality to a world of aesthetics" (Mirsky 118). Woolf's writing was defined as an art with a "narcotic function," "a new and more perfect form of dope" (Ibid.). To Soviet propaganda the use of such labels signaled one of the Stalinist ideological bogeys—"art for art's sake." Once stuck, the label stamped the writer as a hopeless case. Literature under a totalitarian regime has only one function—to serve the people.

The influence of Dostoevsky and Chekhov was also given a "political" spin. Mirsky, or rather a censor's foreign voice, called Dostoevsky "a supreme embodiment of introspection" (Mirsky 108), while in Chekhov the Bloomsbury Group "had found a Russian writer who was completely bourgeois, completely devoid of those distressing rough corners in which, as a result of serfdom, Russian writers used to abound" (Mirsky 115).

Even women's emancipation (the theme that could have made Woolf's essays interesting to the Soviet readership who were oriented toward reshaping the social role of women) was substantially reduced in value by Mirsky's description of the "feminist movement" of the 1910s as "hysterical and abnormal" (Mirsky 27 - 28).

Viewed against such crude aberrations, Mirsky's estimation of Virginia Woolf as "the principal literary expression of Bloomsbury" and "unquestionably a great artist" (Mirsky 117) reads as a piece of comical exaggeration. Anyway, all parts of this caricature portrait must have come together in a provisional censor's mind making up the image of an aesthete woman writer, pathologically introspective, focused on minutest shades of physical and mental suffering. It was enough to take Virginia Woolf off the list of prospective English writers in 1934, and for decades to come. True, there was a feeble attempt to restore the name of Virginia Woolf in the Russian public consciousness in 1937 by printing Jack Lindsay's article "Virginia Woolf,"[13] yet it could not outweigh D. S. Mirsky's knowledgeable exposition.[14] The case of Virginia Woolf could be considered as well as closed. The unwelcome label of aesthete had stuck to her name. Mirsky was repressed in the gulag in 1939, his name fallen into oblivion.

I found an indirect proof of Woolf's's work being blacklisted by the Stalinist authorities many years since, in 1983, while editing her essays on

Introduction

Russian writers for the Moscow journal *Voprosy Literatury*. I discovered then that the 1950 edition of *The Captain's Death Bed and Other Essays* was kept in the so-called special depository of the Lenin State Library in Moscow, and in order to have a glimpse of it you had to provide yourself with a strong certificate testifying to your Soviet residence and a solid job. Unlike the woman speaker in *A Room of One's Own* who was stopped by a gentleman on the threshold of the famous library and denied entrance (*AROO* 11), I did get the necessary letters of reference and enter the quiet chilly corridors of the library special depository. In the room with high barren walls there were a few tables with a dozen readers sitting at them. No one spoke in one's normal voice—you had to whisper. When at last I opened the arrested book, I nearly burst out laughing—so absurd the situation seemed to me. Yet if you think of it, what can better express the subversive character of Woolf's writing? I have recently checked the book—it is still there, though the special depository is now called "Works of limited access."

To go back to the 1940s, it seems few Russian scholars, if any, heard about Virginia Woolf in the next twenty years. Interestingly, the 1962 edition of *Kratkaia literaturnaia entsiklopediia* [Concise Companion to World Literature] gave the wrong date and location of Virginia Woolf's death: "31. III. 1941. Frantsia" [31 March 1941, France].[15] It seems there were no experts around to verify the biographical data.

Limitations on the reception of modernist writers, in general, and Virginia Woolf, in particular, were finally set in the 1950s through the elaboration of a Marxist approach towards Western modernism. Lukács's works served as a theoretical background and a set of guidelines.[16] However, the name of Georg Lukács was not publicized; his works were rather used as a secret piece of sectarian knowledge that was accessible to the apostles of Marxist faith alone than widely circulated among Soviet literary scholars. Yet it is largely with an eye to Lukács's view of modernism as is explicated in his "Ideology of Modernism"[17] that the Soviet methodology of treating realism as a positive alternative to modernism shaped itself in the 1960s in the works of such theorists as Georgii Fridlender.[18] The black-and-white concept of modernism as opposed to realism had become central in Soviet studies of English modernist writers, Woolf included. In a recent interview, Dr. Ekaterina Genieva, President of the Open Society Institute (Soros Foundation, Russia) and the General Director of the Russian Library for Foreign Literature stated that the term "modernism" had been used as a synonym of the anti-humanist and anti-realist trends in arts as late as 1990:

Reinhold

Modernism is another interesting Soviet notion. Today I can use it without getting a nasty feeling of tension inside me. But if we were talking in 1988-1990 I would have done everything possible to avoid using the term. For as soon as you defined this or that work as a modernist text it would mean that you had labeled the thing for good as anti-humanist, anti-aesthetical, anti-something. It is now when the twentieth-century arts dynamic had been analyzed, and the cobwebs swept away, and the periods defined and thoroughly researched that it became clear there was nothing wrong about modernism. Today everyone knows that modernism is a certain trend in arts which emerged for certain particular reasons. It is identified through certain particular features. It creates—I am intentionally using the verb "creates" instead of the trite Soviet term "reproduces"—it re-creates life through myth-making. And there is nothing intrinsically wrong about doing it this way. But they did think it then to be wrong! They were absolutely convinced of it being downright wrong. Those were the times when a word spoken could do away with human life. You realize that a whole constellation of brilliant Soviet translators gave up their lives because they were engaged in translating the works of D. H. Lawrence, Dos Passos, Joyce—whoever...You know they were sent to gulag[19]— for their cosmopolitanism, modernism, and they never came back. So this seemingly innocent notion of modernism did not simply sound but it resonated with all its might. It reminded you of your being squashed between the hammer and the anvil.[20]

Yet the short-lived "ottepel"[21] of the early 1960s also brought about some minor but pregnant changes in the reception of Woolf by academia. Her novels were classified as "psychological";[22] her essays on Russian writers (first identified by D. S. Mirsky thirty years earlier) were referred to, however critically,[23] and her method of writing was found to be akin to impressionism in European painting of the turn of the century. The doublespeak about Virginia Woolf as an official case of a minor suicidal author, on the one hand, and an impressionist novelist, poet of the romantic "moments of being," on the other, emerged among the Soviet anglicists in the mid-1970s as a conflation of ideological clichés and Russian love of arts, French impressionism in particular. (This inadequate conflated image would color the Russian translations of Woolf's work.) From the interview with Dr. Genieva:

> Woolf's writing is of the type that they in the 1970s would call aesthetic, highbrow, useless, leading nowhere but to that very lighthouse, that is, to one's own self. It is about the infinite quest for the heaven and hell in one's psyche. In the Soviet Union at that time it was indeed the hallmark of new writing. Though it came to us after an absurd fifty-year long procrastination, as late as 1986, 1987, or 1990.

Introduction

As the end of the 1970s was approaching, it became clear that translations of modernists' works were underway. It took the joint effort of the younger generation of literary scholars, critics and translators, with whom "nostalgia for world culture," to use Osip Mandelstam's formula of acmeism,[24] had always been great, to breach the wall of ideological aberrations and taboos. After many years' procrastination, Woolf's works came to the Russian reader.

The first translations, however, passed unnoticed. The first of them, Woolf's essay "Lewis Carroll" (1939), came out as an appendix to Nina Demurova's translation of *Alice in Wonderland*.[25] Next were published "Modern Fiction" (1919), "The Russian Point of View" (1925), "The Sentimental Journey" (1932), and "How Should One Read a Book?" (1932) in the collections of essays *Pisateli Anglii o literature* and *Homo legens: Chelovek chitaiushchii*.[26]

In 1983 there was published the first representative collection of Woolf's essays about Russian writers.[27] Twenty years hence, this publication is still referred to by the translators as "a good shot."

1984 saw the first translation of Woolf's fiction. The major Russian literary journal *Inostrannaia Literatura* published *Missis Dalloway* [*Mrs. Dalloway*][28], and it was immediately followed by the first local publication of the original *Mrs. Dalloway*, together with twelve essays.[29]

Virginia Woolf's fiction was eventually finding its way into print in Russia. Since *Flush* came out in 1986[30] running into 50,000 copies, there has been no break in publishing the translations of Woolf's novels, short stories, and essays. Not only the big publishing houses, but also Russian newspapers and literary journals oriented to creative writing took to publishing Virginia Woolf's works. *Literaturnaia Uchioba* covered "Pis'mo k molodomu poetu" [A Letter to a Young Poet] (1932), and the central Russian paper *Literaturnaia Rossiia* publicized a collection of Woolf's diary notes and essays.[31]

Perestroika proved to be a success story for Virginia Woolf's fiction. Thanks to the reading and publishing boom of the late 1980s, *Na maiak* [*To the Lighthouse*] was published in 1988 in the most widely acclaimed Russian literary journal *Novyi Mir* selling an astounding number of 1,100,000 copies.[32] Non-Russian readers may grow skeptical about such fantastic, unbelievable figures, yet it takes one to understand that hundreds of thousands of copies of editions of the works of Kafka, Sartre, D. H. Lawrence, Joyce, Virginia Woolf, and other twentieth-century Western European writers came as a by-product of the reading and publishing boom of 1988-1991 which accompanied *perestroika* in Russia. From my interview with Dr. Genieva:

Reinhold

I remember how happy I was when I first saw a copy of *Novyi Mir* with the translation of *To the Lighthouse*...It seemed then that all of your dreams as a publisher and translator had come true. Those days we turned a deaf ear to what our British and American colleagues were telling us. They thought our joy at having a book published to be idiotic. OK, it came out, so what? With us, it was like creating the world...Why did they publish Virginia Woolf in 1988 in *Novyi Mir*,[33] why not Joyce or Beckett? Well, for the Soviet publishing of the late 80s Virginia Woolf was a better project. You see, Woolf is different, she is a different writer compared to Joyce. There is so much more space, more Lüft in her writing than in Beckett's...The emergence of *To the Lighthouse* in 1988 is significant not only as an instance of cultural memory. Its significance lies in the fact that it has become a kind of watershed (be it big, or small, or medium-size) in the dynamic of Russian literature in its translated form towards the frontiers of European and world culture (I think American culture is deeply rooted in Europe). For all these things are interconnected. You and I worked in one field, others labored in another. Brodskii toiled at his great path in poetry. But what we were all doing together—in our kitchen talks, in dissertations, with our efforts at having this or that essay, or publication brought to light, at keeping this or that fragment intact or unabridged—we were all bringing about not only the *perestroika* but also, the open society which you have mentioned referring to the Open Society Institute (Soros Foundation) as a co-sponsor of the Woolf Across Cultures symposium. If you look at it this way, then the literary date of 1988 will almost overlap with the political, social and psychological changes that were underway then. Yes, 2.5 million copies...And you never know what will become of your words and deeds in the time to come. And this is a great privilege. Just think of it! 2.5 million copies found in the libraries, in universities, on the bookshelves, in the readers' hands: they could have changed someone's mind simply by making him or her think that you can describe the flow of life in a completely different way—well, isn't it fantastic? So it is great that you have identified the year 1988 as a subject of our talk. Today people just do not get it that something can be banned from publishing. Whereas we then were opening—without understanding it clearly—we were opening up the horizons of this world. You ask, why *To the Lighthouse*? Did it change anything in the *perestroika* in the Soviet Union? Sure. A new generation was born.[34]

With the 1988 landslide, Woolf was firmly put on the Russian publishers' list. *Izbrannoe* [Selected Works] came out in 1989,[35] selling an impressive number of 200,000 copies. It went into several reprints with publishing houses all over the country, each time running into more than 100,000 copies.[36] The year 1991 saw the publication of *Komnata Jeikoba* [*Jacob's Room*] in *Inostrannaia Literatura*,[37] and finally, after a ten-year procrastination, the translation of *A Room of One's Own* came to light in 1992 in *Eti zagadochnye anglichanki* [These Mysterious Englishwomen].[38] *Orlando* was published in 1997.[39] By the late 1990s it had become common practice to publish Virginia

Introduction

Woolf's books in translation. Woolf became part of the twentieth-century canon in Russia. Interestingly, the publishing house Azbuka reprinted editions of *Mrs. Dalloway*, *Na maiak* [*To the Lighthouse*] and *Orlando* in the series "Azbuka-Klassika" (2000). *Volny* [*The Waves*], "the most extraordinary" of Woolf's novels, was published in 2001 in *Inostrannaia Literatura* under the heading, "The Twentieth-Century Classics."[40] Woolf's first novel, *The Voyage Out* [Po moriu proch], is the latest publication of her fiction in Russian.[41]

By the early 2000s the total number of copies of Woolf's works published in Russia had reached 2.5 million copies. Though the publishing market had bottomed out in the mid-1990s, and translated fiction today sells a humble number of 2,000 or 3,000 copies, the fantastic figure of 2.5 million copies of Russian translations of Virginia Woolf remains a hard fact. It implies that there is one translation per about twenty adult readers in Russia. Every fifth family seems to possess at least one of her books in translation. To paraphrase *A Room of One's Own*, they will be a great new readership, I said, putting *To the Lighthouse*, by Virginia Woolf, at the end of the shelf, in another hundred years' time.[42]

Notes

[1] D. H. Lawrence, *Jack v debriakh Afriki* [The changed title of *The Boy in the Bush*]. Trans. N. P. Martynova. Leningrad: Mysl', 1927; *Semya Branguenov* [The changed title of *The Rainbow*, part 1]. Trans. Vera Minina. Moscow: Nedra, 1925; *Ursula Branguen* [The changed title of *The Rainbow*, part 2]. Trans. Vera Minina. Moscow: Nedra, 1925; *Synovya i liubovniki* [*Sons and Lovers*]. Trans. Nikolai Shchukovskii. Leningrad: Knizhnye Novinki, 1927; *Fleita Aarona* [*Aaron's Rod*]. Trans. M. Shik. Moscow: Nedra, 1925.

[2] James Joyce, *Uliss* [*Ulysses*]. Fragment (Penelope). Trans. V. Zhytomirskii. Novinki Zapada. Almanach No. 1. Moscow-Leningrad: ZIF, 1925:61-94; *Uliss* [*Ulysses*]. Fragments. Trans. S. Akimov, M. Levidov. *Literaturnaia Gazeta* (1929:20), 2 IX:3; *Uliss* [*Ulysses*]. Episodes 1-6. Trans. I. Romanovich, L. D. Kislova, An. Eleonskaia, V. Toper, N. Volzhyna. *Internatsional'naia Literatura* (1935:1, 2, 3, 9, 10, 11, 12):61-73, 43-50, 55-66, 43-52, 85-95, 54-62, 45-55; *Uliss* [*Ulysses*]. Episodes 7-10. Trans. E. Kalashnikova, N. L. Daruzes, I. Romanovich, O. Kholmskaia. *Internatsional'naia Literatura* (1936:1, 2, 3, 4): 51-69, 52-73, 53-56, 69-91. Quoted from James Joyce, *Dubliners. A Portrait of the Artist as a Young Man*. Introd., commentary E. Genieva. Moscow: Progress Publishers, 1982: 583.

[3] James Joyce, *Dublintsy* [*Dubliners*]. Trans., introd. E. N. Fedotova. Leningrad: Mysl', 1927.

[4] E. M. Forster, *Poezdka v Indiyu* (Istoriia odnogo prestupleniia) [*A Passage to India*]. Trans., introd. L. I. Nekrasova. Moscow: Sabashnikovy, 1927; *Poezdka v Indiyu* [*A Passage to India*]. Trans. V. P. Isakov. Leningrad: Goslitizdat, 1937.

⁵ David Garnett, *Zhenshchina-lisitsa* [*Lady into Fox*]. Trans. I. R. Gerbakh. Leningrad: A. F. Marks, 1924; *Chelovek v zoologicheskom sadu* [*A Man in the Zoo*]. Trans. M. M. Liubimov. Introd. Mikhail Levidov. Moscow: Sovremennye Problemy N. A. Stolliar, 1925.

⁶ Aldous Huxley, *Kontrapunkt* [*Point Counter Point*]. Trans. I. K. Romanovich. Foreword D. Mirsky. Moscow: Khudozhestvennaia Literatura, 1936; *Shutovskoi khorovod* [*Antic Hay*]. Trans. I. Romanovich. Moscow: Goslitizdat, 1936.

⁷ The above refers to the "first wave" of Russian translations of English modernists (the list is far from being exhaustive) and seems to be in accord with the dynamic of the then younger generation of talented Russian novelists such as Yevgenii Zamiatin (1884-1937), Boris Pilnyak (1894-1937), Panteleimon Romanov (1885-1938), and a few others. They were all suppressed after 1928, during the Stalinist purge. On the fate of Russian writers of the 1930s see Robert Conquest, *The Great Terror: Stalin's Purge of the Thirties*. London, Melbourne: Macmillan, 1968: 99, 324-325; Natalya Reinhold, "Martin Amis: 'Real'nost' Pokorno Sledovala za Mnoi'" [Martin Amis: Reality Meekly Followed My Call]. *Voprosy Literatury* (2001:5): 170-171. In terms of literary history, it means that Russian modernism was nipped in the bud. The one Russian modernist of the younger generation who survived, thanks to his exile, is Vladimir Nabokov (1899-1977).

⁸ See V. Azov, "James Joyce." *Sovremennyi Zapad* (1923:4): 210-212; R. Miller-Budnitskaia, "Ob Ulisse James'a Joyce'a" [On Joyce's *Ulysses*]. *Literaturnyi Kritik* (1934:1): 162-179; A. I. Startsev, "Joyce pered Ulissom." [Joyce on the verge of *Ulysses*]. *Internatsional'naia Literatura* (1937:1):196-202; R. Miller-Budnitskaia, "Filosofiia kul'tury James'a Joyce'a" [The philosophy of culture of James Joyce] *Internatsional'naia Literatura* (1937:2):188-209. Quoted from James Joyce, *Dubliners. A Portrait of the Artist as a Young Man*. Introd., commentary E. Genieva. Moscow: Progress Publishers, 1982:586. I. Kashkin, "Joyce." In *Internatsional'naia entsyklopediia*. V. 3. Moscow, 1930; D. Zhantieva, M. Morshchiner, *Sovremennye angliiskie i amerikanskie pisateli* [Contemporary English and American Writers]. *Bibliograficheskii ukazatel' osnovnykh proizvedenii i kriticheskoi literatury na russkom yazyke*. [Bibliographical Index of Major Works and Critical Reviews in Russian] Moscow: Gosudarstvennoe bibliotechno-bibliograficheskoe izdatel'stvo, 1945.

⁹ Translation is considered to be part of the Russian "literary polysystem" (Even-Zohar 45), an art in its own right. Cf. Itamar Even-Zohar, "The Position of Translated Literature within the Literary Polysystem." *Poetics Today* (Spring 1990 11:1): 45-51. See also, the first edition in *Literature and Translation: New Perspectives in Literary Studies*. Ed. James S. Holmes, J. Lambert, and R. Van den Broeck. Leuven: Acco, 1978: 117-127.

¹⁰ D. S. Mirskii, *Intelligentsia*. Moscow: Sovetskaia Literatura, 1934; Dmitri Mirsky, *The Intelligentsia of Great Britain*. Trans. Alec Brown. London: Victor Gollanz, 1935.

¹¹ D. S. Mirsky contributed to *The Criterion*; see his "Chekhov and the English," *The Criterion* (October 1927: VI:4): 292-305; Nabokov referred to him thirty years later in his *Lectures on Russian Literature*, quoting Mirsky's remarks on Dostoevsky and other Russian writers (see Vladimir Nabokov, *Lektsii po russkoi literature* [*Lectures on Russian Literature*]. Moscow: Izdatel'stvo Nezavisimaia Gazeta, 1999: 181, 207.)

¹² A quarter of a century later a Soviet literary scholar, D. G. Zhantieva, would recollect D. S. Mirsky's comment on the Russian influence in the work of Virginia Woolf

Introduction

and leave it unacknowledged in her published doctoral thesis, *Angliiskii roman 20 veka: 1918-1939* [The Twentieth-Century English Novel: 1918-1939]. Moscow: Nauka, 1965: 78-82. Also, see George J. Zytaruk, *D. H. Lawrence's Response to Russian Literature*. Mouton: The Hague-Paris, 1971: 109.

[13] Jack Lindsay, "Virginia Woolf." *Internatsional'naia Literatura* (1937: 11,12). Quoted from I. M. Levidova, "Woolf, Virginia." *Kratkaia literaturnaia entsiklopediia*. Moscow: Gosudarstvennoe Nauchnoe Izdatel'stvo Sovetskaia Entsiklopediia, 1962: 1062.

[14] Lindsay's publication could have been a follow-up to Virginia Woolf's essay "Why Art Today Follows Politics?" in *The Daily Worker*, 14 December 1936; rpt. as "The Artist and Politics" (*CE2* 230-232).

[15] I. M. Levidova, "Woolf, Virginia." *Kratkaia literaturnaia entsiklopediia*. Moscow: Gosudarstvennoe Nauchnoe Izdatel'stvo Sovetskaia Entsiklopediia, 1962: 1062.

[16] See G. Lukács, *Metafizika tragedii* [Metaphysics of Tragedy]. Moscow: Mushaget, 1913; *Literaturnye teorii 19 veka i marksizm* [Nineteenth-century Literary Theory and Marxism]. Moscow: Goslitizdat, 1937; *K istorii realizma* [On the Background of Realism]. Statii 1934-1936. [Articles written in 1934-1936] Moscow: Goslitizdat, 1939; *Bor'ba gumanizma i varvarstva* [The Struggle Between Humanism and Barbarity]. Trans. from the German R. Zazumova. Tashkent: Gosudarstvennoe Isdatel'stvo Usbek SSR, 1943.

[17] G. Lukács, "The Ideology of Modernism." From *The Meaning of Contemporary Realism* (1955). Quoted from *Twentieth-Century Literary Criticism*. Ed. David Lodge. 15th Impression. London and New York: Longman, 1991: 474-487.

[18] G. M. Fridlender, *K. Marx i F. Engels i voprosy literatury* [Marx and Engels and Literary Theory]. Moscow: Goslitizdat, 1962; 2nd ed. Moscow: Khudozhestvennaia Literatura, 1968.

[19] Cf. Valentin Osipovich Stenich, (Smetanich, 1898-1939), translator and literary critic. Between 1923 and 1938 this talented translator from the English, French and German published many works of the then contemporary Western European and American writers, namely *The 42nd Parallel* (1930) by Dos Passos (trans. 1931), *Ulysses* (separate chapters) by Joyce (trans. 1934), *Death in the Woods* (1933) by Sherwood Anderson (trans. 1934), and others. He was sent to gulag in 1938.

[20] We met for an interview on 6 February 2004 at the Russian State Library for Foreign Literature in Moscow (my trans.).

[21] "Ottepel" or "thaw" of 1956-1964 is known as the first post-Stalinist period of liberalization in the Soviet arts.

[22] "Woolf played a significant role in the development of the so-called psychological Western European novel." I. M. Levidova, "Woolf, Virginia." *Kratkaia literaturnaia entsiklopediia*, 1962:1062.

[23] See note 12.

[24] Cf. "[Acmeism is] nostalgia for the world culture." Osip Mandelstam's definition of "acmeism" (from Greek acme = point, a trend in Russian poetry of the 1910s which shaped itself in the work of Sergey Gorodetskii, Mikhail Kuzmin, Osip Mandelstam, early poetry of Nikolai Gumiliov and Anna Akhmatova) is quoted by Nadezhda Mandelstam in her *Vospominaniia. Vtoraia kniga* [Memories. The Second Book]. 4th edition. Paris: YMCA- Press, 1987: 555.

[25] Virginia Woolf, "Lewis Carroll." In Lewis Carroll, *Alisa v strane chudes* [*Alice in Wonderland*]. Trans., commentary Nina Demurova. Moscow: Nauka, 1978:248-250.

Reinhold

[26] Virginia Woolf, "Sovremennaia literatura" [Modern Fiction], "Russkaia tochka zreniia" [The Russian Point of View], "Sentimental'noe puteshestvie" [The Sentimental Journey]. In *Pisateli Anglii o literature*. [English Writers on Literature] Trans. Ks. Atarova. Moscow: Progress, 1981, 276-294; "Kak chitat' knigi?" [How Should One Read a Book?] Trans. Ks. Atarova. In *Homo legens: Chelovek chitaiushchii*. Ed. S. I. Belza. Moscow: Progress, 1983: 254-265.

[27] "Virginia Woolf o russkoi literature" [Woolf on Russian Literature]. Introd., trans. N. Bushmanova (N. Reinhold). *Voprosy Literatury* (1983:11): 188-207; rpt. in *V mire otechestvennoi klassiki* [In the World of Russian Classics]. Moscow: Khudozhestvennaia Literatura (1987: 2): 260-282.

[28] Virginia Woolf, *Missis Dalloway* [*Mrs. Dalloway*]. Trans. Elena Surits. With an Afterword by Ekaterina Genieva. *Inostrannaia Literatura* (1984:4): 70-170.

[29] Virginia Woolf, *Mrs. Dalloway and Essays:* The Sentimental Journey. Jane Austen. Sir Walter Scott. David Copperfield. *Jane Eyre* and *Wuthering Heights*. Lewis Carroll. The Novels of Turgenev. The Russian Point of View. Modern Fiction. Mr. Bennett and Mrs. Brown. On Re-reading Novels. How It Strikes a Contemporary. Introd., commentary E. Genieva. Moscow: Raduga Publishers, 1984.

[30] Virginia Woolf, *Flush*. Trans. E. Surits. Moscow: Izvestiia, Biblioteka Inostrannoi Literatury, 1986.

[31] Virginia Woolf, "Pis'mo k molodomu poetu" [A Letter to a Young Poet]. Ed., trans. N. Bushmanova (N. Reinhold). *Literaturnaia Uchioba* (1986:1): 207-213; "Iz esse i dnevnikov Virginii Woolf" [From Virginia Woolf's Diaries and Essays]. Ed., trans. N. Bushmanova (N. Reinhold). *Literaturnaia Rossiia* (1987:25): 22-23.

[32] Virginia Woolf, *Na maiak* [*To the Lighthouse*]. Trans. E. Surits, introd. E. Genieva. *Novyi Mir* (1988: 9, 10): 100-134, 95-146.

[33] The literary journal that published *Odin den Ivana Denisovicha* by A. Solzhenitsyn in 1962. See A. I. Solzhenitsyn, *One Day in the Life of Ivan Denisovich*. Trans. from the Russian H. T. Willetts with an Introd. by John Bayley. London: David Campbell Publishers, 1995.

[34] See note 20.

[35] Virginia Woolf, *Izbrannoe* [Selected Works]: *Missis Dalloway* [*Mrs. Dalloway*]. *Na maiak* [*To the Lighthouse*]. *Flush*. *Rasskazy* [Short stories]. *Esse* [Essays]. Introd. E. Genieva. Trans. Larissa Bespalova, M. Lorie, E. Surits, N. Vasilieva, et al. Moscow: Khudozhestvennaia Literatura, 1989.

[36] See, for instance, Virginia Woolf, *Missis Dalloway. Na maiak. Flush*. Saint Petersburg: Severo-Zapad, 1993.

[37] Virginia Woolf, *Komnata Jeikoba* [*Jacob's Room*]. Trans. Maria Karp. Introd. E. Genieva. *Inostrannaia Literatura* (1991: 9): 29-127.

[38] Virginia Woolf, *Svoya komnata* [*A Room of One's Own*]. Trans. N. Bushmanova (N. Reinhold) In *Eti zagadochnye anglichanki* [These Mysterious Englishwomen]. Moscow: Khudozhestvennaia Literatura, 1992:78-154; rpt. of 1992 (Moscow: Rudomino, Tekst). See also, the first edition in *Literaturnaia Uchioba* (1989: 6): 168-190.

[39] Virginia Woolf, *Orlando*. Trans. E. Surits. Saint Petersburg: Azbuka, 1997.

[40] Virginia Woolf, *Volny* [*The Waves*]. Trans. E. Surits. *Inostrannaia Literatura* (2001:10): 137-259.

[41] Virginia Woolf, *Po moriu proch* [*The Voyage Out*]. Trans. A. Osokin. Afterword Stuart N. Clarke. Moscow: Tekst, 2002.

Introduction

[42] "She will be a poet, I said, putting *Life's Adventure*, by Mary Carmichael, at the end of the shelf, in another hundred years' time" (*AROO* 164).

Works Cited

Levidova, I. M. "Woolf, Virginia." *Kratkaia literaturnaia entsiklopediia* [Concise Companion to World Literature]. Moscow: Gosudarstvennoe Nauchnoe Izdatel'stvo Sovetskaia Entsiklopediia, 1962: 1062.

Mandelstam, Nadezhda. *Vospominaniia. Vtoraia kniga* [Memories. The Second Book]. 4th edition. Paris: YMCA Press, 1987.

Mirsky, Dmitri. *The Intelligentsia of Great Britain*. Trans. Alec Brown. London: Victor Gollanz, 1935.

Woolf, Virginia. *Collected Essays*. V. 2. London: The Hogarth Press, 1966.

——. *A Room of One's Own*. New York: Harcourt, Brace and Company, 1929.

I

Home Thoughts from Abroad

An Improper Englishwoman: Woolf as a World Writer
Maria DiBattista

In keeping with Virginia Woolf's well-known championing of the overlooked or obscure, we might approach the growing fame and influence of "Woolf Across Cultures," the subject of this symposium, with a detail, perhaps trivial in itself, but one that, if pondered for long enough, might conduct us to the threshold where Woolf's imaginative passages across cultures might be said to begin. In the second chapter of *Orlando*, Woolf's eponymous hero, despondent over his disgrace at Court and the flight of Sasha, the Russian princess, retires to his great country house to nurse his wounds in solitude. There he succumbs to that besetting vice of the Elizabethan nobleman—writing. His biographer discloses that Orlando has long been "afflicted with a love of literature," the "fatal nature" of which was "to substitute a phantom for a reality" (45). Seeking to relieve his disordered mind by populating it with phantoms of his own creation, he retrieves from the huge cabinet that houses his works one thick manuscript and one thin one. The long work, which he will never finish, is called "Xenophila, a Tragedy." The thin one, which he will complete and publish centuries later, is entitled "The Oak Tree" (46).

The literary joke is, of course, jingoistic. "Xenophila" reeks, in its multi-syllabic ostentation and, indeed, in its etymological inspiration, of the foreign. The name seems chosen to parody the ornate diction of high Elizabethan culture (the "contorted cogitations" and "delicate articulation" of Sir Thomas Browne's *Hydriotaphia, Urn-Burial* is a great favorite and model for the bibliophiliac, aspiring writer). To the robust Anglo-Saxon temperament, "The Oak Tree," the only monosyllabic title in the stash of Orlando's unfinished work, clearly recommends itself for its terse and vigorous English, rooted in native idiom as well as native soil. *Xenophila* can claim no such authentic or sturdy provenance. The Greeks had no such word, being generally inhospitable to what was *xenos*, that is odd, unusual, hence foreign, a fact and attitude indicated by the word they did donate to us, *barbarian*, which initially comprehends the non-Greek world and their offending, primitive manners. They did, however, entertain Xenophilos[1] as a masculine name. Perhaps, then, Woolf's feminized transliteration is a sly verbal portent of the sex-change Orlando himself will later undergo. Perhaps, too, Orlando hoped that his tragic representations would eventually convert the (invented) proper name,

Xenophila, into a radiant substantive noun, *xenophilia*, a love of the foreign consecrated by tragedy.

Still, whatever Orlando (or Woolf) intended by this title, the fact remains that, narratively, the tragic story of Xenophila or of the *xenophilia* she might have promoted in the world remained unfinished by Orlando and unknown to us. Is it foolish to wonder why? Xenophila's suspect parentage shouldn't have deterred Orlando from seeking solace in this new word and the work it inspired, for surely an Elizabethan poet would not shy at neologism. Perhaps Orlando lost interest or confidence in the work, as he might have in the word, because he wrongly conceived of *xenophilia* as a subject of tragedy. Perhaps an embodied love of the foreign is more fittingly the material of comedy, a genre which generally entertains happier fates for those enchanted by brave new worlds and their wondrous people.

Certainly the comic note is more characteristic of Woolf's attitude whenever she encounters strangeness, whether in herself or in others. Unlike many other modernists of her generation, she was not especially well traveled nor did her artistic identity depend on the soul-dislocating experience of exile to bring it to independent maturity. *Xenophilia* does not entail for her any physical nor moral act of expatriation but a more homely, if I may risk the pun, relation to the non-British world. Her voyages out were primarily imaginative ones, and while that made her more stay-at-home than Henry James, Conrad, or Joyce, she was as much an international modernist as they. This I hope my title succeeds in encapsulating. I hope, too, that if we could imagine Woolf herself in attendance at this gathering she might actually be pleased by the allegation of impropriety, since she prided herself in being an outsider in relation to such proper British institutions as the Army, the Judiciary, the Church, even the University, all of whose insider customs—and costumes—she satirizes in *A Room of One's Own* and lambasts in *Three Guineas*. Her fiction also betrays an inordinate fondness for those characters who flaunt decorum, perhaps nowhere more superbly than in her indulgent portraits of the reckless Sally Seton, with her power to shock and to make Clarissa Dalloway "feel, for the first time, how sheltered the life at Bourton was" (36), and the interloper Mrs. Manresa, who breaks the ice in the emotionally chilled atmosphere of Pointz Hall with the impulsive vibrations of her own "wild heart." But however we might call up and celebrate the non-British improprieties she champions in her fiction, many might hesitate to proclaim Woolf a world writer. To account for that hesitation—its duration and its content—and to overcome it is the double burden of my title and of my argument.

It is a burden that must be acknowledged and borne by anyone seriously contemplating Woolf as a writer across cultures. Admittedly the mere thought

An Improper Englishwoman

of Woolf extending her imaginative reach and influence across cultures is a heartening and stimulating one, as this symposium and the many scholars and critics assembled here testify. But however happy and productive, it is a thought that should not come unshadowed by the remembrance that Virginia Woolf entered the ranks of world literature wearing the mantle of a London provincial—the lady-novelist from Bloomsbury. This image persists, despite gatherings like this one that brings us together here in Moscow. There is something centripetal as well as centrifugal about Woolf's writing and social imagination that persistently pulls her into the gravitational field of Englishness and all that Englishness entails—its manners, traditions, values, and its humors.

The assessments offered on the occasion of her death, though celebratory and, under the circumstances, respectful of her achievement, tended to confine her to this restricted cultural domain. Stephen Spender, an admiring friend, concludes that "the artistic aims in Virginia Woolf's novels are far more varied than the material, which is somewhat narrow and limited" (426). Limitation is also diplomatically suggested in Malcolm Cowley's review of the posthumous *Between the Acts*, in which he adjudges that "The spirit if not the body of Georgian England survives in her novels" (450). Cowley's is not an untrue nor even unkind pronouncement, although much more is recorded and preserved in that novel, and indeed in all of Woolf's work, however local her settings might be, than the spirit of Georgian England.

This Erich Auerbach understood when, from the lofty and lonely vantage point of scholarly exile, he surveyed the expanse of Western literature from the Hebrews and Greeks to the modern day and awarded her the first place among modernists who inherited and transformed the Western traditions of mimesis. Auerbach was the first critic of comparative instincts to understand the profound and unifying multiculturalism (although this would not be his word, but ours) heralded in Woolf's revolutionary realism. He recognized her audacity in seeking reality in the fidgeting of a restless little boy obliged to hold still as his mother took the measure for a brown stocking and in the thoughts that such a commonplace sight might provoke in a group of vacationers, some of whom have philosophical training and so might ponder the symbolic and human import of such a domestic scene, but most of whom do not and so respond to this moment and its beauty in an undisciplined, but emotionally significant way. As Auerbach almost triumphantly notes in closing his magisterial work, Woolf's novelistic materials might seem somewhat narrow and limited, but that did not prevent her from seeing in and through them "the determining factors in our real lives." In her exploration of the apparently random moment, Auerbach concludes, "something new and elemental appeared: nothing less than the wealth of reality and depth of life in every moment to which we surrender ourselves without prejudice" (552).

Surrender without prejudice—this, I would propose, is the first distinguishing and requisite characteristic of a world writer. To respond to experience unaccompanied by native and personal bias is to enter into life unaided, but also unhindered by the customs and conventions of inculcated ways of thought. In the modernists' unprejudiced surrender to the moment that absorbed them, Auerbach foresaw the triumph of a non-coercive universalism based on the rudimentary and common experiences of everyday life. Auerbach movingly describes the logic of this paradox: "It is precisely the random moment which is comparatively independent of the controversial and unstable orders over which men fight and despair; it passes unaffected by them, as daily life. The more it is exploited, the more the elementary things which our lives have in common come to light. The more numerous, varied, and simple the people are who appear as subjects of such random moments, the more effectively must what they have in common shine forth" (552). To surrender without prejudice is thus to engage that part of the mind unconscious or unregarding of tribal, communal or national divisions and beliefs so that it may experience the moment before it has entered history, behold reality before it has been distorted by ideology. The fruit of this surrender, as Auerbach's language suggests, is the modern epiphany, in which the common life shines forth.

I do not believe Auerbach's choice of Woolf to exemplify this new world writing was an arbitrary one. But her exemplary achievement in excavating the common ground between and across cultures has largely been obscured by the Bloomsburyean garb that has frequently camouflaged her true figure as an author. To appreciate how Woolf achieved her own unprejudiced surrender to the moment and to the common life it bodies forth, I would like to divest her of these garments and to displace, if not completely uproot her from her native ground. So imagined, Woolf appears to me as a writer whose claim to world eminence is justified by her quite personal understanding and incorporation of non-British traditions, traditions that shaped her, as much if not more than Bloomsbury, as a distinctly modernist writer. I want to isolate the two traditions that she continually revisited, as if a second imaginative home: Russian literature and Greek culture, especially its drama.

Both were traditions that attracted her in large part because—in social mores, emotional customs, and in language—they were so utterly different than her own. Their very apartness suggested to her a world richer in realities than were ever dreamed of in Bloomsbury. She returned again and again to the Greeks and the Russian masters for stimulus, sometimes for comfort, but always to extract and ingest morsels of reality or spiritual truth not readily discernible by English moral habits of thought. In Greek literature she found "the stable, the permanent, the original human being" ("On Not Knowing Greek" 28); in Russian literature she was awed in encountering "the soul that is the chief character in Russian fiction"; the soul that "is not restrained by barriers," no matter how well-fortified, and so "overflows...floods...mingles with the souls of others" ("Russian Point of View" 182, 184). Through her reading of the Greeks, which she famously admitted she had no hope of really knowing, and the Russians, whose point of view she recognized as a primary influence on European modernists, Woolf reached back into time and across the European continent to produce her most distinctly and effortlessly modern, yet urgent work. Such imaginative breadth, encompassing cultures remote in time or distanced by space and ideology, qualified her as a world writer and helps us understand the very criteria by which a world writer might be identified and measured: historical depth as well as geographical reach; the imaginative capture within and across cultures of the random moment in which the elementary, thus shared basis of existence manifests itself.

But this is putting the case abstractly, a mode Woolf always suspected. As both novelist and critic, she always subjected working theories and their underlying assumptions to the test of concrete experience. Let me then turn to her own account of an exemplary and characteristically droll instance of such imaginative participation in a life at once foreign and startlingly familiar to her. It is reported in a review of Chekhov's "The Cherry Orchard." Recalling the delights of a 1920 production of the Arts Theatre at St. Martin's Theatre, she muses that there is nothing in English literature in the least like Chekhov's play. "It may be," she speculates, "that we are more advanced, less advanced, or have advanced in an entirely different direction. At any rate, the English person who finds himself at dawn in the nursery of Madame Ranevskaia feels out of place, like a foreigner brought up with entirely different traditions. But these traditions are not (this, of course, is a transcript of individual experience) so ingrained in one as to prevent one from shedding them not only without pain but with actual relief and abandonment" (*E3* 246). Woolf's xenophilia here takes on active emotional form. Her imaginative readiness to shed preconceptions quickly intensifies into positive relief, indeed outright emotional abandon. It is as if her mind at such moments is suddenly released from the force of cultural gravity that has kept it pinioned to its native ground and is spirited into a radically unfamiliar way of life.

This seems almost literally to be the case when Woolf proceeds to describe her reactions to the performance. She reports the sensation of being transported to an imaginative perimeter where "we have reached the end of everything: where space seems illimitable and time everlasting." In this sublime and completely imaginary space, she tries, "quite wrongly" she concedes, "to give effect to my sense that the human soul is free from all trappings and crossed incessantly by thoughts and emotions which wing their way from here, from there, from the furthest horizons—" (*E3* 246). Surrender without prejudice can take no more extreme form than such cross-cultural exhilaration, a deep breathing, as it were, in which all the noxious fumes of chauvinism are exhaled. I deliberately make my own critical metaphors extravagant, because Woolf encourages us, I think, not to shy away from improper, even outlandish retorts to home culture. Examples are legion, but perhaps none more appropriate to this particular setting and audience than her sly parody of Orlando's nativist credulity in believing the tales brought back by imperial adventurers that "the women in Muscovy wear beards and the men are covered in fur from the waist down; that both sexes were smeared with tallow to keep the cold out, tear meat with their fingers and live in huts where an English lord would scruple to keep his cattle" (48). Hirsute, insulated by greasy tallow, brutish in table manners and habitation—it is easy to ridicule such caricatures and a relief to be rid of the actual ignorance, bolstered by self-approving complacency, that conspire in their creation.

And yet Woolf would not be the world writer she is if she did not admit to the more intransigent habits of thought and feeling that can impede our imaginative surrender and allow the random moment to elude us before it has yielded the wealth of life it shelters. Before venturing across cultures, Woolf always pauses to assess not so much the risks, but the inevitable disappointments and failures that await her—or anyone—imaginatively drawn to whatever is foreign to them. Her attempt to describe the "Russian Point of View" in an essay of that name thus opens with this warning: "A special acuteness and detachment, a sharp angle of vision the foreigner will often achieve; but not that absence of self-consciousness, that ease and fellowship and sense of common values which make for intimacy and sanity and the quick give and take of familiar intercourse." Woolf never attempts, much less accomplishes her own acts of translation without acknowledging this moment of hesitation when the mind in its transit suddenly, if not unexpectedly, finds itself in the presence of the utterly different.

Initially, however, the cross-cultural encounter is treated by Woolf as an occasion for reflection and, quite often, open amusement. One such occasion of irrepressible British humor excited her comment in her review of "The Cherry Orchard":

An Improper Englishwoman

> It occurred in the middle of Charlotte's strange speech in the beginning of the second act. 'I have no proper passport. I don't know how old I am; I always feel I am still young,' she begins. She goes on, 'When I grew up I became a governess. But where I came from and who I am, I haven't a notion. Who my parents were—*very likely they weren't married*—I don't know.' At the words I have italicized, Dunyasha bounced away from her to the other end of the bench, with an arch humour which drew the laugh it deserved. Miss Helena Millais seemed to be delighted to have this chance of assuring us that she did not believe a word of this morbid nonsense, and that the old jokes still held good in the world of sanity round the corner. But it was Miss Ethel Irving who showed the steadiest sense of what decency requires of a British matron in extremity. How she did it, since she spoke her part accurately, it is difficult to say, but her mere presence upon the stage was enough to suggest that all the comforts and all the decencies of English upper-class life were at hand, so that any moment her vigil upon the bench might have been appropriately interrupted by a manservant bearing a silver tray. 'The Bishop is in the drawing-room, m'lady.' 'Thank you, Parker, Tell his Lordship I will come at once.' (*E3* 247)

On the outskirts of Chekhov's histrionic world of emotional extremity is the British world of sanity where all spiritual perplexities can be dismissed as the stuff of morbid humor. As a playgoer, Woolf might have shared in the laughter, but as a world writer, she is ready to defect from the known world of custom and decency in which sanity decorously presides and yield to the emotionally foreign, extravagant, highly improper conduct of life that is not only tolerated but *expected* elsewhere.

Still, lurking in this jovial anecdote of an evening spent in the company of Chekhov's characters is a less happy realization. In the moment of cross-cultural identification, Woolf is less hopeful than Auerbach that the unification of cultures and peoples is at hand. Auerbach espouses the aesthetic paradox that in surrender there is victory—and to the victor goes the wealth of life. But readers willing to follow Woolf across cultures find a different, less sanguine paradox awaiting them: it is precisely in the realm of commonly held values, which establishes and maintains the intimacy, sanity and give and take of familiar intercourse in any given culture, that the search for common ground often proves most futile. Only a new understanding of what the common might encompass can resolve the paradox that Woolf's writings pose for us.

We can see Woolf struggling to arrive at this understanding in her great essay "On Not Knowing Greek." The ignorance freely proclaimed in the essay's famous title concerns not only "the difference of race and tongue but a tremendous breach of tradition" (24). Nowhere is this breach more dramatically evident than in our attempts to comprehend the language and agitated emotions of the Greek choruses. What we might call the Woolfian paradox of commonality asserts its obtrusive presence at the very moment when, having shed our traditions, we are ready to hear the Greek tragic chorus voice the common values and shared feelings of their community. Yet instead of discovering what we have in common across cultures, we find ourselves stranded on the brink of utter incomprehension. As Woolf describes it:

> One must be able to pass easily into those ecstasies, those wild and apparently irrelevant utterances, those sometimes obvious and commonplace statements, to decide their relevance or irrelevance, to give them their relation to the play as a whole. We must "be able to pass easily"; but that of course is exactly what we cannot do. For the most part the choruses, with their obscurities, must be spelt out and their symmetry mauled. (30)

"We must 'be able to pass easily'; but that of course is exactly what we cannot do." Woolf quotes, then corrects herself at the very point that, assuming the convivial we, she genially purports to speak for us. But she is also now speaking *to* us in the controlled rhetoric of a writer who knows how difficult such acts of translation are and who warns us that to translate ourselves effortlessly is, as she says, "exactly what we cannot do." The adverb "exactly" functions as an emotional as well as linguistic bar to our presumption that the passage across time and cultures is easily accomplished.[2]

Woolf across cultures is thus a figure precariously straddled over a gap, wide and perhaps unbridgeable, that separates here from there, the known from the unfamiliar world, the native from the foreign, our words for things and for relations from theirs. Being a writer, Woolf hesitates most fretfully on the threshold of language itself, where cultures are most articulate—and most stubbornly themselves. The world writer who seeks for the common life uniting people across cultures finds that words themselves refuse to act as transparent vehicles of common feeling. Woolf typically notices these obdurate opacities in meaning, not in the refined and abstruse vocabulary of elites, but in the ordinary words of everyday life. Let me cite an instance she frequently invokes to illustrate this vernacular divide. In trying to isolate what is unique and virtually untranslatable in the Russian lexicon of feeling, Woolf remarks that the English

> cannot say "Brother" with simple conviction...the English equivalent for "Brother" is "Mate"—a very different word, with something sardonic in it, an indefinable suggestion of humour. Met though they are in the depths of misfortune the two Englishmen who thus accost each other will, we are sure, find a job, make their fortunes, spend the last years of their lives in luxury, and leave a sum of money to prevent poor devils from calling each other "Brother" on the Embankment. But it is common suffering, rather than common happiness, effort or desire that produces the sense of brotherhood. ("Russian Point of View" 179)

An Improper Englishwoman

In an earlier version of this essay, she had explained more fully this difference in emotional address: "The truth is that if you say 'brother' you must say it with conviction, and it is not easy to say it with conviction. The Russians themselves produce this sense of conviction not because they acquiesce or tolerate indiscriminately or despair, but because they believe so passionately in the existence of the soul....And that alone is important; that living core which suffers and toils is what we all have in common. We tend to disguise or to decorate it; but the Russians believe in it, seek it out, interpret it, and, following its agonies and intricacies, have produced not only the most spiritual of modern books but also the most profound" (*E2* 343).

Here what I have called the Woolfian paradox of commonality, a paradox first perceived by Woolf in the context of world literature and culture, takes a curious turn, one that explains her affinity for, and debt to, the Russian point of view to sharpen her own modernist vision. According to Woolf, the Russians have a language, fully expressive of their spiritual outlook, that puts them in direct contact with the soul, the living core in which, she believes, all cultural differences are dissolved in a common fate of toil and striving. They make no effort to clothe the soul in proper garments or festoon it with ceremonial dress. Nothing distracts them from seeing this living core as the fundamental and complex fact of human existence. As a proper Englishwoman, Woolf can only observe and try to describe the rich language and profound works in which this fact is netted and made manifest. She can never approach the soul in the same words, follow it into the deepest recesses of life as the Russians so intrepidly, yet almost casually do.

Still, there are moments when Woolf nevertheless experiences a sensation beyond the capacity of her native culture to produce and her native language to articulate. Such a moment is remembered at the conclusion of her review of that memorable performance of "The Cherry Orchard":

> I do not know how better to describe the sensation at the end of *The Cherry Orchard*, than by saying that it sends one into the street feeling like a piano played upon at last, not in the middle only but all over the keyboard and with the lid left open so that sound goes on. (*E3* 248)

Like a piano played upon at last, Woolf experiences, through Chekhov's great, indisputably *Russian* play, the full sounding of her nature. In this moment of bodily as well as emotional "transport," she is translated into a realm outside language, indeed almost beyond culture, yet finds herself at home with herself in the world in a new way.

Ideological and cultural critics might admonish us about the dangers, not to mention hauteur, of this kind of mutual identification not only across cultures but across historical eras. Woolf's achievement stubbornly defies such reproaches. Certainly Auerbach saw in modernism's embrace of the random moment the chance not only to render "in a very personal way the individual who lives in it," but "also (and for that very reason)...the elementary things which men in general have in common" (552). Readers of Woolf will appreciate how the word common resonates here in a profound way, given the distinctive place that word occupies in her fictional and critical view of the world. What is most valued and yet necessarily most elusive and fugitive in her moral imaginings is our common nature, whether that nature is embodied in the common reader to whom she entrusted, following the precedence established by Dr. Johnson, the task of deciding all claims to literary honors, or whether it is manifested in the subject to which she continually returns in her novels—"the common life which is the real life." This is the common life and common interest that she tirelessly advances in her polemic writings, most ardently at the conclusion of *Three Guineas*: "A common interest unites us; it is one world, one life" (365).

Woolf, then, was not afraid to trust, indeed to venture all her moral credibility on that democratically humble, but morally resonant, imposingly grave word. In enlisting the "common" as her most trusted moral ally and artistic arbiter, she was not flirting with essentialism nor indulging an imperialist fantasy of similitude. It was a word whose origin, history and, if you pardon the redundancy, common usage sanctified her vision of one world, one life. We should also note that this plangent word has its origin in the Latin *communis*, indicating what is shared by all or many and which carries within it a history of mutual obligations (*com*,with + *munus*, services rendered). The word "common" thus emerges out of a communal idea and practice of social and moral barter, a mutual and mutually beneficial exchange of duties, rights, and values. These values bind communities but also affirm the existence of a human order that supersedes as it transcends national or local boundaries. One particular ironic consequence of the paradox of commonality is that at times only a foreign language, as Woolf repeatedly reminds us, can convey an attitude or feeling that we experience but cannot name. Thus she notes how the Greeks fashioned words "which, in so many instances, we have made expressive to us of our own emotions, *thalassa, thanatos, anthos, aster*—to take the first that come to hand; so clear, so hard, so intense, that to speak plainly yet fittingly without blurring the outline or clouding the depths Greek is the only expression" ("On Not Knowing Greek" 37). The sea, death, flower and star: as she intones these clear, hard words for emotions that baffle the expressive power of English, Woolf appears to us as a kind of castaway, thrown up on an unknown shore, picking through shards of a poetic tradition that exert their siren call to her.

But at other times Woolf is lured by those flashes of poetry that leave us "without the support of words" contemplating a "meaning...just on the far side of language": "It is the meaning which in moments of astonishing excitement and stress we perceive in our minds without words; it is the meaning that Dostoevsky (hampered as he was by prose and as we are by translation) leads us to by some astonishing run up the scale of emotions and points at but cannot indicate; the meaning that Shakespeare succeeds in snaring" ("On Not Knowing Greek" 32). Arguably, then, it is on the far side of language where world literature abides, awaiting its readers and common, that is best, interpreters. It is on the far side of language that the genius of Sophoclean drama, Dostoevsky's soul-epics and Shakespeare's theater are co-present. There, too, we might get fitful intimations of something that is not only beyond our local culture but beyond our native stock of words. There we will find "not the thing itself, but the reverberation and reflection which, taken into [the] mind, the thing has made, close enough to the original to illustrate it, remote enough to heighten, enlarge, and make splendid" (32).

Of course it is one thing to undertake such expansive flights beyond the range of clear meanings, another to bring oneself back to earth. To the heightened, enlarged and splendid universe beyond language, perhaps indeed beyond the human capacity for experience, Woolf could only oppose the inclination of her own mind, with its bias for hearty, sensible British "humour." It was humor that Woolf relied on to dissolve what was foreign to her language and experience—the rhapsodes of the Greek chorus, the Russian fraternal hail of brother—and reconstitute them in the idiom and manners of her native English.

Thus even as she celebrates the Russian's spiritual profundity, she suddenly sees, in a spasm of nativist humor, the virtues of a counter-voice, "the voice of protest...the voice of another and an ancient civilization which seems to have bred in us the instinct to enjoy and fight rather than to suffer and understand. English fiction from Sterne to Meredith bears witness to our natural delight in humour and comedy, the beauty of earth, in the activities of the intellect, and in the splendour of the body" ("Modern Fiction" 158). Her English delight in humor and comedy is also thwarted in her encounter with Greek. Tellingly, one of the consequences of not knowing Greek she laments is not knowing when to laugh in reading Greek: "To laugh instantly it is almost necessary (though Aristophanes may supply us with an exception) to laugh in English. Humour, after all, is closely bound up with a sense of the body. When we laugh at the humour of Wycherley, we are laughing with the body of that burly rustic who was our common ancestor on the village green. The French, the Italians, the Americans, who derive physically from so different a stock, pause as we pause in reading Homer, to make sure that they are laughing in the right place, and the pause is fatal. Thus humour is the first of the gifts to perish in a foreign tongue, and when we turn from Greek to Elizabethan literature it seems, after a long silence, as if a great age were ushered in by a burst of laughter" ("On Not Knowing Greek" 37-38). As this historical rhetorical guffaw suggests, only in English humor does Woolf indulge her chauvinism without apology, indeed with something like patriotic relish.

This I think we should take as a healthy sign. We know from Freud that humor functions as a mode of self-defense for the threatened ego, which refuses, he writes, "to be distressed by the provocations of reality, to let itself be compelled to suffer. It insists that it cannot be affected by the traumas of the external world; it shows, in fact, that such traumas are no more than occasions for it to gain pleasure" (Freud 162). He went on to speculate that humor has its origin in the benign parental agency, which, internalized in the Super-ego, "speaks kindly words of comfort to the intimidated ego" (166). Does not humor also incorporate the benign influence of the parental culture, which exerts a salutary centripetal pressure on the centrifugal xenophilic imagination? Humor, we thus might speculate, prevented Woolf from being drawn irresistibly and helplessly into the orbit of the Russians, with their sadness, or the Greeks, who, "with the sound of the sea in their ears, vines, meadows, rivulets about them...are even more aware than we are of a ruthless fate" ("On Not" 39). These were two cultures that in her estimation had penetrated to the very core of life and reported what they saw there without mitigation. But as Freud reminds us, "Humour is not resigned; it is rebellious. It signifies not only the triumph of the ego but also of the pleasure principle, which is able here to assert itself against the unkindness of the real circumstances" (Freud 163). Given her own temperamental disposition to melancholia, Woolf was a writer who in her representations of reality knows how to minister to herself. Rebellious, pleasure-seeking, self-delighting British humor allows Woolf to import what she encounters in other cultures into her own language and writing without being overwhelmed or herself denatured.

So let us return for a last time to our guiding image of Woolf straddled between cultures, suspended between the recognition that we are the same and the knowledge that we are different. This double relation is figured in a brief exchange in *Between the Acts* between Lucy Swithin, the unifier caressing her cross, and the lyric poet Isa, who seeks unity in other spiritual registers. It occurs at the conclusion of the pageant:

An Improper Englishwoman

> "Did you feel," [Lucy] asked, "what he said: we act different parts but are the same?" "Yes," Isa answered. "No," she added. It was Yes, No. Yes, yes, yes, the tide rushing out embracing. No, no, no, it contracted. The old boot appeared on the shingle. (215)

This dynamic counterpoint between yes and no, affirmation and remonstration constitutes the double rhythm that the world writer translates into his or her own national idiom. Isa's "yes" betokens the relief, then active abandon of the mind as it rushes to embrace the foreign, the strange, the excitingly different in hopes of finding in that embrace an elemental nature, the utterly common. The "no" that inevitably follows betokens the necessary counter-movement of the mind withdrawing into its own native, often isolated dwelling. Was there ever an image of defiance and negation more droll, almost pitifully so, than that old boot on the shingle? Yet it is the humor in the image of a homely, dilapidated, but comfortable old boot marooned atop the surviving homestead that makes, Woolf seems to imply, our human and cultural separateness bearable.[3]

Woolf's complex understanding of how cultures interact and influence each other prompts me to propose her as the personification of her own neologism. I salute her as the new Xenophila, the modern writer who loves the foreign both for its own and for our common sake. When I asked a friend of mine who teaches classical literature about this arresting word, he remarked that as a neologism it indeed might be pronounced to sound like a proper name. And then he added, "Something that might interest you is a late commentator of [sic] Euripides. In the *Life of Euripides* attested in the scholia to his extant plays, Euripides is said to have been 'xenophilotatos' (adj. in superlative), because he was much loved by foreigners. [As you can see, in this late attestation the term has passive sense.] Loving foreigners was foreign to our dear ancient Greeks! But nothing could prevent them from being loved by foreigners."[4] In this particular respect, then, Woolf was superior to her dear Greeks, or at least was most like her beloved Antigone, whose self-declared nature was to join in loving. This would be the image of Woolf I would urge her readers to entertain—not Woolf, the English lady of letters, but the cosmopolite Xenophila Xenophilotates, the world writer who, as her writings and this symposium attest, loved and was much loved by foreigners across cultures.

Notes

[1] I am grateful to Paulo Asso for his invaluable help in alerting me to the possible significance of Xenophila. His diligent research revealed the following: "In the 'Paulys Realencyclopädie der classischen Altertumswissenschaft' vol. IX A.2 [Munich, 1983] columns 1565-7, eight men named Xenophilos are listed. I could not find any Xenophila (or Xenophile, as the feminine would sound). As for the adjective 'xenophilos [xenophile] xenophilon' (a form for each gender, m. f. and neut.), it sounds like a completely possible formation, but it is NEVER attested in the extant corpus of ancient Greek literature. Nor is it familiar to me from Modern Greek." Paolo Asso, E-mail, October 12, 2003.

[2] This bar confronts us whenever we attempt to reach across cultures. It is not simply a question, as it is in large part with Greek, that we are separated by such a large historical divide and that we do not even know how the words the choruses are saying are pronounced. Russian literature, which is contemporaneous with our own, suffers a similar, if indeed not greater degradation. We pass no more easily into the Chekhovian delicacies or Dostoevskyen convulsions of the Russian soul than we can be transported into the ecstasies of the Greek chorus. The Russians, too, suffer miserably in translation, a deprivation Woolf regards as catastrophic. In translation, she vividly observes, "the great Russian writers are like men deprived by an earthquake or a railway accident not only of their clothes, but also of something subtler and more important—their manners, the idiosyncrasies of their characters" ("Russian Point of View" 178).

[3] In a comment on this paper, Mark Hussey suggested that Woolf's utopian version of common cause and common nature might have been registered in Lily Briscoe's fantasy of emotionally attaining "the blessed island of good boots" (*TTL* 154).

[4] Paolo Asso, e-mail, June 14, 2003.

Works Cited

Auerbach, Erich. *Mimesis: The Representation of Reality in Western Culture*. Princeton: Princeton UP, 1991.

Cowley, Malcolm. Review of *Between the Acts*. New Republic 6 October, 1941, 440. Rpt. in *Virginia Woolf: The Critical Heritage*. Eds. Robin Majumdar and Allen McLaurin. London: Routledge and Kegan Paul, 1975.

Freud, Sigmund. "Humour." *The Standard Edition of the Complete Psychological Works of Sigmund Freud* XXI, ed. James Strachey. London: Hogarth Press, 1975.

Spender, Stephen. Obituary Notice. *Listener*, 10 April 1941. Rpt. in *Virginia Woolf: The Critical Heritage*. Eds. Robin Majumdar and Allen McLaurin. London: Routledge and Kegan Paul, 1975.

Woolf, Virginia. *Between the Acts*. San Diego: Harcourt Brace, & Co., 1969.

——."The Cherry Orchard" *The Essays of Virginia Woolf*. Vol. 3, 1919-1924. Ed. Andrew McNeillie. San Diego: Harcourt Brace Jovanovich, 1988: 246-49.

——. *The Essays of Virginia Woolf*. Vol. 2, 1912-1918. Ed. Andrew McNeillie. San Diego: Harcourt Brace Jovanovich, 1987.

———. *Mrs. Dalloway*. Harmondsworth: Penguin, 1991.
———. "Modern Fiction." *The Common Reader*. New York: Harcourt Brace, 1953.
———. "On Not Knowing Greek." *The Common Reader*. New York: Harcourt Brace, 1953.
———. "The Russian Point of View." *The Common Reader*. New York: Harcourt Brace, 1953.
———. *Orlando: A Biography*. San Diego: Harcourt, 1973.
———. *Three Guineas*. Oxford: Oxford University Press, 1992
———. *To the Lighthouse*. San Diego: Harcourt, 1981.

Virginia Woolf and Modernism: New Approaches
Peter Faulkner

In my 1977 book in the Methuen Critical Idiom series (published the year after the larger Penguin book on the topic edited by Malcolm Bradbury and James McFarlane) I pointed out that the term Modernism had become current in English literary criticism only in the late 1960s: it made no appearance in the twentieth-century volume of *The Pelican Guide to English Literature*, but was freely used in *The Sphere History* in 1971, particularly in Bernard Bergonzi's opening essay "The Coming of Modernism." I identified the period of Modernism in England as between 1910 and 1930, and took from Stephen Spender's undervalued 1963 book *The Struggle of the Modern* his statements that "Modern art is that in which the artist reflects awareness of an unprecedented modern situation in form and idiom," and that "the principle of reality in our time is peculiarly difficult to grasp, and that 'realism' is not an adequate approach to it" (qtd. 15), relating these statements to Erich Auerbach's great chapter "The Brown Stocking" in *Mimesis* and to other works of post-war criticism. It was only later that I realized the extent that my thinking had been influenced by F. R. Leavis, whose memorably idiosyncratic lectures I had attended as a student at Cambridge. I doubt if Leavis ever used the word modernist, but it seems clear to me that in *New Bearings in English Poetry* Leavis was already in 1932 praising the poetry of Pound and Eliot for what we now call its modernist qualities; the same is true to some extent of his praise of Lawrence's method in *Women in Love* in *D. H. Lawrence, Novelist* in 1955. In my book Virginia Woolf was of course named among the Modernists—not as a "token woman" but as a significant novelist and theorist. The main account of Woolf here was given by my colleague Anthony Fothergill, who wrote on her critical essays. Fothergill emphasized the tension between her attempt to give an accurate account of the modern novelist's enterprise and her Nietzschean suspicion of system, and showed that her explorations were at once tentative and bold. He concluded with the suggestion that we should read the fictions of Joyce, Woolf and Beckett "a little better to read ourselves," which I take to be closely related to his contention that "to understand the modern mind we need to understand the medium in which the mind exists—language" (38). At that time, 1977, I concluded the book with the assertion that no new movement had arrived with the stature of Modernism, and argued that "It is perhaps the high seriousness of their devotion to art which distinguishes the modernists from their successors, who set more store by jokes and language games" (75). History has to some extent overtaken this view, which makes the Modernists sound too high-minded and their successors too superficial. It might be worth remarking, though, that the present suspicion of high-mindedness in English culture is not too far from our traditional philistinism.

By the time that I returned to the discussion of Modernism nearly a decade later, in my Introduction to a selection of critical texts, *A Modernist Reader*, in 1986, I did not feel it necessary to make major changes to my account, though a great deal of scholarship had appeared in the intermediate years, and Postmodernist culture had developed if not exploded. Thus it is perhaps not surprising that a critic of the next generation, Peter Brooker, in his Introduction to *Modernism/Postmodernism* in 1992, found my view over-simple and Spender's formula "blandly reflectionist" (Brooker 2). It is true that we now, rightly, see the word "reflect" as far too simple to describe the relation between art and the not-art from which it is created. But it still seems to me that important questions arise from Spender's formulation: whether there was "an unprecedented modern situation" at the beginning of the twentieth century, and whether this was expressed in the "form and idiom"—as distinct from the subject matter—of the cultural products with which we are concerned. Brooker includes much important critical material in his reader, from such writers as Lukács, Benjamin, Adorno, Berman, Williams, Habermas, Lyotard, Baudrillard, Jameson, Kristeva, Eco and Fuentes, and it is clear that much important scholarship was appearing which was helping to deepen and enlarge discussions of Modernism, especially in the work of Fredric Jameson and Marshall Berman. Jameson's 1982 *The Political Unconscious* is valuable in showing how history, transparently represented in the realistic mode of the nineteenth-century novel, is equally present in modernist writing despite Modernism's emphasis on the individual consciousness. The idea of the political unconscious is a stimulus to the reader to seek out the social implications of texts that seem to want to deny that they embody any. Many of us have I think followed Jameson's lead in thus reading against the grain of modernist aesthetics. Equally importantly, Berman's *All That is Solid Melts into Air* of 1983 certainly succeeded in drawing attention authoritatively to a central aspect of "The Experience of Modernity" (the book's subtitle). For Berman, the first part of *The Communist Manifesto* specifies what were to emerge as the central polarities of the culture of Modernism: "the theme of insatiable desires and drives, permanent revolution, infinite development, perpetual creation and renewal in every sphere of life; and its radical antithesis, the theme of nihilism, insatiable destruction, the shattering and swallowing up of life, the heart of

Virginia Woolf and Modernism: New Approaches

darkness, the horror" (Brooker, 102). There is no denying that such polarities provide much of the energy of modernist creativity.

Brooker's book thus demonstrated the vitality of relevant scholarship in the 1980s, but the index to his book suggests that when it comes to the creative writers, the usual names were holding their own: Eliot, Picasso, Pound, and Woolf are there (though none as frequently as Joyce), together with Beckett, Brecht, and H. D., with James and Yeats in the background. As far as Woolf figures, it is for her remark about "human character" having changed in December 1910 (6), which leads into an awkward discussion of the relationship between the "reactionary ideas" of the male modernists and their writings, which seems to be based on the dubious assumption that because Eliot and the others deplored many aspects of modernity, they could not write about them in a modernist manner. Earlier, Brooker had wanted to detach Woolf from the male writers because of her criticisms of Eliot and Joyce; but there is no doubt that she saw herself as a "Georgian" writer, avoiding the heavy-handed materialism of her Edwardian contemporaries.

Woolf also appears in Jean Radford's contribution to the book, "Coming to Terms: Dorothy Richardson, Modernism and Women." Radford is unhappy about the continuing power, as she sees it, of the canon of Modernism, with Woolf as its "token woman" (96). She draws attention to the problems of feminist critics who do not wish either for women writers to be assimilated to the [male] canon, or to create an alternative canon for women writers. She goes on to attempt to answer the question as to why Richardson is little read (which I believe is still the case) and to suggest ways in which she might be read. One suggestion is that *Pilgrimage* might be read "as a dialogue with other discourses of the period" (Brooker, 101). Thus the activity of Richardson's protagonist is compared to Woolf's in *A Room of One's Own*. Radford ends by commenting on the role of the city in *Pilgrimage*, in relation to Raymond Williams's account in *Writing in Society* in 1983. Anti-urbanism, it is argued, became a constituent element of Englishness at this period. By contrast, Richardson's Miriam Henderson comes back to London at the end of the series, viewing it as a "prairie" rather than a Waste Land (105); from her woman's perspective, the sentimental view of rural England is invalid. Radford's suggestion that *Pilgrimage* should be read in the context of contemporary writing about women is appealing, but it leaves open the question of the reader's response to the text. We are left with the difficult question for the Richardson enthusiast of why so many still read Woolf and so few Richardson. (Dr. Leavis might have attributed it to literary quality, though he would have been reluctant to grant that in Woolf's case.) Is it the result of an academic and publishers' conspiracy? Or dare we admit that there is something about the quality of Woolf's writing that captivates the reader? My view is the latter, but should I be happy with my own captivation? And should I ignore Richardson because she doesn't captivate? This is an issue that deserves further consideration. My impression is that English universities are now producing students who are taught to be more interested in the cultural significance of what they read than in its literary quality. Nevertheless, and happily, Woolf retains a wide readership.

Discussions of Modernism continued and developed. In 1995 Peter Nicholls in his *Modernisms. A Literary Guide* criticized the view of Modernism as "a sort of monolithic cultural formation" (Nicholls vii). His range of reference, both historical and national, was persuasive in this regard, as he moved from Baudelaire, Rimbaud and Mallarmé through to Marinetti and Kafka, and including under the heading "At a Tangent: Other Modernisms," H. D., Stein, Richardson, W. C. Williams, Stevens, Moore and Loy. In "Other Times: The Narratives of High Modernism," Nicholls placed the "belatedness" of Joyce, so aware of his place in the history of fiction, against the stream of consciousness in Woolf, and showed how they were both too "romantic" for the Lewis of that ferocious novel *Tarr*. (102)

Michael Levenson's *Cambridge Companion to Modernism* in 1999 began energetically with the argument that current views of Modernism were distorted and that "A coarsely understood Modernism is at once a historical scandal and a contemporary disability" (Levenson 1). Levenson went on to raise important questions: "Was Woolf's feminism ensnared within a deep class snobbery? Did Eliot's anti-semitism reach down to the roots of his poetry?" But he emphasized that the modernists had to respond to "the pressures of an ugly age" (7). The range of the topics considered is impressive, from Michael Bell on "The Metaphysics of Modernism" through accounts of fiction, drama and poetry to the politics of culture, gender, the visual arts and film. The account of "The Modern Novel" is by David Trotter, who considers Ford, Lewis, Joyce, Lawrence, Fitzgerald, Woolf, Faulkner, Hemingway and Richardson. Its final section, "The Mind Grows Rings," focuses on *Ulysses*, *The Waves* and, unusually and welcomely, Ford's still undervalued *Parade's End*. The selection of these novels supports the view that the modernists were ambitious to produce works that could give comprehensive, though necessarily incomplete, accounts of their times. Trotter argued that the modernist use of parody was followed by or modulated into "a process of psychic and textual additiveness (a proliferation of virtual realities)" (94). As far as Woolf was concerned, he argued challengingly that she was "more interested in cumulative models of selfhood" than recent criticism had been prepared to acknowledge (95).

Virginia Woolf and Modernism: New Approaches

In 2000 Routledge published Peter Childs's *Modernism* in their New Critical Idiom series. The format was larger than Methuen had offered in 1977: 226 pages in all to the earlier 86. Childs devoted the extra room largely to contextualizing material. Thus the first of his three main chapters is entitled "Interpreting and Changing," a title deriving from Marx's well-known statement about the difference between his own—revolutionary—practice and that of previous philosophers, who had been content to try to interpret the world. Childs uses the phrase to introduce a discussion of six thinkers whose interpretations of the world may be said to have changed it, if not for their own, certainly for future generations. The thinkers he discusses are what we might fairly consider the obvious choices: Marx, Darwin, Freud, Nietzsche, Saussure and Einstein. Of these, Saussure is probably the nearest to being a new recruit, which is a reminder that first Structuralism, and then Theory, had their great impact on literary studies in the West in the 1980s and beyond.

A recent theorist whose "Model of Modernism" Childs finds illuminating is Norman Cantor in his 1988 book *Twentieth-Century Culture: Modernism to Deconstruction*. In relation to sexuality and the family, we are told, Cantor argues that "Modernism introduced a new openness with candid descriptions often sympathetic to feminism, homosexuality, androgyny and bisexuality beside a questioning of the constraints of the nuclear family which seemed to hamper the individual's search for personal values" (Childs 19). This is especially interesting as Childs's first reference to feminism. All the six cited sages are male, though Childs is well aware of the importance of feminism in challenging the constitution of the modernist canon. (It is curious that we seem to be able to find in the twentieth century no one single figure equivalent to Mary Wollstonecraft at the end of the eighteenth—perhaps modern feminism had to be a group project?) It is in his Introduction that Childs shows the influence of recent feminist criticism, as when he refers to the "masculinist elitism" of Modernism (22). He remarks that writers like Jean Rhys, Katherine Mansfield, Mina Loy, Dorothy Richardson, Sylvia Townsend Warner and Charlotte Mew "have been added to Virginia Woolf's token inclusion in the Modernist canon" (23), and that critics like Alice Jardine and Rachel Blau DuPlessis have "registered the communality between Modernist writing and *écriture féminine*" as defined by Kristeva and Cixous (23). But Childs resists Andreas Huyssen's argument that there is a "powerful masculinist mystique" inherent in Modernism (24), preferring to allow the possibility of a wider understanding of the term, even if some of the male protagonists of Huyssen's paradigm might not have liked the company they are now placed in.

The contextualization that Childs offers his readers is clearly presented and soundly based, and the emphasis on it is typical of recent approaches. But

Faulkner

he does not neglect more traditional critical exposition. He devotes his second chapter to "Genres, Art and Film," though perhaps surprisingly omitting any consideration of music. Particularly valuable is the devotion of a section to the Short Story—a very important area of modernist activity too often subsumed under The Novel—and of another to Film. Here Childs emphasizes the work of Buñuel and Eisenstein, and relates to the latter's use of montage pages near the end of *Mrs. Dalloway* in which Clarissa's mind ranges over many diverse topics, to recur to "the young man who had killed himself."

The third and final chapter of Childs's book devotes itself to smaller-scale literary criticism, focussing on twelve texts. In accordance with the assertion that Modernism is not so much "a precise label" as "a way of referring to the efforts of many individuals across the arts who tried to move away from established modes of representation" (129), the discussion proceeds under four thematic headings. Thus Charlotte Mew, Katherine Mansfield and D. H. Lawrence appear under "Freedom and Gender," Conrad, James and Ford under "Epistemology and Narration," Woolf, Rebecca West and Eliot under "Identity and War," and Forster, Yeats and Joyce under "Symbolism and Language." The first section enables Childs to return to the topic of feminism, and to pay tribute to critics like Janet Wolff —"Feminism and Modernism" (1990)—and Bonnie Kime Scott—*The Gender of Modernism* (1990). We might want to add earlier Hanscombe and Syers's 1987 *Writing for Their Lives*, together with Gilbert and Gubar's three volumes of *No Man's Land* between 1988 and 1994, and Rita Felski's *The Gender of Modernity* of 1995. All this critical activity means that Childs is in a position to offer another list of women writers previously excluded from the modernist canon: to Woolf and Mansfield are now added May Sinclair, Mina Loy, Rose Macaulay, Jean Rhys, Sylvia Townsend Warner, Edith Sitwell, Anna Wickham and Charlotte Mew. Most readers today would welcome all these names, and to them Childs adds Rebecca West in a later section. But is Mew, fine poet that she is, more modernist than Hardy? And where is H. D.?—she appears only as a founding Imagist with Pound and Aldington (98). Surely the author of the *Trilogy* ought to be celebrated here, a poet who has much in common in sensibility to Woolf, as in Section 29 of "The Walls Do Not Fall":

> We have had too much consecration,
> too little affirmation,
>
> too much: but this, this, this
> has been proved heretical,
>
> too little: I know, I feel
> the meaning that words hide;

Virginia Woolf and Modernism: New Approaches

> they are anagrams, cryptograms, little boxes, conditioned
> to hatch butterflies...

Although Childs's individual discussions are well managed and illuminating, there is clearly something arbitrary about this arrangement: for instance, the placing of Woolf and Eliot under the heading of War means that it is *Mrs. Dalloway* and *The Waste Land* that we encounter, with West's *The Return of the Soldier*. *The Waves* gets only one mention, and *Four Quartets* none at all. We could all suggest different groupings and texts, but that is not perhaps the point: Childs has succeeded in showing the complexities of the ideas he is discussing, and he has expanded the old modernist canon—though no one seems to have been totally discarded. (Overall, the book is clearly about Modernism as it developed in England, so that American writers are present only in the background.)

Childs's account of *Mrs. Dalloway* in the context of the Great War begins with a discussion of the condition then known as shell-shock, relating it to "female" hysteria as well as to the traumatic situations that caused it. He then considers Woolf's idea or ideal of androgyny—"It is fatal to be a man or a woman pure and simple; one must be woman-manly or man-womanly" from *A Room of One's Own* (qtd. 165)—and to consider her technique of psychological "tunnelling." He suggests that Woolf offers three past "sexual possibilities" for Clarissa in the forms of the woman Sally Seton, the unmanly (and therefore perhaps androgynous) man Peter Walsh, and the conventionally manly Richard Dalloway. For the character of Septimus Warren Smith, similarly, there are—or have been—alternative possibilities: his hero-worshipping of his [dead] officer Evans is in tension with his feelings for his wife, to whom he feels no physical response. These psychological complexities, Childs argues, lead the reader to focus on the elusive concept of the self, "which Woolf sees as many-sided and fragmentary but which the Harley Street doctors in the novel, Holmes and Bradshaw, and the War Office Committee see as essentially whole and unified" (167). The discussion is well sustained, and comes back finally to the assertion that "Woolf presents a multi-planar, non-linear view of reality in order to represent the complexity of the modern world, and much of this has to do with the structural dislocation of World War I." Childs then quotes a striking passage from Gertrude Stein to the effect that "the composition of the war, 1914-18, was not the composition of all previous wars" but was "a composition in which one corner was as important as another corner, in fact the composition of cubism" (qtd.175). It certainly seems to be the case that Modernism in England was profoundly influenced by the war, even if the poets who responded most powerfully to it did not employ modernist techniques to convey their agonized responses—with the exception of the sections of Pound's *Mauberley* that deal with the war. Two significant male writers who experienced and wrote powerfully about the war but are still rarely admitted into discussions of Modernism are Richard Aldington and Harold Monro. Aldington usually gets some attention as an Imagist, but his trilogy of novels, *Death of a Hero* (1929), *The Colonel's Daughter* (1931) and *All Men are Enemies* (1932) deserve more attention than it has so far been afforded. Monro, founder of the *Poetry Review* and the Poetry Bookshop, continues to be neglected despite Dominic Hibberd's perceptive 2001 study, *Harold Monro: Poet of the New Age*. When Monro's *Collected Poems* were published posthumously in 1933, T. S. Eliot contributed a critical essay in which he praised Monro's poetry as "more nearly the right thing than any of the poetry of a somewhat older generation than mine except Mr Yeats's" (qtd. 262). Hibberd's description, paraphrasing Eliot, sounds very modernist: "his work had been his own, concerning itself with the world inside the skull, a place of bad dreams and endless questioning" (261).

Finally we come to the *Concise Companion to Modernism*, edited by David Bradshaw and published by Blackwell this year, 2003. As Bradshaw explains, the project of the book is not to define the term, but to give the cultural context in which Modernism developed. Bradshaw is not afraid to use the term Modernism or to make value judgments. His Introduction asserts that Modernism "emerged and flourished" in the "radical and iconoclastic environment" of a time which produced "an efflorescence of ideas" (Bradshaw 1)—his dates are 1880 to 1939—particularly in the twelve spheres with which his book deals, from the Life Sciences, Eugenics and Nietzscheanism through to Physics, Publishing and Reading. Again, if we consult the index we will not be particularly surprised. Along with a range of cultural critics, we find most attention going to Conrad, Eliot, Hardy, Lawrence, Pound, Shaw, Wells, Woolf and Yeats.

Woolf is particularly favored, seven of her works being discussed. The main considerations occur under the headings "Eugenics" and "Reading," and there is an intriguing one under "'Physics." The passage about eugenics is by Bradshaw, and it constitutes a defense of Woolf against the attack on her by Donald Childs in his 2001 book *Modernism and Eugenics: Woolf, Eliot, Yeats and the Culture of Degeneration*, following Suzanne Raitt's argument that Woolf had been unhealthily influenced by the eugenicist attitude of Vita Sackville-West (49). Childs quotes a passage from a letter of 9 January 1915, when she and Leonard had passed "a long line of imbeciles" walking by the river. "It was perfectly horrible," Woolf goes on: "They should certainly be killed" (qtd. 9). Bradshaw's defense is to point out that similar views were

Virginia Woolf and Modernism: New Approaches

being expressed at the time; while this may be true, what we feel in reading the passage is surely something like hysteria: Woolf is profoundly disturbed by what she has seen—who would not be?—and expresses her distress in this aggressive way. At all events, I strongly agree with Bradshaw that this emotive comment should not be taken as commitment to a eugenic program. Bradshaw seems to me more convincing when he goes on to defend passages in Woolf's fiction against criticism by Childs. Childs reads the account in *Mrs. Dalloway* of Lady Bruton's plan to send "young people" to Canada as suggesting Woolf's support for the scheme, but Bradshaw is able to demonstrate that Woolf's irony at Lady Bruton's expense separates Woolf from a positive judgment here, and is part of Woolf's characteristic hostility to imperialist ideologies (52). It is another Bradshaw—Sir William—who proclaims the need to make it "impossible for the unfit to propagate their views," and he is the least sympathetically presented character in the entire novel (53).

A book that is clearly in the background here—though it does not make it into the Select Bibliography—is John Carey's *The Intellectuals and the Masses* of 1992, described by Bradshaw in his chapter on Eugenics as "the most vigorous excoriation of attitudes which were to find monstrous realisation in the racial policies of the Nazis" (34). Carey's thesis is that the writers of the early twentieth century were so disturbed by the massive extension of the reading public and the danger that this might be held to offer to the idea of high culture that they embarked on an assault on the crudity and brutality of the masses which often led them to accept dangerous eugenic attitudes. Carey makes his case by extensive quotation of unsavory sentiments, though his book is marred by a certain philistine populism which shows itself in the use of the term "intellectual"—by an Oxford don—as indicating the self-evidently pretentious. From the present point of view, it is also the case that some of the writers criticized, like H. G. Wells, do not belong obviously to the modernist tradition.

Further into Bradshaw's book we come to a discussion of Physics by Michael Whitworth. Here Whitworth draws attention to the short story "Solid Objects" of 1920. In this strange story, a young man finds "a lump of sea-smoothed glass" on the sea shore, and becomes so obsessed with collecting "fascinating scraps of broken china and peculiar lumps of metal" that he gives up a promising political career (200-1). Whitworth sees his behavior as raising the question, important in twentieth-century science, as to "how these material particularities can be assembled into any sort of pattern without recourse to abstract generalisations; how we move from perceptions to conceptions" (201). Whether we need to relate this question to "descriptionism," as Whitworth does, I am uncertain. We could see the question equally well as one of Woolf's aesthetic preoccupations.

Faulkner

Woolf is presented most positively in the final chapter of the book, "Reading and Modernism," by Todd Avery and Patrick Brantlinger. It is emphasized that she was concerned with the activity of reading throughout her career as a writer, and she is contrasted with the male modernists who were suspicious of the new reading public and addressed themselves characteristically to an educated elite. Although Woolf is presented as sharing the concern with "making it new," she is said to have had a much more positive attitude to the Common Reader, as the title of her books of essays would suggest. This is attributed to her position as a woman excluded from university education, and also, more surprisingly, to her membership of the Bloomsbury Group. Her experience of the Group emerges as a much more liberating and generous experience than is often suggested. The members of the Group are said to have had "an abiding concern with the complex nuances and subtle gradations of aesthetic habitation and of ethical responsiveness to others" (252). For her, we are told, "the reader and the (modernist) writer were—or *might be*—joined by an ethic that promoted sympathetic and noncoercive human relations..." (253). In her 1932 essay "How Should One Read a Book?", Woolf's conclusion was generously liberal: her advice was: "to follow your own instincts, to use your own reason, to come to your own conclusions." Avery and Brantlinger relate this attitude to Woolf's feminist suspicion of male authority, "however heavily furred and gowned," in *A Room of One's Own* (qtd. 253).

This attitude is related to the fluidity of Woolf's novelistic method, especially in *The Waves*, and then, more surprisingly, to the interest of some of the early modernists and the Bloomsbury Group in the new medium of radio. Here Desmond MacCarthy is particularly praised for his series of broadcasts in 1932-1933 on "The Art of Reading." It is noted that his approach was at the opposite extreme from Eliot's as demonstrated at the same time in the lectures that became *The Use of Poetry and the Use of Criticism*. MacCarthy's approach aimed to encourage the reader to make his or her own choices and judgments:

> It is best to enjoy an author before one understands him. Indeed, in my opinion, it is little use trying to understand him before one has enjoyed him...Take then...from every book what belongs to you in it. I'm sure that this is the right way to set about studying literature. True, this method won't necessarily help you to pass examinations or impress others by your cultured conversation, but it is the best way of making literature part of your life and that after all is the most important thing. (qtd. 257)

Woolf, it is argued, was with MacCarthy in her approach to the reader, seeking not "a homogeneity of consent" but rather for "a 'heterogeneity of dissensus' among the multitudes of ordinary, plain, raw, general, low, unkindled, novice,

Virginia Woolf and Modernism: New Approaches

or common readers and 'listeners-in'" (257). Avery and Brantlinger carry through their celebratory mood to the end, suggesting that two kinds of contemporary criticism may prove particularly illuminating for readers of Woolf. One—practised by Anna Snaith and Melba Cuddy-Keane—is looking at the reception of Woolf's work by readers from classes different from her own; the other—by Derek Attridge and Kevin Dettmar—is encouraging us to read modernist texts in a postmodern way, and to discover even more richness when we discard the search for total meaning or philosophical consistency. The reader here seems to be reborn as enthusiast; but might he or she not too easily dispense with the pleasure of the unified text? Here we find ourselves returning to Childs's final sentence (207) about the problematizing of character, representation, reality and "even 'literature'" in postmodern culture, and asking once again what the pleasure of the text, whether Woolf's or another's, can be for us today.

It is evident from the texts discussed that contextualizing is perhaps the most prominent feature of recent critical activity in relation to Modernism. A final question may be raised about the kinds of contextualization that have become usual in recent discussions. Have the contexts we encounter not become too exclusively those of intellectual, at the expense of social and political, history? It is true that most of the chapters in Bradshaw's book relate their ideas to historical events, and we begin the book with a Chronology that includes some political facts, e. g. 1897 Queen Victoria's Diamond Jubilee, 1899 Second Anglo-Boer war (-1902), 1906 Liberal Government elected, 1914 Outbreak of World War I, 1920 League of Nations established, 1924 First Labour Government, 1929 Wall Street Crash, 1936 Spanish Civil war (-1939), 1939 Beginning of World War II. But is this enough to provide an equivalent in historical grounding to the intellectual material covered in detail? This is particularly problematic in the absence of references to the Empire, apart from Ireland: neither "British Empire" nor "Imperialism" is to be found in the index, and although J. A. Hobson does appear—and is indeed praised in a quotation as "by far the most original and penetrating of the new liberal theorists at the turn of the century" (188)—it is for *The Physiology of Industry and Problems of Poverty*, not for his great book *Imperialism: A Study* of 1902. Yet Edward Said's *Culture and Imperialism* had appeared in 1993, and even if it is admitted that the book is less powerful than *Orientalism*, it will hardly do to assume that it has no relevance to the discussion of Modernism. Said himself ends his second chapter, "Consolidated Vision," with a five-page "Note on Modernism." Here he remarks on the emergence of the late-Victorian novel of "frank exoticism and confident empire" in Haggard and Kipling, and how this was followed by the narratives of Conrad, radiating "an extreme, unsettling

Faulkner

anxiety" (227). He goes on to suggest that Conrad, Forster, Malraux and T. E. Lawrence "take narrative from the triumphalist experience of imperialism into the extremes of self-consciousness, discontinuity, self-referentiality and corrosive irony, whose formal patterns we have come to recognize as the hallmarks of modernist culture," the culture also of Joyce, Eliot, Proust, Mann and Yeats. Said's important argument here is that the development of this modernist culture has been seen too often in terms of the internal dynamics of Western society, and not often enough as in part a response to "the external pressures on culture from the *imperium*" (227). Said argues that the Asiatic fever infecting Mann's Venice is an acknowledgement of the vulnerability of Europe to what it had confidently assumed to be its colonial inferiors, and Joyce's Bloom an admission that the English/Irish antithesis needs to admit the necessity of the stranger. Here was Europe belatedly acknowledging the importance of the non-European, "not oppositionally but ironically, and with a desperate attempt at a new inclusiveness" (228). Thus "a new encyclopaedic form" (229) emerged, with three common features: circularity of structure, diversity of materials, and an emphasis on the aesthetic. Said concludes challengingly:

> When you can no longer assume that Britannia will rule the waves forever, you have to reconceive reality as something that can be held together for you by the artist, in history rather than geography. Spatiality becomes, ironically, the characteristic of an aesthetic rather than of political domination, as more and more regions—from India to Africa to the Caribbean—challenge the classical empires and their cultures. (229)

This is an important reminder of the context in which English Modernism emerged, and one that ought not to be neglected merely because the theoretical discourse of empire was only just beginning to emerge at the time.

There is one chapter in Bradshaw's *Modernism* written by a historian, Sarah Wilkinson, but it is entitled "The Concept of the State 1880-1939"—an accurate title, but one suggesting that historical events are not to be its main focus. This is typical of many recent approaches to Modernism which show more interest in theories than in what actually occurred in people's lives in the modern period. We could argue, unfashionably, that it is to the works of fiction themselves that we can go for such enlightenment. But perhaps too we should be pressing ourselves (and our students) to pay more attention to social and political history. If we don't, what does that mean for our (and their) understanding of whatever it is we read? Fortunately, in the case of Woolf, reading *A Room of One's Own* and *Three Guineas* will remind us of the context in which she was writing her fiction, and so preserve us from dehistoricizing and aestheticizing it.

Works Cited

Berman, Marshall. *All That is Solid Melts Into Air*. 1982. London: Verso, 1983.
Bradbury, Malcolm and James McFarlane, eds. *Modernism*. Harmondsworth: Penguin, 1976.
Bradshaw, David, ed. *The Concise Companion to Modernism*. Oxford: Blackwell, 2003.
Brooker, Peter, ed. *Modernism/Postmodernism*. London: Longman, 1992.
Carey, John. *The Intellectuals and the Masses*. London: Faber and Faber, 1992.
Childs, Peter. *Modernism*. London: Routledge, 2000.
Faulkner, Peter. *Modernism*. London: Methuen, 1977.
Faulkner, Peter, ed. *A Modernist Reader*. London: Batsford, 1986.
Hibberd, Dominic. *Harold Monro. Poet of the New Age*. London: Palgrave, 2001.
Jameson, Fredric. *The Political Unconscious*. London: Methuen, 1981.
Levenson, Michael, ed. *The Cambridge Companion to Modernism*. Cambridge: CUP, 1999.
Nicholls, Peter. *Modernisms. A Literary Guide*. London: Macmillan, 1995.
Said, Edward. *Culture and Imperialism*. London: Chatto and Windus, 1993.
Williams, Raymond. *Writing in Society*. London: Verso, 1983.

Virginia Woolf in the U. S. A.
Mark Hussey

Leslie Stephen's household was unusual in its American sympathies and connections; unusual too for "certain related democratic sympathies; a vision, at least in Leslie Stephen's eyes, of what America meant and promised" (McNeillie 41). In 1863, at the height of the American Civil War, Virginia Woolf's father, "tired of the snobbery of the Confederate supporters at Cambridge" (Annan 52), traveled to America. Noel Annan explains that Stephen "realized only too well that this upper-class dislike of the North sprang from dread of democracy" (52). While in America, Stephen established close friendships with prominent intellectuals—Charles Eliot Norton, Oliver Wendell Holmes, and James Russell Lowell. The very first letter in Woolf's published correspondence, written when she was six, is to Lowell, who at the time was American Minister in London.

The now well-known English reaction against Woolf might in a sense be seen as a problem of mis-hearing. Despite her occasional outbursts against humanity in the mass (see Lee, "Offence"), I would argue that Woolf inherited the spirit of her father's profoundly ethical stance toward democracy, and that her foremost early detractors, the Leavises, could not hear in her works the attitudes and principles of that Cambridge critic they very much admired (McKillop 276-77). Two years after his return from America, Stephen attacked the London *Times* for its support of the South in a lengthy pamphlet,[1] anticipating his daughter's later reaction against the newspaper of record for its promotion of the First World War: "I become steadily more feminist," Woolf wrote in 1916 to Margaret Llewelyn Davies, "owing to the Times, which I read at breakfast and wonder how this preposterous masculine fiction keeps going a day longer—without some vigorous young woman pulling us together and marching through it" (*L2* 76). Woolf's analysis of the power of the press to "burke discussion of any undesirable subject," as she put it in *Three Guineas* (162 n16), was a significant thread in the *bricolage* of her 1930s scrapbooks, the source material for much of *Three Guineas* and *The Years*.

Andrew McNeillie has spoken of Woolf's image of America as "a positive space, a place of democracy and futurity, of largely enabling modernity, but one hampered by European traditions, by the haunting shades of English literature" (42). He describes Woolf's America as "an imaginary world" in which she could "extend her speculations, voice the frustrations of what we call a 'modernist' writer and a woman writer" (42-43). In a whimsical article for *Hearst's International* magazine, combined with *Cosmopolitan*, in 1938, Woolf con-

47

cluded that Americans "face the future, not the past." She wrote, "The Americans have swallowed their dinner by the time it takes us to decide whether the widow of a general takes precedence of the wife of a knight commander of the Star of India" ("America" 58). Unlike "the old families who had all intermarried, and lay in their deaths intertwisted, like the ivy roots, beneath the churchyard wall" in *Between the Acts* (7), Americans "never settled down and lived and died and were buried in the same spot" ("America" 58). Concerned as she was throughout her life with the intrinsic connection between democracy and education, Woolf includes in this short article the vision of a fantastic repository of literary manuscripts to contrast with the constraints and hindrances she had described so wittily in *A Room of One's Own*:

> But that immense building which might be a factory or a cathedral—what is that? It occupies a commanding position. In England it would be the King's palace. But here are no sentries; the doors stand open to all. The walls are made of stainless steel, the shelves of unbreakable glass. And there lie Shakespeare's folios, Ben Jonson's manuscripts, Keats's love letter blazing in the light of the American sun. ("America" 59)

Fifteen years after Woolf's death, Leonard Woolf, considering what to do with his wife's papers, wrote to his brother Philip that he was very impressed with the way American universities made writers' papers accessible, and with the intelligence of American students. "I have never come across anything like this here," he continued, "and I feel that if the MSS went to Cambridge or Oxford, they would be stuffed away somewhere and no one would ever look at them again except that one would be shown from time to time to the public under a glass case" (Spotts 500; dated September 17, 1956).

Although I have begun thus to provide a context for Woolf's reception in the United States, so markedly different than that in her own country in the decades immediately following her death, the difference may now well be moot. Witness, for example, the extraordinary work being done on Woolf's texts by British scholars, best exemplified by Julia Briggs's "feminist" edition for Penguin, where English editors dominate, or by the recent *Cambridge Companion to Virginia Woolf*, again dominated by the view from the UK. Jane Marcus, who claimed in 1996 that Woolf is "worthy of world-scale interest as a social thinker" and criticized certain British writers for continuing "to denigrate, scapegoat or ignore Woolf's contributions to social debates and political activities," need not have been concerned about Woolf's re-entry into her home culture in the 1990s ("Wrapped" 19).

I am talking, of course, about the version of Woolf established by feminist academics, but Woolf, as Brenda Silver points out in *Virginia Woolf Icon*, circulates in at least four significant milieux: the academic; that of the "common

Virginia Woolf in the U. S. A.

reader"; that of the self-styled "intellectual" media; and that of popular culture. Given the permeability of boundaries at the start of the twenty-first century, it is an open question which Woolf will be received in new geographies.

One result of the central role played by the U. S. women's movement in Woolf's steady rise in status in the 1970s-1980s was to make Woolf studies virtually synonymous with feminist criticism itself. Patricia Joplin wrote in 1983 that "[I]t would be hard to find any major work of American feminist theory, particularly literary theory, that is not to some degree indebted to *A Room...* There Woolf provided virtually every metaphor we now use. She made available a set of questions, a way of asking them, a possible vision of what lay behind and beyond women's silence" (4). Others have, rightly, warned against drawing too much authority from Woolf (e.g. Bette London, Peggy Kamuf, Trinh T. Minh-ha), but the centrality of Woolf in the foundational structures of American feminist literary criticism is undeniable. Her direct descendants include Kate Millett's *Sexual Politics*, and Sandra Gilbert and Susan Gubar's three-volume *No Man's Land*, works concerned with the impact of the suffrage movement on masculine discourse in the early twentieth century. Woolf's ideas and image are thoroughly imbricated with early works of American literary feminism, such as Joanna Russ's *How to Suppress Women's Writing*, and also inform the work of radical feminist writers such as Andrea Dworkin and Mary Daly. Woolf's metaphors and the issues they illuminate continue to make their presence felt in women's writing: for example,

- we think back through our mothers if we are women
- no common sentence ready for her use
- feminine anger
- women as looking glasses reflecting man at twice his natural size
- Chloe likes Olivia
- anonymity runs in the blood
- interruptions there will always be
- A ____ of one's own

There was intense identification with Woolf among women in the American academy in the early 1970s. Ellen Hawkes Rogat, who published the first challenge to Quentin Bell's representation of Woolf in 1974, wrote of her "pilgrimage" to the Berg Collection of the New York Public Library, where most of Woolf's manuscripts are housed: "In a strange way, her experiences and mine began to reverberate. Not only did her thoughts structure mine, not only were my feelings so often filtered through hers, but I also began to understand, almost vicariously, her responses to experience" ("Visiting"). And she recounts being across the table from a "scholar...who berated his wife, in a

49

strained library whisper, for copying a manuscript too slowly" ("Visiting"). The personal, as Woolf argued in *Three Guineas*, was political.

The relations between biography and fiction were always of particular interest to Woolf, and have also been a prominent feature of Woolf studies from their earliest days. Woolf's writings and her own biography play a salient role in the transformation of autobiography and biography studies that also began in the 1970s.[2] Daniel Ferrer has questioned whether it is possible "in Virginia Woolf's case, to separate the text and what is outside it, the writing and the life?"

> Where could we draw the line in the vast quantity of *intermediate* writings—the diary, the autobiographical fragments, the letters—which occupy such an important place in her *oeuvre* and offer many points of contact with the novels, which they often precede or double? Most critics have been aware of this impossibility of marking a boundary in the continuum which goes from the life to the diary or letters, from the diary to the autobiographical writings; from the autobiographical writings to a novel presented as autobiographical like *To the Lighthouse*; and thence to all the other novels and short stories. (quoted in Anderson 49)

Jacqueline Rose has written in *The Haunting of Sylvia Plath* on the impossibility of assigning final authority to any particular articulation of the subjectivity dispersed across such writers' many and various genres.

At just that moment when challenging new theories of the subject were being received, in translation, in the American university, the women's movement was also attempting to consolidate its arguments in academic programs and to reify women's ways of knowing, women's life-writing, and women's history. At the same time, Woolf was being elevated to a central position in the turbulent cultural politics of the early 1970s through her association not only with feminist criticism but also with the narratives of women's lives privileged through consciousness-raising. In her recent biography of Woolf, Hermione Lee identifies as a risky strategy Woolf's "double approach" in *Three Guineas* to "masculinity as both essentialist and constructed, which it did not try to resolve" (Lee 681) but this unresolved "double approach," I would argue, is the heart of Woolf's politics, which is, after all, the politics of an *artist*. It has been pointed out also by Peggy Kamuf, who describes a "fault line" running beneath *A Room*'s sketch of Professor von X in "the notion of sexual differentiation as a historical production which, if it has produced a privileged masculine subject, cannot also be understood as originating in the subject it only produces" (152). Woolf's skirting of the border of essentialism and construction in both her fiction and non-fiction, as well as in the subject constructed in her autobiographical writings, is what makes her precisely an exemplary figure for

Virginia Woolf in the U. S. A.

American feminism, caught as it has perennially been on the divide between equality and difference, between the urge to deconstruct and eradicate difference, and to emphasize difference as a political strategy.

The intellectual core of women's studies in the US was formed around women's oppression as it ramified into disciplinary research topics. Ellen Messer-Davidow has recently delineated the pathways by which women's studies became "disciplined" by the academy it set out to transform, and although Davidow does not mention her, Woolf figures implicitly in the intellectual history she examines. Despite Jane Marcus's hope that Woolf's name has now "done its cultural work" in the US as an icon of women's studies and feminist theory, and for "all the changing cultural narratives of female madness in the '70s and '80s" (17), and for the "cultural narratives of anorexia and child abuse" (18), Woolf is a permanent part of US feminist discourse. For Marcus, Woolf has too long been "the site of syndromes of desire and despair" (18), but her figure is continually being recast by new generations of readers.[3]

Woolf as writer, as public intellectual, is equal to the demands of new times and places. Davidow describes how feminist standpoint theory developed to "refute the disciplinary epistemology, which . . . claimed that 'only the impersonal, disinterested, socially anonymous representatives of human reason' who used vigorous and value-neutral methods were 'capable of producing [true] knowledge' [quoting Sandra Harding]" (Messer-Davidow 188), and I think at once of Woolf's careful calibration of her narrative stance in her explicitly political writings like *Three Guineas*, the "Introductory Letter" to *Life as We Have Known It*, or even *A Room of One's Own*. The image of Woolf that circulates as straw lady whom cultural critics excoriate for class bias is not the Woolf of her own words wherein are embedded many of the tensions of cultural discourses within which Americans in particular still find themselves enmeshed.

The English reaction against Woolf has been to a large extent shared by the US "intellectual" media (cf. Silver, *Icon*). In England, however, the misogyny and class axe-grinding was allied also with a tradition of anti-Americanism. In 1978, Marcus informed readers of the *Virginia Woolf Miscellany* about a *Times Literary Supplement* editorial entitled "Woolf Whistles" that mocked "our existence, our Americanism, our feminism, our contributors, and Woolf herself ("Woolf Whistles").[4] For English cultural critics, "Woolf" has been a largely American phenomenon and therefore immediately suspect and fair game for mockery. Also in 1978, the *Sunday Times* reviewer of John Lehmann's *Thrown to the Woolfs* asked "Are the Woolfs worth all the fuss we make of them?...does her fiction build up into quite the Mount Everest literary massif which enquiring readers gaze upon with awe? Should the Woolf achievements attract such teams of critical explorers, subsidized by American faculties of English, roping themselves together and planning how they shall reach the summit?" The English lacked the earnestness with which Americans set about the task of reading everything Woolf had written, and although they may have sometimes been baffled by her humor, American feminists understood her politics because they read it in their own accent.

At a 1988 MLA Convention discussion marking the fiftieth anniversary of the publication of *Three Guineas*, Cora Kaplan, an American scholar who had taught for many years in England, remarked that British students disliked Woolf because of her tone; the American working-class writer Tillie Olsen responded that Woolf was addressing her own class, because it was *their* power she sought to subvert. Woolf was more critical of her class and had a more complex relation to it than many of her well-known contemporaries, as Alex Zwerdling points out. Her honesty about class was unusual at the time, a time when—after 1917—the abolition of upper class privilege was more than just a theory. Having matured in a world shaped to a certain extent by the thought of Marx and Engels, Veblen, and Tawney, Woolf moved socially and politically far beyond the boundaries of her Kensington upbringing. An upper-middle-class woman who occasionally displayed her background's casual anti-semitism, she married a Socialist Jew active in the Labour party; a highbrow artist dedicated to experimental fiction, she spent two and a half years teaching once a week in one of London's poorest districts, at Morley College, and throughout her life supported socialists causes, and even published in the *Daily Worker*. Like everything about Woolf, her class consciousness cannot be reduced to simple categories.

The letters that Woolf kept from correspondents who wrote to her about *Three Guineas* demonstrate convincingly that Q. D. Leavis was wrong in saying the essay was "a conversation between her and her friends" (203). In "The Leaning Tower," an essay that began as a paper read to the Workers Education Association, Woolf criticized the Auden generation for its pretense to sharing working-class experience. The only sympathetic piece among responses published in *Folios of New Writing* shortly after Woolf's death in 1941 was by a Welsh miner whose autobiography, *These Poor Hands*, had been published in 1939. B. L. Coombes wrote that he agreed with Woolf that if all the working class has contributed to literature were taken away it would "scarcely suffer," but he continued by saying that "working class writing has not yet become strong on its feet and for the most part is still like an alarmed infant, whimpering at finding itself in strange company and fearing that it may be cuffed before being sent back to its home" (32). He calls on the privileged to help those of the working class to learn to read and write, something Woolf would have

Virginia Woolf in the U. S. A.

agreed was imperative. Among those who wrote to her about *Three Guineas* was a weaver from Yorkshire named Agnes Smith who at first complained that Woolf had excluded working-class women's experience from her essay. Woolf evidently replied immediately, and the women continued their correspondence until Woolf's death in 1941.[5]

Woolf's identification with Bloomsbury "civilization" as exemplified by Clive Bell, made her an easy target for English journalists and critics from the 1950s on, when a number of Bloomsbury memoirs and Woolf's own *A Writer's Diary* were published; the identification is, however, erroneous. In "Virginia Woolf and Offence," Lee documents half a century of class attacks on Woolf, and speculates that their virulent resurgence in the 1990s might have been due to "the continuing domination of masculine critics wielding literary axes…in the universities and on the arts pages" (131). Woolf's class biases have also been examined by American critics within the context of her canonization as a feminist saint. Mary Childers argues that feminist critics have overrated Woolf's political acumen because Woolf aestheticizes politics. Although I would disagree with this estimation, believing Woolf's narrative strategies to be in themselves a subversive politics (along the lines argued in William Handley's "War and the Politics of Narration in *Jacob's Room*"), I think Childers does usefully warn against the overpersonalizing of Woolf as a figure that "tempts some critics to defend her as if she were alive" (Childers 62). "What remains politically remarkable about Woolf," Childers writes, "is that she was frequently more daring in confronting the way her class inflected her feminism than most feminist critics are today, and thus she continues to move us to confront the problem that she poses" (78).

Lee also argues that Woolf's own internal divisions and tensions regarding her class position animate her fiction's subtle exploration of categories. We can look to Woolf herself for a response to charges of elitism and class insularity. In August 1940, she took great care in replying to Vita Sackville-West's son Ben Nicolson, who had written to her criticizing Bloomsbury after the publication of her biography of Roger Fry. Recounting her own efforts to share her learning with the working class at Morley College, and her work with the Women's Co-Operative Guild, as well as the political work of Leonard Woolf and Maynard Keynes, she identifies education as the central, vital issue for democracy: "What is the kind of education people ought to have? That it seems to me is the problem we have got to solve" (*L6* 420).

Raymond Williams described Bloomsbury as a "fraction" that broke away from their own class. "The point is not that [their] social conscience is unreal; it is very real indeed. But it is the precise formulation of a particular social position, in which a fraction of an upper class, breaking from its dominant majority, relates to a lower class *as a matter of conscience*: not in solidarity, nor in affiliation, but as an extension of what are still felt as personal or small-group obligations, at once against the cruelty and stupidity of the system and towards its otherwise relatively helpless victims" (Williams 155). It is, indeed, jarring at times to hear Woolf criticized for elitism when one thinks of some of her contemporaries. For example, T. S. Eliot, in *Notes Toward the Definition of Culture*, warned against the "barbarian nomads of the future [who] will encamp in their mechanised caravans" upon the ground where "ancient edifices" have been destroyed to make room for them (108). Ezra Pound wrote to Marianne Moore that it takes only "about 600 people to make a civilization" (in Zwerdling 110) (the sort of idea mocked by Woolf in *Jacob's Room*, as she later, privately, mocked her brother-in-law, Clive Bell's ideas about "civilisation").[6] In *A Room of One's Own*, of course, Woolf wrote that masterpieces are not single and solitary but "the outcome of many years of thinking in common by the body of the people, so that the experience of the mass is behind the single voice" (an idea she revisited at the end of her life in "Anon"[7]). Among the modernists, Woolf was a radical democrat, and she was an unsentimental democrat. From critics in the 1950s such as Walter Allen, who described moments of illumination in Woolf's fiction as "a succession of short, female gasps of ecstasy," to an English reviewer writing in 2003 that Woolf's are "[i]n many ways...truly terrible novels: inept, ugly, fatuous, badly written and revoltingly self-indulgent" (Hensher), Woolf has always been her own one-person "woman question."

We are now at another turning point in the history of Woolf as icon, as figure in literary history, and as feminist exemplar. In 2003, a transition was effected in the popular imaginary from the monster of Mike Nichols' 1966 movie of Edward Albee's play to the frowning star of Stephen Daldry's movie of David Hare's script of Michael Cunningham's novel *The Hours*. Albee's image of a monstrous woman, and his play's "queering of the heterosexual family" (Silver 114), appearing as it did at a time of rising fear of women's sexual independence, dispersed a complex of associations with Woolf's image and name that have been at the heart of some of the most bitter cultural battles in the US. At *this* cultural moment in the United States, and in England, *The Hours* has served as a lens focusing arguments that have swirled around Woolf throughout the "culture wars" of the 1980s and 1990s, and also, implicitly, arguments about the exhaustion of the US feminist project and the detachment from the social world of its academic practitioners.

Silver details how the self-styled "intellectual" media and some public intellectuals have worked to reclaim Woolf from the "feminists" whose inter-

Virginia Woolf in the U. S. A.

ests are caricatured as reductive, limited, and narrow. Some of the most popular representations of Woolf, such as Eileen Atkins's performance of a script called *A Room of One's Own* written by Patrick Garland, have attempted to contain and resist Woolf's feminism; a widely publicized event organized by the PEN American Center in New York in 2000 was introduced by the novelist Roxana Robinson explaining that Woolf was not a feminist but "had a wide range of interests" (Hussey, "To the Readers"), and this notion that feminism is limiting, reductive, or, worst charge of all, represents women only as *victims* has been used repeatedly to "rescue" an apolitical Woolf, the Woolf of the ubiquitous Beresford portrait, from those scholars who insist on seeing her as a revolutionary.

Following a screening of the DVD "extras" accompanying *The Hours* at the 2003 Woolf conference at Smith College, an audience member pointed out a kind of cognitive dissonance between the version of Woolf represented by various "experts" (including Hermione Lee, Frances Spalding, and Molly Hite) in a short film portrait, and that represented in the movie. Michèle Barrett contrasted the cultural capital accruing to Woolf's image and name in the US with the far more diminished figure she still presents in the UK, but the discussion of *The Hours* both in the press and among Woolf's common readers and her academic devotees has demonstrated her continuing and border-crossing power. Indeed, the fact that Nicole Kidman became the star of a film that began with Meryl Streep in that role is telling in itself.

Just as was the case with Albee's play, it is the movie version of *The Hours* that will now provide most people's point of reference for the figure called "Virginia Woolf." In one of the most insightful articles about *The Hours* phenomenon, Daniel Mendelsohn argued that the film fails to present Woolf "as the confident, gossip-loving queen of Bloomsbury, the vivid social figure, the amusing diarist, the impressively productive journalist expertly maneuvering her professional obligations—and relationships…If anything," he went on, "the film's Woolf is just one half (if that much) of the real Woolf, and it's no coincidence that it's the half that satisfies a certain cultural fantasy, going back to the early biographies of Sappho, about what creative women are like: distracted, isolated, doomed" (19). Mendelsohn quotes from *A Room of One's Own* to illustrate his contention that the film's makers devalue women, in contrast, he says, to Cunningham himself. He quotes these lines from *A Room*: "The truth is, I often like women. I like their unconventionality. I like their subtlety" (Mendelsohn 19). Julia Briggs has pointed out that sixteen days after the first edition of *A Room* was published in England, Woolf changed the word "subtlety" to "completeness" in the second impression of the first edition. She writes, "Woolf's enthusiasm for women had changed: instead of liking their subtlety, she liked their completeness," and comments that "if any textual change could be considered a feminist revision, it must surely be the change from 'subtlety' to the very different claim made for women by 'completeness'" (Briggs 171). Mendelsohn's criticism that *The Hours* gives us only "half" of Woolf seems encompassed already by Woolf's most popular text: *The Hours* may well lack subtlety *and* completeness with regard to "Virginia Woolf," especially as the popular icon "Woolf"—now incarnated in Kidman's performance—bumps up against the "Woolf" constructed by scholars. The tensions at boundaries, the frustrations and sometimes dangers perceived in crossing borders were very much part of Woolf's thinking and of her practice.

The phenomenon of *The Hours* and, more recently, of the (self-) construction of Michael Cunningham as a Woolf scholar, brings once again to the surface the way in which Woolf straddles/explodes/disturbs boundaries between highbrow/popular, masculine/feminine, modernism/mass culture.

In his introduction to a new edition of *The Voyage Out*, published by Random House, Cunningham represents himself as "someone who has written about Woolf" (xxxvi).[8] In a "Reading Group Guide" of the sort that is now found in the latest editions of Woolf's novels, readers are invited to discuss Cunningham's opinion of, for example, Rachel Vinrace as an "engine of perception." His introduction differs, in my view, from those by other novelists in the Harcourt editions, such as Maureen Howard's to *Mrs. Dalloway* or Eudora Welty's to *To the Lighthouse*, by being presented with a veneer of scholarship. Leaving aside many details, let me comment on one point: Cunningham credits "feminist scholars of the 1960s" (xxxv) with bringing Woolf back into fashion, and a few lines later continues: "For those who *had* read her, a cottage industry of sorts grew up, composed mainly of essays and books that claimed that her work, her character, her genius and her suicide could only be understood in light of her lesbianism, her enslavement to Leonard, her mental disorder, her oppression as a woman, and/or the fact that she had survived incest" (xxxvi). This is familiarly dismissive, so that now not only are we faced with what Jane Marcus, reviewing the Shakespeare Head editions of Woolf, has called the "enforced anonymity" of scholars' contributions to the apparatus by which publishers distinguish their editions, but also with the power of one of the literary marketplace's dominant publishers disseminating a representation of Woolf that once again assigns feminist readings to the lunatic fringe—a cottage industry, after all, might as well be a cult.

I have shamefully avoided the charge I was given in my invitation to the Moscow symposium—to comment on Woolf's relation to the twenty-first century American literary scene—but given Woolf's ubiquity, that is probably

Virginia Woolf in the U. S. A.

impossible. Every year, papers at the annual conference on Woolf discuss her continuing presence in the work of Toni Morrison, Paule Marshall, Alice Walker, Julieta Campos, Alice Munro, or Anita Brookner and many others.[9] The intertextualities of Margaret Atwood's recent dystopia *Oryx and Crake* and Woolf's *To the Lighthouse*, from which Atwood takes one of her novel's epigraphs, will no doubt be explored before too long. In closing, however, I'd like to comment on some recent examples of Woolf's continuing presence as a political thinker and public intellectual.

"Seeking the Geopolitical Woolf" in 1996, Susan Stanford Friedman recalled a conversation she had had some years earlier with Mamphela Ramphele, then the vice-chancellor of the University of Cape Town, an anthropologist and activist in the struggle against apartheid in South Africa. Ramphele told Friedman that she longed to write her autobiography, and Friedman urged her to read *Three Guineas*, subsequently sending it to her together with *To the Lighthouse*. Friedman wondered if these books would be "transplantable": "What did they or could they have meant to her in the midst of her geopolitical and personal struggles?" (39). Friedman closed her talk, given at the 6th annual conference on Woolf, by noting that she had just learned of the publication of Ramphele's memoir. "Perhaps there," she speculated," I will find Virginia Woolf International" (39).

In *Across Boundaries: The Journey of a South African Woman Leader*, Ramphele does not mention Woolf by name, but the accuracy of Friedman's speculation is borne out. Ramphele hopes that her story will help women feel good about who they are and turn what is seen as abnormal for women into everyday practice; if successful, "then I would have managed to intimate another possible female destiny" (xii). Ramphele's phrase comes from Carolyn Heilbrun's *Writing a Woman's Life*, a book explicitly and extensively indebted to Woolf. Ramphele recounts challenging Nelson Mandela on the issue of traditional male leadership: "Traditional leadership by its very nature is hereditary and leaves little scope for the democratic election of leaders" (203). She recalls how "his face darkened. He sat up in a regal posture, and said: 'The issue you have raised is too complex to be dealt with cold in the short space of time we have available during this visit'" (but she notes that he rose to the challenge a few weeks later). As Woolf experienced with the reception of *Three Guineas* among her own circle, raising the feminist question at a time of political crisis can evoke more than the usual cold hostility. The issues of *Three Guineas* reverberate also in Ramphele's questions about what happens to women when they assume—as she herself did—positions of power formerly held only by men. Although she does not speak of the mulberry tree or of joining the procession that leads to war, it is clear from Ramphele's memoir that the questions

Woolf asks in *Three Guineas*, and even *To the Lighthouse*'s analysis of the patriarchal family *are* transplantable to other contexts in which patriarchal values and traditions are exposed and challenged.[10]

The most recent example of Woolf's ability to animate contemporary political and intellectual work is Susan Sontag's essay *Regarding the Pain of Others*. Her topic is the spectacle of violence, the effect on viewers of the steady stream of images of violence. Sontag begins by recalling Woolf's strategy of referring in *Three Guineas* to unreproduced photographs of atrocities in the Spanish Civil War. For all the rigor of her argument, and the moral weight given it by Sontag's own activism in war zones, she is hampered by her apparent ignorance of the photographs that Woolf actually *did* include in *Three Guineas* that make the feminist point about gender missing from Sontag's essay.

How Woolf will be read in new geographical and political locations is an open question. We must take seriously what she wrote in "The Leaning Tower": "Literature is no one's private ground; literature is common ground. It is not cut up into nations; there are no wars there. Let us trespass freely and fearlessly and find our own way for ourselves" (18). Woolf's cosmopolitanism, her radical democracy, has deep roots. That those roots can often be found in American soil might explain, at least to some extent, why she has flourished there. Reviewing a now long-forgotten American essayist for the *Times Literary Supplement* in 1917, Woolf wrote of the opportunities available to Americans at the outset of the twentieth century: "…if any one is sceptical as to the future of American art let him read Walt Whitman's preface to the first edition of *Leaves of Grass*. As a piece of writing it rivals anything we have done for a hundred years, and as a statement of the American spirit no finer banner was ever unfurled for the young of a great country to march under" ("Melodious" 81-82). It is worth reminding ourselves of what might have so struck the woman who would go on to write *Mrs. Dalloway, To the Lighthouse, The Waves, Three Guineas,* and *Between the Acts*:

> This is what you shall do: Love the earth and the animals, despise riches, give alms to every one that asks, stand up for the stupid and crazy, devote your income and labor to others, hate tyrants, argue not concerning God, have patience and indulgence toward the people, take off your hat to nothing known or unknown or to any man or number of men, go freely with powerful uneducated persons and with the young and with the mothers of families, read these leaves in the open air every season of your life, re-examine all you have been told at school or church or in any book, dismiss whatever insults your own souls, and your very flesh shall be a great poem and have the richest fluency not only in its words but in the silent lines of its lips and face and between the lashes of your eyes and in every motion and joint of your body…(Whitman 11)

Virginia Woolf in the U. S. A.

Notes

[1] *The Times on the American War* by LS (1865) (Annan 361).

[2] See my chapter on "Biographical Approaches" in Anna Snaith, ed. *Palgrave Advances in Virginia Woolf Studies* (forthcoming).

[3] A sign of Woolf's global reach, in addition to the Moscow symposium and the various Woolf Societies that exist outside the UK and the US (in France, Japan, Korea) is Nicola Luckhurst and Mary Ann Caws, eds. *The Reception of Virginia Woolf in Europe* (NY: Continuum, 2003).

[4] Americans have typically formed the largest contingent at UK Woolf conferences; see, for example, a Fall 1987 report on a conference at Sussex in *Virginia Woolf Miscellany* 29; at the 11th annual conference on Woolf (2001), held at the University of Wales, Bangor, Americans were again present in significantly larger numbers than the locals.

[5] Woolf urged Smith to publish her autobiography with the Hogarth Press, and in fact Smith did publish *A Worker's View of the Wool Textile Industry* in 1944, but not with Hogarth.

[6] According to Quentin Bell, Woolf's opinion was that Clive "has great fun in the opening chapters but in the end it turns out that Civilisation is a lunch party at no. 50 Gordon Square" (*Virginia Woolf* 137).

[7] "'Anon' and 'The Reader': Virginia Woolf's Last Essays." *Twentieth Century Literature* 25. 3 / 4 (Fall/Winter 1979): 356-441.

[8] According to a post by Laura Aimone to the Virginia Woolf listserv (6.23.2003), Cunningham had planned a biography of Woolf for young readers to be published by Chelsea House in a series about gay and lesbian writers (cf. Philip Gambone, *Something Inside. Conversations with Gay Fiction Writers*. U of Wisconsin P, 1993: 151-52.)

[9] Examples (of which there are several more) include Mónica Ayuso, "Remote Inscriptions: *To the Lighthouse* and *The Waves* in Julieta Campos' Caribbean" (Jeanette McVicker and Laura Davis, eds. *Virginia Woolf and Communities* [NY: Pace UP, 1999]: 86-92); Eileen Barrett, "Septimus and Shadrack: Woolf and Morrison Envision the Madness of War" (Mark Hussey and Vara Neverow-Turk, eds. *Virginia Woolf: Emerging Perspectives* [NY: Pace UP, 1994]: 26-32); Barbara Christian, "Layered Rhythms: Virginia Woolf and Toni Morrison" (ibid. 164-77); Beth Rigel Daugherty, "Teaching *Mrs. Dalloway* and *Praisesong for the Widow* as a Pair" (Diane F. Gillespie and Leslie K. Hankins, eds. *Virginia Woolf and the Arts* [NY: Pace UP, 1997]: 175-82; Anne Fernald, "A Room, A Child, A Mind of One's Own: Virginia Woolf, Alice Walker and Feminist Personal Criticism" (Hussey and Neverow Turk, ibid. 245-51).

[10] Ann Murphy and Jeanne McNett, write "The Society of Outsiders still offers perspectives of value to educators and business people as we enter the twenty-first century in a global marketplace, collaborating across borders and cooperating with our competitors. This is a world in which the patriarchal procession is becoming increasingly dysfunctional. As we move into the new century, building on women's achievements during the Twentieth Century, we would do well to rethink the role of our participation in The Society of Outsiders" (324).

Works Cited

Allen, Walter. *The English Novel* (1954). Harmondsworth: Penguin, 1973.
"America, Which I Have Never Seen." Virginia Woolf. *The Dublin Review* 5 (Winter 2001-2): 56-60. First published *Hearst's International*, April 1938.
Anderson, Linda. *Women and Autobiography in the Twentieth Century: Remembered Futures*. London: Prentice Hall/Harvester Wheatsheaf, 1987.
Annan, Noel. *Leslie Stephen: The Godless Victorian*. NY: Random House, 1984.
Bell, Quentin. *Virginia Woolf: A Biography*. Vol. 2 *Mrs Woolf 1912-1941*. London: Hogarth P, 1973.
Briggs, Julia. "In Search of New Virginias." Ann Ardis and Bonnie Kime Scott, eds. *Virginia Woolf: Turning the Centuries: Selected Papers from the Ninth Annual Conference on Virginia Woolf*. NY: Pace UP, 2000: 166-75.
Childers, Mary. "Virginia Woolf on the Outside Looking Down: Reflections on the Class of Women." *Modern Fiction Studies* 38.1 (Spring 1992): 61-80.
Coombes, B. L. "Below the Tower." *Folios of New Writing*. Spring 1941. London: Hogarth Press, 1941.
Cunningham, Michael. "Introduction." Virginia Woolf, *The Voyage Out*. NY: Modern Library, 2001.
Eliot, T. S. *Notes Towards the Definition of Culture*. 1948. London: Faber.
Ferrer, Daniel. *Virginia Woolf and the Madness of Language*. Trans. Geoffrey Bennington and Rachel Bowlby. NY: Routledge, 1990.
Friedman, Susan Stanford. "Uncommon Readings: Seeking the Geopolitical Woolf." *The South Carolina Review* 29.1 (Fall 1996): 24-44.
Handley, William. "War and the Politics of Narration in *Jacob's Room*." Mark Hussey, ed. *Virginia Woolf and War: Fiction, Reality, and Myth*. Syracuse: Syracuse UP, 1991. 110-33.
Heilbrun, Carolyn. *Writing a Woman's Life*. NY: W. W. Norton, 1988.
Hensher, Philip. "Virginia Woolf Makes Me Want to Vomit." *Telegraph* (London). January 24, 2003.
Hussey, Mark. "To the Readers." *Virginia Woolf Miscellany* 55 (Spring 2000): 1.
Joplin, Patricia. "'I Have Bought my Freedom': The Gift of *A Room of One's Own*." *Virginia Woolf Miscellany* 21 (Fall 1983): 4-5.
Kamuf, Peggy. "Penelope at Work." In *Signature Pieces: On the Institution of Authorship*. Ithaca: Cornell UP, 1988.
Leavis, Q. D. "Caterpillars of the Commonwealth Unite!" *Scrutiny* (Sept. 1938): 203-14.
Lee, Hermione. *Virginia Woolf*. NY: Knopf, 1996.
———. "Virginia Woolf and Offence." In John Batchelor, ed. *The Art of Literary Biography*. Oxford: Clarendon Press, 1995. 129-50.
Lehmann, John. *Thrown to the Woolfs: Leonard and Virginia Woolf and the Hogarth Press*. NY: Holt, Rinehart & Winston, 1978.
London, Bette. "Guerillas in Petticoats or Sans-Culotte? Virginia Woolf and the Future of Feminist Criticism." *diacritics* (Summer/Fall 1991): 11-29.
Marcus, "Wrapped in the Stars and Stripes: Virginia Woolf in the U. S. A." *The South Carolina Review* 29.1 (Fall 1996): 17-23.
———. "Woolf Whistles." *Virginia Woolf Miscellany* 11 (Fall 1978).
McKillop, Ian. *F. R. Leavis: A Life in Criticism*. NY: St. Martin's P, 1997.

Virginia Woolf in the U. S. A.

McNeillie, Andrew. "Virginia Woolf's America." *Dublin Review* 5 (Winter 2000-1): 41-55.

Mendelsohn, Daniel. "Not Afraid of Virginia Woolf." *New York Review of Books* 50.4 (March 13, 2003): 17-20.

Messer-Davidow, Ellen. *Disciplining Feminism: From Social Activism to Academic Discourse.* Durham: Duke UP, 2002.

Murphy, Ann and Jeanne McNett, "Women's Learning, Women's Work." Ann Ardis and Bonnie Kime Scott, eds. *Virginia Woolf: Turning the Centuries.* NY: Pace UP, 2000: 317-24.

Ramphele, Mamphela. *Across Boundaries: The Journey of a South African Woman Leader.* 1995. NY: Feminist Press, 1996.

Rogat, Ellen Hawkes. "The Virgin in the Bell Biography." *Twentieth Century Literature* 20.2 (April 1974): 96-113.

——. "Visiting the Berg Collection." *Virginia Woolf Miscellany* 1 (Fall 1973): 1.

Rose, Jacqueline. *The Haunting of Sylvia Plath.* Cambridge: Harvard UP, 1992.

Russ, Joanna. *How to Suppress Women's Writing.* Austin: U of Texas P, 1983.

Silver, Brenda R. *Virginia Woolf Icon.* Chicago: U of Chicago P, 1999.

Smith, Agnes. Letters to Virginia Woolf. *Woolf Studies Annual* 6 (2000): 98-103, 105-06.

Sontag, Susan. *Regarding the Pain of Others.* NY: Farrar Straus Giroux, 2003.

Spotts, Frederic. *The Letters of Leonard Woolf.* San Diego: HBJ, 1989.

Trinh, T. Minh-ha. *Woman, Native, Other: Writing Postcoloniality and Feminism.* Bloomington: Indiana UP, 1989.

Whitman, Walt. Preface to "Leaves of Grass" (1855) [*Complete Poetry and Collected Prose.* NY: Literary Classics of the United States, Inc., 1982. Library of America].

Williams, Raymond. "The Bloomsbury Fraction." *Problems in Materialism and Culture: Selected Essays.* London: Verso, 1980.

Woolf, Virginia. "The Leaning Tower." *Collected Essays* 2. NY: Harcourt Brace & World, 1967. 162-81.

——. *Between the Acts.* 1941. San Diego: HBJ, 1969.

——. "Melodious Meditations." *The Essays of Virginia Woolf* ed. Andrew McNeillie. V2 1912-1918. San Diego: HBJ, 1987: 80-82.

——. *Three Guineas.* London: Hogarth P, 1938.

Zwerdling, Alex. *Virginia Woolf and the Real World.* Berkeley: U of California P, 1986.

The Activist Pens of Virginia Woolf and Betty Friedan
Marilyn Schwinn Smith

My vague consciousness of the connection between the emergence of Second Wave feminism and the re-discovery, re-interpretation, and re-evaluation of Virginia Woolf in the United States was stimulated into an active interest on my reading of the essay by American poet Adrienne Rich, "When We Dead Awaken: Writing as Re-Vision."[1] Written in 1971, before the academy's embrace of Woolf in course curricula, the essay intimated that women had come to Woolf by a route more complex than I had imagined, by something rooted in the inchoate yearnings of their own lives; that Woolf spoke more intimately of women's experience than the academy was prepared to address. Awakened, I began to note a pervasive reference to Woolf by feminist scholars in the late 60s, early 70s.

I was involved, at the time, in an oral history project to recover the feminist history of precisely this period in the area of western Massachusetts where I live. To recover a local piece of the Woolf-feminist history, I invited four women who had been active participants in the Amherst Women's Liberation group to speak about Woolf and the development of their own feminist or activist consciousness. These women convened on a snowy April afternoon, 2003, at Neilson Library, Smith College, each clutching the worn copy of *Three Guineas* she had read in consciousness raising groups of the 60s.[2] They were delighted to discover that each, looking back over the thirty-five years since they met together as young women, had independently selected this book, treasured and dog-eared, to exemplify their relationship with Woolf.

This generation of American women had not come spontaneously to Woolf, nor been trained to be good or even appreciative readers of Woolf. Rather, the social turmoil of the 60s effected a shift in women's lives, enabling them to read with new eyes, looking for new analyses. A seminal event had been the 1963 publication of Betty Friedan's *The Feminine Mystique*. The experience of reading Friedan initiated a deeply personal process, fostered in consciousness raising and support groups, which forged a new, feminist consciousness.[3] With the birth of the Women's Movement in the United States, a generation of women began actively seeking out a new genealogy, dusting off to read forgotten and neglected women of earlier generations. In Virginia Woolf, many women found a voice speaking their own experience. There are multiple factors contributing to the widespread resurgence of interest in Woolf,

Schwinn Smith

well under way by the 1970s. I focus on Woolf's appeal to lay and academic women alike, on her relevancy to the central issues of women's lives in the late 1960s, a relevance that led them to take up and read Woolf outside the academy, but with the seriousness generally accorded authors found within the curricula.

What struck me, this April afternoon, was the central position of *Three Guineas*, a book I assumed had remained unappreciated for much longer. I wondered: might there be something in *The Feminine Mystique* that had prepared the way for such a passionate, decades' long relationship with *Three Guineas*? Might not something in Clarissa Dalloway, redolent of "The Problem That Has No Name," lie behind the power of *Three Guineas* and *The Feminine Mystique* to speak directly to an emergent awareness of the falsity in women's received sense of self? My story, of the activist pens of Virginia Woolf and Betty Friedan, connecting these apparently disparate authors, focuses on the intersection where the artist and activist meet. This focus is grounded in the impetus for personal and social change to which readers respond in the writings of both authors.

The ancient debate over the relative value of words or deeds can be figured as a coin: artist or activist. The flip-flop of this coin suggests a central core, a common vision uniting the artist and the activist. Facing, Janus-like, outwards from each other, they engage the world in different modes, to the same end. Backside hard pressed to backside they are mutually supportive. In the common imagination, Virginia Woolf is an artist, never an activist. Though feminist readings of Woolf have vastly altered her reputation, she remains "artist," noted and chastised for the absence of activism. The case of Betty Friedan seems at first blush miles apart from Virginia Woolf's. Friedan founded national organizations, organized grass-roots initiatives, marched in the streets. Though best known for her writing, for that first book, *The Feminine Mystique*, her reputation remains solidly activist, not artist. Neither characterization does justice.

Woolf and Friedan shared an extraordinary sensitivity to the death-dealing force of their respective cultures. For men sent off to war, this force is literal. Women also experience physical violence, but the more widespread effect of this force on women remains largely invisible, it being a living death. To make this living death visible, and thereby bring into being the conditions under which change can take place, is the task of Woolf's and Friedan's activist pens. Sharing the humanistic value that women, like all people, require not just material well-being and the vote, but full freedom to create themselves, that women, like all people, require not just the material—a room of one's own—but the spiritual—a mind of one's own—Woolf and Friedan had first to bring to light in a new and startling way that fullness of self had been denied to women, even

The Activist Pens of Virginia Woolf and Betty Friedan

where one would least expect it. For minds and selves are what the eponymous heroine of Woolf's first internationally successful novel, *Mrs. Dalloway*, and her descendant, Friedan's American, suburban housewife, appear to lack.

The condition of a woman's mind is of utmost interest to Woolf when she casts from the docks of London into the vast expanse of the open sea a small party of English gentlemen and women (*The Voyage Out* 1915). Much of what Friedan later documents and analyzes in the lives of suburban housewives is presented ironically in the social interactions of this, Woolf's first novel, in Mrs. Elliot's response to Mrs. Thornbury's envy of Miss Allan's knowledge: "But that isn't what women want" (104), and in Hewet's musings on the picnickers: "and Susan—she had no self, and counted neither one way nor the other" (123). Clarissa and Richard Dalloway make a cameo appearance, of which Lytton Strachey famously remarked, "And the Dalloways—oh!—" (Woolf, *Letters* 73; 25 February 1916). Like the introduction of exotic strangers into a closed community, the uninvited appearance of the politician and his aesthetically inclined wife jolts the novel's young heroine out of the habitual condition of her mind: "inextricably mixed in dreamy confusion" (*TVO* 29). The effect of the Dalloways on Rachel Vinrace makes clear to the reader into what desperate straits the condition of her mind, "educated as the majority of well-to-do girls in the last part of the nineteenth century were educated," has led her. "[S]he would believe practically anything she was told, invent reasons for anything she said" (26). So thoroughly ill equipped for independent life— "she really might be six years old" (18)—it seems fated she not survive the voyage out. Clarissa Dalloway, however, does.

If Clarissa is a precursor to the American housewife, let us first ask: who is she? We can say with certainty, that she is a woman of good breeding. That she is lovely. She possesses those qualities of demureness, charm and wit, which make her acceptable to the world of Richard Dalloway. She is *not* manly. In *The Voyage Out*, Clarissa is the wife, whose pedigree Richard exploits to gain access to the ship. She is the wife, whose absence Richard exploits in his attempted conquest of Rachel Vinrace. She is the mother of a daughter and desirous of a son. Together with Richard, she is the butt of Woolf's broadly comic satire, reduced to negligible significance. Why and how should she continue to command Woolf's attention?

The elaboration of Clarissa Dalloway follows the trajectory of Woolf's growing ability to discern the social rhythms of power and subjugation, which shape the condition of a woman's mind. The particular charm and significance of the Dalloways for Strachey lies in Woolf's comic treatment of them. The delicious satire will remain, but something changes. An element of sympathy is injected into the satire, which begins to shift from the person Clarissa Dalloway to the social constructs, which have rendered her so ripe for satire.

Jane Wheare notes an ambivalence between the competing claims of art and activism is present throughout Woolf's career, manifesting itself in Clarissa and Richard's dinner conversation in *The Voyage Out* (ix). In *Virginia Woolf and the Real World*, Alex Zwerdling insightfully charts the development of Woolf's comic technique, and her use of ironic satire. He convincingly argues for the importance of recognizing Woolf's comic technique and irony as a species of social intervention. Irony and satire are, of course, the writer's traditional means with which to shock out of the old, into a new consciousness: the task of the activist pen. Later critics—I note in particular Chene Heady's superb reading of the satirical treatment of Richard Dalloway in *The Voyage Out*—have expanded our appreciation for the political engagement of Woolf's satire. A review of the particular circumstances intervening between the caricature of *The Voyage Out* and the muted satire of "Mrs Dalloway in Bond Street" (1923) suggests why Woolf has transformed Clarissa from pure object of satire, taking her up as a subject, and why she has shifted her attack away from the individual to the social system.

Shortly after recording that Strachey still found *The Voyage Out* "'extremely good' [...] especially the satire of the Dalloways" (*D2* 65), Woolf is so incensed by Desmond McCarthy's approving review (in the *New Statesman*) of Arnold Bennett's collection of essays, *Our Women*, as to vow to work up a piece on Women (*D2* 69). McCarthy espoused Bennett's assessment of upper class women, that "'no amount of education and liberty of action will sensibly alter' the fact that women are inferior to men in intellectual power, and women's indisputable 'desire to be dominated is [...] a proof of intellectual inferiority'" (editors' note, *D2* 339). Under the heading "The Intellectual Status of Women," Woolf responds with what is an outline of the argument she will make again and again in her essays on women, that intellectual inferiority is not the Nature of Women, but that the intellectual condition of Bennett's privileged, upper-class women derives from the deprivation of education and of liberty of action and experience. She counters the gentlemen's assertion "that women are inferior to men in intellectual power" as a fact, which "stares [them] in the face," with the fact, which "stares [her] in the face" (339) of a line of intellectually gifted women reaching back into antiquity. Marshalling her own considerable intellectual capacity, Woolf goes to battle with language as her weapon to expose these so-called facts as an ideological construct; not fact, but the mere *appearance* of fact. Through a judicious balance of rational argument and ironic satire, and sympathy, she lays bare the falsity of received belief concerning the nature of women.[4]

The Activist Pens of Virginia Woolf and Betty Friedan

Spring and summer 1922, Woolf is working in multiple modes: fiction, fantasy and criticism, so she can "vary the side of the pillow as fortune inclines" (*D2* 178). Specifically, she responds to the 1904 biography of entomologist Eleanor Ormerod with a fantasy she re-issues in the first *Common Reader* among "Lives of the Obscure," and drafts a new incarnation of Clarissa, published in *Dial* in July 1923 as "Mrs Dalloway in Bond Street." Both pieces are clearly a continuation of Woolf's preoccupation with the intellectual status of women. The fantasy portrait of Miss Ormerod presents rather than declaims the conditions leading to the obscurity of intellectually superior women. The portrait of the intellectually inferior, if privileged, Clarissa, shopping in Bond Street, takes a subtler, yet potentially more subversive feminist tack. And who is *this* Mrs. Dalloway?

Neither her character nor class has changed. Several of her stock opinions are given a reprise, notably on the topics of suffrage and the decisive importance of appearance. She muses: "How then could women sit in Parliament? How could they do things with men? For there is this extraordinarily deep instinct, something inside one; you can't get over it; it's no use trying" ("Mrs Dalloway" 147). Judging by this inarticulateness, we might say she has no intellect. Or, we might want to say she has not a mind of her own. The thoughts rolling through her consciousness, as she walks along Bond Street on the way to purchase the gloves herself, are cast in the words of men: Hugh Whitbread, Sir Dighton, Jack Stewart, Shelley, Fitzgerald, Richard Dalloway, a mysterious Phil, Shakespeare (whose Sonnets she knows by heart), old Uncle William who is remembered for saying "a lady is known by her gloves and her shoes."

With a mind thus inventoried with the words of men, Clarissa filters even her thoughts about the female body through a man's alien perspective. Thinking of Hugh Whitbread's wife's illness, she concludes: "Milly is about my age—fifty—fifty-two. So it is probably *that*, Hugh's manner had said so, said it perfectly" (147). Or, when first sympathizing with the "shop-girl" in the glove shop: "Still it seemed tiresome to bother her—perhaps the one day in the month, thought Clarissa, when it's agony to stand. 'Oh, don't bother,' she said" (151). Clarissa's natural urge is to offer the shop-girl a more pleasant holiday venue than the probable room in Brighton:

> to send her to Mrs Lumley's right in the country (and it was on the tip of her tongue). But then she remembered how on their honeymoon Dick had shown her the folly of giving impulsively. It was much more important, he said, to get trade with China. Of course he was right. And she could feel the girl wouldn't like to be given things. (151)

No mind of her own; thoughts on the female body filtered through a male gaze; delimited by her reproductive function. We can confidently say, Clarissa is "feminine."

Clarissa's portrait in the 1925 novel is more ambiguous, drawn with a large dose of sympathy. The conditions of her life remain the same, as Woolf announces with the novel's title, *Mrs. Dalloway*. A significant shift, however, has occurred in Woolf's relationship with her subject. The novel has barely begun before we hear the lament:

> Oh, if she could have had her life over again! [...] She would have been interested in politics like a man [...] Instead [...] she had the oddest sense of being herself invisible, [...] not even Clarissa any more; this being Mrs Dalloway. (29)

Clarissa begins to look like a prime candidate for America's post-war suburbia, subject to the feminine mystique.

A generation later, Friedan chooses, like Woolf, to focus on a particular stratum of women. Well aware of the far more desperate conditions of working class women or of African American women, Friedan concentrates on the plight of the privileged American housewife.[5] What Woolf had depicted, Friedan documents. A scholar and professional journalist, Friedan bases her work on numerous interviews and a review of professional research. The actual words of actual women cited by Friedan uncannily echo the words spoken by Woolf's fictional women. Culling the pages of *The Voyage Out*, *Mrs Dalloway*, *The Feminine Mystique* and the letters Friedan received in response to its publication,[6] one can compile a lengthy list of correspondences. Friedan's use of words spoken in real life endows them with a power not present in fiction. Reading Woolf's fictional dialogues through the lens of Friedan's quotations endows Woolf's fictive world with greater credibility.[7] An example, striking for its resonance with Clarissa: "I feel so empty somehow, useless, as if I don't exist" (Friedan, *Feminine* 232). Looking back over forty years, Friedan recalls that April morning in 1959 when "the problem" became clear to her, listening to a young woman say, as might have Clarissa: "I'm Jim's wife, and Janey's mother, a putter on of diapers and snowsuit, a server of meals, a Little League chauffeur. But who am I, as a person myself?" (Friedan, *Life* 104).

When Friedan, as Bettye Goldstein, entered Smith College in the fall of 1938, she conceived herself a budding author, yet it was not clear which direction her writing would take. Goldstein's first year themes and poems drew on details of campus life. She wrote about the conditions of bourgeois life that drive one to contemplate suicide. In addition to her personal pieces, Friedan

The Activist Pens of Virginia Woolf and Betty Friedan

thought and wrote during these formative years about world events. Contemplating a world on the brink of war, she wrote poems speaking with the soldier's voice. Her experience of a Smith education sharpened her social awareness, developed her analytic skills and launched her into the world of public involvement.

Yet, like Woolf, she was deeply ambivalent about an apparent antagonism between art and activism. Referring to a freshman essay written in January of 1939, historian Daniel Horowitz writes:

> [Bettye] wondered about the relationship between commitments to creativity and political action. She speculated on what would have happened if Emily Dickinson had left her house in Amherst to witness social problems, and if Virginia Woolf had chosen to struggle with social misery rather than focus so much on style. (45)

Goldstein would have been referring to the novel, *Mrs. Dalloway*, a book included in the syllabus of the required composition course.[8] Goldstein's critique of Dickinson and Woolf, that they did not engage broader issues of social justice, is standard for that time. Her musings are notable as evidence that she is seeking among the works of creative writers models for socially engaged writing. Goldstein does not know that Woolf has just published, in 1938, her most impassioned, socially engaged work, *Three Guineas*.

In April of 1939, just four months after Goldstein speculates on Woolf's focus on style rather than social misery, Woolf herself writes:

> One is living all the time in relation to certain [...] conceptions. Mine is that there is a pattern hid behind the cotton wool. And this conception affects me every day. I prove this, now, by spending the morning writing, when I might be [...] learning to do something useful if war comes. I feel that by writing I am doing what is far more necessary than anything else. ("Sketch of the Past" 73)

Simultaneously, the two women writers, a generation apart in years, actively contemplate how best to bring their talents and abilities to bear on a very real and very troubled world. Both pondered a life of words or a life of deeds.[9]

Different in so many fundamental ways, Woolf and Friedan share an understanding of the nature of women, which places education for women at the very heart of their respective careers. Education is the means to a mind of her own, to an intellectual self, to an individuality. The centrality of education, its motivating impetus to Woolf's as well as Friedan's writing, deserves re-emphasis.

Woolf's preoccupation with the subject of a woman's education extends over the course of her writing career. In *The Voyage Out, Jacob's Room, To the*

Schwinn Smith

Lighthouse, A Room of One's Own, The Pargiters and the tract that she develops out of it, *Three Guineas,* Woolf rehearses the wound inflicted by depriving women of an education. Education, to the extent it either furthered or delimited a woman's full use of her mind, lies at the heart of Woolf's feminism, at the heart of her adumbration of the nineteenth century's Woman Question: "what does a woman want?", a question continuing to haunt us into the twenty-first century.

Addressing the 13th Annual Conference on Virginia Woolf, Smith College President Carol Christ sums up the critical difference that education in the modern sense has wrought between the sexes, the difference Woolf articulated in *Three Guineas.* Despite the numerous similarities and advantages shared by the daughters and sons of educated men, the daughter "does not have an independent identity as an educated woman, but a dependent identity fixed through family relationship" (7). The debate about education for women, whatever its economic underpinnings, is largely a debate on the nature of women. Do they have minds? So long as one can ask, as St. John Hirst asks Rachel Vinrace in *The Voyage Out*: "Can one really talk to you? Have you got a mind?" (141), it does not matter what pragmatic advances are made in the material condition of women: attaining the right to vote or to the professions.

Christ identifies Woolf's separation, through her concept of the common reader and the common mind, of philosophy and literature from an institutional tradition. She conjoins them, rather, to her imaginative experience (12-13). Education can be technical, vocational, any sort of training. Woolf's focus is the *life* of the mind, in opposition to the *regulation* of the mind which formal education represents. She writes: "I feel sometimes for hours together as though the physical stuff of my brain were expanding larger and larger—throbbing quicker and quicker with new blood—& there is no more delicious sensation than this" (*PA* 178). With this mental life, Woolf situates herself as well as her construct—the common reader rather than the academic—at the very center of intellectuality.

> I think I see for a moment how our minds are threaded together—how any live mind is of the very same stuff as Plato's & Euripides. It is only a continuation & development of the same thing. It is this common mind that binds the whole world together; & all the world is mind. [...] I feel as though I had grasped the central meaning of the world, & all these poets & historians & philosophers were only following out paths branching from that centre in which I stand. (*PA* 178-9)

Any restriction on the life of the mind spells, for Woolf, a living death.

In her opening chapter, "The Problem That Has No Name," Friedan pursues the same argument that Woolf had. Material amelioration in the condition

The Activist Pens of Virginia Woolf and Betty Friedan

of women's lives, liberation through technology from the labor-intensive drudgery, liberation from repressive sexual mores, even bestowing the privileges enjoyed by the upper classes, these apparent improvements exacerbated woman's condition: by obscuring reality, by giving a false sense of betterment, by rendering woman's wound—her lack of a self—nameless. The activist works for material betterment; the artist, for spiritual. Woolf and Friedan share an awareness of an often-overlooked fact: the two must go together, not one at the expense of the other. Their mutual emphasis on education is for spiritual, as well as material, liberation.

Friedan makes frequent reference to the attack on women's education contained in Lundberg and Farnham's 1947 *Modern Woman: The Lost Sex* (*Feminine* 37, 111, 150, 184). Often cited as the starting point for her book, Friedan's 1957 questionnaire of her college classmates had been conceived in the hope of disproving Lundberg and Farnham's influential thesis that "quality education made women frustrated" (Horowitz 193). In her prefatory note, Friedan writes: "The answers given by 200 women to those intimate open-ended questions made me realize that what was wrong could not be related to education in the way it was then believed to be" (7).

In *The Feminine Mystique*, Friedan is aligned most closely with Woolf's activist pen. I suggest *The Feminine Mystique* and *Three Guineas* have been such influential texts largely due to their style, an impassioned, ironic rhetoric designed to go beyond analysis and to awaken a new understanding. Woolf and Friedan use their activist pens to dispel inherited, illusory notions of woman's nature, to remove the filter of archaic beliefs. The activist pen roots out what reason cannot reach: unconsciously held belief. I cite at length a passage from *The Feminine Mystique* both for its resonance with *Three Guineas* and its relevance to the difficulty of seeing clearly not the illusions of previous generations, but the illusions of one's own.

> The glorification of 'woman's role', then, seems to be in proportion to society's reluctance to treat women as complete human beings; for the less real function that role has, the more it is decorated with meaningless details to conceal its emptiness. This phenomenon has been noted, in general terms, in the annals of social science and in history—the chivalry of the Middle Ages, for example, and the artificial pedestal of the Victorian woman—but it may come as somewhat of a shock to the emancipated American woman to discover that it applies in a concrete and extreme degree to the housewife's situation in America today. (Friedan, *Feminine* 229)

Unable to read as a student the satire of *Mrs. Dalloway* nor yet familiar with *Three Guineas*, Friedan had criticized Woolf as a stylist. Yet, it is with a Woolfian irony (doubtlessly indebted to her youthful sensitivity to Woolf's style)[10] that, twenty-five years later, Friedan criticizes fascist and capitalist culture, excoriating, to quote Horowitz, "the powerful social forces in America that celebrated motherhood and a child-centered home in an attempt to keep educated women out of the work force" (53). In what sounds like a mixture of Clarissa's loss of identity and the analysis of the later *A Room of One's Own*, Friedan ironically depicts the American suburbia of the 1950's:

> The more a woman is deprived of function in society at the level of her own ability, the more her housework, mother-work, wife-work, will expand—and the more she will resist finishing her housework or mother-work, and being without any function at all. (Evidently human nature abhors a vacuum, even in women.) (230)

> There are no true walls or doors; the woman in the beautiful electronic kitchen is never separated from her children. She need never feel alone for a minute, need never be by herself. She can forget her own identity. (235)

Creativity is the premier value shared by Woolf and Friedan, the *telos* toward which they direct their desire for liberty of mind and experience for women. It is not, therefore, surprising that irony should be a distinctive quality of their activist pens. Irony and satire facilitate in the reader a creative leap across boundaries set by belief and tradition. They effect a transformation, comparable to Kuhn's paradigmatic shift, not possible by means of logic and reason, which must remain within the bounds of given rules, definitions *and* beliefs.

Creativity enabled Woolf and Friedan to make connections where the weight of cultural practice resisted. Irony assisted the transmission of their vision. A case in point is their ability to recognize policies toward women as patriarchal which their respective societies preferred to recognize only as properties of alien political systems. The analysis of fascist policy toward women was neither new nor obscure. Horowitz documents Friedan's exposure during her junior year at Smith College to progressive critiques of "Hitler's reactionary policy toward German women, which would remove them from political life, relegating females to the home and 'the three K's—Kinder, Küche und Kirche' [...]" (53). What was new was Friedan's creativity *and* willingness to recognize a parallel to her own culture in the demonized "Other" (Nazi Germany), a willingness already matched by Woolf in *Three Guineas*.

Friedan has fought her entire career against the condition of living death (absence of self, absence of creativity) she documents in *The Feminine Mystique*. A repeated theme in her college essays is spiritual barrenness, often labeled "Sunday afternoon." Spiritual barrenness and a consequent living death are central, as well, to Woolf's writing, notably in the evolution of Clarissa

The Activist Pens of Virginia Woolf and Betty Friedan

Dalloway's characterization. Death lurks barely beneath the glittering surface of Clarissa's life. "Why go on?" asks Clarissa in the glove shop in Bond Street, and answers in the next breath, "for one doesn't live for oneself" ("Mrs Dalloway" 152). She continues to muse: "Thousands of young men had died that things might go on" (152-3), thus compounding her sense of worthlessness, that she should see no reason to go on.

This living death, there being no self for which to live, is transformed in the 1925 novel, where its impetus toward suicide is transferred onto the war veteran, Septimus Smith. Woolf's disturbing doubling of Clarissa with Septimus, suggesting that a society hostess (Bennett and McCarthy's privileged woman) should be so damaged by the conditions of upper class life as to be explicable by analogy to the trauma of war, can be visualized in a coin image. Bound together by a shared core, they face Janus-like in opposing directions: Clarissa toward life, Septimus toward death.[11] A link between *Mrs. Dalloway* and *Three Guineas* can be traced through expanding circles radiating out from the "living death" at the coin image's core.

Before Chene Heady identified so clearly the political satire in *The Voyage Out*, even before Alex Zwerdling established the thread of social engagement running across the whole of Woolf's career, an early feminist reading of *Mrs. Dalloway* had identified both political and social critique, not the portrait of an individual, as the novel's subject. Recognizing that "wars, madness, the love of suffering and pain, adherence to an abstract, hierarchical, authoritarian set of values and means of organization are linked [in *Mrs. Dalloway*] to death," Lee Edwards understood the relation of the novel to *Three Guineas*. Edwards was able to see the novel as a fictional treatment of what Woolf "treats more abstractly in *Three Guineas*, a network that ties all forms of oppression to each other, [...]" (162, 171). Edwards also identified precisely how Woolf does this, by stepping outside assigned meanings and given truths, a move that renders one "vulnerable to the charge that you fail to comprehend the meaning of the word at the center of your discussion. Thus, Virginia Woolf is not generally regarded as a political—or indeed even a social—novelist" (163). Though Friedan may not have read *Three Guineas*, one may speculate that her early reading of *Mrs. Dalloway* exposed her to the social analysis made explicit in the later work.

Woolf's closing sentence of "The Intellectual Status of Women" crowns that argument with reference to master-slave relations (342). This is the move made by mid-nineteenth century American feminists, who compared the condition of women to that of American slaves. As a rhetorical device, the move is designed to expose an invisible evil by equation with an all-too-visible evil. The power of the move derives from the analogy of a condition of seeming well

73

being—the white, feminine, idealized woman—with an impossible, undeniably unacceptable condition—the dehumanized slave. The doubling of Clarissa with Septimus, no less shocking or controversial than the slave analogy, also makes this move. It is the more subversive tack I referred to earlier.

Friedan's text also employs this move, or creative leap, or paradigmatic shift. Like Woolf's social analysis, Friedan's critique of American social reality focuses on psychological damage: the erasure of self wrought by slave culture, war culture, patriarchal culture. Friedan's text updates, in light of the post-war revelations, the repertoire of analogues—positing as double to the American housewife, not merely a survivor of slavery or war, but of the slave and death camps of Nazi Germany.[12]

Converted from doubting and judging themselves as individuals, Second Wave feminists in the United States turned a critical and questioning eye on the larger societal, not personal, factors which determined the conditions of women's and men's lives. What may explain the impact of *Three Guineas* in the United States is the fact that it was written in opposition to war. This was the position of American women in the late 1960s. Many of these women, awakened into a new consciousness about the illusory nature of the feminine mystique, were also women participating in the anti-Vietnam war movement. Friedan, writing after World War II, was not writing against war and her cultural critique was less far reaching. Woolf's radical critique of patriarchal and militaristic culture, a critique too radical for many of her own generation, spoke eloquently to this later generation, to these women who came together on an April afternoon in 2003, after thirty-five years, reading Woolf again, in opposition to yet another American war.

Notes

[1] Rich turns to Woolf as a guide for learning to write the female self. She notes in particular the attention Woolf draws to the necessity women feel to disguise their own voice.

[2] A video tape of this event, "A Celebration of Valley Feminists," third in the lecture series *Woolf in the Valley* organized by Marilyn Schwinn Smith, is held by the Sophia Smith Collection, Neilson Library, Smith College. The panelists are Brett Averitt, Arlyn Diamond, Lee Edwards and Lorna Peterson.

[3] I mention in passing, the serendipitous linkage of Woolf and Friedan in an imaginative evocation of American culture of the 60s, "Understanding the Feminine Mystique," in Charles Boebel's "From *Orlando Ever After*" (49-50).

[4] *Virginia Woolf as Feminist*, Naomi Black's study of *Three Guineas* and its genesis across Woolf's career, appeared in print after this paper was delivered. Black cites "The Intellectual Status of Women" as Woolf's "earliest feminist publication in a nonfeminist

The Activist Pens of Virginia Woolf and Betty Friedan

location" (100). Tracing the constancy of Woolf's feminism to its fullest expression in *Three Guineas*, Black confines her analysis to non-fictional writing. My linkage of the MacCarthy exchange to the genesis of *Mrs. Dalloway* follows a separate, not contradictory trajectory. Both arguments lead to *Three Guineas*.

[5] Woolf's awareness of the conditions of lower class women's lives can be found scattered throughout her writings. Her "Introductory Letter to Margaret Llewelyn Davies" is particularly compelling. Friedan's early work as a labor journalist exposed her to the lives of working women. See in particular the reference to this period on page 9 of her essay, "The Way We Were—1949" and chapters 5-7 of Horowitz, *Betty Friedan*.

[6] See in particular her essay, "Angry Letters, Relieved Letters."

[7] Woolf's "Introductory Letter to Margaret Llewelyn Davies" makes clear her familiarity with the actual words of working women.

[8] Among the English Department papers, housed in the Archives of Smith College, are course syllabi and notes taken at departmental meetings regarding books suggested for specific courses. It is possible to determine that *Mrs. Dalloway* was taught at Smith Goldstein's freshman year, 1938-1939.

[9] Noting that Woolf's feminist activism was manifested through her pen, Black cites other instances of Woolf's awareness that "writing was still how she could best serve" (49).

[10] In a chapter titled "Discovering the Life of the Mind," Friedan lists Woolf, together with Thomas Mann and James Joyce, as authors of the "marvelous new kinds of books" which thrilled her to read at Smith College. She recalls having read *A Room of One's Own* while at Smith (*Life* 35), though most probably after writing her 1939 essay referred to above.

[11] See Smith, "Narration, Memory, and Identity" for a discussion of trauma and the life-death opposition in the Clarissa-Septimus dyad.

[12] Black is sensitive to the premium Woolf places on creativity and the psychological dimension of Woolf's analysis. See in particular pages 57, 62, 71.

Works Cited

Ardis, Ann, and Bonnie Kime Scott. *Virginia Woolf: Turning the Centuries: Selected Papers from the Ninth Annual Conference on Virginia Woolf.* New York: Pace UP, 2000.

Black, Naomi. *Virginia Woolf as Feminist*. Ithaca, NY: Cornell UP, 2004.

Boebel, Charles. "From *Orlando Ever After: A Dramatic Speculation*." Ardis and Scott 40-55.

A Celebration of Valley Feminists. Videocassette. Sophia Smith Collection, Neilson Library. Smith College. Northampton, MA.

Christ, Carol. "Woolf and Education." Welcome and Plenary Address. 13th Annual Conference on Virginia Woolf. Smith College. Northampton, MA. June 5, 2003.

Editors' Note. *The Diary of Virginia Woolf*, 339.

Edwards, Lee R. "War and Roses: The Politics of Mrs. Dalloway." *The Authority of*

Schwinn Smith

    Experience: Essays in Feminist Criticism. Ed. Arlyn Diamond and Lee R. Edwards. Amherst, MA: U of Massachusetts P, 1977, 160-77.

English Department, Papers. Archives, Neilson Library. Smith College. Northampton, MA.

Friedan, Betty. "Angry Letters, Relieved Letters." *It Changed My Life*, 20-7.

———. *The Feminine Mystique.* New York: Dell, 1963.

———. *It Changed My Life: Writings on the Women's Movement.* New York: Random House. 1976.

———. *Life So Far.* NY: Simon & Schuster, 2000.

———. "The Way We Were—1949." *It Changed My Life*, 8-16.

Heady, Chene. "'Accidents of Political Life': Satire and Edwardian Anti-Colonial Politics in *The Voyage Out.*" *Virginia Woolf Out of Bounds.* Ed. Jessica Berman and Jane Goldman. New York: Pace UP, 2001, 97-104.

Horowitz, Daniel. *Betty Friedan and the Making of* The Feminine Mystique: *The American Left, the Cold War, and Modern Feminism.* Amherst, MA: U of Massachusetts P, 1998.

Kuhn, Thomas S. *The Structure of Scientific Revolutions.* Chicago: U of Chicago P, 1962.

Lundberg, Ferdinand, and Marynia F. Farnham. *Modern Woman: The Lost Sex.* New York: Grosset & Dunlap, 1947.

Rich, Adrienne. "When We Dead Awaken: Writing as Re-Vision." *College English* 34.1 (1972). Rpt. in *American Poets in 1976.* Ed. William Heyen. New York: Bobbs-Merrill, 1976. Rpt. in *On Lies, Secrets, and Silence. Selected Prose 1966-1978.* By Adrienne Rich. New York: Norton. 1979, 31-49.

Smith, Marilyn Schwinn. "Narration, Memory, and Identity: *Mrs. Dalloway* at the End of the Century." Ardis and Scott 158-65.

Wheare, Jane. Introduction. *The Voyage Out.* By Virginia Woolf. ix-xxxvi.

Woolf, Virginia. *The Diary of Virginia Woolf.* Ed. Anne Olivier Bell. Assisted by Andrew McNeillie. Vol. 2. 1920-1924. New York: Harcourt Brace Jovanovich, 1978.

———. "The Intellectual Status of Women." Appendix III. *The Diary of Virginia Woolf*, 339-42.

———. "Introductory Letter to Margaret Llewelyn Davies." *Life As We Have Known It.* Ed. Margaret Llewelyn Davies. London: Hogarth, 1931, xv-xxxix.

———. *Letters: Virginia Woolf & Lytton Strachey.* Ed. Leonard Woolf and James Strachey. 1st American ed. New York: Harcourt Brace, 1956.

———. *Mrs. Dalloway.* New York: Harcourt Brace, 1981.

———. "Mrs Dalloway in Bond Street." *The Complete Shorter Fiction of Virginia Woolf.* Ed. Susan Dick. London: Hogarth, 1985.

———. *A Passionate Apprentice: The Early Journals 1897-1909.* Ed. Mitchell A. Leaska. New York: Harcourt Brace Jovanovich, 1990.

———. "A Sketch of the Past." *Moments of Being.* Ed. Jeanne Schulkind. 2nd ed. New York: Harcourt Brace, 1985.

———. *The Voyage Out.* Ed. with Introduction and Notes by Jane Wheare. London: Penguin, 1992.

Zwerdling, Alex. *Virginia Woolf and the Real World.* Berkeley: University of California Press, 1986.

II

Translation

"The meaning on the far side of language": Walter Benjamin's Translation Theory and Virginia Woolf's Modernism
Makiko Minow-Pinkney

In her essay on "The Russian Point of View," Virginia Woolf expresses doubts "whether, for all their enthusiasm, the English can understand Russian literature" (*CE*1 238). Elsewhere, referring to British enthusiasm for the Greeks, she mockingly asks: "with what slight resemblance to the real meaning" are they "forever making up some notion of the meaning of Greek?"(*CE*1 1). In the case of "a literature so alien as the Russian" (246) which can be approached only by translation, Woolf's doubt becomes paramount. My first encounter with Woolf was a Japanese translation of *To the Lighthouse* when I was a young student: I was immediately enthralled, and Woolf became *the* author for me. But how could it be possible to understand in translation a text whose writing is renowned for its poetic beauty? In the light of Woolf's words mentioned above, could any foreigner ever hope to understand Woolf? In this essay I shall explore the translatability of literary work, drawing particularly on Walter Benjamin's theory of translation. My discussion will be extended also to Woolf's modernist aesthetics, for Benjamin's translation theory, which has a strong resonance with Woolf's aesthetics, offers a new perspective from which Woolf's modernism can be understood.

The issue of translation is integral to modernism. In relation to this inherent connection between the two, I would like to mention briefly the specific context of translation in Japan. It is not too far-fetched to argue that translation is at the core of the Japanese modern self. The modernization of feudal Japan happened towards the end of the nineteenth century, triggered by pressure from the West. Since then modernity, modernism and postmodernism have happened with amazing speed in a short space of time. Translation played a crucial role here: Western texts translated into Japanese during the period of modernization served as a model; ideationally and stylistically, that is, they helped to create modern Western concepts in the Japanese language and a new modern writing style, through which, more crucially, the creation of new, "modern" subjectivity was undertaken.[1] To achieve modernity, Japan had to reject its own discursive past and force itself to emulate, or rather, recognize the foreign as its own true origin. By this process of Lacanian *méconnaissance* or misrecognition at the level of the entire nation, Japan constructed a modern self. Dislocation from the origin, a present self which no longer coincides with one's past, the longing for an authenticity which resides in the foreign land—these anxieties of modern Japan are also those of translation as such. The anxiety of the language of modernity and the anxiety of translation perfectly coincide in Japan.

The examination of the development of "modern" poetry in Japan reveals this misrecognition (conflation of "origin" and "foreign") in its conception; Japanese "modern" poetry starts when the West (particularly France in this case) was recognized as a distant, unreachable origin. Seeking "the essential constitution of Japanese modernism" in the 1920s, Hosea Hirata suggests that

> the anxiety of translation lies at the nucleus of modernism in Japan; one may even claim that anxiety single-handedly constitutes and defines the modernist text in Japan. If we are to define "modernity" as the anxiety of the past and the impulse toward the patricide of history, we should be able to extend the idea that the anxiety of translation is essential to the constitution of Japanese modernism to modernism in general. (185)

Indeed, disowning their own "parents," the Wellses, Bennetts and Galsworthys, the orphaned modernist writers in England sought their true "origin" in far-away places and times, in translation. For Woolf, "the year 1860 was a year of empty cradles...the reign of Edward the seventh was barren of poet, novelist or critic...it followed that the Georgians read Russian novelists in translation" (*CE*1 122). The English moderns recognized an identity in foreign writers, not their own people. "No one but a modern, no one perhaps but a Russian," Woolf writes, has the same rather peculiar perspective on life. Therefore "to write of any fiction save theirs [Russians'] is a waste of time" (*CE*2 109).

Gayatri Spivak describes her experience as a translator in terms of an erotic encounter with the other: "Translation is the most intimate act of reading. I surrender to the text when I translate" (178). And yet, however eagerly translators try to abandon themselves and merge their identity into the other's, translators cannot help ending up causing a fundamental change in the other too. Woolf compares Russian authors read in translation to men deprived of their clothes by an earthquake or in a railway accident; they are "stripped of their style" and "nothing remains except a crude and coarsened version of the sense" (*CE*1 238-9). In Walter Benjamin's famous essay "The Task of the Translator" (1923), the original text, once translated, appears to be wearing a "royal robe with ample folds" (76). Woolf suggests nakedness and Benjamin a regal luxury, but what each is pointing at is really not so different, for the sovereign body of the original in Benjamin must, one would think, be suffering from a feeling of chill or nakedness in its gorgeous folds which—"overpowering and alien" in Benjamin's phrase—somehow remain ill fitting to its body. The common premise of these two metaphors is our classical notion of trans-

"The meaning on the far side of language"

lation, which Barbara Johnson summarizes as follows: "the separability of style and thought and the priority of the signified over the signifier...Faithfulness to the text has meant faithfulness to the semantic tenor with as little interference as possible from the constraints of the vehicle. Translation, in other words, has always been the translation of meaning" (Johnson 145). The possibility of translation is based on the opposition of signifier and signified, and the prioritizing of the latter over the former. What Derrida terms "an absolutely pure, transparent and unequivocal translatability" (*Positions* 20) can be posited only on the premise of the transcendental signified. Thus the translator's dream of perfect translatability is deeply rooted in what Derrida calls "logocentrism." The paradox of this is that it is precisely that very logocentrism and its most significant aspect, "phonocentrism," which at the same time render that dream unattainable. Phonocentrism privileges speech over writing because of its immediacy to the source of meaning, and thereby guarantees the full presence of meaning uncontaminated by a vehicle of representation; and it thus puts translation in its place for being doubly distanced from the presence of meaning. So logocentrism guarantees translatability but at the same time it makes translation impossible. Derrida's philosophical enterprise to understand signification as différance deconstructs the clear cut differentiation between signifier and signified and thus unsettles the notion of translatability.

If the non-identity between signifier and signified initiates the linguistic process of ceaseless shifts from signifier to signifier, seeking a signified, and meaning results from this process rather than from being located in the fixed signified, there is no stable meaning to be transported in translation. The replacement of one signifier with another is also the very process of translation. If being non-identical, foreign to itself is the essential condition of signification, language can signify only on condition of the carry-across operation of translation. Hence Barbara Johnson's remark: "Derrida's entire philosophic enterprise...can be seen as an analysis of the translation process at work in every text" (Johnson 146). However, logocentrism is incorrigible and motivates the signifier's movement to find and settle on one signified. This desire of linguistic enterprise is also the desire of translation: a wish to master différance and overcome foreignness. So translation posits the transcendental signified as a guarantor of translatability but at the same time it derives its necessity from the fact that such a transcendental signified is missing. Translatability exists on the premise paradoxically of both the presence and absence of the transcendental signified.

Walter Benjamin's "The Task of the Translator" demonstrates such poststructuralist notions well before the time of poststructuralism but it also gives us a unique and different way of understanding translation and translatability.

Minow-Pinkney

Written as an introduction to his own translation of Charles Baudelaire's *Tableaux Parisiens*, Benjamin's concern is not with any kind of work but a literary, particularly poetic work whose essential substance is "what it contains in addition to information...the unfathomable, the mysterious, the 'poetic,' something that a translator can reproduce only if he is also a poet" (70). He endeavors to remove translation from the idea of transmitting information ("This is the hallmark of bad translations" [70]). He distinguishes "the intended object" from "the mode of intention" in language: the way in which the intended object is approached, the mode of signification, the value of the word, its connotations and associations, the images the word evokes, the word's relationship with other words, etc.—these are specific to each language, even though the intended object may be the same. What translation is concerned with is the mode of intention, not the intended object. "The task of the translator consists in finding that intended effect [*Intention*] upon the language into which he is translating which produces in it the echo of the original" (77). Benjamin contends: "translation, instead of resembling the meaning of the original, must lovingly and in detail incorporate the original's mode of signification...For this very reason translation must in large measure refrain from wanting to communicate something, from rendering the sense..." (79). So Benjamin's idea of translation does not comply with our classical notion of translation, which Barbara Johnson described as the translation of meaning. Translation is engaged with nothing but the modes of intention which are the essential content of a literary work. Hence Benjamin's enigmatic assertion: "Translatability is an essential quality of certain works," which means, he adds, "a specific significance inherent in the original manifests itself in its translatability" (71). How translatable a certain work is, is a gauge of how essential the modes of intention are to the work, namely, the degree of the poetic quality of the work. Translatability is the mark of the highest poetry. Thus with translatability and the poetic becoming identical, the necessity of translation acquires a totally new significance in Benjamin's theory.

According to Benjamin, what translation wishes to realize is "pure language," which does not seem to be quite the same as the transcendental signified. What is this pure language? In his earlier unpublished paper "On Language as Such and on the Language of Man" (1916), Biblical references are said to be explicit, but the later essay, "The Task of the Translator," does not present its arguments in theological terms. Nonetheless, it is not difficult to imagine Biblical backgrounds in his theoretical notions. Adopting the problematics of loss of "mourning and melancholia" as an interpretative dominant, we could approach his notion of "pure language" as Paradisaic language before the Fall, lost and yearned for by mankind. However, there is another story of

"The meaning on the far side of language"

mankind and language in the Bible—the story of the tower of Babel. Prior to his discussion on Benjamin's essay, Derrida comments on this story: "[the] tower of Babel does not merely figure the irreducible multiplicity of tongues; it exhibits an incompletion, the impossibility of finishing, of totalising, of saturating, of completing something on the order of edification, architectural construction, system and architectonics" (165). In the light of these aspects of the story pointed out by Derrida, if we approach Benjamin's translation theory in terms of the problematics of "incompletion," his somewhat enigmatic arguments on the relationship of the original, translation and pure language seem to make clearer sense than if approached within the interpretative hold of "mourning and melancholia."

God's punishment of humanity and the dissemination of the people and their language all over the earth means "scattering," but dissemination also implies that each fragment is carrying a remnant of the original whole; what is lost is the "totality" as Derrida mentions, but the original survives "concealed and fragmentary" as Benjamin says of "pure language" (80). So in translation "the great motif of integrating many tongues into one true language is at work" (77), "of making both the original and the translation recognizable as fragments of greater language, just as fragments are part of a vessel" (79). So Benjamin posits a "kinship of languages," "which is to manifest itself in translations" (74). The kinship "rests in the intention underlying each language as a whole—an intention, however, which no single language can attain by itself but which is realized only by the totality of their intentions supplementing each other: pure language" (74). We should surely interpret his "supplement" in a Derridean sense here. Benjamin writes "pure language" is "concealed in concentrated fashion in translations" (77); the task of the translator is "to release in his own language that pure language which is under the spell of another, to liberate the language imprisoned in a work in his re-creation of the work" (80). So the original is incomplete until it "is able to emerge as pure language" (80) after being supplemented by translation. Hence the original's call for translation; the original needs the detour of translation. Long before Derrida, Benjamin's argument was already deconstructing the hierarchy of the original and translation.

The goal of translation is to achieve "a final, conclusive, decisive stage of all linguistic creation" (75), which is "pure language." The original language has the natural unity between content and language "like a fruit and its skin" (76). This organic unity is responsible for language's constant state of flux as well as its infinite power to change and survive. Translation, by losing this organicity, Benjamin argues, "ironically transplants the original into a more definite linguistic realm…" (76). "Pure language" retained in each language in a fragmentary manner is concealed and "weighed with a heavy, alien meaning. To relieve it of this, to turn the symbolising into the symbolized...is the tremendous and only capacity of translation" (80). What Benjamin is saying here is, in other words, that the translation's task is to eliminate (or at least reduce) the linguistic movement of différance—the very signifying process ("the symbolising" in Benjamin's phrase)—which produces "a heavy, alien meaning" and obfuscates the pure language. So this pure language when finally realized, he writes, "no longer means or expresses anything but is, as expressionless and creative Word, that which is meant in all languages" (80). When Benjamin talks of the foreignness of languages of which translation is a provisional solution, he surely means not only the foreignness between languages but the foreignness within language as the essential condition of signification: the foreignness which prevents any given language from being self-identical, namely what Derrida terms as différance. Benjamin asserts that translation is a "way of coming to terms with the foreignness of languages" (75). It is a way of reducing it, of halting the constant flux, the shifting movement of différance. In translation in which the amorphous capacity of language for signification is reduced, "the original rises into a higher and purer linguistic air" (75). Pure language means non-signification. So in order for translation "to allow the pure language...to shine upon the original all the more fully" Benjamin recommends "a literal rendering of the syntax which proves words rather than sentences to be the primary element of the translator" (79). The linearity to which différance destines language causes signification but at the same time delays the arrival of meaning; it is the hindrance which blocks the light of pure language. So Benjamin writes: "the sentence is the wall before the language of the original, literalness is the arcade" (79).

If the incompleteness of the system of signs is at the core of Benjamin's translation theory, incompleteness is also a noticeable characteristic of modernist art. Modernist fiction was often accused of the lack of a complete "rounded" character, a fragmentary style of writing and the lack of a clear narrative plot with a proper conclusion. Post-impressionist paintings scandalized viewers by their unfinished, sketchy appearance. Gertrude Stein writes in *The Autobiography of Alice B. Toklas* that "Cézanne had come to his unfinishedness and distortion of necessity, Matisse did it by intention" (46) and tells an amusing anecdote about Cézanne's portrait of a woman: "It was this picture that Alfy Maurer used to explain was finished and that you could tell that it was finished because it had a frame" (39). So without the frame, one wouldn't be able to tell if it was finished. According to *The Autobiography*, this happened to be the very picture under whose stimulus Stein wrote her *Three Lives*. (Stein also mentions that not long before starting *Three Lives*, she began translating

"The meaning on the far side of language"

Flaubert's *Trois Contes* as an exercise in literature, suggesting not only the influence of foreign literature on this modernist text but inherent connections between translation and her modernist writing.)

Discussing Chekhov in "The Russian Point of View," it is the "inconclusiveness" of his stories which particularly attracts the modernist Woolf's attention: "These stories are inconclusive" (*CE*1 241), Woolf writes: "the end is not there." "Nothing is solved, we feel" (242). The great realist Tolstoy is most comprehensive and seems to capture almost every aspect of life: "Nothing seems to escape him" (244); "Everything is astonishingly clear and absolutely sharp" (245). And yet even he disturbs the foundations of life and brings in uncertainty by posing a question devastatingly fundamental and yet difficult to answer and thus leaves the text inconclusive:

> "Why live?" There is always at the centre of the book some Olenin, or Pierre, or Levin who gathers into himself all experience, turns the world round between his fingers, and never ceases to ask, even as he enjoys it, what is the meaning of it, and what should be our aims. (246)

Woolf's attention to the inconclusiveness of the Russian mind and literature would, in turn, throw some light on the particular nature of the unfinishedness of modernist art. The other related characteristics which appear in Woolf's writing on Russian fiction are its spirituality: "it is the soul that is the chief character in Russian fiction" (242); its profundity: "If we want understanding of the soul and heart where else shall we find it of comparable profundity?" (*CE*2 109); and its honesty: "an honesty for which we can find no match save among the Russian themselves" (242). It is the comprehensive and compassionate mind of the Russian whose preoccupation is the soul's "relation to things outside themselves" (251) and not with each other that makes them ask a question to which " there is no answer" (*CE*2 109). "[I]f honestly examined life presents question after question which must be left to sound on and on after the story is over…" (*CE*2 109). And it is on this that the modernist finds affinity with the Russian: "there may be no answer to these questions, but…let us never manipulate the evidence so as to produce something fitting, decorous, agreeable to our vanity" (*CE*1 242). So the moderns, too, leave their works incomplete by refusing to put a false end to their unfinishable quest for the absolute meaning of human existence.

If the novel is understood as the form which has developed when the immanent meaning of human being is no longer given in an organic homogeneous world, the quest for the ontological certainty of human being is inherent to the novel, and the realist novel tries to solve the problem by presenting a narrative whose protagonist finds in the end self-verification and a place in his/her living circumstances. As the organic unity of society further disintegrates with industrialization, technological revolution, and the weakened power of religion which used to give assurance to the ontological status of human being, the realist novel form becomes increasingly strained to give a convincing answer. For the moderns the contrivance of realist narrative becomes simply a lie and pretence.

Here perhaps we remember the Hungarian critic Georg Lukács, a contemporary of Woolf and Benjamin, who condemned modernism as a literary form leading only to a further decadence of modern society in which separation and isolation were the norm. Thus he championed realism as the only credible novel form which could demonstrate a higher mode of the individual's original unity with the self, integrated in the organic world as it is supposed to have existed in the epic world. Though his rejection of modernism may now be obsolete, the reason for his importance as critic, according to Tony Jackson, is that Lukács was one of the first critics to read realist fictions in a modernist way; that is, he recognized their increasing difficulty in finding a genuine immanence rather than its simulacrum. In *The Theory of the Novel* Lukács writes:

> An empty immanence, which is anchored only in the writer's experience and not, at the same time, in his return to the home of all things, is merely the immanence of a surface that covers up the cracks but is incapable of retaining this immanence and must become a surface riddled with holes. (92)

When modernism emerged as a new literary form which was concerned to expose the very "cracks" and "holes" in the narrative text, Lukács rejected it because he could only see in it alienation, despair and hopelessness. "He could value only a literature that would try to forge a new anchor for the old idea of the self" (Jackson 166). And it was Tolstoy for him who was great enough to be just able to forge such a new anchor and "created a form of novel which overlaps to the maximum extent into the epic" (Lukács 145). Interestingly, in *The Theory of the Novel* and in "The Russian Point of View," published roughly contemporaneously (the former in 1920, the latter in 1925), Lukács and Woolf admire the same great achievement of Tolstoy from almost opposite perspectives. Lukács's enthusiasm for Tolstoy lies in his capacity as a realist novelist to close up "cracks" and "holes," while for Woolf, the immensity of Tolstoy, who "most enthrals us and most repels" (*CE2* 246), resides in his capacity to open up "cracks" and "holes" by asking "Why live?"

Let's look briefly at *Anna Karenin*. Such a "crack" or "hole" seems to appear in Chapter 20, Part 5, entitled "Death." Why is this the only titled chapter? Does it indicate its pivotal importance to the novel as a whole? Or does it

"The meaning on the far side of language"

suggest some anomaly of the chapter in relation to the novel? This chapter depicts Levin coming face to face with his own death through his brother Nikolai's death, which brings his agnosticism to its crisis point and precipitates him into agonizing ontological uncertainty: "So he lived, not knowing and not seeing any chance of knowing what he was and for what purpose he had been placed in the world" (826). Tormented by these questions, Levin's life becomes a desperate search for the answers, until he finds God at the end of the novel. This makes a sharp contrast to the story of Anna who ends her life by suicide in utter nihilism, condemning every human existence including her own. With her selfhood disintegrated, Anna ends up ejected from the society which has been the sole grounding reality of her whole existence. This is the exact opposite of the ideal ending of the projected subject of a realist novel which is supposed to provide the protagonist with a self-verification in relation to others in her/his living circumstances, or return her/him to "the home of all things" (in Lukács's phrase) as in the case of Levin.

"Death" marks the limits of this realist novel which seems to include almost everything—love, passion, marriage, family life, economics, politics, agriculture etc.—and every point of view, even of a horse and its rider, Vronsky, fused into one or the point of view of Laska, Levin's dog. As Woolf noted: "Nothing seems to escape him. Nothing glances off him unrecorded" (*CE*1 244). But the novel cannot write about death with internal knowledge as it does so confidently about other subject matters. The chapter offers merely Levin's response to death. This representational limit of the omniscient novel, in fact, also appears with "birth." It can be approached only externally from the point of view of Levin who is helplessly and anxiously waiting outside the labor scene; even the experience of Kitty who gives birth does not appear there. Both "death" and "birth" are off-limits to representation. So the chapter titled "death" is a crisis point not only of Levin but also of the omniscient realist narrative: a hole from which the whole realist text and Levin's selfhood could start to unravel.

The incompleteness of language and its endless process of signification, according to Benjamin's theory, calls for the supplement of translation which could halt the movement of différance and shed the clogging meaning it produces in order to allow pure language to emerge. So too does a realization of the incompleteness of narrative text in relation to the absolute meaning of human being call for a new literary form that could address the very lack and aim for the absolute meaning to emerge. Here arises the necessity of modernism which supplements the inadequacy of realist narrative by bringing to the surface of the text the very lacuna which the realist text represses and conceals from itself. But because what modernism supplies, in fact, is the very hole

87

of the narrative representation, this makes the modernist text explicitly incomplete. Modernism is a decision to choose the possibility that "the horizon widens; the soul gains an astonishing sense of freedom" (*CE*1 242), as Woolf writes on the inconclusive Russian novels, rather than a false completeness.

As mentioned earlier, Benjamin makes translatability and the quintessential quality of literariness—"the unfathomable, the mysterious, 'the poetic'"—almost synonymous; neither translation nor the poetic is concerned with transmitting information, with their engagement being with what Benjamin calls "the mode of intention." If the poetic is primarily translatable, or indeed is translatability itself, the foreignness of languages is not a hindrance to understanding. Woolf, too, refers to poetry as something that we understand without being hampered by linguistic barriers. Discussing Aeschylus in her essay "On Not Knowing Greek," she writes:

> To understand him it is not so necessary to understand Greek as to understand poetry. It is necessary to take that dangerous leap through the air without support of words which Shakespeare also asks of us…we know instantly and instinctively what they mean…The meaning is just on the far side of language. It is the meaning which in moments of astonishing excitement and stress we perceive in our minds without words; it is the meaning that Dostoevsky (hampered as he was by prose and as we are by translation) leads us to…(*CE*1 7)

"Poetry" in Woolf's writing usually means poetry written in prose rather than in verse. Woolf names some novelists as "poets" because "there is poetry in novels" (*CE*2 96), she claims. Among them are Tolstoy, Emily Brontë, Melville, Hardy, and Sterne. Novels achieve poetry through various means, according to Woolf, but perhaps the most distinctive kind she discusses is what she calls "the poetry of situation rather than of language" (94) which is found in *War and Peace* or *Wuthering Heights*. So these novels do not even rely on language for effecting poetry. In "The Narrow Bridge of Art," she calls "the variety of the novel which will be written in time to come" "poetry" (*CE*2 225). *The Waves*, as we know, is her own attempt to write "a playpoem" (*D*3 203) envisaged as such a new kind of novel. She writes in her diary about the novel still referred to as *The Moths*:

> The idea has come to me that what I want now to do is to saturate every atom. I mean to eliminate all waste, deadness, superfluity: to give the moment whole; whatever it includes…Waste, deadness, come from the inclusion of things that don't belong to the moment; this appalling narrative business of the realist: getting on from lunch to dinner: it is false, unreal, merely conventional. Why admit anything to literature that is not poetry—by which I mean saturated?…I want to put everything in: yet to saturate. That is what I want to do in *The Moths*…made transparent. (*D*3 209)

"The meaning on the far side of language"

Her emphasis is on the moment. Poetry is presented as belonging to the moment in contrast to the linear continuity of narrative, which she dubs "waste, deadness, superfluity" and "false, unreal, merely conventional." Poetry expresses the central idea of her ambition which her modernist aesthetics wishes to achieve. What is notable is her word "saturate"—poetry as saturation. Saturation implies totality, fulfilment and completion in contrast to an incomplete state which would start the chain movement of shifting signs and is thus inherent in linear narrativity. Interestingly, in the passage I quoted earlier, Derrida also uses the same word in order to suggest the implication of the story of Babel, which is, he writes: "the impossibility of…saturating."

It seems clear that what Woolf means by "poetry" is also related to her famous "moments of being" which she writes about in "A Sketch of the Past"—the privileged moments of revelation which used to catapult her whole being out of the continuum of everyday life, causing either despair or rapture, which, Woolf thinks, made her a writer and from which all her writings fundamentally derive. If Woolf's poetry is non-verbal and constitutes her central notion of modernist aesthetics, it is reasonable to infer that the aesthetic ambition expressed by the painter Lily in *To the Lighthouse* also refers to this "poetry" of Woolf's: "Phrases came: visions came. Beautiful pictures. Beautiful phrases. But what she wished to get hold of was that very jar on the nerves, the thing itself before it has been made anything" (*TTL* 209). One of her diary entries of the time when she was writing these words for Lily reads: "Suppose one could catch them [thoughts] before they became 'works of art'? Catch them hot and sudden as they rise in the mind…Of course one cannot; for the process of language is slow and deluding. One must stop to find a word. Then there is the form of the sentence, soliciting one to fill it" (*D*3 102). There is another entry made two years later about her frustration with "the process of language": "But what a little I can get down with my pen of what is so vivid to my eyes, & not only to my eyes: also to some nervous fibre, or fan like membrane in my spine" (*D*3 191).

To catch such a "jar on the nerves," sensation conveyed "to some nervous fibre," "the thing itself" before being put through "the process of language" is her modernist project. So Woolf's modernist aesthetics present the verbal process as a problem, pointing to the fundamental antithesis between Lily's "the thing itself" and "the transmuting process" (*D*3 102) of art, because, as Jacques Lacan writes in *Écrits*: "the symbol manifests itself first of all as the murder of the thing" (104). After the words of Lily's wish, "to get hold of…the thing itself," the original holograph draft reads: "the germ, in painting, in knowing, of all art and affection" (qtd. in notes for *TTL*, ed. Lee, 257)—Lily /Woolf wish to get hold of the very source of art which, perhaps like a germ in another sense, can be transmitted directly through physical contact or through the air.

In discussing Aeschylus, Woolf writes: "we know instantly and instinctively" what the words of his play mean (*CE*1 7); it is a mysterious communication involving both the psychic and the somatic levels of our being ("instinctively"), and it is the understanding which happens without delay ("instantly"). The linear process of linguistic signification which is an infinite deferring of the meaning becomes redundant to such a communication. Hence Woolf's well known condemnation of the linear narrative of the realist novel as "waste, deadness, superfluity" (*D*3 209). Polarized against the instantaneous and intuitive poetry is the drudgery of narrative business, adhering to "a formal railway line of sentence, for its convenience" (*L*3 135-36) as Woolf wrote to her French painter friend, Jacques Raverat, or in *The Waves* what Bernard calls "a biographical style" (184), which he regards as a necessary convenience but a lie. Here we should remember Benjamin's emphasis on the importance of "words" rather than "sentences" in translation. The syntax and sentences, namely, the linearity of language, are for him "the wall" blocking the light of pure language and he recommends "a literal rendering of the syntax" by concentrating on words (79). Thus for both Woolf's poetry and Benjamin's pure language the linearity of the signifying process is a waste and deadness to be got rid of. For Benjamin, "A real translation is transparent" (79). Woolf, too, wanted her modernist experimental "playpoem" *The Moths/The Waves* to be free from the clogging meaning of the signifying process, to be "transparent."

The difference between Woolf and Benjamin on this matter is that Benjamin's idea of pure language is close to the Romantic notion of symbolism which aspires to transcend the materiality of language, while Woolf tries to take poetry back to the somatic level before language. Therefore what is meant by Woolf's poetry could also be approached in terms of what Julia Kristeva posits through her concept of the semiotic, which she theorizes as taking place in the complex of bodily drives linked to the pre-Oedipal primary processes. Though heterogeneous to the symbolic, the semiotic is vital in order for the sign to be not an empty but a meaningful one, invested with the affect of the subject, because the semiotic, as a kind of lining, connects the abstract sign to the bodily drives. Kristeva, too, privileges "poetry" because this aesthetic form, situated directly over the schism between the two competing modalities of the symbolic and the semiotic, tries to give the semiotic as much dominance as possible.

So poetry can be communicated regardless of the foreignness of its language, paradoxically because the quintessence of the poetic does not belong to the realm of language. The poetic—"rhetoricity" (in her word)— is also what

"The meaning on the far side of language"

Gayatri Spivak emphasizes in her essay on translation as something the translator must care for, because, she argues, it indicates "the limits of its language" (181), "the silence between and around words" (179); silence occurs because "rhetoric or figuration disrupt logic"—the logic which "allows us to jump from word to word by means of clearly indicated connections" (178-9). This is Spivak's version of what Kristeva theorizes as the semiotic disruption of the symbolic which can be witnessed in the avant-garde poetic text and in which subjectivity itself is unravelled before it is reconstructed in a new form. Spivak insists: "Language is not everything. It is only a vital clue to where the self loses its boundaries" (178). In this area of silence the magic of communication happens. We remember here that in *The Voyage Out*, a would-be novelist, Terence's ambition is to write "a novel about silence." Spivak uses the metaphor of textile and describes this disruption of the logic of text (Kristeva/Lacan's "the symbolic") by rhetoricity (the semiotic) as "fraying." The task of the translator, therefore, is "to facilitate [the] love between the original and its shadow, a love that permits fraying" "the selvedges of language-textile" (178) so that the interweaving of the two texts can happen. As translator one needs to unravel oneself and one's language first. Spivak writes: "First…the translator must surrender to the text" (181). Here arises the question of the politics of translation which Spivak's essay entitled "The Politics of Translation" addresses, but I do not have space here to discuss this issue.

Benjamin writes: "for the sake of pure language [the translator] breaks decayed barriers of his own language" (80). "He must expand and deepen his language by means of the foreign language" (81). This is exactly what modernist experimentalism advocates. The moderns had a sense of crisis that the language they inherited had become bleached, drained of physical substance, inert and invisible. In order to regenerate language, the Russian futurist Viktor Shklovsky advocates the introduction of foreignness and incomprehensibility into it. In his rousing manifesto "The Resurrection of the Word" in 1914, he insists that one must reject the false transparency of the "glassy armour of familiarity" of language (44) and reactivate the materiality of words by defamiliarization in order to recover the figurality of words and thus rework language into poetry: "we have become too used to setting up comprehensibility as a necessary requirement of poetic language" (46). The hallmarks of modernist experimentalism—complex form, difficult style, and recondite allusions from far-flung sources—certainly disrupt the smooth familiarity of one's language into unnatural alienness. Modernist writing is deliberately unnatural, as if it is a language of translation; "organised violence upon ordinary language," which is Roman Jakobson's definition of modernist poetry, might be a description of a bad translation. The new language of the Russian futurist "is incomprehensible, difficult...It is not even like Russian..." (46), announces Shklovsky, because the futurist artist "has broken it down and mangled it up" (46). Such destructive vocabulary is not peculiar to the futurists. Woolf too, in "Mr Bennett and Mrs Brown," urges the "smashing and crashing" because, "at whatever cost to life, limb and damage to valuable property, Mrs Brown must be rescued" (*CE*1 333). Thus the "prevailing sound of the Georgian age" is, Woolf claims, "the sound of breaking and falling, crashing and destruction." The result is that "Grammar is violated; syntax disrupted" (*CE*1 334).

Spivak's metaphor for what is essential for good translation, "fraying of the language-textile," is less violent than Benjamin's breaking "decayed barriers of his own language," but it, too, indicates some kind of breaking up; it reminds me of Bernard in *The Waves* referring to the "torn bits of stuff, stuff with raw edges"(184). His desire is to attend to these torn bits of stuff with raw edges which "the biographical style" neatly tacks together to keep the civilized fabric of social life. Here again the interests and project of modernism and translation seem to overlap.

So Spivak contends that communication between two texts and two subjects happens in "the silence of the absolute fraying of language" (181), "beside language, around language" (178) beyond "the limits of its language" pointed at by the rhetoricity of the text. Woolf writes that the meaning of poetry "is just on the far side of language" and that "we perceive [it] in our minds without words" (*CE*1 7). Spivak says that in translation meaning "hops" into "the spacey emptiness" between two languages where the self gets perilously close to losing its boundaries—"risky fraying" (178). Woolf, too, talks of "the dangerous leap through the air without the support of words" (*CE*1 7) which we need to take in order to understand poetry. A "leap" and a "hop" are "dangerous" (Woolf), "perilous" and "risky" (Spivak). But there is a chance for a fortunate or daring achievement too. "Risk" and "chance" are the words through which Derrida brings translation and poetry together. Speculating on the possibility/impossibility of translating the word "deconstruction," Derrida ends his letter to a Japanese friend:

> The chance...would be that another word...can be found in Japanese to say the same thing,...to speak of deconstruction...in a word which will be also more beautiful.
>
> When I speak of this writing of the other which will be more beautiful, I clearly understand translation as involving the same risk and chance as the poem. How to translate 'poem'? a 'poem'? (8)

"The meaning on the far side of language"

According to Benjamin and Woolf, as I have been examining, poetry is translatable. In fact the poetic—the quintessence of literariness—is translatability itself and this absolute translatability means paradoxically the needlessness of translation and the impossibility of translation at the same time. It is similar to the proper name, which, as Derrida points out, referring to a singular, unique existence, is not an empty sign and lies outside the semantic system of a language and therefore makes translation redundant and impossible at once. What else can one do except, as Derrida does in the letter, repeating the word (tautology) or chanting the word? If poetry resides in the realm of silence outside language where understanding occurs "without the mediation of meaning" (Benjamin 82), the only and crucial role of the translation of poetry is to provide "a vital clue" (Spivak 78) to this area of silence and contribute to the realization of "pure language—which no longer means or expresses anything but is…that which is meant in all languages" (80) and in which, therefore, total communication exists.

Note

[1] One of the crucial moments in Japanese modernization was the movement called *genbun itchi*, encouraged by the establishment which was pressing the country towards modernization. Kojin Karatani argues that the movement means more than "unifying spoken (*gen*) and written (*bun*) languages" as it is usually translated and interpreted; it is rather the reforms that abandoned the classical or "literary" Japanese employed in written texts by doing away with Chinese characters (Kanji). *Genbun itchi* represents the invention of a new ideology of writing as equivalent with speech, that is, what Derrida terms phonocentrism, inherent in Western metaphysics. Karatani regards the movement of *genbun itchi* as corresponding to the emergence of "abstract thought and language" that, Freud argues, is simultaneous with that of (Western) subjectivity—the "interiority." For more on *genbun itchi* movement, see Karatani 39-54.

Works Cited

Benjamin, Walter. "The Task of the Translator." *Illuminations*. Ed. Hannah Arendt. Trans. Harry Zohn. London: Fontana Press, 1973. 70-82.

Derrida, Jacques. *Positions*. Trans. Alan Bass. London: The Athlone Press, 1981.

——. "Des Tours de Babel." *Différance in Translation*. Ed. and trans. Joseph Graham. Ithaca: Cornell UP. 1985. 165-207.

——. "Letter to a Japanese Friend." *Derrida & Différance*. Ed. David Wood and Robert Bernaconi. Coventry: Parousa Press, 1985. 1-8.

Hirata, Hosea. *The Poetry and Poetics of Nishiwaki Junzaburo: Modernism in Translation*. Princeton: Princeton UP, 1993.
Jackson, E. Tony. *The Subject of Modernism: Narrative Alterations in the Fiction of Eliot, Conrad, Woolf, and Joyce*. Michigan: Michigan UP, 1994.
Johnson, Barbara. "Taking Fidelity Philosophically." *Différance in Translation*. Ed. and trans. Joseph Graham. Ithaca: Cornell UP. 1985. 142-48.
Karatani, Kojin. *Origins of Modern Japanese Literature*. Forward. Fredric Jameson. Trans. Brett de Bary. Durham and London: Duke UP, 1993.
Lacan, Jacques. *Écrits: A Selection*. Trans. Alan Sheridan. London: Tavistock Publication Ltd., 1977.
Lukács, Georg. *The Theory of the Novel*. Tran. Anna Bostock. London: Merlin Press, 1971.
Shklovsky, Viktor. "The Resurrection of the Word." *Russian Formalism: A Collection of Articles and Texts in Translation*. Ed. Stephen Bann and John E. Bowlt. Edinburgh: Scottish Academic Press, 1973. 41-47.
Spivak, Gayatri Chakravorty. "The Politics of Translation." *Destabilizing Theory: Contemporary Feminist Debate*. Ed. Michèle Barrett and Anne Philips. Cambridge: Polity Press, 1992. 177-200.
Stein, Gertrude. *The Autobiography of Alice B. Toklas*. Harmondsworth: Penguin Books Ltd., 1966.
Tolstoy, Leo. *Anna Karenin*. Harmondsworth: Penguin Books Ltd., 1978.
Woolf, Virginia. *The Waves*. London: The Hogarth Press, 1976.
———. *Collected Essays*. Vol. 1 and 2. Ed. Leonard Woolf. London: The Hogarth Press, 1966.
———. *The Diary of Virginia Woolf*. v3. Ed. Anne Olivier Bell. London: Hogarth Press, 1980.
———. *A Change of Perspective: The Letters of Virginia Woolf: 1923-1928*. Ed. Nigel Nicolson. Assistant ed. Joanne Trautmann. London: Chatto & Windus Ltd., 1968.
———. *To the Lighthouse*. Text ed. Stella McNichol. With an introduction and notes by Hermione Lee. Harmondsworth: Penguin Books Ltd., 1992.

Mediating Virginia Woolf for Korean Readers
Myunghee Chung

In his Rede Lecture in 1942, E. M. Forster, Woolf's most respected friend, seems to "transmit some honour to her" (5). Actually this situation is rather ironic, as Forster mentions in the lecture. Definitely the occasion of the Rede lecture should be "the greatest honour" for Forster, rather than Woolf. In addition, Forster says Woolf "would receive the homage a little mockingly, for she was somewhat astringent over the academic position of women" (5). From this first moment in which she is evaluated as a dead writer, the critic is very conscious of her sex. Forster's definition of her, as a very sensitive, esoteric, poetic aesthete, is not unrelated to her sex. Especially when he defends her against "extreme Feminism" (33), he points out that she is after all "not only a woman" (34), but also a lady who has "much less to complain of, and seems to keep on grumbling from habit" (33). Here her sex, class, and intellectuality internally crisscross over her being. Thus, she cannot but be quite problematic in her relationships with the university, other women, her society, and furthermore, her own country.

All the seeds of sixty years of critical conflict over Woolf are already present in Forster's remark. Perhaps now we should positively appropriate her controversial ambiguities. I wish in this paper to briefly look into Woolf criticism and suggest a more inclusive and capacious thinking paradigm both for Korean and Western readers. To elucidate this paradigm, it is important to go over what the earlier critics of Woolf have set up, starting with Forster.

Despite Forster's sincere intention to honor her in the Rede lecture, he is repeating the general critical attitude toward her at that time. Malcolm Cowley comments on her last book, *Between the Acts*, by indicating that even though Woolf brilliantly represents old England before the war, she presents an unreal and beguiling illusion with no concern about the real world (176). In 1942, F. R. Leavis again says that she has "a sensitive mind whose main interests are not endorsed by the predominant interests of the world it lives in, and whose talent and professional skill seem to have no real public importance" (180). He continues, she is only cultivating the "bubble of the private consciousness" (180). Forster provides a likely summary of their opinions: "she is like a plant which is supposed to grow in a well-prepared garden bed" (3). She is an aesthete who "selects and manipulates her impressions" (9), and "enforces patterns on her books" (10). Moreover, she has "no great cause at heart" (10).

In a word, she is only concerned with the inner world, even if one is to put it positively. Or she is only a woman writer who is trapped in a narrow, private and feminine space. There is still the Victorian division between the public, real and male world and the private, unreal and female world. The private world is closely aligned to pathological aestheticism. All these critics warn against Woolf's penchant for the inner or illusive world and "aesthetic brooding" (Leavis 180). Still Forster insists that she escapes from being a pathetic aesthete, because she likes "writing for fun" (10).

Her contemporary critics are in a way fortunate: Leavis and Cowley could lightly ignore her and Forster could generously patronize her. Now, however, it has been taken for granted that Woolf's novels present formidable difficulties to many readers. Her difficulties are great not just for Koreans due to their language differences. In *Virginia Woolf: A Critical Reading*, Avrom Fleishman begins his foreword with the fear readers must have had in reading her. He points out that Woolf is "a learned author" (x). She has educated herself not only with the help of her intellectual father and his library, but also been brought up to feel "at home in a notoriously bookish milieu" (x). "She made a cumulative synthesis of the sentiments, values, and perceptions of her tradition" (x). Forster also acknowledges "the breadth of her knowledge and the depth of her literary sympathy" (18). Her high aristocratic intellectuality and consequent difficulties in her reception may have been disparaged in the 1930s, identifying Woolf with "a literary and cultural elite and elitism" (Silver 8). Now her texts demand "learned readers," and Fleishman calls for the productive and critical analysis of her texts. Some perceptive critics can explain her difficulties and thus help readers to understand and enjoy her works easily and comfortably.

Citing James Naremore's *The World Without a Self* (1973), Fleishman suggests that Naremore answers Empson's complaint that Woolf's "dissolved units of understanding had been coordinated into a system" (qtd. Fleishman ix). They seem to agree on the fragmentariness of her writings and think it necessary to restructure them. In his introduction to the book, Naremore is saying that Woolf's novels contain "other, stranger characteristics" (1). Among these, he points out "erotic sensibility" and "a watery element" of her writing. "Reading her, one sometimes has the impression of being immersed in a constantly moving liquid, immersed so deeply that the people and things in her books become muffled and indistinct, like blurred and ghostly shadows" (2). About her fluid style, I completely agree with him. As she has defined the new novel in "Modern Novels," "there would be no plot, little probability" (33) and everything is vague and slippery.

Mediating Virginia Woolf for Korean Readers

Naremore explains this characteristic more like a gender difference. It is because she is seeing an unusual and different world probably, and partly due to her unusual "way of seeing" things (2). So to speak, what she wants to represent is "a world without a self—watery, emotional, erotic, generally associated with the feminine sensibility" against "the world of the self" (245). In this paper, I do not ask why a world without a self is feminine, nor refer to Sigmund Freud either.[1] I simply want to point out that Naremore makes due effort to explain Woolf's distinctive writing style. Thus, he wants to get rid of readers' unnecessary fear and normalize or mediate her texts for them. Her different world or different vision of the world brings out her unusual characteristics and makes it difficult for readers to follow. And he closely analyzes her writerly and intellectual quality without any seemingly obvious prejudice. So-called modernists rather intentionally vie for elitism and this kind of mediation is usually presumed to be necessary for James Joyce, as for Woolf. With this help, readers can conclude with admiration that she is a great writer, almost the Judith Shakespeare whom she has envisaged in *A Room of One's Own* (117-8). Fleishman suggests rather optimistically that Woolf's difficulties will be resolved with such perceptive critical essays as Naremore's and that these essays will establish her as one of "the enduring masters of fictional art" (x). It is quite certain, however, that as a critic he wrote before the advent of Poststructuralism.

Here I confess that I greatly owe my interest in and love for Woolf to such critics as Naremore, Fleishman, Lucio Ruotolo, etc. I believe they greatly contributed to establishing her reputation as a master modernist in English literature. But there is something strange about it. As Forster distinguishes Woolf as a woman from Woolf as a writer and Woolf as a lady, she is contradictorily defined according to her various social and cultural titles. However innocently Naremore names Woolf's sensibility as feminine, that adjective cannot but bring about various connotations, whether good or bad. Woolf's gender has been implicitly emphasized and it still may connote her image as a female writer who may not have any concern about the outside world, probably until Alex Zwerdling. In *Virginia Woolf Icon*, Brenda Silver points out Woolf "has become the site of conflicts" "in debates about art, politics, sexuality, gender, class, 'the canon,' fashion, feminism, race, and anger" (3). After reader-response criticism and post-structuralism, it seems rather natural for readers to appropriate any great author with their various critical tools and to produce their diverse meanings. The greater the authors are, I believe, the more disparate claims their texts can incorporate. Thus, this phenomenon seems another proof that Woolf is a great master of art. Still, it is very interesting and rather disconcerting to find that those debates have often represented her with radically irreconcilable and equally persuasive images. Moreover, another interesting thing is that Woolf is almost ridiculously popular. Is it despite or due to her various conflicting meanings? In the foreword to Silver's book, Catherine R. Stimpson says that Woolf "has become more and more famous" after her death (xi).

In Korea, we are facing a similar situation. Woolf has become more and more famous since I completed my PhD and returned home. I was never taught Woolf in graduate school here. I read *To the Lighthouse* on my own and tried hard to make sense out of it. In the United States, I came across her work for the first time in a class of my doctoral course (1985). Now most of the graduate schools in Korea read her, primarily *To the Lighthouse* and *Mrs. Dalloway*, in courses on the Twentieth-century English Novel. I must be fortunate and foresighted to have chosen to write a dissertation on her. Despite her popularity, however, there still is some tension, or what Silver calls "anxieties" in discussing Woolf in the Korean academic world (4). It is absolutely due to the negative fear and suspicion of feminism in general and its association with Woolf's feminism. As in the United States, there are also some small battles over what kind of feminism Woolf's is. And there is something else, a rather old-fashioned, more complicated and deep-rooted sense of anxiety working against her. Here in Korea arguments over her with the subject of art, gender, politics, canon, and feminism are going on fiercely under the water on a small scale. And she still seems a very dangerous and entrapping territory that demands an explanation or an elaborate story about your inclination and motivation towards her.

In the Korean English Department, Woolf does not have a Fleishman, nor a Naremore yet, or if she does, there are only a few. As sixty years back in England, her aestheticism, high-brow elitism and private vision are still problematic and may be a great obstacle to acknowledging her as a master modernist. First of all, our present situation as a divided country and several tyrannical soldier-turned-presidents' governments have driven intellectuals towards Marxism and realistic novels. Novelists should have their substance, "essential and successful concern" directly from "life" (Leavis 180). In Marxist Lukács- and Leavis-oriented criticisms in Korea, Woolf has been a fragile aesthete who has only domestic, frivolous, trivial concerns and did not care for the outside real world. Just as in Leavis's and Cowley's criticisms, she may be a wasteful and irresponsible imitator, rather than a writer. Of course there is Joyce, to whom nobody here denies his being a great aesthete. But Bloom, the hero of *Ulysses*, does not suffer deadly criticism from the conflicts over whom Mrs. Dalloway is going to invite or whether she is invited or not to some special party (*MD* 43-5; 178-80). Joycean man at least represents the trivial life of

Mediating Virginia Woolf for Korean Readers

modern everyman, while Woolf's characters are trapped and limited in some esoteric English social class and circle of life. Now I am translating *Between the Acts*. Many colleagues ask me why and how I am doing it, since the novel is famous for its Englishness.

This view explains some hesitancy in the Korean academic world about Woolf. A retired colleague told me about her rather odd, but repetitive and consistent experience. Through her teaching years, many of her bright students had shown interest in Woolf and wrote master's theses on her. When they had to choose topics for their dissertations, however, they seldom chose her as a lifelong object of study. Eventually they turned to presumably more solid and substantial male novelists such as Joseph Conrad, D. H. Lawrence, and especially, Joyce. This is not unrelated to the long-standing cultural presumption that high culture is associated with the masculine and low culture with the feminine. Since one's dissertation is closely related to one's job opportunity after graduation, Woolf may not be a high enough writer and will have less market value than other male writers. There are always some distancing and satirizing, rather than sympathetic, glances towards her. Since I have written a dissertation on Virginia Woolf (here my gender definitely contributes), my colleagues (mostly men) love to pretend being afraid of Woolf and me. They usually make a joke out of her name that is synonymous with the pronunciation of "wolf." This make-believe fear is not that innocent, as Fleishman supposes readers to have discovered in confronting Woolf's formidable intellectuality. Edward Albee did his job of instilling this concept of fear quite well even in Korea.

Silver insists that Albee's play, *Who's Afraid of Virginia Woolf*, makes Woolf and his play's title "household words, 'part of the coinage of everyday speech'" in the United States (102). Despite this popularity, she notes the play's "emphasis on fear" (103). Despite Woolf's acknowledged stardom, Silver argues that Woolf's name becomes "synonymous with the power to elicit fear" (103). Thus Woolf is again evoking fear in the general public. First of all, it may be because Woolf is a highbrow writer, "the upper-middle class, snobbish, intellectual aristocrat" (103). As Fleishman has already pointed out, it is understandable that her elitism must be just as scary as that of male modernists. Woolf's experimental fictions may evoke fear in both common and seasoned readers just like other modern and postmodern experimental novelists. This must have been partly intentional: she had always wanted to be considered a serious writer and was afraid of being regarded as an easy and frivolous "scribbling dame."[2] Thus, one of the possible interpretations of Albee's play is that her status of being an intellectual writer is ridiculed and readers are encouraged to challenge her. Silver also points out that the childlessness of the couple in the Albee play and Woolf's childlessness strongly connote homosexuality and its reference to the Bloomsbury group which is so often associated with and identified with her (111-12). The play definitely reflects a general fear at the time of the homosexual as well as of the childless woman with feminist ideals. Thus, Woolf's popularity is inseparable from the fear she evokes, and this fear is strongly and deeply tainted by her gender. Intellectuality in woman is always threatening. Moreover, it is presumed to desexualize woman and interfere with her female destiny as a mother.

The fear Silver points out can be double-edged: it might be real fear of Woolf's intellectuality and strong feminism and at the same time, only a pretension of fear which is a simple parodic gesture. Still there must be some underlying fear even in the ignoring and satirizing gesture. In her book, Silver says that she is going to explore "the conflicting constructions of Virginia Woolf as cultural icon" (4). And she finds a rather consistent pattern, the underlying dynamics between binary oppositions, beauty and terror, sex and intellect, etc., whether it is in order to celebrate or criticize Woolf. Despite Silver's brilliant retracing of Woolf's reception in America and her thorough research, her conclusion seems to me too simple and repetitive, almost disappointing. The iconic representations of her always move around with complex combinations of these categories. And her multifaceted iconic power is derived from her crossing over those fixed categories that define the proper woman in a patriarchal society. And this border-crossing monstrosity can raise fear, but it also triggers strong attraction. To any modern woman, I think it is really frustrating to find the evidence that gender is a major source of problems. Woolf's gender interferes with her intellectuality.

As in the United States, Woolf is also a star, a celebrity, and a cultural icon in Korea. Her madness and suicide are just another oddity that powerfully attracts people's interest. Many people know her name and have probably read some of her novels. She is a popular figure, and people are curious about her rather uncommon life. A few years ago a publishing company approached me with a suggestion to translate a biography of Woolf, and we chose Hermione Lee's *Virginia Woolf*. I thought it would be nice for the graduate students to have her biography, so I was the first to translate a biography of hers in Korea. Still, I strongly doubted the publisher's opinion that Woolf was popular in Korea and that common readers would read the book. Lee's book was published here in two volumes. Interestingly, only the first volume was printed in a second edition; it seemed that readers preferred it over the second. The other day, however, the publisher accounted for the difference: many began reading her with great zeal, but later, things became too complicated. Thus, they stopped reading and did not go to the second volume at all. From the beginning, they do not have to read her full story. The "Woolf icon and star" can be

Mediating Virginia Woolf for Korean Readers

created and produced with "partial images, acts, and words" (Silver 272). They do not have to finish reading her biography or novels in order to like and popularize her. Nobody cares for the authentic Woolf. Instead, they like to use her "to support particular social, cultural, and/or political ends" they have in their mind (Silver 212).

Although multifaceted iconic figuration here in Korea is much simpler than in the United States, still her popularity seems overwhelming and almost embarrassing. Silver remembers "growing up at a time when Virginia Woolf had already achieved canonical status" (xv). As I have already mentioned, however, it is strongly doubtful even now whether Woolf is a prominent public figure in the Korean literary world. I think there seems to be a somewhat parallel relationship between the reception of her in the academic and public worlds in the United States and Great Britain. But here we seem to have a kind of discrepancy between the ways Woolf is received by the so-called high academic culture and popular culture. A few years ago, *The Years* was, interestingly, a best seller just as in the United States of 1937. Nobody could clearly explain why it happened. My graduate students still complain about the absence of plot in Woolf's novels. How is it possible for the general public to enjoy reading her works? Even so-called professionals encounter difficulties, trying to deduce some adequate meaning out of them. What do they see there they like or identify with? This is a really weird phenomenon in popular culture. The academic world, including myself, sends suspicious glances towards the best seller stardom of Woolf.

No translation of Woolf was a best seller except for *The Years*. And this is really inexplicable. The novel has such a loose structure that we cannot easily identify it with the regular novel. It is another of Woolf's experiments with her narrative style. She seems to have gone through two major stages of experimentation. *To The Lighthouse* marks the conclusion of the first. I assume that Woolf's second experimentation with narrative techniques began with *The Waves*, continuing through *The Years*, and perhaps ended with *Between the Acts*. In these novels, she uses the usual narrative strategy of going towards a center as in her former novels, *To the Lighthouse* and *Mrs. Dalloway*, and then, scatters that movement into an unending repetitive rhythm. In her diary she commented on the way *The Waves* was shaping itself.

> What interests me in the last stage was the freedom and boldness with which my imagination picked up, used & tossed aside all the images & symbols which I had prepared. I am sure that this is the right way of using them—not in set pieces, as I had tried at first, coherently, but simply as images; never making them work out; only suggest. (*D4* 10-11)

Woolf's narrative style changed with *The Waves*, and *Between the Acts* came as a culmination point in her ever-changing style. She does not provide a structure typically expected of novels, but critics like Empson and Fleishman suggest that their structure can indeed be discerned by readers with adequate insight. In a word, readers do need to do more work with Woolf's novel than with the more traditional novel in order to have an aesthetic appreciation. But this is exactly what Woolf is against in *Between the Acts*. In the novel, its narrator clearly satirizes the effort of Streatfield who wants to summarize and conclude the content of the pageant didactically. The novel also distances the anonymous voice of Miss La Trobe at the end of play. Just like Mr. Streatfield, she tries direct communication. "Let's talk in words of one syllable, without larding, stuffing or cant. Let's break the rhythm and forget the rhyme. And calmly consider ourselves" (218). And her concluding speech is that "we act different parts but are the same" (251). Yet any interpretation, even that of the author, will not have any absolute power in Woolf's novels. The two directions within the novel, unity and dispersal, are never resolved but seem more like a structuring principle of the novel as such. Thus, many people try to figure out widely different and various explanations of this best seller phenomenon. Probably the title looks rather attractive. Or the timing was perfect. At the moment of publication, Koreans were suffering from an economic crisis and the somewhat ascetic and realistic tone of the novel appealed to their general mood. Or perhaps it is that the vulgar and simplified messages of feminism were abstracted from the book and have played their due roles. We are inclined to judge her being a best selling author as "a degrading commodification of literature" (Silver 80). While her respectability is relatively precarious, tentative, and not completely safe in the academic world, how can she properly be understood and enjoyed in the popular world?

Just as in America, her iconic power in Korea also comes from her popularized pictures. The other day, one cinema-major student said to me that he had learnt about the Virginia Woolf Society of Korea (VWSK). I was so surprised and thrilled to know that he was aware of our society and of Woolf. I asked him how it was possible. He told me that he saw the poster for the conference of the VWSK last spring. The VWSK had used her picture for the poster of the biannual conference and it had such an unusual iconic power that he remembered it. Just as in America, feminism in Korea has also helped popularize Woolf among common readers. *A Room of One's Own* is very popular and there are several translated versions. Moreover, its dramatic version in Korean was quite popular among the so-called oppressed housewives about ten years ago, and was again performed on stage this year. Of course, it is just the title that the play shares with the source text. The author, a Korean female writer, com-

Mediating Virginia Woolf for Korean Readers

pletely rewrote it using stories of various Korean historical heroines; Woolf's essay just inspired the play and lent it its name. I myself visited the theatre ten years ago and met the script-writer who had produced a dramatized version of Woolf's book. She was watching the kids of the housewives who came to the play. She believed that her play and the women's act of coming to the theatre for rooms of their own would change Korean women's life. I also wanted to believe that and wished her the best of luck. Anyway, this play has definitely contributed to championing Woolf as a mother-goddess of women's rights in Korea just as in many other English-speaking countries. Any Korean housewife can use the phrase, a room of one's own, for their own advantage, even without knowing its source or its precise meaning in the context of the whole book. Now movies based on her novels, or works inspired by her novels, like *The Hours*, also help any common viewers in Korea know at least her name.

Recently in Korea, all of Woolf's writings are being translated by academic professionals. What I mean by "professional" here is someone who has studied Woolf and English literature as a scholar and thus, presumably, is able to mediate Woolf for the Korean common reader. This presumption is precariously authoritative and also, quite problematic, especially in the present postmodern world. Still, the intervention of professionals is clearly motivated by high-minded good intentions. They want to deliver a "readable and enjoyable" Woolf to Korean readers. Thus, academics need not have false anxieties, nor should common readers idolize false images of her. They are eager to promote lupine studies in the academic world and offer the necessary information to the popular world for enjoying her properly. They believe the more people know about Woolf, the less will she serve as a grotesque object of admiration or undercutting. And this re-visionary understanding will eventually bring about some helpful change in Korean literature. Yet, this good intention belies a rather audacious hypothesis: Woolf is too difficult to be digested without help either by the academics or the common reader. And some professionals know the better, if not the best or the truest, Woolf. Thus they are set on explaining things more like Naremore and Fleishman in the 1970s of the United States.

The VWSK was actually incubated by these translation projects and very deeply involved in establishing and disseminating the proper Woolf among Korean readers. Its primary aim is to complete the translation of all her novels. Although some of them, like *Mrs. Dalloway* and *To the Lighthouse*, have been translated several times, we recently translated those two novels again. This year *The Waves* will be published for the first time. Then, *Between the Acts*, *Orlando*, *Jacob's Room*, *Night and Day*, and *The Voyage Out* will follow. *Jacob's Room* and *Night and Day* will also be first time translations. Some of her diaries and letters have been selected and translated in a series accompanying the novels. The selection principle is to help the reading and understanding of her novels. Also, *A Room of One's Own* has been translated anew, and *Three Guineas* is under way. These translations are addressed not to the academic world within the Ivory Tower alone, but also to the common reader. Thus, the VWSK wants to provide a "decent" Woolf, so that we do not have to be afraid of her any more. The present task of translation is supposedly to trigger people's interest in reading the real Woolf. Then, people will be able to overcome fear, prejudices and idolization whether due to her gender, feminism, or intellectual aristocracy.

In August 2003, the VWSK published the first volume of Woolf's short stories in Korean. It is a two-volume edition of her *Collected Short Stories*, with the second volume coming out in December. It came as the first cooperative project aimed at disseminating Woolf for common readers. General responses from the public are fairly encouraging: the best-known bookstore in Seoul has chosen it for this month's book among 3000 new books, and the publisher has sold out the first 2000 volumes, deciding to add another 1000 volumes to the first edition and thus to publish a second edition together with the second volume at the end of this year. Still, the general response is sharply divided: some of my colleagues at school commented with obvious disappointment that her short stories are after all rather conventional and old-fashioned. On the other hand, many students and the so-called "common readers" are happy with these short stories and expressed their enthusiasm ardently. Why? First of all, they are thrilled by the fact that they can enjoy reading her. Secondly, her stories can after all be readable and digestible. They seem simply amazed at the fact that she has written such amusing and "real" stories too. These responses may be partly due to our editing policy. We have chosen to put rather easily readable stories at the beginning and to finish the volume with more experimental pieces. And we are going to apply the same editing principle to the second volume. The VWSK begins to wield its power over the consumption of Woolf in Korea.

Through these activities, the VWSK has clearly assumed the authority to define Woolf in Korea, and has implied that her reception in this country has so far been misdirected and should be updated. The so-called Woolfians in Korea laid claim to her writings in order to say a word of truth about her. Not just the process of the translation, but also the very sequence of translations published are meant to establish priorities among Woolf's writings, and the accompanying annotations cannot but imply critical evaluation. The VWSK will definitely disclose a desire for some specific re-visionary rearrangement of all her writings. Yet this rearrangement cannot but be naturally and automatically appropriating Woolf for some specific interpretation. And the latter seems

Mediating Virginia Woolf for Korean Readers

to run contrary to the postmodern inclination towards multiplicity, and even to Woolf's possible intention for her novels.

In his publication of *A Writer's Diary* (1953), Leonard Woolf seemed to intend to keep his wife within the framework of the image of a writer. Similar to Leonard, the VWSK most of all wants to inform readers about the proper Woolf as a professional writer. And it wants to facilitate analyses similar to those of Naremore and Fleishman to encourage academic studies and to help readers to understand her writings. Her modernist works demand guidance, and her frequently discussed feminism is too naively simplified instead of including its complicated two-edged aspects. If her bourgeois inclinations repulse many so-called conscientious intellectuals who are involved in Marxist-oriented and more activist movements through the difficult political and social upheavals here, her concern for the real world should be brought forward. Yet its well-meaning mediation is doomed to fail. Silver points out that Leonard's effort ironically facilitates a shift of her status "from writer to personality to star" (97). Silver remarks that nobody can prohibit her dissemination, nor stop "a proliferation of uncontainable Virginia Woolfs" (116).

Silver notes that she distrusts "those who would fix her into any single position, either to praise or blame her" (5). I agree with her. Unlike her, though, the intervention of the VWSK wishes to correct and redirect Woolf's hesitant reception in the academic world and her strange popularity in the popular world with our translation works. The question is whether it is possible to control her images and dissemination. When the head of our major publishing company here suggests that it will make readers' access much easier if they can have some medium such as translators' personal history of meetings with her, we clearly understand what he means, but we hesitate. If things work out, the Korean academic Woolfians can disseminate her as widely as they plan and also be "capitalizing on" her being a star (Silver 116). In any case, this star thing is beyond any control, as Silver points out. How about that sincere idea of the "real" Woolf that the VWSK has in mind?

What the VWSK is doing now will not go far from what Silver names the iconic appropriation of Woolf. But its motive is not to resolve various conflicting and contradictory claims over her and thus suggest the final and authentic Woolf. Now in Korea, any Woolf reader feels rather puzzled and embarrassed in confronting the extremely diverse and multiple proliferations of her meanings just as in the United States. Yet Korean readers do not have any social and cultural codes to interpret or organize the meanings like native English speakers. Nor will their language gap allow them to meet her directly. Here only a few academicians or professionals have access to her writings. Thus the VWSK wants to contribute at least by providing the first materials for understanding and judging her. I do not believe our translations and annotations will have the final say on Woolf. Our annotations, on the contrary, will urge Korean readers to read her novels with emotional detachment, just as Woolf has done in her texts with what she is saying, describing, suggesting and claiming. And I think this is really a healthy gap for readers to have. Moreover, her writings most of all have the power to produce innumerable versions of her meanings. And it wholly depends on the readers whether they choose to read or accept the intervening explanations for their understanding. Just as Woolf's texts do not have any authority in explaining their meanings, the translator's positive mediation cannot dictate anything. Still, that mediation can provide a loose and tentative frame of reference even for just a while, just like Woolf's texts are always there as a substantial and final framework for multiple meanings in the past, the present and the future.

The VWSK clearly realizes that our translations and annotations are giving a version of Woolf and that we cannot control the various and fantastic readings of her. Silver declares "we cannot stop the proliferation of Virginia Woolfs or the claims to 'truth' or authenticity that accompany each refashioning of her image" (5), but a really important and problematic question is who will have the authority to define and control Woolf's meanings (Silver 9-10). Now no critic will audaciously claim that Woolf is a narrow-minded invalid. Julia Briggs points out that it is really difficult to understand how Leavis "silently" omitted Woolf "from the Great Tradition," "chiefly on the grounds that her work lacked moral purpose" (xvi). It is incomprehensible why Leavis cannot see Woolf's deepest concern for the coming war in *Between the Acts*. Still this definition was and will be possible and will contribute to shaping her representative images. Like Silver, I strongly oppose any efforts "to fix [Woolf] into any single position." Still, I believe some loose boundary should be drawn which may include and reserve some space for various claims. At least it can offer a starting point for readers. Fleishman, Naremore and Ruotolo have contributed greatly to re-thinking Woolf as a major and serious, not second-rate modernist. Unlike Forster's and Leavis's, their approaches analyze positively the critical difficulties and challenges Woolf's texts presented to them. Thus, despite all that postmodern anxiety of authority, I think it is important to offer some reasonably critical and balanced background for a general introduction of Woolf, especially for non-English-speaking readers.

In her criticism of *Between the Acts*, Gillian Beer says Woolf finds that "words are always communal" (131). That seems quite reasonable and understandable. When foreigners are reading translated writings, however, it is really frustrating. How can they go into her communal experiences, such as the Englishness she represents, with communal words? If words are historically

Mediating Virginia Woolf for Korean Readers

laden with cultural meanings, how can non-native speakers go into the closed circuit? Should Korean readers be acquainted with English culture and its historical past in order to understand her? Many critics point out that Woolf's last novel reveals "a strong feeling of nostalgia for an older English culture" (Zwerdling 308) and "a longing for a more lyrical and impersonal existence than that provided by the chaotic and destructive reality of the thirties" (Lee 207). She wishes to establish a viable English collective identity in confronting the coming war. According to some recent critical remarks, however, Woolf is "not nostalgic" (Beer 404). She shows that the continuity of English history or culture is a fiction just as much as that of English identity.[3] Culture is not something solid you inherit intact from the past. Culture itself is "a medley" of acquired fragments (*BTA* 90). Her notion of cultural common life does not presuppose some naïve notion of original unity or wholeness before history like the idealistic dreamer, Mrs. Swithin. Those fragments which people acquire artificially and belatedly compose the continuity of history.

In *Between the Acts*, Woolf reiterates many cliché norms and cultural fragments which produce certain differential attributes in human culture. They seem to offer some superficial connection to isolated characters in this helter-skelter novel. Oddly enough, she seems to approve the common binary opposition between reality and fantasy in addition to using patriarchal notions of women. She may provoke the anger of many feminists and postmodernists. In the novel, various communal and arbitrary signs of culture, words, clothes, sexuality, social and family titles, have the power to produce certain emotions and responses, which can then connect the characters in the novel. Although there is a clear tension between Isa and Giles and they never talk to each other, Isa can feel proud and connected to her husband when she is repeating the cliché phrase, "the father of my children" (14). In the same way, the senior Oliver feels grateful to his daughter-in-law, Isa, "for continuing" him (18). Then, is Woolf endorsing this communal sign of producing a community? Probably. Unlike her insistence on being an outsider in *Three Guineas* (105-114), her diaries and letters reveal a deep and almost obsessive affection for Englishness, London and England, even if these are an only fictional geography (*D5* 263, 353; *L6* 466). She, however, clearly worried that these communal signs could strategically be manipulated to provoke certain tyrannical actions, such as English patriotism and, furthermore, Nazism. Her repetition (her re-representation) rather comically and painfully discloses the fictiveness and thus, the underlying subversive power of those notions.

The VWSK wants to follow "Woolf's sense that the capricious and the fugitive may be the only way of holding things together" (Beer 128). It wants to suggest the style of "orts, scraps, and fragments" which will allow space for possible extreme meanings to float freely (*BTA* 188). We do not worry about the possible fixity of these readings. The free, slippery style of Woolf will not get pigeon-holed either through any critic's definition, or any specific cultural and social ideology. Her texts will take on various interpretations and may temporarily offer some space for them. Yet, her writings will not be reduced into any single shape. And that is the most amazing aspect of her writing. In her book, Silver's main point is not Woolf's border-crossing. She argues that multiple and monstrous border-crossings in various iconic figurations of Woolf create "a way of imagining otherwise" (269) and, thus, "allow us to see, and think and speak and act differently" (272). Woolf's reiteration of all those cultural fragments in the cesspool of Pointz Hall also invites her readers to imagine a new symbolic landscape for England and probably for the whole world. Woolf says that words will rise "above the intolerably laden dumb oxen plodding through the mud" (*BTA* 212). Even if the artist is only a dumb ox struggling heavily with the long literary history, still "wonderful words" can float freely, "without meaning" (212). As Beer points out, Woolf is producing "another idea of England" "as mixture and common place" (147) where "divisions" are "chalk marks only" (*TG* 163). That is why she is globally loved, admired, and appropriated positively.

Notes

[1] According to Freud, the Oedipus Complex is a necessary stage for a human child to adopt a proper cultural gender corresponding to his biological sex. He discovers, however, that this process in girls is not as complete as in boys ("The Passing of the Oedipus-Complex" 170-71). While a boy's Oedipus complex is perfectly replaced by the superego, a girl either reluctantly abandons, only represses or keeps it forever. Thus a girl's "super-ego is never so inexorable, so impersonal, so independent of its emotional origins as we require it to be in men" ("Some Psychological Consequences of the Anatomical Distinction Between the Sexes" 182). In addition, femininity without the proper super-ego frequently lacks a sense of justice, conscience, reason or a social self. Naremore's "world without a self" is very close to Freud's femininity which is still emotional and imbued with infantile sexuality.

[2] In her essay, "A Scribbling Dame," Woolf harshly criticizes Eliza Haywood as an unreadable and non-professional woman writer and labels her "a scribbling dame." Woolf always rejected literary critics' patronizing attitude that frequently compromises aesthetic judgment in order to discover forgotten woman writers.

[3] In *The Myth of the Modern*, Perry Meisel points out that Pointz Hall is doubling Forster's *Howards End* in *Between the Acts*. He says, however, that we cannot call Woolf's act "borrowing or theft," because "proper authority" is "little more than a transpersonal function" (182). He insists that Bloomsbury and Woolf always reject a sense of property and proper identity.

Mediating Virginia Woolf for Korean Readers
Works Cited

Beer, Gillian. *Virginia Woolf: The Common Ground*. Ann Arbor: The U of Michigan P, 1996.
Briggs, Julia. "The Story So Far…" *Virginia Woolf: Introductions to the Major Works*. Ed. Julia Briggs. vii-xxxiii. London: Virago Press, 1994.
Cowley, Malcolm. "England under Glass." *The New Republic*, 6 October (1941): 440. Rpt. in *Virginia Woolf: Critical Assessments*. Ed. Eleanor McNees. Vol. IV. Mountfield, East Sussex: Helm Information, 1994. 175-77.
Fleishman, Avrom. *Virginia Woolf: A Critical Reading*. Baltimore: Johns Hopkins UP, 1975.
Forster, E. M. *Virginia Woolf*. New York: Harcourt, Brace and Company, 1942.
Freud, Sigmund. "The Passing of the Oedipus-Complex." *Sexuality and the Psychology of Love*. Ed. Philip Rieff. New York: Simon & Schuster, 1997. 166-172
———. "Some Psychological Consequences of the Anatomical Distinction Between the Sexes." *Sexuality and the Psychology of Love*. Ed. Philip Rieff. New York: Simon & Schuster, 1997. 173-183.
Leavis, F. R. "After *To The Lighthouse*." *Scrutiny*, 10, January (1942): 295-8. Rpt. in *Virginia Woolf: Critical Assessments*. Ed. Eleanor McNees. Vol. IV. Mountfield, East Sussex: Helm Information, 1994. 178-80.
Lee, Hermione. *The Novels of Virginia Woolf*. London: Methuen, 1977.
Meisel, Perry. *The Myth of the Modern: A Study in British Literature and Criticism after 1850*. New Haven and London: Yale UP, 1987.
Naremore, James. *The World Without a Self: Virginia Woolf and the Novel*. New Haven and London: Yale UP, 1973.
Silver, Brenda R. *Virginia Woolf Icon*. Chicago: The U of Chicago P, 1999.
Woolf, Virginia. *Mrs. Dalloway*. New York: Harcourt Brace Jovanovich, 1953.
———. *A Room of One's Own*. New York: Harcourt Brace Jovanovich, 1957.
———. *Between the Acts*. New York: Harcourt Brace Jovanovich, 1969.
———. *Three Guineas*. New York: Harcourt Brace Jovanovich, 1966.
———. *The Diary of Virginia Woolf*. Ed. Anne Olivier Bell. Vol. 4, Vol. 5. New York: Harcourt Brace Jovanovich, 1982, 1984.
———. *The Letters of Virginia Woolf*. Ed. Nigel Nicolson and Joanne Trautmann. Vol. 6. New York: Harcourt Brace Jovanovich, 1980.
———. "Modern Novels." *The Times Literary Supplement*, 10 April 1919. Rpt. in *The Essays of Virginia Woolf*. Ed. Andrew McNeillie. Vol. 3. New York: Harcourt Brace Jovanovich, 1988. 30-37.
———. "A Scribbling Dame (Eliza Haywood)." *Virginia Woolf: Women and Writing*. Ed. Michèle Barrett. New York: Harcourt Brace Jovanovich, 1979. 92-95.
Zwerdling, Alex. *Virginia Woolf and the Real World*. Berkeley: U of California P, 1986.

Translation of Virginia Woolf in Korea
Hee Jin Park

The Korean poet In-whan Park (1923-56) is famous for his poem "Merry-go-round and a Lady." He was known as a so-called "modernist" after the War and sang intellectually of his sadness for all disappearing things. After the first and second World Wars, everyone had been suffering from anxiety and nihilism and so it was only natural that he should have appealed to contemporary readers emotionally. In-whan Park referred to Woolf a couple of times in the above poem ("Drinking a glass of liquor we talk about Virginia Woolf's life …" "We have to listen to Virginia Woolf's sad story…"). I suppose that this poet might have happened to read a newspaper article about Woolf's suicide and that he was shocked by the news. It is not probable that he could have read any of Woolf's works considering his age, but interestingly enough this poem contributed to introducing Woolf to Korea and ever since then she has come to be well known, loved and perhaps even feared by Korean people.

It was probably in the early 1970s that we began to read Woolf in university classes, along with James Joyce and William Faulkner. Let me digress briefly by including my personal history here as it might throw some light on Woolf's introduction to our universities. When I was about to write my MA thesis (1967) my advisor suggested to me that I might write my paper on Woolf. He had never given a lecture on Woolf, but I guess he thought it would be good for me to read Woolf simply because I was a female student. He added that when he was a middle school boy, Woolf's *The Years* (1937) was published and became one of the best sellers in English-speaking countries. I went to the States in 1967 for further study, wrote both my MA thesis and PhD dissertation on Woolf, returned to my country (1979), and until I retired last year I taught Woolf in classes at both the undergraduate and graduate levels.

Until the late 1970s the readers of Woolf were strictly limited to academics and even they used to complain that Woolf was too difficult. At first she was received as a modernist. But in the 1980s she was reintroduced as the godmother of feminism and the scope of her readers widened to include readers whose intrinsic interest was in feminism rather than in Woolf. And this spring through Michael Cunningham's novel, *The Hours*, and Stephen Daldry's film of the same name, Woolf was revived again in Korea as in other countries.

We are now living in the era of multiculturalism. It goes without saying that language, as the heart in the body of culture, is closely intertwined with the culture that uses the particular language. Naturally the relationship between language and culture has been a controversial subject. Prominent linguist Edward Sapir maintains that language is a guide to social reality. He goes on to state that language powerfully conditions our thinking largely about social problems and processes. He goes further to emphasize that we human beings are very much at the mercy of the specific language which has become the means of expression for their society. Sapir insists that it is quite an illusion to imagine that one adjusts to reality essentially without the use of language and that language is merely an incidental medium for solving particular problems of communication or reflection. He puts a strong stress on the fact that the real world is to a large extent unconsciously built up on the language habits of the community (Sapir).

He goes on to cite more specific instances. He contends that even comparatively simple acts of perception are very much more at the mercy of the social patterns called "words" than we might think. And then in reference to one situation that supports his contention, he says, "If one draws some dozen lines, for instance, of different forms, one perceives them as divisible into such categories as 'straight,' 'crooked,' 'curved,' 'zigzag,' because of the designating suggestion of the linguistic terms themselves." He concludes we human beings see and hear and experience to a great extent as we do because the language habits of our group render certain choices of interpretation inclined beforehand (Ibid.)

Another distinguished linguist, Benjamin Lee Whorf, goes one step further than Sapir and elaborates his view as follows. He found that the background linguistic system (in other words, the grammar) of each language is not merely a reproducing instrument for expressing ideas but rather is itself the shaper of ideas, the program and guide for the individual's mental activity for his or her analysis of his or her mental stock in trade. He argues that idea formulation is not an independent work, strictly rational in the old sense, but is part of a particular grammar, and differs, to some extent, in different grammars. His argument proceeds that we dissect nature along lines laid down by our native languages. If we follow his argument, we come to the conclusion that our thinking method is controlled by the system, the so-called "language." According to this argument, there can be neither true bilingualism nor perfect translation.

As we continue to examine Whorf's work, eventually we encounter his view of the relationship between language and *Weltanschauung*. He proposes that in a sense language reflects the world view, *Weltanschauung*, of the people who speak that language. This is called "linguistic relativity." If we go one step further we can say that language controls the speaker's world view. We call this kind of assertion "linguistic determinism" (Carroll 213). If Whorf's

Translation of Virginia Woolf in Korea

linguistic determinism makes sense, it may be possible to control people's thinking through language. George Orwell's famous novel *1984* is based on this hypothesis. In order to leave no room for complaints the government devises a new language, the so-called "Newspeak," and forces people to speak this language. As long as they speak this language no one can voice anti-government ideas at all because there is no means to express the discontent with this language.

On the other hand, Greenberg insists that language tries to adapt itself to the changing culture. Hockett, like Whorf, takes the opposite view, namely that thinking influences language.[1] But several scholars, such as Feuer or Fearning, assert that we can understand various kinds of culture despite their difference of time and place, and that, as Mead supposed, man's effort or anguish for existence is quite identical across cultures. Hoijer joins this group and says that no culture can stand alone and isolated, and that among cultures there are similarities to a large extent. He proposes first that the propagation of culture shows the fact that cultural interchange is possible and in fact was possible, and secondly, as all cultures are based on the common physiological, psychological, and social characteristics, culture exchange is successful. Accordingly, communication between cultures is not such an impossible thing as Whorf insists.[2]

This problem cannot be said either to have been proved or to have been contradicted, as Carroll points out in the following quotation:

> In the writer's talk with a number of contemporary American linguists, he encountered a considerable skepticism. One individual characterized Whorf's propositions as "untested generalizations." Many linguists think Whorf's ideas represented too much of an extrapolation from available data. (Carroll 45-46)

So we can launch into our task of translation without much reservation.

Translation, probably the most integral part of inter-cultural relations, is starting to be featured as an independent subject of study. In keeping with this world-wide trend, cultural studies has recently emerged in Korean academia, and numerous universities have made curriculum revisions towards interdisciplinary courses, Translation Studies being one of them; a couple of graduate programs in translation-training have been launched, and some foreign language departments offer courses in translation, both literary and technical. Nevertheless, in our country Translation Studies is still in its infancy, not quite a discipline in its own right.

There have been desultory translations of Woolf's works from as early as 1965 in Korea. If a translator perceives his or her role as partly that of "improving" existing translations, that is indeed often the reason why we undertake translations of the identical works for the second or third time. Certainly an implicit value judgment underlies this position. In 1994 a prestigious publishing company ("Sol," which means pine tree in Korean) launched a long-term project for translating the complete works of Virginia Woolf, a project I was involved in. I gathered together Woolf scholars in Korea and managed to translate *To the Lighthouse*, *Mrs. Dalloway*, *A Room of One's Own*, and *Selected Essays and Diaries* in 2 volumes. The translations of *The Waves*, *Between the Acts*, *Three Guineas*, and *Selected Letters* are to come out soon, hopefully this year. As of now the translating team, along with some other Woolf scholars, have just finished translating Woolf's short stories (*The Complete Shorter Fiction of Virginia Woolf*, second ed., ed. Susan Dick 1989). The first volume just came out this August, and the response of the readers is enthusiastic, to our surprise and happiness. The translation of *The Waves* is expected to be published this year, and the second volume of the translation of short stories is to come out in January 2004.

Our team has not been exposed to contemporary translation theory. But we know that there is an anti-theory theory too, at least the kind that says translations do not need any theory (Robinson). We comfort ourselves with this theory, but our team works with a kind of rule of its own. When readability and word for word translation are in conflict with each other, we have decided to choose readability, but on condition that loyalty or even submission to the text is always the first object to accomplish. We try to avoid the translation strategy that prizes the utmost clarity and easy readability, because that use of the most familiar language turns out frequently to be the most prejudicial. And we keep in mind that just a little bit of literal translation can be sauce for the dish when translating a foreign text.

Inevitably, there are endless problems in translations. Among them, the problem of translations between non-related cultures is clearly one of the most crucial. There is an interesting study on one of the various planes of meanings a word has, which is related to association. Osgood and Suci experimented with quantitative measurement of meaning and submitted an article under the title "Factor Analysis of Meaning" (Osgood 325-38). In a comparable experiment of word association, when words such as "father" or "mother" are given in an experiment, the experimentee will show similar responses. For example, from "father" he or she might get a response of "strong," "hard," "dirty," "empty," "excitable," "bass," "active," "cruel," "bitter," etc. On the other hand from "mother" he or she might get a response of "weak," "soft," "clean," "full," "calm," "treble," "passive," "kind," "sweet," etc. Of course, strictly speaking, these epithets are not the meaning of the words. But a simple word

Translation of Virginia Woolf in Korea

like "father" or "mother" has a host of modifiers behind it. There are other meanings of the word too.

In relation to this, one thing is noticeable: the result of the evaluation is different according to the difference in cultural background. Even though it was not included in the Osgood and Suci experiment, the simple word "dog," for example, will elicit very much different responses depending on the nation's cultural background. The existence of such connotative meanings of words contributes to the difficulty of translation. Although we can translate the words it is not easy to translate the host of psychological associations interwoven with the words. In the meaning of a word there is always another plane of meaning like association or impression.

I have just finished translating *The Waves*. The translating process was, I confess, a long journey of torture and joy. Everybody knows *The Waves* is intrinsically difficult to read both from the point of view of content and writing technique, not to mention the task of translation itself. And even though it is classified as a novel for the sake of convenience, as we all know, it is poetry within the framework of a novel. Nevertheless, from time to time it occurred to me that in addition to the inherent nature of the work, the non-relatedness of the two languages, namely English and Korean, makes the job quite demanding. Marguerite Yourcenar, one of the French translators of *The Waves*, might not have had such language difficulty caused by the non-relatedness of the two languages as I had. I can perceive that the text to be translated seems to be at her fingertips, because she treats the text so freely, at one time shortening and at other times lengthening it at her will. On the other hand, I find myself clinging desperately to the text, trying hard to translate word for word accurately. I presume this phenomenon partly arises from the non-relatedness of the two languages. We can glimpse the translator Yourcenar's grasp of the text to be translated from the following:

> And blushing yet scornful, in the oldest condition of raw rapture and scepticism, I took the blow; the mixed sentences; the complex and utterly unprepared for impact of life all over, in all places at the same time. (*TW* 218)

> Plein à la fois (et bien étrangement) de dédain et de honte, de scepticisme et d'enthousiasme, j'ai accepté ces coups de poing de la vie: ce mélange de sensations troubles entièrement imprévues, qui tombent sur moi partout et tout le temps. (*Les Vagues* 247)

Park

I will cite one more example where the French translator shows her courage by not sticking to word-for-word translation. This speaks to the fact that the text to be translated is at her fingertips.

> Yet if someone had but said: "Wait"; had pulled the strap three holes tighter—he would have done justice for fifty years, and sat in Court and ridden alone at the head of troops and denounced some monstrous tyranny, and come back to us. (*TW* 129)

> Et pourtant, si quelqu'un avait serré la courroie d'un cran de plus, il aurait fait honneur à l'Angleterre pendant cinquante ans; il aurait présidé des conseils, chevauché à la tête des troupes, dénoncé de monstreux abus de justice, et enfin, il nous serait revenu. (*Les Vagues* 151)

Note that the phrase, "if someone had but said: 'Wait';" has completely disappeared in her translation. In a word, she could be that courageous, but I cannot. Note also the word "Angleterre" has been added, which Woolf did not use herself. On the other hand, if we look at Japanese translations, we find many similarities between their translation and ours.

Some of the minor problems we Korean translators are facing when we translate English texts are: 1. Cultural difference. Koreans are very fastidious about the seniority problem and the order of seniority is overemphasized in Korean. In English it is not; instead, gender difference is stressed. So while English has only "brother" and "sister," Korean has four words for brother and sister stressing the seniority. Korean has only one word for "nephew" regardless of gender, but in English they differentiate between male and female, "nephew" and "niece." 2. Punctuation difference. In Korean we use only commas (,) and periods (.). On the other hand, Woolf uses colons (:) and semi-colons (;) pretty often while we do not use them at all. 3. Grammar difference. In Korean we have no passive voice. 4. Idiomatic use of color is different too: "purple with rage" (English): "blue with rage" (Korean). As a matter of fact, in pure Korean (not the word derived from Chinese) we have only one word for both the English words "blue" and "green."

One of the noticeable characteristics of Korean translation of Woolf is that almost all of the translation is done by Woolf specialists. In a sense it is encouraging, considering the character of Woolf's works. Translation is an odd and secretive art. There are numerous elements which make it so odd an art. Here let me cite just a couple of them. To begin with, a work of literature is not intended to be translated into another language. Secondly, a translator embodies someone else's thoughts and images by writing in another language. It is an odd art for certain. Translation is a hidden art in the sense that usually the translator is not well respected and in that (s)he is not well paid at all. Nevertheless

Translation of Virginia Woolf in Korea

it is an art and it requires aptitude, practice, talent, and general knowledge. Translation, like any other cultural practice, entails the creative reproduction of values, involving far more than simply word-for-word transfers from SL (source language) to TL (target language). It is a recreation of a text, an entirely creative process of making a text no longer "foreign" but intimately comprehensible to the target readership. A translation always communicates an interpretation, that is, an interpretation on the part of the translator. A foreign (translated) text is altered by the translator and supplemented with features peculiar to the culture specifics of the target language. Translation is a very serious and really difficult art, not only an odd and concealed one.

Of course Woolf scholars are not supposed to be the only or the best qualified translators of Woolf. But personally I think that in Woolf's case it is almost inescapable that Woolf scholars should do this job. And what they may lack in some specific qualities such as aptitude, talent, or practice, they make up for in their passion for and special knowledge of Woolf.

A translation of a work into another language is somehow always bound to be incomplete. Since John Dryden explained the situation back in the seventeenth century ("There are so few who have all the talents which are requisite for translations" [Wechsler 9]) not much has changed. But think where we would be if we were not only unable to read the Bible or the ancient classics, but also if the writers we could read had themselves read no more than a few of the great writers and thinkers of the past and their time. We would be unenlightened, thirsty for knowledge, hungry for art. Yet works are translated, often to great acclaim. There are many authors whose works have been transposed through translations from one context to another so successfully that they have become canonical figures in multiple literatures. For example, we find Shakespeare as a canonical figure in literatures across the world, a situation that has come into existence through successful translation.

In any case, it is an undeniable fact that we are heavily indebted to translations for our access to the literature of the world. It allows us to enter the minds of people from other times and places. It is a celebration of otherness, as Wechsler has properly pointed out, a truly multicultural event without all the balloons and noisemakers. And it enriches not only our personal knowledge and artistic sense, but also our culture's literature, language and thought.

We, Korean translators of Woolf, are of one faith with the translators who translated the King James Version of the Bible:

> Translation it is that openeth the window, to let in the light;
> that breaketh the shell, that we may eat the kernel;
> that putteth aside the curtain, that we may look into the most holy place;

> that removeth the cover of the well, that we may come by the water.
> (Wechsler 11)

Woolf scholars in Korea strongly believe in the fact that our efforts to introduce Woolf to Korea through translation will also help Korean readers look into the mind of Virginia Woolf and discover the deep well of meaning hidden within her writing. This is not an easy task, but we look upon her works as we would look upon a tree and do our best to preserve the branches, the roots, and the trunk, although to our regret some of the leaves are to be removed. As an American translator from French, Rosemary Waldrop said translation is like "wrenching a soul from its body and luring it into a different one" (Wechsler). Once a month Korean Woolf Society members meet regularly to read the works of Woolf in order to widen our scope of understanding her. Hopefully as a result of these meetings we will continue translating Woolf and in so doing make her known widely and appreciated properly in Korea. For us, translating Woolf is a labor of love which we perform not with hopes of fame, fortune, or applause, but because of our desire to share the works of an author whom we admire and respect. We want to open a window and shed light onto the works of this extraordinarily gifted writer.

Notes

[1] See "Chinese versus English: An Exploration of the Whorfian Thesis," in Hoijer 122.
[2] See Hoijer, "The Sapir-Whorf Hypothesis," in Hoijer 94.

Works Cited

Baker, Mona. *In Other Words: A Coursebook on Translation*. London & New York: Routledge, 1992.
Bassnett, Susan. *Translation Studies*. London & New York: Methuen & Co. Ltd., 1980.
Carroll, J.B. *The Study of Language: A Survey of Linguistics and Related Disciplines in America*. Cambridge, Mass.: Harvard UP, 1953.
——, ed. *Language, Thought and Reality: Selected Writings of Benjamin Lee Whorf*. Cambridge, Mass.: The M.I.T. Press, 1956.
Hoijer, H. ed. *Language in Culture: Proceedings of Language and Other Aspects of Culture*. Chicago: U of Chicago P, 1954.
Osgood, C.E. & G.J. Suci. "Factor Analysis of Meaning." *Journal of Experimental Psychology*, 1955: 325-38.

Robinson, Douglas. *Translation & Taboo*. Northern Illinois: Northern Illinois UP, 1996.
Sapir, E. "A study in phonetic symbolism." *Journal of Experimental Psychology*, 1929, 12: 225-39.
Schulte, Rainer & Biguenet, John (eds). *Theories of Translation: An Anthology of Essays from Dryden to Derrida*. Chicago: U of Chicago P, 1992.
Venuti, Lawrence. *The Scandals of Translations: Towards an Ethics of Difference*. London & New York: Routledge, 1998.
Weschsler, Robert. *Performing without a Stage: The Art of Literary Translation*. North Haven, CT: Catbird Press, 1998.
Woolf, Virginia. *The Waves*. 1931. Harmondsworth: Penguin, 1964.
Yourcenar, Marguerite. trans. *Les Vagues* by Virginia Woolf. Paris: Editions Stock, 1974.

Hermeneutic Lacunae and Ways of Dealing with Them in Translating *Mrs. Dalloway*

Galina Yanovskaya

If you ask me how Virginia Woolf's works translate into Russian I would say that adequate translation is hardly possible because I am sure one should read her works in the original with one's eyes, and soul and mind open.

Due to their modernist intention, Woolf's texts are known to resist linear reading and still more, linear translation. In the latter case, as I argue in this paper, there accumulates the so-called hermeneutical lacunae effect which comes down to blocking the implied extra semantic signals and this, in its turn, results in the deformation of the reader's cognitive response.

Proceeding from this assumption I claim that an alternative complex strategy of hermeneutical coupling of all semantic units can be used as a way to ward off the unwelcome lacunae effect. The latter approach allows us to read Woolf's texts at least at two levels: the narrative level (which constitutes the surface of the textual space of a work), and the meta-narrative level, which includes the means of expressing the author's intention and her reflection of the creative process. I am going to show the difference between the two strategies by analyzing several fragments from *Mrs. Dalloway* in the original and in translation.

As is known, twentieth-century literature and arts have made ample use of the palimpsest technique.[1] That it can open a new perspective in the strategies of reading and translation is prompted by the analysis of Woolf's writing. Let me quote a passage from a well-known Russian translation of *Mrs. Dalloway*:

> "Dai mne ruku, siad' so mnoi riadom" (Peter Walsh ne uderzhalsia i, vleziaia v taksi, sunul bedniage monetu) i "Pus't' smotriat, pus't' vidiat, ne vsio li ravno?"—voproshala ona, i prizhimala k grudi kulak, i ulybalas', priacha shilling v karman, a liubopytnye vzgliady stiralis', vychiorkivalis', a prokhodiatschie pokoleniia—krugom mel'teshili i tolkalis' prokhozhie—ischezali, kak listia, chtoby moknut' i pret', stanovias' peregnoem dlia toi vechnoi vesny. (Woolf, *Missis* 83)

> "...give me your hand and let me press it gently" (Peter Walsh couldn't help giving the poor creature a coin as he stepped into his taxi), "and if some one should see, what matter they" she demanded;...and all peering inquisitive eyes seemed blotted out, and the passing generations—the pavement was

crowded with bustling middle-class people—vanished, like leaves, to be trodden under, to be soaked and stepped and made mould of by that eternal spring— (*MD* 72)

Let us make some preliminary observations. The reader of the Russian translation seems to be trapped by a linear translation strategy, and is unable to grasp the message, for his/her attention is glued to the two instances of direct speech ("give me your hand" and "if some one should see, what matter they"), hence it seems there is no logic in the image of "the passing generations," which sounds odd and unpredictable. It happens so because only the denotative meaning of the key word "coin" is translated but all the other meanings, including the one of "creating new words or expressions," are left untranslated. Similarly, other words in the fragment reveal themselves as potent signifiers when translated with the whole semantic halo. Let Russian readers look at the same fragment of the target text with the extra signifiers indicated in square brackets. Linear translation does not explicate the additional meanings of the key words, yet they keep their signifiers:

"Dai mne svoiu ruku i dai mne pozhat' eio nezhno " (Peter Walsh ne cmog uderzhatsia, chtoby ne dat' bednomu poetu monetu [pomoch bednomu poetu sozdat' novye slova] "i esli kto-to uvidit, kakoe im delo?" voproshala ona... i vsio vsmatrivaiutschiesia liubopytnye [issledovatel'skie] glaza kazalis' vycherknutymi [stiortymi, promoknutymi promokashkoi, pachkaiuschimi, zatemniaiuschimi], i prokhodiatschie pokoleniia – trotuar [mozaichnyi pol] byl perepolnen suetiaschimsia narodom srednego klassa - ischezli, kak listia [nasledstvo], chtoby na ikh meste poyavilis' sleduiutschie, chtoby vpitat'sia, nastoiatsia i vzrykhlit' pochvu [prevratit'sia v prakh, vylitsia v formu, sozdat' obraz] etoi vechno dliatscheisia vesny [istochnika]—

For the English-speaking readers, the semantic halo of key words is given in square brackets:

"...give me your hand and let me press it gently" (Peter Walsh couldn't help giving the poor creature a coin [helping the poor poet to create new words] as he stepped into his taxi), "and if some one should see, what matter they" she demanded;...and all peering inquisitive eyes seemed blotted out [wiped off, absorbed by a blotter, soiling, darkening], and the passing generations—the pavement [mosaic floor] was crowded with bustling middle-class people—vanished, like leaves [inheritance], to be trodden under, to be soaked and stepped and made mould [turned into dust, poured out into a form, made an image] of by that eternal spring—

Hermeneutic Lacunae

Now, we can easily reconstruct the implied meaning of the fragment: we are talking about the mystery of the creative act and the stages of modeling a figure, shaping the text as some form, palimpsest, manuscript over the rubbed off "text" of the past.

As Mallarmé used to say, the poem is shaped not from ideas, but from words. This explains why it becomes possible for the twentieth-century reader to take an "outside position" towards his/her own language, and to play on words while discovering at the same time that a word has multiple meanings; in other words, the language starts generating itself.

Two tendencies become visible in texts imitating spontaneous speech, to which all seemingly incompatible modernist writers' works of the early twentieth century belong, i. e. that of segmentation and splitting up of the utterance, and that of structural compactness (Vygotskyi 83-84). To put it differently, a message is both abridged at the level of verbal explication, as well as dissipated at the extra-linguistic, referential level. The syntax is both simplified as well as complicated. The abridgement of the message by omitting the name of the subject of speech in the speaker's inner monologue (for he/she knows it very well) combines with the message getting dissipated via various predicates and going round one more time about the same thing. "On the one hand, long windy speculations expose the individual's epistemological search and identify ever new aspects in it. On the other hand, this type of discourse is structured as 'discourse for others'" (Kovtunova 185).

The increased functional and semantic role of such prosody-oriented, super-segmental means as *semantic caesura*, which is indicated in the text with a certain punctuation mark, is determined by the factors listed above. The most "obtrusive" marks in Woolf's idiolect are dashes, brackets and semicolons. As analysis shows, their frequent use cannot be defined as a characteristic feature of the flow of speech of a certain personage or type of speech as a whole. Most probably, we can define this aspect as part of the author's intention, which is why it is appropriate in this paper to refer to the analysis of such a linguistic and stylistic phenomenon as "parceling," which explains the use of the semicolon. From a great variety of constructions to which the parceling method is applied it seems possible to identify some intentional units which are different in level, depth and frequency of "filling in" semantic caesurae.

The most obvious of these is aimed at enhancing the reader's sensory experience by focusing on the shades of feeling, and drawing his/her attention to the things the reader is supposed to see, hear and feel by imaginatively interacting with the text in question (Silman). Let us build on the lexical units in the following fragment of the Russian translation of *Mrs. Dalloway* by providing their semantic paradigms:

Yanovskaya

> Kakoi svezhyi [chistyi, krepkii, silnyi, prokhladnyi], kakoi spokoinyi [tikhii, bezvetrennyi, mirnyi, umirotvoriaiutschii, uspokaivaiutschii], tische [besshumnee, spokoinee, nepodvizhnee], chem seichas, konechno, byl vozdukh rannim utrom; kak shlepok [legkii udar, vzmakh kryliev, kolykhanie] volny [moria, vnezapnoi mysli, vzmakha, znaka]; kak potselui [kasanie] volny…prokhladnyi [ziabkii, znobiatschii, unylyi] i rezkii [ostryi, silnyi, pronzitel'nyi, tonkii] i (dlia vossemnadtsatiletnei devochki, kakoi ona togda byla) torzhestvennyi [pyshnyi, vazhnyi]…

Compare this to the text in the original:

> How fresh [clean, strong, hard, cool], how calm [quiet, windless, peaceful, conciliatory, soothing], stiller [more noiseless, more tranquil, more fixed] than this of course, the air was in the early morning; like the flap [slight blow, wave of the wings, heaving] of a wave [the sea, a sudden thought, sweep, sign]; the kiss [touch] of a wave; chill [sensitive to cold, shivering, dull] and sharp [acute, strong, piercing, thin] and yet (for a girl of eighteen as she then was) solemn [splendid, important] …" ([*MD* 1])

Due to the use of trivial characteristics "fresh," "calm," "still" in the above passage, the situation of figurative and sensory insufficiency shapes itself, which can be qualified as the base. The prearranged communicative task of the given situation can be determined as follows: "how much and to what extent was the air like that…then?" or, to be more exact, "how could it be…that she has defined it now and then?" The intentional semantic caesura remains open both in the heroine's, as well as the author's and reader's minds. The use of the semicolon slows down not only the given triad, but also the narration itself. It is still uncertain as to how to close: to continue a dull, trivial set of definitions (like the ones in brackets) or to blow up with a completely new cluster of tropes. The outburst, however, takes place: now the parceling unit can be understood by the reader both literally and metaphorically due to the so-called sensory sufficiency.

Let me emphasize the following: the intentional pause in the given case helps to destroy not only the inner form of a word and utterance, but it also provokes in the first place the destruction of the inner form of narration. Thus, the readers of the source text (presumably native speakers), in whose consciousness all the shades of meaning stir up as a unity of some sort, not only synthesize the general meaning of the message, but face a completely new narrative tone. It baffles them, at that. One is deceived in one's expectations, since the message which seems to have just exploded with the subtlest shades of meaning, gradually subsides, getting back into the old track. The same happens to the whole narrative mode: they both continue sparkling off with smaller details but these are weak attempts to regain former suggestiveness. The shades

Hermeneutic Lacunae

of meaning get weaker, and the message that seemed to be running non-stop suddenly stops short as if the phrase stumbled over the intentional caesura in "the kiss [touch] of a wave." What remains are separate traces, or echo-like recollections of the form that has just been made and destroyed. Then another "explosion" of yet another "base" will follow, and then another "theme" will fade away but anyway, the semantic caesura once shaped as a semicolon will continue to remind the reader of the implied meaning of every other narrative unit. What this writing mode ultimately comes to is the intention of making the reader forget about linear reading and apply a new strategy of retrospective reading.

Let me give an example of a parceling structure as a model of the reverse type—theme-base-segmentation. Compare a fragment of the target text:

> ...kto-to [nekto, liuboy, kazhdyi, vsiakii, ty] chuvstvuet/sh [otschutschaet, ispytyvaet, osiazaet, perezhyvaet, vidit, osoznaiot] dazhe posredi ulichnogo dvizheniia ili prosnuvshis' nochju, Klarissa byla uverenna, osobennuiu [osobuiu, iskliuchitel'nuiu, detal'nuiu, obstoiatel'nuiu, trebovatel'nuiu] tishynu [molchanie, zamiranie, uspokoenie], ili vazhnost' [torzhestvennost', znachitel'nost']; neopisuemuiu pauzu [ostanovku, peredyshku, zameshatel'stvo, nereshytel'nost', tsezuru]; ozhydanie [tomlenie, neizvestnost'] (no eto mozhet byt' eio serdtse, vzvolnovannoe, govoriat, influentsei) pered tem kak Big Ben udarit [porazit, prodiot na um, osenit, pronzit, pustit korni, otchekanit, otpechataet, vycherknet]

to the same passage in the source text:

> one [somebody, anybody, everybody, anyone, you] feels [becomes aware of, experiences, perceives, worries, sees, realizes] even in the midst of the traffic, or waking at night, Clarissa was positive, a particular [special, exceptional, detailed, thorough, exacting] hush [silence, dying out, soothing], or solemnity [significance, importance]; an indescribable pause [stop, respite, confusion, indecisiveness, caesura]; a suspense [languor, uncertainty] (but that might be her heart, affected, they said, by influenza) before Big Ben strikes [hits, comes into somebody's mind, dawns upon, runs through, takes root, mints, prints, crosses out, begins to play]. (*MD* 2)

Let me skip over the detailed commentary, and limit myself to some general observations.

First, we see in the given passage, though in reverse order, all the above mentioned principles in operation. "The theme" (action aspect) creates the tense atmosphere of expectation, whereas "the base" (temporal aspect) brings the musical theme to a close.

Second, the interplay of various shades of meanings explicitly appeals to the reader's senses and mind, as well as to his/her creative experience (see potential semantic signals in "to realize," "detailed," "caesura," "to dawn upon," "to come into somebody's mind," "to print," "to cross out").

If we take into account the principle of semantic dissipation, thanks to which the implied meaning of one parceling unit becomes explicit in the following examples (with or without extra auxiliary parts of speech, which update the semantic paradigm), then the emergence of an emotional, narrative and mental "outburst" seems to be logical:

> Kakie my glupye [bezrassudno rastrachivaem (vremia)], dumala ona, peresekaia Viktoria strit. Odnim nebesam tol'ko izvestno, pochemu kazhdyi ... vidit [vstrechaet, ponimaet, provozhaet, sledit, rasporiazhaetsia, zabotitsia, razbiraetsia, obnaruzhyvaet, dovodit do kontsa] eto tak, sovershaia [proizvodia, sostavl'aia, pobuzhdaia, predpolagaia, vozmetschaia, kompensiruia, naviorstyvaia, sobiraia, vydumyvaia, smiriaias', reshaia, maskiruia], stroia [sozdavaia, polagaias', osnovyvaias', sviavaia gniozda, formiruia, konstruiruia, stilizuia, sochiniaia] eto vokrug kazhdogo..., oprokidyvaia [kuvyrkaias', vyviortyvaia, privodia v besporiadok, vzjerosgyvaia] eto, tvoria [sozdavaia, sozidaia proizvedenie iskusstva/mirozdanie, vozvodia v zvanie tvortsa/avtora] eto kazhuiu sekundu zanovo [snova, opiat', vnov' i vnov']...

Compare to the source text:

> Such fools [spending (time) in vain] we are, she thought, crossing Victoria Street. For Heaven only knows why one [anybody, everybody, somebody, someone, you] loves [wants, cherishes] it so, how one sees [meets, understands, sees off, watches over, is in command of, takes care of, looks into, finds, completes; the noun "diocese" in this case is implicitly connected with the preceding one: "For Heaven only knows…" —and leads the narration to the sacral level] it so, making it up [creating, combining, impelling, suggesting, compensating, making up for, collecting, inventing, resigning oneself, deciding, disguising], building [creating, depending upon, being founded on, building nests, forming, constructing, styling, composing] it round one, tumbling [somersaulting, slipping out, getting into a mess, tousling] it, creating [making, constructing a piece of art/the universe, raising to the creator / author title] it every moment afresh [anew, one more time, over and over again]...
> ([*MD* 2])

If, however, the discourse is arranged as nomination, as is the case with the Russian translation of *Mrs. Dalloway*, the above quoted passage reads as an illogical one, beyond semantic paradigm and context. The latter is the result of the so-called semantic or hermeneutical lacuna, which comes to block-up the implied semantic signals and the reader's cognitive function. The text loses its suggestiveness. Graphically the difference can be represented as follows.

Hermeneutic Lacunae

Fig. 1. Semantic hermeneutical lacunae

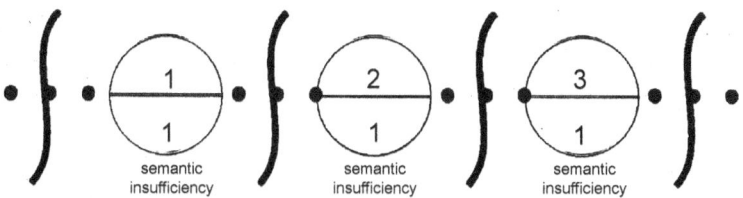

Fig. 2. Hermeneutical coupling

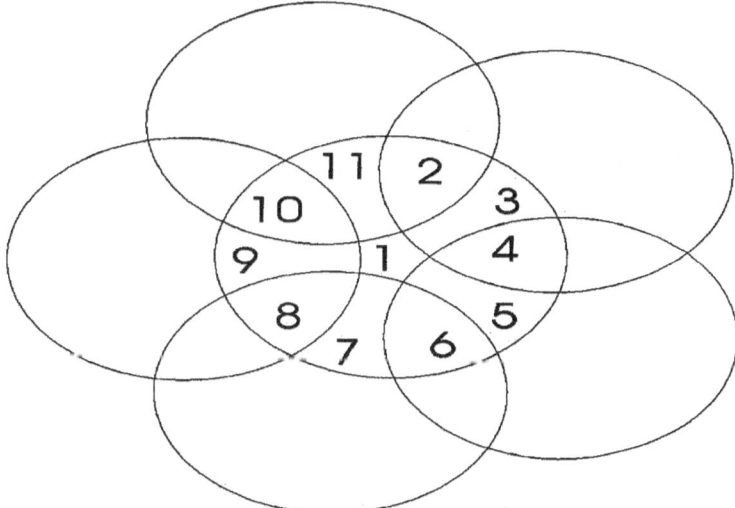

From this point of view Woolf's discourse can be identified as *incantation* which endlessly varies and modifies closely related semantic fields and paradigms. It clarifies the intention of the novel as the one about how the novel can be written and received by the reader. The reverse also holds: this is the novel about what could not have been written and the way it could not have been received by the reader. The latter is justified by a further analysis of parceling.

Let us turn to what I think is a vivid example:

V glazakh [vzgliadakh, tochkakh zreniia] liudei, v kachanii [kolebanii, vzmakhe, ritme] strannichestve [zvuke tiazhiolykh shagov, potope], i trudnom puti [sharkanie][(1)]; v riove [grokhote, mychanii] i game [shume, sumatokhe, vzryve smekha][(2)]; ekipazhei [karetok pishutschikh mashinok], avtomobilei [kolesnits], avtobusov [soedinit' neskol'kikh punktov], vagonov [furgonov, avangard], reklamnykh agentakh snuiutschikh [khitriatschikh, uviortyva-

Yanovskaya

jutschikhsia] i idutschikh mernym shagom[3]; dukhovykh mednykh orkestrakh [objedinenie,zaviazka, usy, sviaz', obramlenie][4]; sharmankakh [organakh, finansirujutschikh pliticheskie aktsii][5]; v triumfe [zvuke pobedy, torzhestve idei] i pozviakivanii [sozvuchii, alliteratsii] i neobychno [stranno, neznakomo] vysokom penii [zvone, shume, sviste, gudenii, zhuzhanii, vospevanii] aeroplana [vozdushnogo zamka] nad golovoi [u istoka reki, v rubrike, razdele, podzagolovke] bylo vsio, chto ona lyubit[6]; zhiz'n' [obraz reki, rod zaniatii, zhizneopisanie, biografiia, voodushevlenie, natura][7]; London[8]; etot moment [mig, sekundu, mgnovenie, chastitsu, dvizhutschuiu silu, impul's] ijunia.[9]

Compare to the source text:

In people's eyes [their looks, their points of view], in the swing [hesitating, flap, rhythm], tramp [sound of heavy steps, tread], and trudge [shuffling][1]; in the bellow [crash, lowing] and the uproar [noise, bustle, outburst of laughter][2]; the carriages [carriages of typewriters], motor cars [chariots], omnibuses [to unite some items together], vans [caravans, vanguard], sandwich men shuffling [dodging, evading] and swinging[3]; brass bands [union, outset, ties, connection, frame][4]; barrel organs [bodies financing political actions][5]; in the triumph [the sound of victory, in rejoicing of ideas] and the jingle [consonance, alliteration] and the strange [queer, unknown] high singing [ringing, noise, whistle, buzz, hum, glorifying] of some aeroplane [castle in the air] overhead [at the river-hear, in the heading, part, subtitle] was what she loved[6]; life [the way of life, occupation, one's life description, biography, inspiration, nature][7]; London[8]; this moment [instant, second, in a flash, particle, motive power, impulse] of June.[9] (*MD* 2)

Let me make some comments on the above. Without repeating the previously made observations, which are fully applicable to the given passage, I would like to emphasize other points—in particular, the inaccurate motivation of semantic paradigms, and the inaccuracy of their explication by means of punctuation marks. I mean that of all the variety of paradigms it is possible to distinguish three central nexuses: rhythm and sound; people and cars; the general and the particular. These three are alternately combined both within the framework of a separate parcelling unit, as well as the whole passage.

Every new combination is slightly shifted towards predominance and characterization. This is the only regularity we can observe. Shifts occur within the limits of one semantic nexus. See modifications in the nexus "rhythm plus sound":

- rhythm plus sound
- sound plus rhythm

Hermeneutic Lacunae

- rhythm plus sound
- sound (crescendo) plus rhythm (major)
- sound (diminuendo) plus rhythm (minor)
- combinations 4 and 5 plus the sound pitch.

Thanks to the possible range of combinations there shapes itself the changing panorama of visual and sound images of the city. Moreover, it is the reason for us to be able to see, hear and reproduce them all by way of summing up and perhaps completing the narrative. In any case, the open-end fragmented structure tends to completed form.

Semantic completion is found in parcelling units 7, 8 and 9: "life, London, this moment in June," which are linked by subject-cum-location-cum-temporal characteristics. Yet, it is only the illusion of completion that they create by means of building on suggestiveness, since they contradict the previous units, which seem to be closed. See unit 6, which ends with "what she loved." According to the logic of syntactical-semantic subdivision of the sentence, parcelling units 7, 8 and 9 have to be indicated with semicolons, to distinguish them from unit 6. How meaningful then can be the use of the semicolon in the given context? The more so that in the previous sentence a similar syntactical-semantic situation is fixed with the help of a semicolon. I think we will have again to explicate potential semantic signals of the creative process of writing, that is, *rhythm, carriage of a type-writer, uniting some items together, vanguard, outset/connection/frame, consonance/alliteration, glorifying, castle in the air, heading/subtitle, one's life description/biography, impulse.*

The author's intention is visible here. It comes down to "[expressing] life" in separate sounds, "[showing] London," "[fixing] this moment" or, at least, shaping the illusion of this message. Thanks to the intentional replacement of colon with semicolon the circumstantial interdependence of units 1-6 and 7-9 is cancelled, their determination through cause and effect relations, as well as explanatory and complementary ones gone. As a result of this experiment, units 1-6 become a subject, whereas units 7-9 turn into a predicate. In other words, the content of units 1-6, that is, "life," "London," is predicated with "this moment."

Secondly, the birth of intention is registered in the analyzed example. The appropriate semantic signs show us this (exposition, heading, life description, etc.). It is not difficult to refer them to a certain category of literary terms, as they metonymically remind us of the genre, composition and artistic means—in other words, to poetics of creative work (see the above listed examples).[2] Here the broken line of the origin of intention is implicitly and explicitly marked: it will pick up centripetal force, convert itself into the energy of movement, become an episode, event or narrative line, message, sketch (motor

Yanovskaya

car, airplane, barrel organ) and will gradually fade away as the uproar of the street in London.

Summing up, I would like to emphasize the following: the given examples cannot be qualified as word-for-word or literal translation—they rather serve as working illustrations and can be used by professional translators in their commentaries on Virginia Woolf's texts, which obviously need no less commentary than the works of Joyce.

Notes

[1] From L f Gk palimpsestos (*palin* again + *psao* rub smooth).
[2] This idea shaped itself in discussion with my research supervisor, Prof. V. I. Greshnykh, on 24 March 2000.

Works Cited

Kovtunova, I. I. *Poeticheskii Syntaksis* [Poetry Syntax]. Moscow, 1986.
Semionova, L. V. "O Raschlenenii Syntasicheskoi Struktury kak Istochnike Ekspressivnosti" [On Splitting Up Syntactic Structure as a Source of Expressiveness]. In *Voprosy Sintaksisa Angliiskogo Iazyka* [Aspects of English Syntax]. Gorky: Gorky State University (1975: 1).
Silman, Tatiana. *Zametki o Lirike* [Notes on Lyrics]. Leningrad, 1977.
Vygotskyi, L. S. *Myshlenie i Rech* [Thinking and Oral Discourse]. Moscow and Leningrad, 1934.
Woolf, Virginia. *Missis Dalloway* [*Mrs. Dalloway*]. Trans. Elena Surits. In *Izbrannoie* [Selected Works]. Moscow: Khudozhestvennaia Literatura, 1996.
Woolf, Virginia. *Mrs. Dalloway*. NY: Vintage, 1992.

Holland and Virginia Woolf: The Reception of Virginia Woolf's Translated Work in the Netherlands
AnneMarie Bantzinger

Although theories about translation can fill whole libraries and no doubt do, one can always put them aside and add a personal point of view. Translating should be a creative and at the same time an impersonal affair, as difficult a task as writing itself.

While researching the subject of the translation of Virginia Woolf's work in the Netherlands for the International Symposium in Moscow, I never came across a clear idea or a conscious decision from either the translators or their reviewers regarding what exactly they were looking for or what they were aiming at. As can be seen, the bulk of the translations of Woolf's work into Dutch were published between the years 1976 and 1988. I looked for book reviews and essays about specific translations during this period, ignoring the biographical summaries and the retelling of the novel under review.

To put the reception of her translated work in perspective, I briefly looked at the reception of her original work between the two World Wars, that being the time most of her writings were published in Great Britain. Any attention given to Woolf in the Netherlands—in either newspapers or magazines—would show up in Nijhoff's *Index op Nederlandsche Periodieken van Algemeene Inhoud*.[1] I decided to start looking for information starting with 1925.[2]

In the time span of those seventeen years I found fourteen entries.[3] I also looked at other literary magazines of the day: *Critisch Bulletin II* had three entries,[4] *De Vrije Bladen* had one,[5] as had *Werk & Criterium*[6]; *Forum*[7] had one entry in about the same period (1925-1941). Two of the editors of *Forum* were Edgar du Perron (1899-1940) and Menno ter Braak (1902-1940). The article in *Forum* was written by Elisabeth de Roos (1903-81), a Dutch literary critic and wife of E. du Perron. Her article is worth a closer look[8] since De Roos writes with great insight about Virginia Woolf's writing in general and some of her novels specifically. Her article is divided into two chapters. In the first she talks about the way Woolf writes, emphasizing her role as a female author. In the second part she uses different novels to explain the specific style and method of Woolf's writing, using *The Waves, Orlando, A Room of One's Own, Mrs. Dalloway* and *To the Lighthouse* as examples. In this context it is worth noting that in 1933, when de Roos wrote her article, the novels and the essay were available to her in English.

Bantzinger

Her husband, E. du Perron, was an important figure in the literary circles of his time. Among his published work are his letters[9] in which I found a few references to Virginia Woolf. Most of these references had to do with ordering books to be sent to him in Paris where he was living at the time.[10] In these letters, or on postcards in some cases, he asks H. Mayer[11] to please send him the latest novel *Mrs. Dalloway*[12] also asking for *Orlando*[13] and on 19 July, 1935 he refers to *Mrs. Dalloway* in a letter to another friend showing that he has read it.[14] Thus it is quite understandable that Elisabeth de Roos, also a literary critic, would write an article about Virginia Woolf, especially considering the access she had to some of Woolf's novels. After all, did not Woolf herself make a note in her diary on 8 May, 1935 while on a tour in Holland, about the "immense profusion of highly civilized shops, English, German and French books equal to Dutch" (*D4* 310). From 1 till 8 of May, 1935 Woolf, her husband Leonard and their marmoset Mitz visited Holland. Their visit passed unnoticed; only Mitz could draw a crowd and "attracted even greater attention than she did back home" (Nunes 51). On the whole Virginia was very much impressed by Holland. She loved the weather, the cleanliness and the towns they visited, "all next door,—I mean towns are only across 6 fields" (*L5* 389). She loved the architecture and in a letter to her sister Vanessa she describes "the colours, the canals, the tulips and the flowering trees, weeping their reflection into the water" (Ibid.). She further writes that she "has seen some of the best Rembrandts in the world; and Vermeers" (Ibid.). In this positive and optimistic mood she praises the Dutch bookshops with their abundance of foreign literature. In hindsight one can only wish that she and not Mitz had attracted the crowds.

Returning to the Dutch literary men of the day I looked at the work of a close friend, literary and personal, of Du Perron, Menno ter Braak who would certainly have known about Woolf as well. However, he did not write about Woolf. I could find no reference about her in his published writings, letters, diaries, essays or otherwise.

Another possible source of information was the "Vestdijk Kring" (Vestdijk Circle) a group of admirers of Simon Vestdijk (1898-1971). I asked them whether they knew Vestdijk had written about Woolf. Vestdijk, a prolific writer and critic, did write criticism and essays on European literature.[15] However, although his widow Mieke Vestdijk and their son Dick looked into his unpublished work and in his library, he did not write about her and they found no books by her.[16]

The lack of interest in the work of Virginia Woolf is beginning to be apparent. It will get further substantiation on studying the thesis by Roselinde Supheert called *Yeats in Holland. The Reception of the Work by W. B. Yeats in*

Holland and Virginia Woolf

the Netherlands before World War II. I started to realize that not only was there little interest in Virginia Woolf before World War II but one could generalize this lack of interest to English literature as a whole. Supheert too looked at literary magazines, newspapers, books, unpublished writings, letters, and combed through University and private libraries and found little interest in "modern" English literature. In fact the case for Yeats in Holland is better because he had a group of admirers, such as A. Roland Holst, P. N. van Eyck and J. C. Bloem, all members of the Dutch literary field of the day. Another point worth noting is that teaching of English in general was not high on the academic agenda, that "in the early decades of the twentieth century, Dutch Anglistics was still in its infancy" (Supheert 233) and that "degrees in English were only awarded from 1921 onwards" (Ibid.). Also "literature from the nineteenth and twentieth centuries was no important feature" (234). After this conclusion, it is understandable that the publications of "modern writers" can not be found at university libraries given the fact the subject was not taught. In yet another example from Supheert's work, referring to the University of Utrecht Library's Anglia catalogue (a unique record of acquisition), she writes "modernist writers are rare in the Anglia catalogue" (47). "Woolf, Forster, Eliot and Lawrence, remain undiscovered until 1932, when all a sudden some of their work is acquired" (48). In the Amsterdam University Library, Supheert found in the catalogues of the 1920s and 1930s "Woolf totally absent" (49). One has to add to this fact that "the educated class could and did read English—although French rather than English was the primary foreign language; however, the Dutch critical scope was fairly narrow and conservative" (96-97).

Knowing now how scarce the attention to Woolf's work was between the two World Wars, let us see whether the reception of her translated work was any better.

After the publication of Quentin Bell's biography of Virginia Woolf, and even more so after her diaries and letters started to appear in published form, the interest in Woolf in Holland took off. Interest in her as a person grew, especially regarding her connection with Vita Sackville-West.[17] However, interest in her novels was a different matter. As most of the translations of her work appeared between approximately 1976[18] and 1988, it makes sense to look at the reception of her translated novels and other writings during this time period.

Most public and university libraries[19] in Holland have a subscription to a cutting service. This service provides cuttings from major newspapers and weekly magazines, which proved to be the best sources of information on this subject.

I will take you through the translated works in order of publication in the Netherlands. (See Appendix 1.) *Mrs. Dalloway* was Virginia Woolf's first novel to be translated into Dutch. In 1948 Nini Brunt translated it for the publishing house G. A. van Oorschot in Amsterdam. The staff of G. A. van Oorschot are unable to trace the history of this translation. Their archives have recently been transferred to the National Literary Museum in The Hague and are not yet available to the public. A member of van Oorschot's staff suggested that the decision to translate *Mrs. Dalloway* was probably not a very conscious one.

It is very likely that one of the authors they published had suggested the translation. He estimated that not more than two thousand copies had been printed.[20] In an article about Woolf, Mr. Wim Simons writes in *Utrechts Dagblad*, a regional newspaper, that Woolf does not sell well because "she writes very difficult books" (here and otherwise my trans.), and "the real devotees will read her work in the original language." In the same vein, James Brockney writes in *Het Vaderland* that the publisher van Oorschot was twenty years too early with this translation. The fact that it took thirty-two years before a reprint was published is reason enough to suggest the book was not a great success. Or, to put it more strongly, the first edition seems to have been forgotten. After the second edition was published in 1980, Dorinde van Oort writes in *NRC-Handelsblad*:

> There is every reason to welcome Nini Brunt's translation of Virginia Woolf's first mature novel *Mrs. Dalloway* with joy. It is a pity we have had to wait for this translation for so long. *Mrs. Dalloway* would have been a suitable and representative introduction for the Dutch readers; more suitable than the books previously translated into Dutch: *A Room of One's Own, A Writer's Diary* and the pseudo-biographies *Orlando* and *Flush*.

Van Oort finds the translation itself to be "good Dutch, beautiful in style and rhythm." She points out some questionable parts of the translation, mainly specific words. For example, she states that, "debatable is the translation of the word 'meaning' when Septimus is looking at England from the train window and thinks 'that the world itself is without meaning.'" She also remarks on some sloppiness of the translation of the word "idea" as if it had said "ideal" which makes the sentence incomprehensible. She observes that the word "since" does not always translates into "sinds" (since) but also into "omdat" (because) and "a great deal" does not only mean "een groot deel" (a great deal) but also "heel wat" (quite a lot). She ends her review with the remark:

> Every translator has his blind spots. When will the time come that we have someone look at their work, just to prevent these kinds of minor flaws, flaws that can so easily be spotted by someone else?

Holland and Virginia Woolf

Publisher G. A. van Oorschot can not recall why they decided to publish a translation of *A Room of One's Own* either. *Een Kamer voor Jezelf* (*A Room of One's Own*) translated by C. E. Waals-Nachenius did not sell well at all. The time was clearly not ripe for such a feminist work. Later, as can be seen by the several republishing dates,[21] it sold much better, and continues to be popular today. The latest reprint was published in 2003.[22] In the several book reviews and essays about *Een Kamer voor Jezelf* I found none that commented on the translation.

Then, in 1976, twenty-eight years after the publication of the translation of *Mrs. Dalloway* and eighteen years after the translation of *A Room of One's Own*, a translation into Dutch of *Orlando* was first published. Hannemieke Postma writes in *NRC-Handelsblad*:[23]

> Hurrah and cheers, finally, for the first time a book by Virginia Woolf has been translated into Dutch, a joyful fact that should be celebrated wholeheartedly. *Orlando* was published in 1928, so we have been waiting for this translation for almost 50 years.

This proves again that the first two translations, i.e. *Mrs. Dalloway* (1948) and *Een Kamer voor Jezelf* (1958), were forgotten in 1976 when *Orlando* was first published in the Netherlands. Postma blames the Bloomsbury craze "rampant for several years now"[24] as the reason for the sudden interest in translating the works of Virginia Woolf, and calls *Orlando*:

> Woolf's least serious novel and looking at what else will be published shortly, *Flush* and *A Room of One's Own* by De Bezige Bij and *A Writer's Diary* by De Arbeiderspers, consequently none of her great novels will be available for the Dutch reading audience, which is a pity. Of course the grandiose masterpieces like *To the Lighthouse* and *The Waves* are very likely untranslatable, but why not try *The Voyage Out*? Anyway, perhaps some day it will happen. I sincerely hope so. The novels of Virginia Woolf are in my opinion the most important written in this century—and although *Orlando* is a typical Woolf novel, it cannot be considered as representative. Of course I cannot explain in a few words what makes her work so special. (Ibid. 39)

It would have been very nice indeed if she could, but in this context the following is more relevant since she does have some remarks about the translation as well. She writes:

> still—and it seems unavoidable—*Orlando* is nicer in English. Gerardine Franken really did take much care in the translation, but Woolf's irony is so light that it gets lost in the translation. Sometimes the Dutch seems clumsy there where the English is more light-footed.

Bantzinger

She gives a couple of examples and adds that without the English text next to the translation, the Dutch becomes hard to understand. She ends her review with the hope that her criticism does not discourage the reader and adds that we can look forward to the translation of the complete works of Virginia Woolf.[25]

In a review in *De Nieuwe Linie* of March 1977 Daniël Robberechts cries out:

> What is the matter with Dutch publishers who decide—except for her *A Writer's Diary* and an essay—to publish her lesser work first? To answer this question one has to get under the skin of the publisher. "How to sell Virginia Woolf to the Dutch public?" The first argument to publish *Orlando* is the fact that this book was her first work that sold very well in England. Her cousin Quentin Bell wrote in his biography of her: "from the publisher's point of view this book was perfect."[26] Up until *Orlando* many people thought her novels tough to crack. *Orlando* changed all that. One could read a book by a 'difficult' author and find it easy, pleasant and it had a narrative as well.

The second argument for publishing *Orlando* was the whiff of scandal surrounding this book. The translation of *Portrait of a Marriage* (*Portret van een Huwelijk*[27]) had been a great success, and it added to the excitement of reading *Orlando*. The publisher, De Bezige Bij, who published *A Portrait of a Marriage* in translation, writes on the flap "of course Virginia Woolf wrote *Orlando* because she was inspired by the sexual appeal of Vita Sackville-West."

Robberechts goes on to criticize the lack of background information. He writes in the same review that "a lot of references will escape the Dutch reader who is not familiar with British history, literature and biography. The publisher is silent about those matters."

In *NRC-Handelsblad*, Pierre Dubois, in a book review of *Orlando*, speaks kindly about this translation. In his opinion the translator carried it out "with great care." He also hopes it will be an encouragement to read more of a writer whom he calls "certainly one of the most important of this century."

In the same year, 1976, a translation of *A Writer's Diary* (*Schrijversdagboek*) was published. Wim Simons writes in *Utrechts Nieuwsblad*: "this is an important book because it offers a glimpse of the writer at work." He is very pleased with this translation. He is especially pleased with the notes and the short postscript provided by the translator, Joop van Helmond. He hopes that because of the translation the Dutch readers will be challenged to read more of this unique writer.

James Brockney writes in the same vein in *Het Vaderland*. He talks about the general decline in reading for which he blames television or the possibly even more dangerous competition of bestsellers. He does see a steady growth

Holland and Virginia Woolf

of interest in the works of Virginia Woolf, especially now that the translations of her work appear regularly. In this context this translation is very useful and interesting, says Brockney.

In 1988, eleven years after the publication of *Schrijversdagboek*, Daniël Robberechts writes that he finds something very awkward in the Dutch version of *A Writer's Diary*. He looked up several quotes in the complete edition of the *Diary*, as edited by Anne Olivier Bell, looked them up in *A Writer's Diary* as edited by Leonard Woolf, then compared them with the Dutch translation. He writes: "It is amazing to have to conclude that the Dutch translator has taken very little trouble to represent the original accurately (was it because it isn't a purely literary work?)"

Nienke Begemann has another criticism. She writes:

> I have to confess I don't understand why De Arbeiderspers published this book in the first place. This writer's diary deals with writing and reading of books that are not available in Dutch and I think people interested in the matter can also read the English version.

In an even sharper criticism, she adds: "The translation does not strike me as having the clear intention to copy the style of Virginia Woolf: brevity, the accuracy of phrasing and the certainty are lacking. The Dutch is rendered full of miserable little words and sentence for sentence one can point out some error." But she continues by saying:

> Still, we should not get downhearted. I only wish that, if we really have to go along with this second wave of Bloomsbury enthusiasm, someone would make a good translation of one of Virginia Woolf's best novels. And that does not include *Orlando*. Who will translate *The Waves* or *To the Lighthouse* or *Mrs. Dalloway*? Then there will be at least one more reader of her work...[28]

It is interesting to note that like Dorinde van Oort would later do in 1980 she asks for a translation of *Mrs. Dalloway* in 1977, apparently unaware of the 1948 translation.

Then came *Flush*. Quentin Bell, in his biography of Woolf, says it was one of her least read books (Bell 2:175). The Dutch version of *Flush*—with only one edition—is called excellent by Jacques den Haan. He continues saying that "the translator succeeded in overcoming problems of the erudition and subtle use of language, a trademark of Virginia Woolf."[29] Peter van Zonneveld praises this as a very readable translation. Dr. J. Kuin starts his review in *De Volkskrant* by pointing out why the need for translations is more urgent now than ten years previously:

Bantzinger

A different view on what to teach and what the children in secondary school should know is starting to emerge. The ability to speak about all kinds of subjects and to produce the correct pronunciation has become a higher priority than being able to read difficult texts. Therefore more and more books are translated to give the students the opportunity to get acquainted with texts originally written in foreign languages. It is very likely that someone who was interested in Woolf ten years ago would have preferred to read her in English. Now even such a charming and light-footed little work as *Flush* has been translated into Dutch, indeed in an excellent way, worthy of the book.

He adds that "as in *Orlando*, Woolf plays with her knowledge of English culture in a superior way, here centred on the Victorian era. The Dutch reader may need some help with this and such aid is offered to him in the translator's notes and a postscript by Thomas F. Staley. Whoever prefers the cheap English edition of the Penguin series has to do without that help."

Three Guineas (*Geachte Heer*) presents one big problem in translation. Maaike Meyer finds the drastic deviation from the original title "difficult to stomach."[30] *Geachte Heer*, the Dutch title, means "Dear Sir" in English. Otherwise she praises the translation of the text. The second edition bears the literally translated title, *Drie Guineas*.

A Haunted House/Mrs. Dalloway's Party in Dutch published under the title *Maandag of Dinsdag* (*Monday or Tuesday*) with the subtitle *Verzamelde Verhalen* (Collected Stories) saw only one edition (see Appendix 1A). It is wonderful that the publisher took the trouble to publish some of Woolf's shorter fiction. However, there seem to be no reviews or any other kind of attention given to this collection. Add the fact that the book was printed only once and it seems that, sadly, it did not sell very well.

In the March 23, 1979 "Classics" column in *NRC-Handelsblad* Nienke Begemann discusses *To the Lighthouse*. The reviewer uses the original since no translation had been published at this time. Relevant in this context—the reception of and attention to Woolf in Holland—is the fact she calls this novel a milestone much more so than *Mrs. Dalloway* or *The Waves*: "*To the Lighthouse* stands straight-up just as the beacon from the title, an illumination which inspires and which remains with you..." Another comment on the translation of the title of *Naar de Vuurtoren* (*To the Lighthouse*) comes from Mirjam van Hengel in *Het Financiële Dagblad*. She writes that "the title has the power of a surname and each translation of it sounds grotesque."

The collection of Woolf's stories and essays on women and literature *Women and Writing* gets the highest praise from Diny Schouten in *Vrij Nederland*.[31] In contrast to the source text, however, Schouten finds the translation, *Schrijvende Vrouwen*, exceptionally bad. She argues that even without the original, the editors of this Synthese Series, which claims to be a scholarly

Holland and Virginia Woolf

publication "should have spotted the numerous problems with the translation." Doris Grootenboer in *Algemeen Dagblad* also finds the translation "wooden and bad" but at the same time she is pleased to get acquainted with Woolf's original and feminist ideas in Dutch.

Sixty years after the first publication of *Jacob's Room*, a Dutch translation, *Jacob's Kamer*, appeared but it did not sell very well. Just one reprint was published in 1986. Nienke Begemann in *NRC-Handelsblad* writes, "the book has been translated into very readable and carefully phrased Dutch with just a few stumbling blocks." She continues: "anyway it is more important that people who want to read Virginia Woolf's novels in Dutch, and I assume there are still more, can now start at a beginning."[32] Considering Woolf wrote two novels before writing *Jacob's Room* (*The Voyage Out* and *Night and Day*) and that there were quite a few novels and essays already translated into Dutch in 1982, to call this translation "a beginning" I find a somewhat awkward remark.

Next in this chronological overview of the translated work of Virginia Woolf we find *Moments of Being*. The Dutch translation was published as *Wezenlijke Momenten*. With just one printing and no reviews, this translation met with a lacklustre reception.

The Waves published under the Dutch title as *De Golven*, with one reprint in 1991, did only slightly better, although the reviews I found are positive. Lucienne Stassaert writes in *De Nieuwe*: "except for a few minor flaws the translator has understood the 'Woolfian music' exceptionally well."[33] J. F. Vogelaar in *De Groene Amsterdammer* finds the same in this translation and describes it as "doing justice to the tone and rhythm of language of this book."[34] Marja Brouwers advocates a separate review of the translation to do justice to the translator's work. "The translator," she writes, "has to make so many decisions having to do with the nature of literary Dutch as opposed to the English." Brouwers praises this translation by Gerardine Franken as "being in general accurate and readable, at the same time keeping much of the poetic glaze."

Franken herself has spoken about the translations of the works of Virginia Woolf. She says in her interview with Annemiek Neefjes in *Vrij Nederland* that, "translating Woolf is a struggle, but a nice one. Everything fits, everything she writes, she writes for a reason." Franken also admits that, "although taking meticulous care with the translation, she would now do things differently."

I would like to end this survey with a curious case. I refer to the two different translations into Dutch of *The London Scene*, published by two different publishers and with two different titles. *Over Londen* (meaning "About London") was first published in the Netherlands in 1983. In the course of my research I only found two copies of this charming book in Dutch university libraries.[35] This publication has the five original stories[36] as published by Frank Hallmann. The second translation *Geheim Londen*[37] (meaning "Secret London") has six stories.[38] Curious also is the fact that this book can usually be found in the travel section in bookshops as well as in libraries.

Scanning the field of the translated work of Virginia Woolf in Holland one cannot escape the conclusion that the translation of Virginia Woolf's work in Holland has been a haphazard and coincidental affair. Choices seem to have been made randomly. (The translation of *Mrs. Dalloway* might be an example of this.) In some cases, such as that of Franken, they are the result of the venture of an individual who started to translate even before a publisher was found. The fact that the same translations have been used over the years seems to indicate that publishers have not dared to risk their money investing in a new translation.

To add to the range of obstacles, the general public in Holland do not seem to be avid readers of psychological novels and may find Woolf's novels too difficult. As shown, there are only some novels by Virginia Woolf with several reprints. The impact that the movies (*Mrs. Dalloway*, *Orlando* and lately *The Hours*) have had on the sale of Woolf's books, needs more investigation.

One also must not forget the ability of the educated Dutch to read foreign literature in the original language. Books in foreign languages have always been widely available and especially after World War II, teaching of English has featured highly in the school curriculum. This can also help to explain the meagre interest in the translated work of Woolf.

Finally, as recently as 2003, still using the same translations, another reprint of the translated "classics"—*Mrs. Dalloway*, *Orlando* and *A Room of One's Own*[39]— was published in one volume: a hopeful but not a very convincing sign of interest in the work of Virginia Woolf in translation in Holland.

Appendix 1

Original title and date of publication	Dutch title, publisher, dates of publication, translator
Mrs. Dalloway (1925)	*Mrs. Dalloway* Amsterdam: G.A. van Oorschot, 1948 Amsterdam: De Bezige Bij, 1980, (BBLiterair), 1981, 1983, 1985, 1995, 1996 (Orlando Reeks), 2003. Translation: Nini Brunt

Holland and Virginia Woolf

A Room of One's Own (1929)
    Een Kamer voor Jezelf
    Amsterdam: G.A. van Oorschot, 1958
    Amsterdam: De Bezige Bij, 1977, 1979, 1983, 1985 (Pocket no. 22), 1996, 2003.
    Translation: C.E. van der Waals-Nachenius

Orlando (1928)
    Orlando
    Amsterdam: De Bezige Bij, 1976, 1977, 1984, 1987 (Pocket no. 40), 1993, 1995, 2003.
    Translation: Gerardine Franken. Postscript: James Naremore. Poemlines: Koos Schuur

A Writer's Diary (1953)
    Schrijversdagboek
    Amsterdam: De Arbeiderspers, 1976 (part 1 and 2) Privé Domein no. 37
    Amsterdam/Antwerpen: Atlas, 1999.
    Translation, postscript and notes: Joop van Helmond

Flush (1933)
    Flush
    Amsterdam: De Bezige Bij, 1978 (BBLiterair).
    Translation: Gerardine Franken

To the Lighthouse (1927)
    Naar de Vuurtoren
    Amsterdam: Bert Bakker, 1980, 1981, 1982.
    Amsterdam: Maarten Muntinga, Febr. 1988, (Rainbow Pocketbooks Series 52), April 1988, 1990, 1992.
    Translation: Jo Fiedeldij Dop. Poemlines: Dolf Verspoor

Three Guineas (1938)
    Geachte Heer
    Amsterdam: Feministische Uitgeverij Sara, 1980.
    Drie Guineas
    1985.
    Translation: Introduction, Part I and Part II: Janneke van der Meulen. Part III: Ank van Wijngaarden

Monday or Tuesday (1921)*
    Maandag of Dinsdag. Verzamelde Verhalen
    Amsterdam: Bert Bakker,1981.
    *For contents see appendix 1A
    Translation: Jo Fieldeldij Dop

Women and Writing (1925 etc.)
    Schrijvende Vrouwen
    Amsterdam: De Arbeiderspers and Wetenschappelijke Uitgeverij b.v.,1981.

Bantzinger

	Translation: Mouring Lindenberg
Jacob's Room (1922)	*Jacob's Kamer* Amsterdam: Bert Bakker, 1982. Amsterdam: Maarten Muntinga, 1986 (Rainbow Pockets Series no. 35). Translation: Jo Fiedeldij Dop
Moments of Being (1976, 1985)	*Wezenlijke Momenten* Amsterdam: De Bezige Bij, 1982. Translation: Leonoor Broeder Introduction and footnotes: Jeanne Schulkind
The London Scene (1975)	*Over Londen* Amsterdam: Tabula, 1983. Translation: Carol Limonard
The Waves (1931)	*De Golven* Amsterdam: De Bezige Bij, 1985 (BBLiterair), 1991 (Pocket no.78). Translation: Gerardine Franken
The London Scene (1975)	*Geheim Londen* Amsterdam: Byblos, 2000. Translation: Catalien and Willem van Paassen

Appendix 1A

MAANDAG OF DINSDAG
Subtitle: *Verzamelde Verhalen* (Collected stories)
Amsterdam: Bert Bakker, 1981.
Translation: Jo Fiedeldij Dop, Amsterdam
Cover: Donald Janssen, GVN, Rijswijk
Typography: Max van Os, Amsterdam
Printing: Tulp, Zwolle
ISBN 90 6019 8220

This translation drew from three collections:
Monday or Tuesday London: The Hogarth Press, 1921
A Haunted House London: The Hogarth Press, 1944
Mrs. Dalloway's Party London: The Hogarth Press, 1973

Contents

Mrs. Dalloway in Bondstreet	"Mrs. Dalloway in Bond Street" (1922-1925)
Entrée in de wereld	"The Introduction" (1922-1925)
Een spookhuis	"A Haunted House" (1917-1921)

Holland and Virginia Woolf

Maandag of Dinsdag	"Monday or Tuesday" (1917-1921)
Een ongeschreven roman	"An Unwritten Novel" (1917-1921)
Voorouders	"Ancestors" (1922-1925)
Het strijkkwartet	"The String Quartet"(1917-1921)
Kew Gardens	"Kew Gardens" (1917-1921)
De stip op de muur	"The Mark on the Wall" (1917-1921)
De nieuwe japon	"The New Dress" (1922-1925)
De jachtpartij	"The Shooting Party" (1926-1941)
Lappin en Lapinova	"Lappin and Lapinova" (1926-1941)
Vaste voorwerpen	"Solid Objects" (1917-1921)
De dame in de spiegel	"The Lady in the Looking-Glass" (1926-1941)
De hertogin en de juwelier	"The Duchess and the Jeweller"(1926-1941)
Momentopnamen:	"Moments of Being:
'De spelden van Slater hebben geen punten'	'Slater's Pins Have No Points'" (1926-1941)
De man die zijn naasten liefhad	"The Man who Loved His Kind" (1922-1925)
Het zoeklicht	"The Searchlight" (1926-1941)
De erfenis	"The Legacy" (1926-1941)
Samen en apart	"Together and Apart" (1922-1925)
Een samenvatting	"A Summing-up" (1922-1925)

Reference for English titles and dates:
The Complete Shorter Fiction of Virginia Woolf. Ed. Susan Dick. London: The Hogarth Press, 1985.

Notes

This article could not have been written without the encouragement of Natalya Reinhold (Moscow, Russia), MaryLou Barisas-Winder (Rome, Italy), Viora Buia (Malden, The Netherlands), and Helen Winder (Silver Spring, U.S.A.) looked at the text with a critical eye. Thank you Roselinde Supheert for your time and thesis, Volkert Groothoff, librarian at the Utrecht University Library, for your suggestions. A special thanks for their support to Willem, David and Martine.

[1] *Nijhoff's Index op Nederlandsche Periodieken van Algemeene Inhoud (Nijhoff's Index on Dutch periodicals of general content)*. Gravenhage: Martinus Nijhoff, 1925-1941. The list of magazines and newspapers used for this Index is too long to quote for this article. Over the seventeen years about 60-65 different magazines and newspapers are listed in this Index.

[2] In the University Library of Utrecht volumes of *Nijhoff's Index* run from 1909 till 1970.

[3] Ten entries under the heading "Woolf, Virginia"; the other four under "English Literature." Four were book reviews about a specific novel. 1925, *Mrs. Dalloway*; 1930, *A Room of One's Own*; 1934, *Flush*; 1938, *The Years*. The other ten were simply called "Virginia Woolf" or "The Novels of Virginia Woolf."

Bantzinger

[4] 1930, *A Room of One's Own*; 1934, *The Common Reader*; *Flush*; *Mr. Bennett and Mrs. Brown*; *Night and Day*; *Orlando*; *The Waves*; 1941, *A Room of One's Own*, *The Waves*. Verkruijse, P. J. Amsterdam: Thespa, 1975. *Bibliografische beschrijvingen, analytische inhoudsopgaven en indices/2 Critisch Bulletin II*.

[5] 1936. Geerds, J. F. Sicking, J. M. J. Amsterdam: Thespa, 1975. *Bibliografische beschrijvingen, analystische inhoudsopgaven en indices/3, De Vrije Bladen*.

[6] 1939. Hoogerhuis, S. S. Amsterdam: Thespa, 1975. *Bibliografische beschrijvingen, analytisch inhoudsopgaven en indices/4, Werk & Criterium*.

[7] 1933. *FORUM, Maandschrift voor Letteren en Kunst*. [Monthly magazine for Literature and Art] Onder leiding van Menno ter Braak, E. du Perron en Maurice Roelants, Rotterdam: Nijgh & Ditmar N.V., 2de Jaargang, no.1, 1933.

[8] Roos, E. de. *De Manier voor Goede Verstaanders, I. De Manier bij Virginia Woolf, II.* [A Word to the Wise is enough, I. After the Manner of Virginia Woolf, II.] *FORUM*, Rotterdam: Nijgh & Van Ditmar N.V., 1933: 43-49.

[9] Perron, E. du, *Brieven V., 2 mei 1934 – 31 oktober 1935*. Amsterdam: G.A. van Oorschot, 1979.

[10] e.g. *Brieven III*, "Bellevue December 15, 1932" du Perron writes..."Virginia Woolf I shall not buy; the money is just not there..." 505.

[11] Employee at the publishing firm Nijhoff, The Hague, the Netherlands.

[12] See *Brieven V*, 256, Paris, March 26, 1935 (postcard): "also please one copy of *Mrs. Dalloway* by Virginia Woolf (from the Hogarth Press). Is there also a cheap pleasant edition of *Orlando* (not Tauchnitz)? What do these small books of the Hogarth Press cost? Mrs. Dalloway you can in any case send..."

[13] See *Brieven V*, 262, Paris, April 1, 1935 (postcard): "do you have news already about *Mrs. Dalloway*," 277, Paris, April 8, 1935 (postcard): "From the Woolfs at 5/ just *Mrs. Dalloway*..."

[14] See *Brieven* V, 408, Paris, July 19, 1935 letter to W. L. M. E. van Leeuwen. In this letter du Perron compares Joyce's *Ulysses* with *Mrs. Dalloway*. Therefore he must have received his copy and read it.

[15] See e.g. Vestdijk, Simon. *Lier en Lancet. Essays over Emily Dickinson, James Joyce, Paul Valéry, Rainer Maria Rilke e.a.* Rotterdam: Nijgh & Van Ditmar N.V., 1939.

[16] We exchanged several emails about this question. Ra.albers@worldonline.nl (secr. Vestdijk Kring).

[17] Nicolson, Nigel. *Portrait of a Marriage*. London: Weidenfeld and Nicolson, 1973.

[18] Except for *Mrs. Dalloway* and *A Room of One's Own*, all other translations date from 1976 and after.

[19] Public libraries in Bilthoven, Groningen, Hilversum, The Hague and Utrecht. University libraries in Amsterdam, Groningen and Utrecht and my private collection. (AMB)

[20] Until this date (September 2003) I have been unable to trace exact numbers printed of any publication. These numbers apparently belong to the realm of closely guarded business secrets.

[21] *Een Kamer voor Jezelf*, 1977, 1979, 1983, 1985, 1996, 2003.

[22] *Mrs. Dalloway, Orlando, Een Kamer voor Jezelf. (Mrs. Dalloway, Orlando, A Room of One's Own)*. Translations: Nini Brunt, Gerardine Franken, C.F. van der Waals Nehenius. Amsterdam: De Bezige Bij, Amsterdam, 2003.

[23] Postma, Hannemieke. *NRC-Handelsblad*, November 14, 1976.

[24] I take this to mean from 1972 after Quentin Bell's biography of Virginia Woolf was published.
[25] There is no complete translation of her work in the Netherlands today, August, 2003.
[26] Bell, Quentin. Vol. II, 140, "8,104 copies in the first six months."
[27] *Portret van een Huwelijk*, Amsterdam: De Bezige Bij, 1975. (BBCargo). Translation: Gerardine Franken; Poemlines: Cees Buddingh.
[28] Begemann, Nienke. *NRC-Handelsblad*, June 24, 1977.
[29] Haan, Jacques den. *Het Parool*, June 24, 1978.
[30] Meyer, Maaike. *De Volkskrant*, March 24, 1981.
[31] Schouten, Diny. *Vrij Nederland*, July 18, 1981.
[32] Begemann, Nienke. *NRC-Handelsblad*, May 5, 1982.
[33] Stassaert, Lucienne. *De Nieuwe*, February 13, 1986.
[34] Vogelaar, J.F. *De Groene Amsterdammer*, February 12, 1986.
[35] University Library of Amsterdam and the University Library of Groningen. No copies can be found in public libraries.
[36] *De haven van Londen* ("The Docks of London," December, 1931), *Het tij van Oxford Street* ("Oxford Street Tide," January, 1932), *Huizen van beroemde mensen* ("Great Men's Houses," March, 1932), *Abdijen en kathedralen* ("Abbeys and Cathedrals," May, 1932), '*Dit is het Lagerhuis*' ("'This is the House of Commons,'" October, 1932) *Good Housekeeping*. See McVicker 143.
[37] *Geheim Londen*, Amsterdam: Uitgeverij Byblos, 2000. Translation: Catalien en Willem van Paassen.
[38] *De havens van Londen* ["The Docks of London"], *De stroom van Oxford* Street ["Oxford Street Tide"], *Waar grote mannen woonden* ["Great Men's Houses"], *Abdijen en kathedralen* ["Abbeys and Cathedrals"], '*Dit is het Lagerhuis*' [" 'This is the House of Commons'"], *De roep van de straat* ["Street Haunting: A London Adventure"] 1927 *Yale Review*. See McVicker 143.
[39] Woolf, Virginia. *Mrs. Dalloway, Orlando, Een Kamer voor Jezelf* [Mrs. Dalloway, Orlando, A Room of One's Own]. Amsterdam: De Bezige Bij, 2002. Translation: Nini Brunt, Gerardine Franken, C.E. van der Waals-Nachenius.

Works Cited

Begemann, Nienke. "*Schrijversdagboek 1 & 2.*" [A Writer's Diary 1 & 2] *NRC Handelsblad*, June 26, 1977.
——. "*Naar de Vuurtoren*" [To The Lighthouse]. *NRC-Handelsblad*, March 23, 1979.
——. "*Jacob's Kamer*" [Jacob's Room]. *NRC-Handelsblad*, May 14, 1982.
Bell, Quentin. *Virginia Woolf, A Biography*. New York and London: Harcourt, Brace Jovanovich, 1972.
Borre, Jos. "*Ik wil een beeld schetsen van het hele leven*" [I want to sketch an image of life itself]. *Hervormd Nederland*, September 27, 1980.
Brockney, James. "*Een Kamer voor Jezelf*" [A Room of One's Own] and "*Schrijversdagboek 1 & 2*" [A Writer's Diary]. *Het Vaderland*, November 19, 1977.
Broeder, Leonoor. "*Een sterk ontwikkeld gevoel voor plaats*" [A strongly developed

Bantzinger

sense of place]. *De Volkskrant*, September 4, 1998.

Brouwers, Marja. "*Schrijvende Vrouwen*" [Women and Writing]. *Vrij Nederland,* July 26, 1986.

Byvanck, W.G.C. "*Virginia Woolf en haar roman Mrs. Dalloway*" [Virginia Woolf and her novel *Mrs. Dalloway*]. *Amsterdamsch Weekblad*, 25 Juli, 1925.

———. "*Virginia Woolf*" [Virginia Woolf]. *Handelsblad*, October 8, 1927.

———. "*Virginia Woolf*" [Virginia Woolf].*De Stem*, X, 1930, 279-281.

———. "*Virginia Woolf*" [Virginia Woolf].*De Stem*, XIV, 1934, 993-1001.

Dick, Susan ed. *The Complete Shorter Fiction of Virginia Woolf*. London: The Hogarth Press, 1985.

Dubois, Pierre H."*Orlando*" [Orlando]. *NRC-Handelsblad*, February 26, 1977.

Geerds, J. F. & J. M. J. Sicking *Bibliografische beschrijvingen, analytische inhoudsopgaven en indices/3*. Amsterdam: Thespa, 1975. *De Vrije Bladen*. Woolf, Virginia, 13 (1936) 10, 31.

Grootenboer, Doris. "*Schrijvende Vrouwen*" [Women and Writing]. *Algemeen Dagblad*, December 11, 1981.

Haan, Jacques den. "*Hondenliefhebster*" [Doglover]. *Het Parool*, June 24, 1978.

Hengel, Mirjam van. "*Naar de Vuurtoren*" [To The Lighthouse]. *Het Financieel Dagblad*, February 12, 1999.

Hoogerhuis, S.S. *Bibliografische beschrijvingen, analytische inhoudsopgaven en indices/4. Werk & Criterium* Amsterdam: Thespa, 1975. *Werk en Criterium*. Woolf, Virginia, W1(1939) 12, 27, 28, 29.

Houts, Tine van. "*Geachte heer, val dood...*" [Dear Sir, drop dead...]. *Het Parool*, November 21, 1980.

Houwaard C. "*Woolf, Virginia, Engelsch schrijfster*" [Woolf, Virginia, English writer]. *De Stem*, XXI, 1941, 562-567.

Huffel, A.J. van. Jr. *Nijhoff's Index op Nederlandsche Periodieken van Algemeenen Inhoud*. Gravenhage: Martinus Nijhoff.

Hughes, R. "*Virginia Woolf. Three Guineas*." *De Stem*, XVII, 1938, 1161-1165.

Kuin, dr. J."*Flush*" [Flush]. *De Volkskrant*, September 9, 1978.

Lambrechts, An-Marie."*Schrijvende Vrouwen*" [Women and Writing]. *De Standaard*, October 9, 1981.

McVicker, Jeanette. "'Six Essays on London Life': A History of Dispersal." Part 1. *Woolf Studies Annual* 9 (2003): 143-65.

Meyer, Maaike. "*Geachte Heer*" [Three Guineas]. *De Volkskrant*, March 24, 1981.

———. "*Schrijvende Vrouwen*" [Women and Writing]. *De Volkskrant*, August 22, 1981.

Neefjes, Annemiek. "*Interview met Gerardine Franken. Vertalers over de Schrijver die ze het liefst vertalen. 'Bij Woolf staat niets er zomaar'*" [Interview with Gerardine Franken. Translators about the Writer whom they like to translate best. "With Woolf there is nothing for no reason"]. *Vrij Nederland*, August 2, 1997.

Nunes, Sigrid. *MITZ, The Marmoset of Bloomsbury*. New York: Harper Flamingo, HarperCollins Publishers, 1998.

Oever, Annie vanden. "*Een Bedorven Leven*" [A Spoiled Life]. *De Groene Amsterdammer*, September 21, 1988.

Oort, Dorinde van. "*Mrs. Dalloway*" [Mrs. Dalloway]. *NRC-Handelsblad*, July 7, 1980.

Panhuijsen, Jos."*Woolf, Virginia. De romans van...*" [Woolf, Virginia. The novels of...]. *Boekenschouw*, XXVII, 1933, 154-157.

———. "*Woolf, Virginia, en haar The Years*" [Woolf, Virginia, and her The Years].

Holland and Virginia Woolf

Boekenschouw, XXXII, 1938, 25-30.
——. *"Engelsche Letterkunde.—Cultuurgidsen. Virginia Woolf, Three Guineas."* [English Literature.—Gultural Guide. Virginia Woolf, Three Guineas]. *Boekenschouw*, XXXII, 1938, 214-219.
Perron, E. du. *"BrievenV."* 2 mei 1934, 31 oktober 1935, Amsterdam: G.A. van Oorschot, 1979.
Peters, Carel. *"De Transparante Envelope. Het Werk en de Betekenis van Virginia Woolf"* [The Transparent Envelope. The Work and the Meaning of Virginia Woolf]. *Vrij Nederland*, October 23, 1976.
Postma, Hannemieke. *"Orlando"* [Orlando]. *NRC-Handelsblad*, November 14 and 19, 1976.
Robberechts, Daniël. *"Orlando"* [Orlando]. *De Nieuwe Linie*, March 11, 1977.
——. *"Schrijversdagboek 1 & 2"*[A Writer's Diary]. *De Groene Amsterdammer*, September 21, 1988.
Roos, Elisabeth de. *"Virginia Woolf en haar A Room of One's Own"* [Virginia Woolf and her A Room of One's Own]. *Amsterdamsch Weekblad*, Juni 28, 1930.
——. *"Engelsche Letterkunde: Virginia Woolf, Vera Brittain, Gertrude Stein"* [English Literature: Virginia Woolf, Vera Brittain, Gertrude Stein]. *Groot Nederland*, 1934, I, 267-272.
——. *"De Manier voor Goede Verstaanders, I"* [A Word to the Wise is enough, I], *"De Manier bij Virginia Woolf, II"* [After the Manner of Virginia Woolf, II]. *Forum*, 1933, 43-49.
Roscam Abbing, Marja. *"Virginia Woolf als werkende vrouw"* [Virginia Woolf as a working woman]. *Hollands Diep*, August 28, 1976.
Ruyters, Jann. *"Verlokkende Ongrijpbaarheid van Virginia Woolf"* [The Enticing Elusiveness of Virginia Woolf]. *Trouw*, October 1, 1998.
Schouten, Diny. *"Schrijvende Vrouwen"* [Women and Writing]. *Vrij Nederland*, July 18, 1981.
——. *"Wezenlijke Momenten"* [Moments of Being] and *"Over Londen"* [The London Scene]. *Vrij Nederland*, May 21, 1983.
Simons, Wim J. *"Orlando"* [Orlando] and *"Een Kamer voor Jezelf"* [A Room of One's Own] *Utrechts Nieuwsblad*, June 11, 1977.
Stassaert, Lucienne. *"Geachte Heer"* [Three Guineas]. *De Nieuwe*, November 7, 1985.
——. *"Over Londen."* [The London Scene]. *De Nieuwe*, February 13, 1986.
Steenhuis, Aafke. *"Achter de Elegantie De Bezetenheid"* [Behind the Elegance the Madness] and *"Een Kamer voor Jezelf"* [A Room of One's Own]. *De Groene Amsterdammer*. September 21, 1988.
Supheert, Roselinde. *Yeats in Holland,The Reception of the Work by W.B.Yeats in The Netherlands Before World War II*. Utrecht: Costerus New Series 104, 1995.
Veire, Frank van de. *"De Golven"* [The Waves]. *De Standaard*, June 21, 1986.
Verkruijse, P.J. *Bibliografische beschrijvingen, analytische inhoudsopgaven en indices/2*. Amsterdam: Thespa, 1975. "Woolf, Virginia."*Critische Bulletin II. Common Reader* 5 (1934) 292, 7 (1936) 329. *Flush* 5 (1934) 289-290,292. *Mr. Bennett and Mrs. Brown* 5 (1934) 291. *Night and Day* 5 (1934) 291. *Orlando* 5 (1934) 290-291, 12 (1941) 164. A Room of One's Own 1 (1930) 39-41. 12 (1941) 163. *Three Guineas* 9 (1938) 205-309. *The Waves* 5 (1934) 289. 12 (1941) 164,166. *The Years* 7 (1936) 158.
Verroen, Sarah. *"Een Literair Karakter"* [A Literary Character]. *Het Vaderland*, January

Bantzinger

30, 1982.

Vogelaar, J.F. "*Jacob's Kamer*" [Jacob's Room]. *De Groene Amsterdammer*, September 21, 1988.

——. "*De Golven*" [The Waves]. *De Groene Amsterdammer*, February 12, 1986.

Vos, Marjoleine de. "*Mrs. Dalloway*" [Mrs. Dalloway]. *NRC-Handelsblad*, April 13, 1999.

Vos van Steenwijk W. de. "*Woolf, Virginia, Engelsch schrijfster.*" [Woolf, Virginia, English Writer]. *De Delver*, XI, 1937, 28-32.

Wells, H.G."*Virginia Woolf*" [Virginia Woolf]. Handelsblad, December 15, 1928.

Wit, Augusta de. "*Virginia Woolf*" [Virginia Woolf]. *Nieuwe Rotterdamsche Courant*, April 24, 1929.

——. "*Nieuwe Engelse Boeken,*" "*Boeken*" [New English Books, Books]. *Nieuwe Rotterdamsche Courant*, April 9, 1930.

Woolf, Virginia. *The Letters of Virginia Woolf. The Sickle Side of the Moon.* 1932-1935. Ed. Nigel Nicolson. Asst. Ed. Joanne Trautmann. London: The Hogarth Press, 1979.

Woolf, Virginia. *The Diary of Virginia Woolf.* Vol. 4. Ed. Anne Olivier Bell. London: The Hogarth Press, 1982.

Zeeman, Michaël. "*Lussen rond een denkbeeldige lijn. Het Schrijversleven van Virginia*" [Loops around an Imaginary Line. The Writer's Life of Virginia]. *De Volkskrant*, October 18, 1996.

Zonneveld, Peter van. "*Orlando*" [Orlando], "*Een Kamer voor Jezelf*" [A Room of One's Own] "*Flush*" [Flush]. *NRC-Handelsblad*, June 2, 1978.

Miyeko Kamiya's Reproduction of Modernist Writing Style: Kamiya, Virginia Woolf, and the Problem of the "Monstrous" Voice

Hogara Matsumoto

I Introduction

Miyeko Kamiya (1914-1979) is widely known in Japan as a person who demonstrated her versatility as a psychiatrist, a translator, an essayist, and a Virginia Woolf scholar. As a psychiatrist, Kamiya disinterestedly devoted herself to the good of the leprous patients in Japan's largest leprosarium, Nagashima Aiseien. As a multi-lingual with a good command of French, English, German, Greek, Latin, and Japanese, she translated Marcus Aurelius's *Meditations*, Michel Foucault's *The Birth of the Clinic: An Archaeology of Medical Perception* and his *Mental Illness and Psychology*, and Virginia Woolf's *A Writer's Diary,* edited by Woolf's husband, Leonard, into Japanese. As an essayist, Kamiya wrote essays on such various topics as humanity, family, and her experiences abroad. As a Woolf scholar, she left a scholarly achievement in Woolf studies by publishing a renowned paper, "Virginia Woolf: An Outline of a Study on her Personality, Illness and Work," originally written in English, in the Swiss journal *Confinia Psychiatrica* in 1965; her book written in Japanese, *Virginia Woolf Studies*, which contained further notes, professional articles, and experimental creative writing on Woolf's mental problems and works, came out posthumously in 1981 in Japan.

Kamiya's approach to the modernist woman writer Virginia Woolf is often regarded as entirely psychiatric; however, it embraces all of Kamiya's versatile talents. In fact, despite Quentin Bell's comment in *Virginia Woolf: A Biography* that the "Japanese psychiatrist Mme Miyeko Kamiya is, I believe, preparing a pathography of Virginia Woolf and this may enable us to know whether psychiatry could have helped her" (20), Kamiya herself defined her studies, to be collected in *Virginia Woolf Studies*, as an exploration of Woolf's "anthropographie" rather than "pathographie"; in other words, Kamiya intended her approach to be not merely a medical record or a doctor's diagnostic paper but a comprehensive examination of Woolf the writer from multiple points of view: Woolf's family background, personality build-up throughout her life, mental problems, and artistic creativity (*Virginia Woolf Studies* 138-139). This desire to embrace all aspects of Woolf can be seen in Kamiya's wish to complete her studies after the publication of all five volumes of Woolf's *Diaries* and six volumes of *Letters* since she considered the biographical materials produced by the novelist herself to be the most important sources for her "anthropographical" research. Regrettably, Kamiya passed away before the final three volumes of Woolf's *Diaries* and the last volume of the *Letters* came out. What is left to us, therefore, is only a part of Kamiya's study, academic papers and notes, in the form of "work in progress."

Interestingly, in addition to her scholarly work on Woolf, Kamiya also wrote the fictional "Virginia Woolf's Autobiography" ("VWA") written in the style of memoir, though the draft was left unfinished; although "VWA" is a fictional work, it is included in Kamiya's *Virginia Woolf Studies*. In writing "VWA," Kamiya referred to Bell's *Virginia Woolf: A Biography*, Woolf's *A Writer's Diary*, as well as her autobiographical writings such as "A Sketch of the Past," "Reminiscences," and "22 Hyde Park Gate" as well as the first two volumes of Woolf's *Diaries* and the first four volumes of the *Letters* mentioned above. At first glance, Kamiya's "VWA" seems to be just a summary or a rewrite of Woolf's biographical facts based on her diaries and memoirs, but a close examination reveals that it is actually a highly strange and enigmatic text. What we find in "VWA" are the problems inherent in translation and a dense, oscillating voice that reveals Kamiya's own "monstrous," conflicting selves as a psychiatrist, literary scholar, woman professional and wife, as well as Woolf's similar conflicts and her ambivalent feelings about her family and past including her traumatic sexual experiences. In short, the vacillating voice of "VWA" reflects Kamiya's strong will to understand and express Woolf's "madness" by identifying with Woolf's traumatic experiences under a tyrannical father, sexually abusive brothers, and authoritative doctors, while we can also find Kamiya's tendency to detach herself from Woolf, thereby making Woolf's first person narrative voice sound like that of a highly neurotic person who has neither a definite view of self nor a clear sense of past. This is especially true when we compare Kamiya's "VWA" with the autobiographical writings by Woolf. Kamiya's problematic "treatment" of Woolf's voice as that of a neurotic patient foregrounds not only her attitude to Woolf but also the problem of translation. By eventually showing that it was her mental illness that enabled Woolf to be an artistic writer and that a trace of "madness" lies within every person's mentality, Kamiya, in her interdisciplinary study, presents the unstable subjectivity that reflects her "monstrous' sense of self, Woolf's agonized voice, their social positions, and the gap between different cultures. If we consider the significance of the fluctuating subjectivity using Marianne DeKoven's idea of "the

The Problem of the "Monstrous" Voice

irreducible self-contradiction...of modernist form" (20) that suggests female modernists' fear about, and desire for, the revision of culture set forth in *Rich and Strange: Gender, History, Modernism*, we can view the oscillating voice in the light of literary criticism; through DeKoven's argument, the unstable voice found in the "translated," that is, figuratively interpreted, voice of "VWA" can be regarded as something close to Kamiya's unconscious yet modernistic manifestation of her complex "consciousness": anxiety and hesitation about pursuing a profession, fear of being considered as "unwomanly," and strong desire to produce brilliant achievements. The modernist subjectivity reproduced or disclosed in an odd manner in "VWA" suggests both Kamiya's ambivalent position and conflicted sentiment as a renowned psychiatrist and a woman trapped in the patriarchal system of Japanese society as well as Woolf's state of mind as a professional writer and a neurotic patient.

In what follows, I will first introduce the experiences that went into creating Kamiya's complex personality she herself called "monstrous": her international background, her young days that awakened her desire to become a professional psychiatrist, and the limitations she encountered in the conservative atmosphere of Japanese society. Then, I will touch on the problem of translation that non-native scholars inevitably face and emphasize the problem of the writing style inherent in the translation of the narrator's voice. Finally, I will examine Kamiya's "VWA" by comparing it with Woolf's autobiographical writings and other biographical materials. My analysis shall show that the vacillating voice found in "VWA" is closely associated with the problem of translation; in the process of translation and reproduction of Woolf's voice, I will argue, Kamiya's "monstrous" sense of self is translated into, yet not fully fused into, the ambivalent feelings of Virginia Woolf, thus evoking the ambivalent position of an elitist Japanese female psychiatrist who helped introduce Western culture into Japan.

II Kamiya's "Monstrous" Sense of Self

Throughout her life, Kamiya felt she existed between two worlds: between Japan and the West, between life as a professional and life as a woman. This sense of belonging to no man's land helped develop her complicated personality.

When Kamiya was nine years old, her family left Japan for Switzerland as her father was sent there by the Ministry of Foreign Affairs as a Japanese representative to the Board of International Labor Organization; her family resided in Geneva for three and a half years. What she encountered there was not only a conflict between Western culture and Japanese culture but also a conflict between her parents' expectation and what she desired to be. As a child, she lived under the pressure of the statement of Japanese governmental officials and her parents that her family members were "representatives of Japanese culture" and that they were supposed to behave themselves so as not to "disgrace the Japanese nation" (*Pilgrimage* 33, 36; *The Significance of Being* 79).[1] Repeatedly criticizing such nationalistic ideas prevalent in Japan's imperialistic age, Kamiya, later in her life, reflected on the influence of her childhood experience in a cross-cultural environment and her knowledge of the gulf between languages acquired therein:

> It is inevitable that my short stay in Switzerland left a profound impression on my mind and made me "un-Japanese-like," and that even now it is easiest for me to think, read, and write in French, and I am favorably inclined toward European culture. (*Pilgrimage* 59)

This sense of divide among her many different languages and her different cultures seems to have stayed with her her entire life. She emphasizes the importance of not being trapped in a particular system by assuming that it might be highly possible for "a person who perfectly fits in one system to stop thinking about what one's language consists of and what lies behind the language as if a spell were cast on one" (*Pilgrimage* 66). In other words, her school days in Switzerland and her college life in the United States led Kamiya to consciously evade being stuck in one system. This ability to stand apart from any one cultural system allowed her to cast a critical eye on both Japan and the West while at the same time it gave her a conflicted sense of self.[2]

In her twenties, a new source of conflict started to grow inside Kamiya; as a young Japanese woman, she was pressed to make a choice either to pursue a profession or to get married. It was when she was put in a sanatorium for treatment of her tuberculosis and was confronted with her own mortality that she finally made up her mind to pursue her career as a medical doctor because her doctor told her not to get married until she had turned thirty years old and time had proved that she had completely recovered from her illness (*The Significance of Being* 84). Yet the problem of marriage continued to put her in a difficult situation throughout her twenties. Although she was aware that marriage might prevent her from pursuing her career, she found that her "femininity"[3] attracted the attention of young men and that she was also attracted to some of them. The question of whether she should continue her studies or marry someone continued to torment Kamiya even after she started to attend medical school (*Diaries and Letters* 25); at the same time, she experienced another difficult situation. While she studied as a medical student, she found it difficult to suppress her desire to read literature and write literary

The Problem of the "Monstrous" Voice

works, a desire she had cherished since she was in Tsuda Women's College as an English major (*Diaries and Letters* 53-54; *Diaries of My Young Days* 119-120). Her dilemma persisted until she eagerly started writing essays and professional articles later in her life.

Kamiya eventually did marry but not until after she established her career as a psychiatrist. Though she had an understanding husband, Kamiya consistently sensed the tension between her wish to visit the leprosarium and her duty to stay home as a housewife and mother. As Virginia Woolf argued that it was necessary for a woman writer to kill the cult of Victorian womanhood, "the Angel in the House" (Woolf, "Professions for Women," *CE2* 286), similarly Kamiya had to deal with her "calling" as a psychiatrist and the duties assigned to Japanese women in a patriarchal society (*Diaries and Letters* 126-127).

Reflecting on the conflict between her desire to pursue a career and the immense pressure of Japanese society, Kamiya analyzed her own mentality as "divided" (*Diaries and Letters* 51) or even "schizophrenic" (*Diaries and Letters* 70). Accordingly, the stress of bearing the tension between these two different spheres made her think of herself as not only complex but also "monstrous"; Kamiya wrote in her diary on March 2, 1944:

> I can concentrate on my study these days. At the same time, my mind is dominated by an impulse to create something of my own inside myself. I shall be drained of my energy by what I have learned so far, what I will learn from now on, and everything I learn. As long as I was born into the world as a "monster" as well as a woman, it should be natural to demonstrate my own peculiarity. I do not need to imitate men, nor do I need to imitate women. But still, I do not need to content myself with behaving as someone who has no sex. I shall be myself, so far as circumstances permit. I shall burn with my feminine sentiment, masculine intellect, and cowardice. Who cares if I do. It is all myself: an active, haughty high school girl possessed by an appetite for knowledge; a pietistic, timid being detached from secular affairs in my years of illness and recuperation; and a realistic, hard-working medical student, who was at the same time attracted to literary expression. (*Diaries and Letters* 51)

Kamiya's "monstrous" sense of self, in short, suggests her divided yearning for two different worlds: man's world and woman's world, masculine intellect and feminine sentiment, and medicine and literature. It may be possible to conclude, then, that her sense of "monstrosity" can be construed as relating to the image of "female monster" discussed in Sandra M. Gilbert and Susan Gubar's *The Madwoman in the Attic: The Woman Writer and the Nineteenth-Century Literary Imagination*. Kamiya, who was familiar with such Greek mythological figures as Medusa and Circe, might have internalized the image of "female monster" that is represented in the writings of male authors as the aggressive Other demanding their autonomy and desire (Gilbert and Gubar 34-35). Her "monstrosity," however, should not be considered as merely a manifestation of her deviation from society's norms; it also represents her duality or "hybridity" as "a radical heterogeneity" that involves "fusion, the creation of a new form" (25) defined by Robert J. C. Young or "otherness" as "productive ambivalence" defined by Homi Bhabha that "enables a transgression of [the] limits from the space of that otherness" (38). In short, the oscillating, dual identity that contains a sense of "otherness" suggests a newer sense of subjectivity that is not trapped in one system and, therefore, may be capable of presenting a counter-narrative to the dominant culture and expressing an undiscovered aspect of Kamiya.

Kamiya's dual sense of self resembles Virginia Woolf's ambiguous position bordering on the boundary between an upper-middle class woman belonging to a group of elitist intellectuals called the Bloomsbury Group and a rebellious feminist who wrote *A Room of One's Own* and *Three Guineas*, between her sense of identity as a professional woman writer and her ambivalent sense of yearning for the Victorian "Angel in the House" expressed in "Professions for Women," and between a sense of sympathy toward the people of other races and classes and a sense of fear or contempt toward them.[4]

Kamiya's conflicted desires and Woolf's ambivalent position argued above are strangely reflected in the fluctuating narrative voice observed in Kamiya's "VWA." Yet before analyzing "VWA," I will discuss the problem of translation; as Kamiya experiences a sense of "discrepancy" between two different languages, translation cannot be a transparent process to express something in a different language or to simply change something from one language to another. Woolf's use of the "stream of consciousness" technique, that is a notable characteristic of her modernist writing style, also makes the translation of her writings especially problematic. As Makiko Minow-Pinkney, in her brilliant *Virginia Woolf and the Problem of the Subject*, argues that the "stream of consciousness" technique "allows the novelist's discourse to move from a character's interior world to the exterior world (or vice versa) in a homogeneous medium, which produces a continuous indeterminacy" (*Virginia Woolf* 54-55), and as Ban Wang discusses that Woolf's "stream of consciousness" technique shows "the ways in which consciousness, or various forms of subjectivity of characters...are constructed in language, discourse, systems of signification" (Wang 178) rather than representing an individual character's private consciousness as private and "autonomous" (Wang 177), in Woolf's writing, the importance of the voice or the writing style cannot be overemphasized because the narrator's voice always interplays with the consciousness of other characters or social, political, and linguistic forces from within or with-

The Problem of the "Monstrous" Voice

out. In short, the medium of translation, including the translation of the voice or the writing style, is another factor that makes the voice of "VWA" embrace otherness.

III Japan and the Problem of Translation[5]

In her "Reading, Misreading and Virginia Woolf's Voice," Makiko Minow-Pinkney rightly asserts that "the anxiety of the language of modernity and the anxiety of translation perfectly coincide in Japan" ("Reading" 111). As Minow-Pinkney suggests, Japan has attempted to construct a modern self since the end of the nineteenth century, and for Japan, translation of Western texts and ideas was an important way to achieve modernity. That is why the concept and quality of translation have been eagerly discussed in Japan. What is significant in Minow-Pinkney's paper is that she discusses the problem of translation by claiming that it is "interpretation" and is even "misreading" in many cases, showing that translation is a site where the concept of Derridean *différance* is at work. Therefore, as Minow-Pinkney concludes, a Virginia Woolf translated into Japanese is "an offspring of the marriage of two radically different languages and cultures, resembling both and yet different from both: a reproduction with a difference, with the power to grow and speak on its own" (115). If Minow-Pinkney's argument is correct, "VWA" can be considered as a newly reproduced offspring of Kamiya, the cosmopolitan Japanese scholar, and the original English Virginia Woolf text. However, here we have to emphasize a point Minow-Pinkney does not mention in her paper. It is true that translation is a difficult and problematic process because two different languages and the desires of two different writers (the original author and the translator) are negotiated and interplayed in the text; yet what makes the translation of Woolf's works still more difficult is that her writing style is especially unique due to her adoption of "stream of consciousness" technique in her autobiographical writings and diaries as well as novels. An analysis of the writing style designed by the translator is highly important because it reveals how the translator interprets the original text.

A similar problem of translation can be observed in Arthur Waley's translation of Lady Murasaki's *The Tale of Genji* (1925). It is a well-known fact that Virginia Woolf had a close relationship with Waley, a British orientalist, as E. M. Forster had introduced him to the members of the Bloomsbury Group (Rosenbaum 319); also well-known is the rising European interest, especially modernists' interest, in Japanese arts during the first two decades of the twentieth century, as, for example, William Butler Yeats and Ezra Pound were profoundly influenced by an American orientalist Ernest Fenollosa's works on such Japanese arts as Noh theater.[6] Woolf read Waley's translation of *The Tale of Genji* and wrote a book review of the Japanese eleventh-century novel for *Vogue* in 1925. Also, Woolf scholars might be familiar with Woolf's references to Lady Murasaki in "Women and Fiction" and *A Room of One's Own* and her assessment of Lady Murasaki as a "great figure from the past" (*AROO* 104) that woman writers should think back through.[7] In fact Catherine Nelson-McDermott discusses the possible influence Lady Murasaki's *The Tale of Genji* might have had on Woolf's *Orlando: A Biography*, focusing on the problems of gender and sexuality in both texts. More important for my argument, however, is the fact that the Bloomsbury Group members, highly influential intellectuals who received the modernist works of James Joyce and Marcel Proust with applause, played a vital role in the reception of *The Tale of Genji*. As a result, the British public assumed that *The Tale of Genji*, *Ulysses*, and *A la recherche du temps perdu* represented "a new kind of literature that shared similar literary values"[8] (Nakamura 27), that is to say, those of literary modernism. According to Nakamura, Waley's writing style in his translation of *The Tale of Genji* was "intellectual and elegant," evoking an image of "Proustian" writing style in the reader (28). It is also noteworthy that Waley, in his preface to *The Tale of Genji*, remarks that Amy Lowell, a leading imagist and modernist poet, wrote the introduction to the *Diaries of Court Ladies of Old Japan*, which contains the diary of Lady Murasaki. In other words, modernist writers and Bloomsbury Group members were deeply involved in the reception of Japanese eleventh-century woman's writings.

Their interest in Lady Murasaki's writing indicates their high estimation of her stylistic technique as well. Waley's style, Nakamura argues, was intentionally adopted in order to subtly reveal the motive and strategy of the new literary movement: first, it was an attempt to shed light on the depth of human psychology; secondly, it aimed at reviving a sophisticated taste for aestheticism; thirdly, it acknowledged and stressed the importance of a sense of time; and lastly, it attempted to capture the public interest in a fashionable society (28). What is important here is that through the process of translation the voice of the author, the intention of the translator, and even the ideas of the translator's contemporaries emerge. In other words, translation, again, is not "a word-by-word rendering of the source text" (Reinhold 10), nor is it a process to express something in a different language in a simple manner. Translation, in short, should be regarded as transformation of the source text in terms of a target language and culture with the effect comparable to that in the source culture and language; the process of translation, that inevitably produces a dual voice, needs to be historicized. In analyzing the translated text, we have to pay close

The Problem of the "Monstrous" Voice

attention not only to the words the translator chooses to use but also to the writing style the translator develops.

Seen in this light, we can say that the narrative voice and the writing style of Kamiya's "VWA" deserve most careful attention. "VWA" is a product created out of Kamiya's examination of Virginia Woolf's autobiographical writings, *A Writer's Diary*, and Bell's *Virginia Woolf: A Biography*. "VWA," a text written in Japanese, therefore should make use of the process of literal translation and figurative interpretation from several different perspectives: language, psychiatry, Kamiya's "monstrous" sense of self acquired out of her life bordering on the boundaries between two different worlds, and her understanding and diagnosis of Woolf's mentally traumatized life.

IV Kamiya's "Virginia Woolf's Autobiography": the Monstrous Voice and Modernism

We will begin our discussion by referring to previous Woolf studies that touch on Woolf and Kamiya. Two scholars have discussed the relationship between Virginia Woolf and Miyeko Kamiya, and both of them take up "Virginia Woolf's Autobiography" as an important text. Sei Kosugi, in "Woolf and Psychiatry: In Relation to Miyeko Kamiya and M. Foucault," argues that "notions of madness that Kamiya acquired in the process of reading and translating Foucault are reflected in her Woolf studies, which expounds the integrity and creativity of the world of madness" (14). Here Kamiya is considered to have performed a humanistic reading of Foucault, and consequently in Kosugi's reading, "VWA" is construed as an attempt to "reconstruct the pathological world of patients as an organic whole through the eyes of the patients themselves" (14). While Kosugi thus treats "VWA" as an aesthetic reproduction of the "mad" yet artistic mind of the patient by stressing the influence translating Foucault's works had on Kamiya, Masami Usui, in "Miyeko Kamiya's Encounter with Virginia Woolf: A Japanese Woman Psychiatrist's Waves of Her Own," presents a biographical and feminist reading of "VWA" by emphasizing the similarities behind the two women's painful life experiences and motives of their writings. What is illuminating in Usui's argument is that she argues that Kamiya, out of her empathy with Woolf, "recreat[es] Woolf's voice as a victim of sexual abuse" (4) by manipulatively evoking a sense of anger in the voice of "the narrative I" so that the narration would "articulate the core of Woolf's trauma" (7). Usui also claims that Kamiya "encod[es] Woolf's lesbian tendencies, mental breakdown, and creativity" (10) in "VWA," mentioning the presence of a young woman with "schizo-affective psychoses" who probably desired Kamiya as a lover and who showed an exceptional artistic talent.

Both scholars' readings are fruitful, uncovering a new aspect to Kamiya's work and thereby suggesting a reconsideration of Woolf's works in a new light. My aim in this article, however, is to show that Kamiya creates a monstrous, dual voice and consequently develops a strange writing style in "VWA." Close attention to her writing technique shall betray Kamiya's twofold attitudes, that is, her oscillation between her "empathy" with Woolf (as Usui suggests) and her detachment from Woolf.

The most striking difference between Kamiya's "VWA" and Woolf's autobiographical writing is that the mode of writing of "VWA" is quite prosaic whereas the narrator of "A Sketch of the Past" delineates her memories of the past in a poetic, impressionistic manner, displaying keen and delicate senses of sight and hearing that also awaken the reader's sense of aesthetic perception. This dissimilarity naturally leads to the pronounced difference in the narrators' voices. When Woolf says in the essay that her memories are "sensual" and therefore entice her into "ecstasy" and "rapture," her sense of self seems to be embedded in the beautiful scenes of her childhood memories:

> But to fix my mind upon the nursery—it had a balcony; there was a partition,...The quality of the air above Talland House seemed to suspend sound, to let it sink down slowly as if it were caught in a blue gummy veil. The rooks cawing is part of the waves breaking—one, two, one, two—and the splash as the wave drew back and then it gathered again, and I lay there half awake, half asleep, drawing in such ecstasy as I cannot describe. (*MOB* 65-66)

In the narrative "I" in "such ecstasy as I cannot describe," Woolf's past sense of self and her present sense of self merge. In other words, the past sense of "ecstasy" is revived and rejuvenated in the present sense of the narrator. Of course, the momentary unification of the past rapture and the sensation of the present might be invented as part of the narrator's illusion since "her memories may have been reworked because memory is not reliably objective in anyone," as Thomas C. Caramagno remarks in his discussion of "A Sketch of the Past" (140). What is important here, however, is that Woolf depicts vivid memories of her childhood and also makes the narrator of the essay relive the past memories once again, thus uniting the present moment and the past.

In "VWA," in contrast, the past experiences of the narrator are oddly detached from the narrator. For example, the past events are narrated from the past viewpoint. When the narrator writes about the letters her brother Thoby sent from Cambridge, she talks about a friendship he was building up with Lytton Strachey and Saxon Sydney-Turner. Then she introduces Leonard Woolf, a man who becomes her husband later, thus: "There was a certain

The Problem of the "Monstrous" Voice

Woolf, a strange man with brilliant brain" (*Virginia Woolf Studies* 60-61). It is questionable as to why the narrator separates the past from the present so strictly even though she may be looking at Thoby's old letters while writing her autobiography. What is more, her past experiences are often described as stories told by her family or episodes the narrator finds in her own diary but actually does not remember. In short, the narrator is alienated from them, and her voice and writing style un-color the experiences. For instance, the narrator writes, "I had not been allowed to study since November, 1896, but I recovered gradually; *my diary says* that I started to study history and German in February, 1898, and 'a little Greek' in March, by permission of Dr. Seton" (*Virginia Woolf Studies* 55; italics mine). In "VWA" Kamiya generally makes the narrator's memory vague especially before, during, and after her mental breakdown (*Virginia Woolf Studies* 52, 66). This may be understandable if such descriptions are adopted due to her advanced knowledge of mental illness as a psychiatrist, as she states in "Notes on Virginia Woolf's Pathography" that "it is quite normal for a patient not to remember things that happened while her/his mental illness was progressing fast" (*Virginia Woolf Studies* 201). Kamiya, however, makes the narrator's memory unclear even in referring to the events that happened while the narrator was in good health:

> The next year, in 1899, I started to keep a diary again when I visited Warboys parsonage in Huntingdonshire in the neighborhood of my Stephen cousin. This time I wrote my diary using a pen with a fine point and in a meandering manner so that it might be illegible to anyone. Also I *appear to have attempted* to deceive others by pasting pages of my diary on the leaves of Watts' *The Right Use of Reason*. (*Virginia Woolf Studies* 89; emphasis added)

According to Kamiya's narrative above, the narrator does not remember the episode well. True, one does not remember one's teens completely, but Woolf's own description of the episode firmly contradicts Kamiya's way of narrating the story. Woolf's version of the same episode goes like this:

> A sudden idea struck me, that it would be original useful & full of memories if I embedded the foregoing pages in the leaves of some worthy & ancient work, the like of which might I knew be bought at St Ives old Curiosity Shop for the sum of 3d. So one day a week or two ago, A. & I drove over there; & demanded old books;...(*PA* 159)

Clearly Woolf has a vivid memory of the episode; as seen in her other autobiographical writings, her sensation and enhanced consciousness brighten and even speed up the narration. Compared with Woolf's own voice and writing style, it is obvious that Kamiya intentionally manipulates the narration of "VWA" and makes the narrator lose her memories of the past events irrespective of the fact whether they happened during her mental illness, or in her healthy state of mind. Moreover, as the narrator's vague sense of memory persists throughout the text, it produces another effect; that is, the narrator's voice and subjectivity start looking somewhat indefinite and unreliable.

Through Kamiya's repression of the narrator's memory, the narrative voice becomes not only obscure but also neurotic. In referring to Woolf's mental illness, Kamiya tends to use strong words. At the very end of "VWA," the narrator describes how she felt when her father, Sir Leslie Stephen, died:

> In my sorrow was a deep sense of irritation as well as a sense of guilt. My brothers and sister looked too carefree, and the letters of condolence made me angry because they seemed to miss the point. I felt I was all alone and arrested by a sense of fear. I kept on writing to prove that I didn't go mad again, but I may have been mad already then. (*Virginia Woolf Studies* 66)

It is true that "VWA" was left unfinished by Kamiya, but such an ending conveys the impression that the narrator is "mad." In addition to her amnesiac "symptoms," here the narrative "I" admits and declares that she may have been "mad." In referring to her own mental problem, Woolf uses the word "mad" twice in *A Writer's Diary*, but in her autobiographical essays she only uses the word "mad" when she talks about her cousin Jim Stephen. In short, Woolf usually does not mention her "madness" in public writings. It is, therefore, unmistakable that Kamiya the author makes the narrator of "VWA" a neurotic patient rather than a person who has a definite sense of her past and present self.

The ending quoted above certainly reflects Kamiya's view of Woolf as a patient who suffered from mental illness. Here it may be necessary to ascertain precisely how Kamiya analyzed Woolf's illness. In the concluding part of "Virginia Woolf: An Outline of a Study on her Personality, Illness and Work," Kamiya arrives at a diagnosis:

> Unmistakably the course of the illness and its general structure indicate it [her illness] to be manic-depressive psychosis. But we cannot overlook the schizoid and schizophrenic elements both in the personality and the illness, above all the "Präcoxgefühl" that emanates from her whole being, especially her persistent sense of living in "glass-walled room" alone and unable to have real communication with others, as is often expressed in her diary. (Kamiya, "Virginia Woolf" 200)

Kamiya clearly sees Woolf as manic-depressive and also schizophrenic; however, I'm not saying that Kamiya, like the authoritative doctor of the Bradshaw type in *Mrs. Dalloway*, suppresses the voice and subjectivity of her patient in the text and makes Woolf an invalid. As Usui points out, due to

The Problem of the "Monstrous" Voice

Kamiya's empathy for Woolf's mental problem as the source of her creativity, Kamiya's original motive should have lain in shedding a new light on how a patient's mind works to create a work of art (2). Also, Kamiya is known as a "humanistic" psychiatrist as Kosugi rightly suggests (14). Yet, as I have discussed above, a peculiar writing mode shaped by Kamiya makes the narrator amnesic, and consequently, the narrative voice of "VWA" is made somewhat neurotic. The narrator's loss of memory and her neurotic voice, I argue, represent a unsettling subjectivity of the narrative "I"; just like Kamiya's own "monstrous" sense of self, in the unstable subjectivity is embraced Kamiya's empathy with Woolf's traumatic experiences as woman and patient, Kamiya the doctor's diagnosis of Woolf's illness, and Kamiya's attempt to revive Woolf's voice.

The writing style and the narrator's voice adopted by Kamiya might be close to what Marianne DeKoven discusses in *Rich and Strange* as "the aesthetic of *sous-rature*—the unsynthesized dialectic or unresolved contradiction that characterizes modernist form" (25, italics DeKoven's). In this book DeKoven rightly stresses the intersection of "social scope" and "aesthetic stature" in modernism, that is, "unresolved contradiction" between political radicalism and aesthetic interest in modernist form (19), building on the arguments of Luce Irigaray and Jacques Derrida. In her argument of "rich and strange" characteristics of modernist writing, DeKoven maintains that female modernists' writing generates "self-contradiction" (20), namely, a conflicted tension between their desire for the revision of the male-dominated social systems and their fear that they might be punished for possessing such a dangerous desire. More interestingly, according to DeKoven, such modernist writing style is very well practiced in the representations of "pathologically unreliable first-person narrative"; DeKoven cites, for example, Charlotte Perkins Gilman's "The Yellow Wallpaper" and Woolf's *The Voyage Out* in which the "rich and strange" representation of the South American jungle is closely associated with the deranged vision of feverish heroine Rachel. In both texts, the heroines, swamped by the tension between matrimonial institutions of the patriarchal society and their own desire to escape from it, fall into a subconscious, dream-like vision; the vision is narrated in a modernist style, that is, ambiguously and disruptively, evoking a "rich and strange" atmosphere.

Then, not only the neurotic voice of the narrator but also the conflictual oscillation observed in the writing style in Kamiya's "VWA" can be regarded as a modernistic manifestation of how Kamiya's "monstrosity" and Woolf's rebellious yet anxious subjectivity resonate; in "VWA" Kamiya and Woolf's political motives and their aesthetic practices are certainly interconnected in a complex, "rich and strange" way. In Kamiya's reproduction of Woolf's modernist mode of writing, that is, the narrative 'I''s oscillating voice, we can see how the modernist writing style is figuratively transmitted from Woolf to Kamiya through their similarities: their pride as professionals, their critical, rebellious attitudes toward the conservative, patriarchal social systems, and their willingness to strive persistently to cross the border between countries, genders, and professions. The unstable voice and subjectivity found in "VWA" suggest that the problems Woolf faced are still unsolved and of critical importance in contemporary Japan, and that the making of the complex subjectivity of this Japanese female intellectual, in terms of her academic interest in the English woman writer, the constraints imposed on women, and the social prejudices roused against the women who transgress the socially accepted feminine propriety, needs to be historicized, as a textual practice, through the examination of her works as well as her life. In short, the possibility of modernist writing style can be reconsidered in a newer, different light in a foreign land.

V Conclusion

In summary, Miyeko Kamiya's "Virginia Woolf's Autobiography" is a highly problematic text that suggests the problems of gender, translation, and literary criticism. In Kamiya's "VWA," we can find a vacillating voice that reveals Kamiya's conflicted, "monstrous" sense of self and desire as a professional psychiatrist and a Japanese woman in a patriarchal society, as well as Kamiya's "empathy" with Woolf's experiences as a modernist professional writer, a woman, and a patient suffering from mental illness. The oscillating voice in "VWA" also reflects Kamiya's treatment of Woolf as a psychiatrist, as well as Kamiya's will to identify with Woolf. In other words, through her psychiatric analysis and the process of translation that inevitably produces differences from the original text, Kamiya makes the voice or the writing style of the narrator sound like that of a neurotic patient who does not have a definite sense of self or a clear sense of the past. This ambivalence in the unstable voice of "VWA" can be construed as Kamiya's reproduction of Woolf's modernistic, vacillating writing style when we refer to Marianne DeKoven's argument of the "unresolved contradictoriness" (21) in modernist form that unveils female modernists' desire for radical social change and their fear about punishment for possessing such dangerous desire. The modernist writing style in "VWA," created out of Kamiya's ambivalence, in short, may disclose a complicit, textual relationship between the two female writers, who possess a sense of Otherness.

The Problem of the "Monstrous" Voice
Notes

[1] All English translations of Kamiya's works which were originally written in Japanese are mine.

[2] In her diary on March 10, 1939, Kamiya criticizes the "idealistic" aspect, "easygoing atmosphere," and material comfort of American society (*Diaries and Letters* 8).

[3] Ota discusses "feminine" aspects of Kamiya and their relation to her "monstrosity" by citing examples from Kamiya's memos.

[4] For Woolf's representation of other classes see Endo; for her representation of other races, see Matsumoto.

[5] In this section I will mainly discuss the problem of translation associated with the Japanese texts; however, recently Woolf scholars have pointed out that Virginia Woolf was actually interested in, and even influenced by, the problem of translation. For example, Natalya Reinhold argues that encountering "cultural Otherness," especially through Russian writers by experiencing the process of translation, had a profound effect on her writing practice and her strategy as a modernist writer.

[6] For further discussion on Fenollosa's influence on W. B. Yeats and Ezra Pound, see Miyake.

[7] Woolf refers to Lady Murasaki as a precursor of the woman writer; however, it is a mistake to think of Lady Murasaki's presence in eleventh-century Japan as a proof that Japanese women were powerful figures then, or Japan was a liberal country. In reality the ladies-in-waiting at Mikado's (Emperor's) court had no way but to find favor with Mikado or other powerful lords; moreover, a sophisticated literary sense required of the ladies at court was acquired to help them send love poems to the lords and win their favor. For further information on *Tale of Genji*, see Nakamura.

[8] All English translations of Nakamura's work in Japanese are mine.

Works Cited

Bhabha, Homi. "The Other Question." *Contemporary Postcolonial Theory: A Reader.* Ed. Padmini Mongia. London: Arnold, 1997.

Caramagno, Thomas C. *The Flight of the Mind: Virginia Woolf's Art and Manic Depressive Illness.* Berkeley: U of California P, 1992.

DeKoven, Marianne. *Rich and Strange: Gender, History, Modernism.* Princeton: Princeton UP, 1991.

Endo, Fuhito. "'Are we not all prisoners?': Pastoral as Allegory in *Mrs. Dalloway.*" *The Journal of Social Sciences and Humanities* [Jinbun Gakuho] No. 302. Tokyo: Tokyo Metropolitan University. (1999): 43-89.

Gilbert, Sandra M. and Susan Gubar. *The Madwoman in the Attic: The Woman Writer and the Nineteenth-Century Literary Imagination.* New Haven: Yale UP, 1979.

Kamiya, Miyeko. *Diaries and Letters* [*Nikki/Shokanshu*]. 1982. Vol. 10 of *A Collection of Kamiya Miyeko's Works* [*Kamiya Miyeko Chosaku-shu*]. Tokyo: Misuzu, 1996.

———. *Diaries of My Young Days* [*Wakaki-hi no Nikki*]. 1984. Supplementary Vol. [Hokan] of *A Collection of Kamiya Miyeko's Works.* Tokyo: Misuzu, 1996.

———. *Pilgrimage* [*Henreki*]. 1980. Vol. 9 of *A Collection of Kamiya Miyeko's Works.*

Tokyo: Misuzu, 1996.

———. *The Significance of Being [Sonzai no Omomi]: A Collection of Essays, 1971 1979.* 1981. Vol. 6 of *A Collection of Kamiya Miyeko's Works.* Tokyo: Misuzu, 1996.

———. "Virginia Woolf: An Outline of a Study on her Personality, Illness and Work." *Confinia Psychiatrica* 8 (1965): 189-205.

———. *Virginia Woolf Studies [Vajinia Urufu Kenkyu].* 1981. Vol. 4 of *A Collection of Kamiya Miyeko's Works.* Tokyo: Misuzu, 1990.

Kosugi, Sei. "Woolf and Psychiatry: In Relation to Miyeko Kamiya and M. Foucault." *Virginia Woolf Review* 15 (1998): 1-15.

Matsumoto, Hogara. "Mrs. Manresa and *Between the Acts*: Woolf's Figurative Use of Race." *Virginia Woolf Review* 15 (1998): 44-58.

Minow-Pinkney, Makiko. "Reading, Misreading and Virginia Woolf's Voice." *Re: Reading, Re: Writing, Re: Teaching Virginia Woolf: Selected Papers from The Fourth Annual Conference on Virginia Woolf.* Eds. Eileen Barrett and Patricia Cramer. New York: Pace UP, 1995. 108-115.

———. *Virginia Woolf and the Problem of the Subject.* New Brunswick: Rutgers UP, 1987.

Miyake, Akiko, ed. *A Guide to Ezra Pound and Ernest Fenollosa's Classic Noh Theater of Japan.* Orono: The National Poetry Foundation, 1994.

Lady Murasaki. *The Tale of Genji.* Trans. Arthur Waley. Boston: Houghton Mifflin Company, 1925.

Nakamura, Shinichiro. *The World of* The Tale of Genji *[Genji Monogatari no Sekai].* Tokyo: Shincho-sha, 1968.

Nelson-McDermott, Catherine. "Virginia Woolf and Murasaki Shikibu: A Question of Perception." *Virginia Woolf Miscellanies: Proceedings of the First Annual Conference on Virginia Woolf.* New York: Pace UP, 1992. 133-144.

Ota, Yuzo. *Starting from a Sense of Loss [Soshitsu kara no Shuppatsu].* Tokyo: Iwanami Shoten, 2001.

Reinhold, Natalya. "Virginia Woolf's Russian Voyage Out." *Woolf Studies Annual* 9 (2003): 1-27.

Rosenbaum, S. P., ed. *The Bloomsbury Group: A Collection of Memoirs and Commentary.* Toronto: U of Toronto P, 1995.

Usui, Masami. "Miyeko Kamiya's Encounter with Virginia Woolf: A Japanese Woman Psychiatrist's Waves of Her Own." *Doshisha Literature: A Journal of English Literature and Philology* 43 (2000): 1-26.

Wang, Ban. "'I' on the Run: Crisis of Identity in *Mrs. Dalloway*." *Modern Fiction Studies* 38, 1 (Spring 1992): 177-191.

Woolf, Virginia. *Collected Essays.* Ed. Leonard Woolf. 4 vols. London: The Hogarth Press, 1966-1967.

———. *Moments of Being.* Ed. Jeanne Schulkind. San Diego: Harcourt, 1985.

———. *A Passionate Apprentice. The Early Journals: 1897-1909.* San Diego: Harcourt, 1990.

———. *A Room of One's Own.* San Diego: Harcourt, 1981.

Young, Robert J. C. *Colonial Desire: Hybridity in Theory, Culture and Race.* London: Routledge, 1995.

III

Orlando on an International Stage

Orlando and Literary Tradition in Japan: Sex Change, Dressing and Gender in *Torikaebaya Monogatari*

Noriko Kubota

To the Japanese reading public, Virginia Woolf has been a fascinating novelist for over seventy years, and *Orlando* has a long history of reception in Japan as her first work translated into Japanese. Various aspects of the literary tradition in Japan can be clarified when we consider the publication of *Orlando* in Japanese in 1931. The purpose of this paper is to draw a possible comparison between *Orlando* and *Torikaebaya Monogatari*, a Japanese classical novel written in the twelfth century, and to reconsider the literary tradition in Japan, which corresponded with *Orlando* both covertly and overtly.

Before considering this in detail, I would like to survey the overall situation of Virginia Woolf's work translated into Japanese. Woolf is one of the few novelists whose works are readily translated into Japanese. Except for *The Voyage Out*, all of Woolf's novels have been translated in Japan for more than seven decades. In addition to her novels, some of her essays, as well as *Moments of Being*, have been translated. The latest translation of Woolf's work is her collection of essays entitled "yamai ni tsuite" (*On Being Ill*), which was translated by Shizuko Kawamoto and published in December, 2002. Her biographical and dramatic works *Flush* and *Freshwater* are also translated into Japanese.

Another remarkable feature concerning the translation of Woolf is that some of her works have been translated several times by various translators of different generations (Table 1). The subtle and delicate style of Woolf's writing attracted many translators to transplant her exquisite writing into the equivalent style of Japanese. Japanese is a language with varied modes of style and enormous quantities of vocabulary, so it is thought to be suitable to express a "spontaneous flow" of feelings and an inner state of mind. Among Woolf's novels, *Mrs. Dalloway* lends itself most to translation: it has been translated six times by six translators over the past fifty years. It is surprising that after the first translation of *Mrs. Dalloway* was published in 1954, five other Japanese translations of this novel succeeded one another in the next few decades. *To the Lighthouse* was translated four times by different people from 1949 to 1977. There are three translations of *The Waves*. Even the essay genre has featured conspicuously: *A Room of One's Own* has been translated three times over six decades.

Title	Year of Publication	Translator	Publisher
Night and Day	1977	Noriko Kamei	Misuzu Shobo
Jacob's Room	1977	Keiko Izubuchi	Misuzu Shobo
Mrs Dalloway	1954	Minoru Osawa	Mikasa Shobo
Mrs Dalloway	1955	Akira Tomita	Kadokawa Shoten
Mrs Dalloway	1956	Ichiro Ando	Kawade Shobo
Mrs Dalloway	1974	Akira Osawa	Kodansha
Mrs Dalloway	1976	Ineko Kondo	Misuzu Shobo
Mrs Dalloway	1998	Ai tanji	Shueisha
To the Lighthouse	1949	Minoru Osawa	Ondori-sha
To the Lighthouse	1956	Sakiko Nakamura	Shincho-sha
To the Lighthouse	1976	Chise Ibuki	Misuzu Shobo
To the Lighthouse	1977	Tadamasa Ito	Kaimei Shoin
Orlando	1931	Masanobu Oda	Shun-yun-do
Orlando	1983	Yoko Sugiyama	Kokusho-Kankohkai
Orlando	2000	Shizuko Kawamoto	Misuzu Shobo
The Waves	1943	Yukio Suzuki	Shonan Shobo
The Waves	1953	Minoru Osawa	Kawade Shobo
The Waves	1976	Shizuko Kawamoto	Misuzu Shobo
The Years	1958	Minoru Osawa	Mikasa Shobo
Between the Acts	1977	Yayoi Toyama	Misuzu Shobo
Flush	1979	Keiko Izubuchi	Misuzu Shogakukan
Freshwater	1992	Toshio Nakajima	Kobian Shobo
A Room of One's Own	1940	Ichiro Ando and Masami Nishikawa	Aoki Shoten
A Room of One's Own	1984	Kayoko Muramatsu	Shokado
A Room of One's Own	1988	Shizuko Kawamoto	Misuzu Shobo

Table 1: A List of Publication of Virginia Woolf's Major Works Translated into Japanese

Orlando has been translated into Japanese by three different translators so far, and it is worthy of note that *Orlando* was the first full-length translation into Japanese among all Woolf's works. It was published in 1931, only three years after the publication of the original work. This is an interesting fact, as the other novels of Virginia Woolf were not introduced into Japanese until after her death, although the "Time Passes" section of *To the Lighthouse* and some of her short stories were translated during her lifetime. The second of Woolf's novels to be translated was *The Waves*, which was translated by Yukio Suzuki in 1943. Thus, it can be said that *Orlando* was translated in Japan at an outstandingly early date. Moreover, another interesting matter is that it was chosen

Orlando and Literary Tradition in Japan

as the first work of Woolf's to be translated into Japanese in a situation where many reviewers treated it as *jeu d'esprit*, and the Japanese translator himself recognized that *Mrs. Dalloway* and *To the Lighthouse* were "so far the most renowned ones among Mrs. Woolf's numerous works" (Oda 4; my translation).

One possible reason for *Orlando*'s early translation could have been an interesting literary trend in Japan: there has been a literary tradition of sex change, though it seems to be somewhat latent. The climax of the story in *Orlando*—the sex change of the hero—was not, therefore, such an unusual or rare story for the Japanese reading public. An example of this tradition of sex change is to be found in *Torikaebaya Monogatari*, which is one of the earliest Japanese novels, published in the twelfth century. After the modernization of Japan in the 1860s, and especially from the end of the nineteenth century onwards, a lot of classics of Japanese literature written in the eleventh and twelfth centuries began to be published, among them *Torikaebaya Monogatari*.

Year of Publication	Editor/translator and Publisher
1890	Takejiro Noguchi ed. Tokyo: Hakubunkan.
1891	Kokubun Jiten Series. Soshi Omiya ed. Tokyo: Hakubunkan.
1903	Katsura Maruoka and Daisaburo Matsushita eds. Tokyo: Itakuraya shobo.
1909	Katsura Maruoka and Daisaburo Matsushita eds. Tokyo: Meibunsha.
1914	Yoshikata Ikebe ed. Tokyo: Hakubunkan.
1925	Yoshinori Yoshizawa tr. Tokyo: Ochobungakusosho kankokai.
1925	Kochu Nihon Bungaku Taikei Series. Kokumintosho kabushikigaisha ed. Tokyo: Kokumintosho.
1929	Kokubungaku Chushaku Sosho Series. Shinobu Orikuchi ed. Tokyo: Meichokankokai.
1929	Taneo Sasakawa ed. Tokyo: Hakubunkan.
1937	Gendaigoyaku Kokubungaku Zenshu Series. Yasunari Kawabata tr.Tokyo: Hibonsha.
1947	Koten Hakkutsu Series. Hideo Odagiri ed. Toyko: Shinzenbisha.
1960	Koten Nihon Bungaku Zenshu Series. modern translation. Tokyo: Chikuma Shobo.
1960	Shukusatu Nihon Bungaku Zenshu. modern translation. Tokyo: Nihon Shuhosh.
1971	Torikaebaya Monogatari. Tokyo: Shintensha.
1972	Shin-ichiro Nakamura tr. Tokyo: Kawade Shoboshinsh.
1976	Eiichi Mitani ed. Tokyo: Kadokawa Shoten.
1978	Hiroshi Kuwabara ed. modern translation. Tokyo: Kodansha.
1983	Heian Koki Monogatarisen Series. Osamu Otsuki ed. Tokyo: Izumi Shoin.
1992	Osamu Otsuki et al eds. Tokyo: Iwanami Shoten.
1993	Seiko Tanabe ad. Tokyo: Kodansha.
2002	Youhei Misumi and keiko Ishino eds. modern translation. Tokyo: Shogakukan.

Table 2: A List of Major Publications of Torikaebaya Monogatari in Modern Japanese

Kubota

As the original work was written in Old Japanese, the modern version of the *Torikaebaya Monogatari* text has been published repeatedly alongside the modern translation of the novel, and sometimes the adapted version of *Torikaebaya Monogatari* (see Table 2).[1] As a result, we have various kinds of modern versions, several translations into modern Japanese and various adaptations of the text.

Another example concerning sex change or cross-dressing in Japanese literary tradition is to be found in Kabuki plays. Kabuki has been one of the most popular genre of plays in Japan, and its most characteristic feature is that all actors are men; male actors play the roles of women in female costumes, so cross-dressing and cross-sex are at the heart of Kabuki.

Thus it can be said that the Japanese reading public provided a good cultural milieu for the reception of a translation of *Orlando*. In order to further research the reception of *Orlando* in Japan, I would like to compare and examine *Orlando* and *Torikaebaya Monogatari* with a view to sex change, dressing and gender.

Torikaebaya Monogatari was translated into English in the early 1980s, given the title *The Changelings*. The word "changelings," however, has a slightly different connotation, and I prefer to use the original Japanese title *Torikaebaya Monogatari* in my discussion. "Monogatari" means a tale or a novel, and "torikaebaya" is a subjunctive phrase, meaning "I would like to exchange." It is based on a remark of the father of the protagonists and will be referred to later on.

Although the oldest version of *Torikaebaya Monogatari* is not extant today, it was proved to be published in the Heian era, which was a golden age in Japanese literature. In the same era, *The Tale of Genji*, thought to be the greatest masterpiece of Japanese literature, was published, at the beginning of the eleventh century, and *Torikaebaya Monogatari* was said to be much influenced by *The Tale of Genji*. It may be an interesting coincidence that Virginia Woolf wrote a review of the English translation of this great Japanese novel by Arthur Waley in 1925.[2]

Torikaebaya Monogatari is a story set in the aristocratic world of old Japan. The most striking characteristic of the plot of the novel is that the two protagonists—a sister and a brother—experience a sex change, and they experience the sex change twice. They are lovely children and very much alike in their features. The boy is shy and timid, and has all the "feminine" traits the age imposed on girls in those days. The narrator of *Torikaebaya Monogatari* explains that "as the children matured, the boy became surprisingly shy. Not only did he avoid the eyes of any lady-in-waiting who was the least unfamiliar to him, but he even felt ill at ease and embarrassed in the presence of his father"

Orlando and Literary Tradition in Japan

Figure 1. The Picture-Scroll of The Tale of Genji (painted in the twelfth century).

(*Torikaebaya Monogatari* 14). He likes playing with dolls and those kinds of games that girls are supposed to like.

On the other hand, the female protagonist is extremely active; she is fond of riding and archery and playing with other boys. She is also very good at playing the flute, which was considered an instrument for men and is also good at composing and reciting Chinese-style poems, which belongs to the sphere of men's fundamental learning. In a word she has all the "masculine" characteristics.

Of their own accord, they gradually begin to dress in the clothes of the opposite sex. In those days, dress was extremely differentiated according to the sex; typical female clothes were called juuni-hitoe consisting of twelve layers of kimono garments as is seen in the famous picture roll of *The Tale of Genji*[3] (Figure 1). Long hair is another qualification for female beauty. Based on their behavior and dress, everybody outside their family takes the female protagonist as a boy, and the male protagonist as a girl. Their father deplores his children's so-called abnormality—to use his word—but he has no choice than to let it pass. He wishes he could exchange the sexes of his children so they could recover their normal state. Furthermore, the title of the novel is based on this remark. When their coming-of-age ceremonies draw near, both children are requested by the emperor to serve as courtiers in the emperor's court. The request of the emperor possesses an absolute power, so their father resolves to approve of the present state of both children and to exchange the children's identity for them to survive court life. They are forced to celebrate their coming-of-age in exchanged identities. Here their first formal sex change happens.

After the ceremonies, the girl disguises herself as a man and works in the court as a high-ranking official, while the boy waits upon a royal princess as a court lady. Both make a great success in the court, and of course nobody finds out their secret. In the course of time, the female protagonist is given the position of Chunagon (a kind of high-ranking official for men), and begins to be called Chunagon. Chunagon, as a man, has to get married and lives a married life with the daughter of an aristocrat, although there is no physical contact between them. Then, another crucial accident happens when Chunagon is talking to one of her colleagues alone. The colleague, named Saisho, has been notorious for flirting with women around him, and is in love with the male protagonist working as a court lady, yet commits adultery with Chunagon's wife. Now he is also attracted to the beauty of Chunagon who is disguised as a man, and he makes love to her. At the beginning of this scene, Saisho feels sexual love towards his "male" colleague Chunagon, but in the end he finds that he has loved a woman. The twist of sexuality in this scene is highly interesting. Now the secret of Chunagon—her true sex—is disclosed to the man and, more than that, she gets pregnant and gives birth to a boy in secret.

On the other hand, the male protagonist serves as a court lady, and gradually falls in love with the royal princess he is serving, and his identity is disclosed to the princess herself. Eventually both protagonists make a final resolution to exchange their identities again and recover the life of their own sex. This is the second formal sex change for the protagonists. They serve in the court again happily ever after. When the novel closes, only Saisho is in a state of depression for his wrongdoings, and here we can see a concept of retribution, which is one of the representative ways of thinking in those days in Japan.

As is seen from my brief survey of the story, the sex change, which occurs twice, makes up the main plot of the novel. The plot of sex/gender change functions for the protagonists to recognize and reconsider their own gender. The identity of the female protagonist remains a complete and harmonious whole, being an active girl and dressed as a boy in the stage of her girlhood. Her natural inclination makes her adopt boys' clothes and she does not feel any discrepancy within her identity as she lives within the small circle of her own family; her dressing as a boy is not considered to be cross-dressing, which has the power to invade and destroy patriarchy. But the golden age finishes when she reaches the coming-of-age, exchanges her identity with her brother and begins to serve in the court of the emperor as a man. This change of sex and the various changes of her life following the sex change reveal that the female protagonist has to be strongly conscious of her own gender, of her being

Orlando and Literary Tradition in Japan

changed into a male. The retarded gender consciousness shows that it is the society itself which puts emphasis on the gender difference and which forms the concepts of gender within one's self. The perception of gender of the female protagonist here reminds us of Orlando's first recognition of her own gender. It is when she is on board an English ship heading for England, after leaving Turkey where she turned into a woman, that she becomes fully conscious of being a woman. The narrator of *Orlando* says:

> It is a strange fact, but a true one, that up to this moment she had scarcely given her sex a thought. Perhaps the Turkish trousers which she had hitherto worn had done something to distract her thoughts; and the gipsy women, except in one or two important particulars, differ very little from the gipsy men. At any rate, it was not until she felt the coil of skirts about her legs…that she realized with a start the penalties and the privileges of her position. (*O* 108)

Although she experiences sex change, she behaves as though she did not differ much from men in Turkey. It is "a complete outfit of such clothes as women then wore" (*O* 108), meaning 'the dress of a young Englishwoman of rank" (108) that makes her conscious of her own gender. In both cases the recognition of their own gender comes far later than when the cross-dressing or sex change really happens. The society to which they belong—the emperor's court or the English ship—is a rather important factor for both protagonists' forming of gender consciousness.

In *Torikaebaya Monogatari*, Chunagon, the female protagonist, disguises herself as a man from the coming-of-age onward, and her dressing is thought to be cross-dressing with the danger of trespassing upon the gender boundary. Her uneasiness derived from living as a man in a male-oriented world increases, and she gradually becomes distressed and pessimistic. At the same time, however, it should be noted that she can liberate and develop her inherent abilities such as inclination towards scholarship, logical thinking and open-hearted temperament better in a man's world. Thus, she experiences double identity: she experiences what men could do and what women could not do at that period.

The second sex change can be said to be more significant than the first one for the recognition of gender. When the female protagonist gets pregnant, she has to depend on a man whom she happens to sleep with. In those days polygamy was prevalent and women were forced to live entirely dependent lives as one of their husbands' wives. As is requested by her partner, Chunagon, the female protagonist, stops living as a man, and begins to wear female clothes. That is, she returns to her original sex—a female. However, she is no longer a mere woman but a woman who knows the life of a man and what the male gender truly is. The female protagonist here recognizes the vain state of women through her experience of being a man and resolves to deny such a dependent kind of life. As the last month of her pregnancy draws near, she thinks: "It seems I must remain as I am. There is nothing I can do. And how wearisome it is, too!,...To go on constantly waiting and thinking is not to my liking" (114). Chunagon, the female protagonist, resolves to be a nun after delivering her child. It is dramatically ironical that Chunagon makes this disinterestedly cool observation, while Saisho, her partner, is convinced of her being in a satisfactorily dependent and placid state. He does not doubt her dependence upon himself at all. Compared with Saisho's other partner, Yon no Kimi, her self-awareness is remarkable. Being in a similar situation—both are Saisho's partners and both are pregnant—their responses are extremely different. Yon no Kimi knows nothing other than to rely on him, and her lack of awareness is thought to be common to women generally in those days. In contrast, Chunagon's recognition of her own state, even in pregnancy, is based on her experience of being a man. Thus, it can be said that Chunagon has attained a new gender-awareness.

This significant scene reminds us of Orlando's new awareness after he becomes a man: "She remembered how, as a young man, she had insisted that women must be obedient, chaste, scented, and exquisitely appareled. 'Now I shall have to pay in my own person for those desires,' she reflected, 'for women are not (judging by my own short experience of the sex) obedient, chaste, scented, and exquisitely appareled by nature. They can only attain these graces, without which they may enjoy none of the delights of life, by the most tedious discipline...'" (*O* 110). Here the experience of both sexes leads Orlando and Chunagon in *Torikaebaya Monogatari* to new awareness.

In *Torikaebaya Monogatari* the female protagonist finally runs away from Saisho's house, leaving her baby behind, and finds a new life. This episode means that she denies her role as a dependent wife in search of her true self, sacrificing her position as mother. Chunagon attains a higher conception of gender through two sex changes.

The final point I would like to discuss concerns dressing in both novels. Lemoine-Luccioni states in *La robe* that clothes are the language of the body (32), and the intricate and inseparable connection of the person and the clothes he/she wears is rather common in literature of those days in Japan. This way of thinking can be traced particularly in *Torikaebaya Monogatari*. In this twelfth-century novel, the delicate beauty of the attire represents the beauty of a person. The narrator explains the femininity and exquisite beauty of the male protagonist in his boyhood, by describing the boy's dressing: "...her [male protagonist's] complexion was as beautiful naturally as if it had been deliber-

Orlando and Literary Tradition in Japan

ately made up; and *her side locks*, dampened by perspiration, *fell in a cascade of curls, as if someone had set them.* She was lovely and charming...her appearance was perfect without it [cosmetics]...She [male protagonist] was tall and slender, and infinitely captivating. Her appearance was set off to advantage *by the pale and subdued pattern of the luxurious silk robe she wore over six delicate layers of white underrobes lined in pale violet.* She [male protagonist] was elegant *from the tips of her sleeves to the hem of her robe*" (*Torikaebaya Monogatari* 18; emphasis added). From these passages we know that the innocent beauty of the male protagonist is represented through the minute description of the boy's sensitive "feminine" dressing, including the description of attractive locks, as the locks are thought to be a key factor defining female beauty. The garment of the female protagonist—male attire—is also minutely described: the narrator explains *her* beauty and brilliance through the description of her exquisite dressing as a boy. In this scene, the father of the protagonists, feeling anxious about his children, peeps in at his daughter:

> *Over robes of various colors*, he [the female protagonist] was wearing *a pale green brocade hunting outfit lined in light blue, with violet brocade trousers lined in red.* His [the female protagonist's] face was round, his complexion extraordinarily beautiful, and his eyes lovely. His radiance filled the air all about. It was as though *his charm overflowed right down to the hem of his trousers.* When Sadaijin [their father] saw this beauty, so stunning that he could not tear his eyes away from the lad, he was so moved that the tears he had shed and his grief were both forgotten, and despite himself he smiled slightly. " (*Torikaebaya Monogatari* 19; emphasis added)

Thus, there are many descriptions of attractive attire in this novel, showing how the attire becomes identical with the person who wears the garments. Following are two other examples about the beauty of the protagonists revealed after they begin to serve in the court:

> The ladies-in-waiting wore five pale-red robes lined in plum red over unlined kimonos. In addition some wore red and purple silk brocade tunics, and others three layers of pale green robes. In the midst of these many ladies *clad in every possible hue* sat Chunagon [female protagonist], respectful and dazzling, *with the deep red shades of his purple brocade trousers glinting beneath his tunic.* More than usual, his brilliance, his encompassing charm, his captivating winsomeness, seemed unparalleled." (*Torikaebaya Monogatari* 39; emphasis added)

The second example is about the male protagonist:

> *Over strikingly beautiful red and purple silk brocade robes, in colors of progressively greater intensity from top to bottom,* Naishi no Kami [the male protagonist] was wearing *an all-red robe, and this was crowned with a formal*

silk brocade robe, white on the outside and deep purple within. With her face masked behind and a fan red on one side, purple on the other, she looked so like Chunagon one could hardly tell them apart. (*Torikaebaya Monogatari* 39; emphasis added)

Sandra Gilbert and Susan Gubar have pointed out that "[we] are what we wear, and therefore, since we can wear anything, we can be anyone" (327). What they say about the dressing of Orlando can also be applied to *Torikaebaya Monogatari*. It should be noted that both protagonists in *Torikaebaya Monogatari* look fine in the robes of their opposite sexes: Chunagon [the female protagonist] in a robe for men, and Naishi no Kami [the male protagonist] in attire for women. Here cross-dressing works in order to reveal their real selves. Wearing the costumes of the opposite sexes, the two protagonists of *Torikaebaya Monogatari* cross the boundary of sex, and trespass and deconstruct the boundary of gender, as Orlando remains Orlando whether *he* [Orlando] wears men's costumes or *she* [Orlando] wears women's costumes.

I would also like to examine the peculiar aspect of the reception of *Torikaebaya Monogatari* in the first half of the twentieth century. While the various versions of this novel were published one after another, *Torikaebaya Monogatari* was not valued highly in academic literary circles before the Second World War, when conventional morality was still dominant in Japan. A most influential scholar at that time named Sakutaro Fujioka criticized the novel in 1904, saying that it is "abominably degrading" (Fujioka 279; my translation). Since then his point of view has become influential, but in spite of this canonical view, the publication of the novel has not been undermined. Several renowned authors have been interested in this novel and have translated it into modern Japanese. Yasunari Kawabata, a Nobel prize-winning writer, got interested in the novel and published a modern translation in 1937. Shin-ichiro Watanabe, another eminent author and critic of French literature, published a new translation in 1972. Seiko Tanabe, another well-known contemporary writer, published a new version of the novel addressed to teenagers. Considering this acclaim from well-known novelists and repeated publication of the text in various forms, it can be said that this reflects the novel's popularity among the Japanese reading public and that the literary tradition of sex change has continued, although somewhat latently.

Torikaebaya Monogatari has been an important factor in constructing this literary tradition in Japan, so it is quite understandable that *Orlando* is what the Japanese reading public wanted to be first of Woolf's oeuvre translated into Japanese. From this survey of sex change, cross-dressing and gender recognition in *Torikaebaya Monogatari*, we see some parallels with *Orlando*. Both novels resonate across cultures and across times.

Orlando and Literary Tradition in Japan

Notes

With special thanks to Ms. Sarah Moate, Prof. Natalya Reinhold, and Prof. Mark Hussey who made valuable suggestions for this paper, which is indebted to the 2002-2003 special study grant of the Graduate School of Tsuru University.

[1] The major publications of modern versions, annotations, and translations of *Torikaebaya Monogatari* are listed in Table 2. As to the adaptations of the text, many literary works adapted from *Torikaebaya Monogatari* have appeared in various kinds of novels and sometimes in comic books.

[2] Virginia Woolf wrote a review essay entitled "The Tale of Genji," contributed to *Vogue*, late July 1925, 66: 2,53,80. Arthur Waley's translation of this novel was published in six volumes from 1925 to 1933, with Woolf's review featuring in the first volume.

[3] Picture roll is a major genre of transcription of classical novels from the tenth to the sixteenth century. The picture roll of *The Tale of Genji* is one of the most famous and popular picture rolls in the Heian Era.

Works Cited

Fujioka, Sakutaro. *Kokubungaku-Zenshi* [*A Complete Literary History in Japan*]. Tokyo: Tokyo-Kaiseikan, 1904.
Gilbert, Sandra and Susan Gubar. *No Man's Land: The Place of the Woman Writer in the Twentieth Century. Volume 2: Sexchanges*. New Haven: Yale UP, 1991.
Lemoine-Luccioni, Eugenie. *Ifuku no Seishin Bunseki* (trans. Washida, Seiichi and Osamu Kashiwagi Trs.). Tokyo: Sangyo-Tosho, 1993. Trans. of *La robe: essai psychanalytique sur le vetement*. Paris: Le Champ freudien, 1983.
Oda, Masanobu. Introduction to *O-lando* [*Orlando*]. Tokyo: Shun-yun-do, 1931.
The Changelings [*Torikaebaya Monogatari*], trans. Rosette F. Willig. Stanford, California: Stanford UP, 1983.
Torikaebaya Monogatari, author unknown, written in the late twelfth century.
Woolf, Virginia. *Orlando*. London: Penguin Books, 1993 (1928).

Constantinople: Virginia Woolf at the Crossroads of the Imagination
Julia Briggs

I Imagination

In *A Room of One's Own*, the novel is described as "leaving a shape on the mind's eye, built now in squares, now pagoda shaped, now throwing out wings and arcades, now solidly compact and domed like the Cathedral of Santa Sofia at Constantinople" (64). Was Woolf thinking of *Orlando*, her most recent novel, in which the third pivotal chapter is actually set in Constantinople, or was it *To the Lighthouse* that seemed to her so "solidly compact and domed"? But for Woolf, Santa Sofia was not merely "very solid," it was also "very shifting" (*D3* 218): "like a treble globe of bubbles frozen solid, floating out to meet us. For it is fashioned in the shape of some fine substance, thin as glass, blown in plump curves; save that it is also as substantial as a pyramid...beautiful, evanescent and enduring" (*PA* 347). That was how the great mosque (or cathedral) had appeared to her when she had first visited it, with Vanessa and Violet Dickinson, in October 1906. And as Lyndall Gordon has shown, it became a metaphor for "delicacy of treatment with strength of form" (111-2): that paradox of weight and weightlessness, of granite and rainbow dominates Woolf's sense of *To the Lighthouse*, just as it dominates Lily Briscoe's artistic aims, so that her portrait of Mrs. Ramsay parallels the novel itself. Lily too envisages her painting in terms of a paradox: "She saw the colour burning on a framework of steel; the light of a butterfly's wing lying upon the arches of a cathedral." And when she takes her painting up again, ten years later, she experiences the same sense of contradiction: "Beautiful and bright it should be on the surface, feathery and evanescent, one colour melting into another like the colours on a butterfly's wing; but beneath the fabric must be clamped together with bolts of iron" (54; 186).

Historically speaking, Santa Sofia is itself a series of paradoxes: formerly a great Christian church built by Justinian at the height of the Byzantine Empire, inheriting the mantle of Rome after its fall, it stands at the crossroads of East and West, not simply geographically, but spiritually too, since after 1453, it became the greatest mosque in Constantinople. The city itself became the seat of the Caliph, spiritual leader of the Moslems, just as it was the seat of the Patriarch of the Greek Orthodox Church. It stood not only on an East-West axis (where Asia met Europe met Russia; where Moslem met Christian

Orthodox met Catholic), but also a North-South axis: high in the gallery of Santa Sofia is a runic inscription, dating from the tenth century, which records that the Vikings too reached Constantinople. The city, modern Istanbul, thus stands at the crossroads—and not merely of the imagination.

Of course, Woolf thought of the structure of *To the Lighthouse* in various ways, also picturing it in terms of the "H" figure she had drawn in her notebook as she began writing, a figure which corresponds to the long-short-long beams of the lighthouse, as well as to the novel's three-part structure; yet looking back from the late thirties, she recalled its composition in terms of "Blowing bubbles out of a pipe" (*MOB* 81), and her early memories of Constantinople also surface within the novel itself. In her 1906 journal, the young Virginia Stephen had recorded that "the most splendid thing in Constantinople" was "the prospect of the roofs of the town seen from the high ground of Pera. For in the morning a mist lies like a veil that muffles treasures across all the houses & all the mosques; then as the sun rises, you catch hints of the heaped mass within; then a pinnacle of gold pierces the soft mesh…and slowly the mist withdraws, & all the wealth of gleaming houses & rounded mosques lies clear on the solid earth, & the broad waters run bright as daylight through their midst" (*PA* 351).

In *To the Lighthouse*, as Nancy walks with Minta Doyle "along the road to the cliff" and down to the beach, she repeatedly catches Nancy's hand; each time she does so, Nancy wonders "What was it she wanted?" For a moment, Nancy shares her author's vision of "the whole world spread out beneath her, as if it were Constantinople seen through a mist." It seems that she must ask "'Is that Santa Sofia?' 'Is that the Golden Horn?'" as unidentified forms emerge from the mists—"a pinnacle, a dome; prominent things, without names." But when Minta drops Nancy's hand to run down the hillside, "whatever it was that had protruded through the mist, sank down into it and disappeared" (81). But what is it that emerges from the mist as Minta clasps Nancy's hand? Is it Minta's hopes for the future, her excitement at her impending engagement, which she communicates through touch, or is it a sexual charge that briefly unites these two young women on the threshold of life? In the third section of the book, Nancy's younger sister Cam again links Constantinople with form or design emerging from chaos, as drops of joy illuminate "the dark, the slumbrous shapes in her mind; shapes of a world not realised but turning in their darkness, catching here and there, a spark of light; Greece, Rome, Constantinople" (205)—moments of civilization redeemed from the nightmare of history.

Virginia Woolf at the Crossroads of the Imagination
II Gender and Genre

Constantinople had figured glancingly in *Mrs Dalloway* as a site of sexual crisis, the place where Clarissa, "through some contraction of this cold spirit,...had failed" her husband (34, 129). It may be that both here and in *To the Lighthouse* we should read the city as standing for love between women, as David Roessel has argued (402), though it may equally signify the return of the repressed, the visible rising of desire from the mists of the unconscious. But in *Orlando*, Woolf's next novel, Constantinople was quite explicitly linked with women, and women who love women from the moment of its inception. Before she had even decided what that book was to be about, or that it would portray her beloved Vita (Sackville-West), Woolf wrote a preliminary sketch for it in a diary entry for March 1927, only weeks before the publication of *To the Lighthouse*. It was to be called "The Jessamy Brides," and would focus on lesbian love: "Two women, poor, solitary, at the top of a house ... the ladies of Llangollen...Sapphism is to be suggested...The Ladies are to have Constantinople in view. Dreams of golden domes" (*D3* 131). Were those golden domes the voluptuous curves of the female body? In the event, most of this scheme was abandoned, as self-censorship transmuted homosexual into heterosexual love. Almost the only element to survive was Constantinople itself: with its "Dreams of golden domes," it became both the literal and, arguably, the psychic centre of *Orlando*, a place of transit from one state of being to another, from manhood to womanhood—it was a natural setting for transition, both geographical and spiritual.

Sent as ambassador to Constantinople, Orlando enjoys exactly the same view of the city that Virginia had described in 1906, and Nancy had glimpsed as she held Minta's hand; he gazes down from his house, "entranced. At this hour the mist would lie so thick that the domes of Santa Sofia and the rest would seem to be afloat; gradually the mist would uncover them; the bubbles would be seen to be firmly fixed; there would be the river; there the Galata bridge" (*O* 84).

Vita's ancestors, the Sackvilles (whose history *Orlando* incorporates) had often acted as ambassadors abroad, but it was actually her future husband, Harold Nicolson, who was attached to the British Embassy in Constantinople when he first proposed to her in January 1912 (Glendinning 44). He was in the diplomatic service, and it was his second posting. The couple began their married life in Constantinople in October 1913, living in a "wooden Turkish house, with a little garden,...and such a view over the Golden Horn, and the sea, and Santa Sophia!" (Glendinning 69)—exactly the view that had so delighted

Virginia (and would later entrance Orlando). The city, which Vita had expected to find "beastly," turned out to be "lovely":

> She has an early morning of her own,
> A blending of mist and sea and sun
> Into an indistinguishable one,
> When Saint Sophia, from her lordly throne
>
> Rises above that opalescent,
> A shadowy dome and soaring minaret,
> Visible though the base be hidden yet
> Beneath the veiling wreaths of milky shroud...

("Morning in Constantinople," *Collected Poems* 201, cited Roessel, 403)

Vita and Harold came back to England for the birth of their son Ben in August 1914. With the outbreak of war, they would not return, but both of them remembered the city with affection—Vita wrote eight poems on *Constantinople* (1915, privately printed), and Harold wrote a romantic thriller about the old Ottoman empire, *Sweet Waters* (1921), which included portraits of himself and Vita. During his posting, Harold had learned something of the extraordinarily complex rivalries between Greece, Turkey, Russia and the West in that part of the world, and thereafter his expertise would be called upon when plans for its future were discussed—as at the Paris Peace Conference of 1919, at San Remo in 1920 and Lausanne in 1922.

In *Orlando*, the hero reaches the summit of his success as a man in Constantinople, scaling the heights of that world of male honors that Woolf alternately giggled over and despised. Like various historical Sackvilles, and indeed like her own father, Leslie Stephen, Orlando is dubbed Knight Commander of the Order of the Bath (KCB), and at the same time acquires the grandest of British aristocratic titles, being crowned duke (as some of the Sackvilles had been). Orlando celebrates the occasion publicly, with a grand reception and a display of fireworks; privately, he consummates a clandestine marriage to the gypsy Rosina Pepita (in reality, Vita's grandmother), who apparently bears him several children (though the book's time scheme scarcely allows for this). Yet at the climax of his achievements as a man, both professionally and personally, Orlando once more falls into a deep coma during which a revolution takes place not only around him, but also within him: "The Turks rose against the Sultan...set fire to the town, and put every foreigner they could find, either to the sword or the bastinado" (95). There are, perhaps, distant echoes of Shelley's *The Revolt of Islam*, of Vita's (then unpub-

Virginia Woolf at the Crossroads of the Imagination

lished) novel *Challenge* (which Woolf read in June 1927) and of the actual political crisis of Chanak in September 1922.

Orlando, meanwhile, awakes to find himself a woman. This startling transformation is heralded by a change of genre—from fiction or mock-biography to a form expressly designed to present transformation: the Jacobean, or more precisely, the Jonsonian masque. Woolf's sense of the appropriateness of the court masque as a form within her fantasia had already been reflected in the first draft, which includes two references to masques that were subsequently changed or deleted. During the fair on the ice of the opening chapter, there is a performance before King James of "a masque by one of the popular Elizabethan poets—Jonson, Shakespeare or another" (Woolf *O: Holograph*, 38). But it is particularly linked with Ben Jonson since, as Orlando listens, "Something was already being said about the Chariot of love" (Woolf, *O: Holograph*, 40), words that recall Jonson's "Celebration of Charis," and the stanza that begins "See the Chariot at hand here of Love" (which Woolf would have known from Quiller-Couch's *Oxford Book of Verse*, though it is not, in fact, a masque but a sequence of poems in the form of a triumphal procession). This episode is later replaced by a performance of *Othello*, which, with its allusion to the eclipse (viewed by Vita and Virginia together), brings together both Orlando's jealousy of Sasha and the jealousy that Vita aroused in Virginia.

The second masque to appear in Woolf's manuscript is performed as part of the celebrations for Orlando's new honors—Milton's *Comus* (Woolf, *O: Holograph*, 102, though later cut out of the scene). Milton's poetry was as familiar to Woolf as Shakespeare's; she had quoted the invocation, "Sabrina fair, Listen where thou art sitting…" from *Comus* in her first novel, *The Voyage Out*, where its underwater imagery had contributed to Rachel's growing delirium (309). Milton's masque includes Jonsonian elements (among them, the figure of Comus himself, derived from "Pleasure Reconcil'd with Virtue"), but it was not structured on such simple lines as Jonson's masques were, and it seems to be the Jonsonian masque that provided Woolf with the format she used to mask Orlando's mysterious change of sex.

Jonson invented the "antimasque," in which a group of undesirables (such as witches in "The Masque of Queens") appear and identify themselves, only to be dismissed by the forces of virtue: it is this structure that Woolf employs for the "Masque of Truth" in *Orlando*, but with the added twist that her vices or antimasquers are figures traditionally considered virtues: Chastity, Purity and Modesty are bid "Avaunt! Begone…!" (96). At times during this episode, Woolf's continuous prose threatens to slither into Jonsonian rhymed couplets:

183

"Hide deeper, fearful Truth.
For you flaunt in the brutal gaze of the sun
things that were better unknown and undone;"

"those who prohibit; those who deny;
those who reverence without knowing why;" (*O* 96, 97; my re-alignment)

While Woolf clearly grasped the structure, and even the tone of the stage directions in the Jonsonian masque, it is difficult to tell when she first encountered the form. Nearly ten years previously, Lytton's mother, Lady Strachey, had read to her from Jonson's masques: "They are short & in between she broke off to talk a little...I enjoyed it," her diary entry records (*D*1 106). Had she remembered them ever since? Though she discussed Jonson's comedies in her essay "The Elizabethan Lumber Room" (*The Common Reader* 1925), she did not refer to his masques. A great deal has been written, and more might be said on the subject of Orlando's sex change, but let us instead adopt Woolf's example, as she appropriates a dismissive manoeuvre from Austen's *Mansfield Park*: "let other pens treat of sex and sexuality; we quit such odious subjects as soon as we can" (98).

III Religious Conflict

Leaving Constantinople, Lady Orlando goes to live among the gypsies in Bursa (or Broussa), the old capital of the Ottoman empire, visited by Virginia Stephen in April 1911, when she travelled out to help Vanessa who had a miscarriage while on holiday there with her husband Clive and lover Roger Fry. Out in the wilderness, the gypsies offer an alternative society; untroubled by social hierarchy, authority or law, a way of life that constitutes a utopian vision in the novel as a whole, since the great determinants of class and gender are here temporarily in abeyance. Class does not exist among the gypsies, and gender is less conspicuous as everyone wears Turkish trousers, so that "the gipsy women, except in one or two important particulars, differ very little from the gipsy men" (108). For a while, Orlando can disappear amongst them, yet their differences of outlook remain a source of tension: her urge to write, her worship of nature and her very different cultural experiences set up anxieties on both sides. The issue of religious difference, avoided in the Constantinople scenes, now arises: though Orlando tries to sort it out through open discussion, "much bad blood was bred between them. Indeed, such differences of opinion are enough to cause bloodshed and revolution. Towns have been sacked for less, and a million martyrs have suffered at the stake rather than yield an inch upon any of the points here debated. No passion is stronger in the breast of man

Virginia Woolf at the Crossroads of the Imagination

than the desire to make others believe as he believes. Nothing so cuts at the root of his happiness and fills him with rage as the sense that another rates low what he prizes high" (105).

A hundred years ago, the themes of religious conflict, intolerance and violence were as closely associated with Constantinople as they are with Jerusalem today. *Orlando*, Woolf's most optimistic fiction, lightens these themes, presenting them amusingly; but when she had first turned to the question of faith in her 1906 journal, she observed that "it was not ten years ago that the Turks and Armenians massacred each other in the streets" (*PA* 357). Such massacres had indeed taken place in 1894 and 1896. Leonard Woolf recalled one of his earliest teachers being highly exercised over them:

> The terrible stories and Mrs Cole's passionate indignation had a great effect upon me: for the first time I had, I think, a vague feeling or dim understanding of the difference between civilisation and barbarism. I could almost see the helpless Armenians being bayoneted by the Turkish soldiers and the women and children fleeing and floundering through the snowdrifts. And I had a shadowy feeling ... that each of these victims was a person, like me an 'I'. (*Autobiography* 388)

It was, of course, Clarissa Dalloway who notoriously "cared much more for her roses than the Armenians. Hunted out of existence, maimed, frozen, the victims of cruelty and injustice (she had heard Richard say so over and over again)—no, she could feel nothing for the Albanians, or was it the Armenians?" (*MD* 132). No excuse is offered either for Clarissa's failure of sympathy, nor for her ignorance. In fact, both Albania and Armenia had been ravaged by armies of occupation during the First World War, although their problems remained substantially different. The Armenians became the victims of Turkish genocide once again in 1915, in the wake of a massive defeat inflicted on the Turks by the Russians. In retaliation, the Turks drove the Armenians from Eastern Anatolia, and there were continued attacks on them in 1919, when their numbers were further decimated by famine. In a moment of Clarissa-like coldness, Woolf wondered how her friend Janet Case could get so exercised over "the quantities of Armenians. How can one mind whether they number 4,000 or 4,000,000? The feat is beyond me" (*D1* 271).

Although her words are chilling, Woolf may be being no more than honest about the sincerity of the gestures we make towards sufferings that we cannot alleviate. She put this question more directly to herself two years later, while thinking about the War Reparations Committee, and the civil war in Ireland, where "People go on being shot & hanged...The worst of it is the screen between our eyes and their gallows so thick. So easily one forgets it – or I do ...Is it a proof of civilisation," she wonders, "to envisage suffering at a distance?" (*D2* 100). "Who remembers the Armenians today?" Hitler had cynically asked (MacMillan 377); perhaps Clarissa's forgetfulness helps us to remember them.

IV At the Crossroads of Past and Future

Constantinople suffered a series of political crises in the years following the First World War, and in the debates over its future, Vita's husband Harold Nicolson, had a small but significant part to play. Given his expertise in that area, it was inevitable that he should be at the great Peace Conference of 1919 (as he described in his book, *Peacemaking*, 1919). There, he worked closely with the Greek prime minister Eleutherios Venizelos, as the delegates tried to determine the fate of the old Ottoman empire: the Turks had allied themselves with Germany in 1915, and had subsequently shared their defeat. In April 1919, Venizelos, buoyed up by British and French encouragement, sailed into the Turkish port of Smyrna, with the further intention of embarking an army of invasion in mainland Turkey—Turkey and Greece had a long history of religious and territorial rivalry. In the panic that ensued, the British entrusted the task of restoring order in the interior to a young, blue-eyed and highly charismatic Turkish officer who had already distinguished himself at the Dardanelles, and was currently in Constantinople—his name was Kemal Mustafa Ataturk. He left immediately for the Anatolian mainland, where he set about co-ordinating a nationalist movement (MacMillan 369-72; 433-4).

Meanwhile, back in Paris, Lloyd George and Georges Clemençeau pored over Harold Nicolson's maps, trying to construct a workable future for Thrace, Constantinople and Anatolia. In March 1920, British troops entered Constantinople where they arrested leading nationalists, but Ataturk, who had now established his headquarters at Ankara, responded by arresting any Allied officers within range. The conference at San Remo, and the treaty of Sèvres that was its outcome granted Smyrna and Thrace to Greece, and gave France and Italy demarcated areas of influence in Anatolia. The Sultan's representative signed, on behalf of the Turkish people, but Ataturk had different plans. The following year, he renegotiated the border between Turkey and the new Russian Soviet, a border that has lasted till the present. He rejected all proposals for peace with Greece unless Greek troops withdrew entirely from the Turkish mainland (MacMillan 449).

From their base at Smyrna, Greek forces were spreading into the interior, but Ataturk was biding his time. In August 1922, he marched his nationalist army to Smyrna and the sea, watching complacently while the Greek quarter was burnt to the ground—"a disagreeable incident," he called it (MacMillan

Virginia Woolf at the Crossroads of the Imagination

451). The sudden collapse of the Greek forces left British and French troops in Constantinople and at the straits unprotected; while the British approached the empire for help (and failed to get it), the French marched their men out of Chanak, on the Asian side. There was an unpleasant scene between the French prime minister, Raymond Poincaré, and Lord Curzon, the prickly British foreign secretary. As endless lines of Greek refugees poured out of Turkey and Thrace, a peace conference was hastily called and Curzon set off at once, with Harold Nicolson in tow. At Lausanne they were joined by Poincaré, and the new Italian representative, M. Mussolini, "a small brown gentleman in a brown suit and very white shirt-cuffs" (*Some People* 204).

When the British and French invited representatives of the Sultan in Constantinople to attend, Ataturk responded by abolishing the Sultanate. Though he did not actually attend the conference in person, he dominated its proceedings; unlike the Allied powers, he was negotiating from a position of strength, having established military control of mainland Turkey. Unlike earlier conference decisions, the Treaty of Lausanne made no attempt to protect Armenian or Kurdish minorities in Turkey (Armenia itself was now a Soviet republic, under the rule of the Bolshevik Commissar for Nationalities, one Joseph Stalin—see MacMillan, 449). The treaty ceded to Turkey Turkish-speaking territories from Eastern Thrace down as far as Syria, and set up a compulsory transfer of populations, Muslims being returned to Turkey in exchange for the Greeks who were fleeing for their lives. Turkey was heading for the future, as Ataturk transformed the fallen empire into a new secular state, based on the Turkish language, rather than on shared religion. By 1923, the last foreign troops marched out of Constantinople. The Sultan had already gone into exile, and the Caliph would soon follow him. Ataturk had established himself at Ankara, the new capital of the new Turkey he was creating—the man who gave birth to a nation, or the first of the new dictators, depending on your point of view.

Harold Nicolson's book of memoirs, *Some People*, gives the Lausanne conference an air of broad farce by focusing on "Arketall," Curzon's hastily acquired, laconic and permanently drunken valet, in charge of the Marquis's foot-rest and his wardrobe. Nicolson's account begins at Victoria Station where "on the linoleum of the gangway Lord Curzon's armorial dressing-case lay cheek by jowl with the fibre of Miss Petticue's portmanteau" (*Some People* 187; compare "a piece of a policeman's trousers lying cheek by jowl with Queen Alexandra's wedding veil," *O* 55). At the Conference, Lord Curzon had to cope not only with the intransigence of the Turks, but with the evident decline of his valet, who finally leaves under a cloud, having hidden or mislaid all his master's trousers. Curzon's death, three years after the conference, left

Nicolson free to write this affectionate, gossipy account of him. In September 1927 Virginia Woolf wrote a review of *Some People* for the *New York Herald Tribune*. Her delightful account is entitled "The New Biography," and contrasts the truth of fact ("of granite-like solidity") with the truth of fiction ("of rainbow-like intangibility"), arguing that they are fundamentally incompatible. So far, no biographer has been subtle or bold enough "to present that queer amalgamation of dream and reality, that perpetual marriage of granite and rainbow …But Mr Nicolson with his mixture of biography and autobiography, of fact and fiction, of Lord Curzon's trousers and Miss Plimsoll's nose, waves his hand airily in a possible direction" (229, 235).

As her diary reveals, Nicolson's method in *Some People* stimulated Woolf to wonder whether she too could not sketch, "like a grand historical picture, the outlines of all my friends. I was thinking of this in bed last night…" His example opened a door for her, suggesting "a way of writing the memoirs of one's own times during people's lifetimes. It might be a most amusing book. The question is how to do it. Vita should be Orlando, a young nobleman…& it should be truthful; but fantastic" (*D3* 156-8). This is the first time Orlando is mentioned by name. The rest is literary history. Behind Woolf's fiction, as always, lay an extraordinary range of reading, a weight of serious thought and knowledge, worn so lightly that we are scarcely aware of it: the butterfly wing of fiction, fantasy and imagination is, after all, always underpinned by the stone arches of history and politics, and held in by the iron bands of fact.

Works Cited

Glendinning, Victoria. *Vita: A Biography of Vita Sackville-West*. New York: Alfred Knopf, 1983.
Gordon, Lyndall. *Virginia Woolf: A Writer's Life*. Oxford: Oxford UP, 1984.
MacMillan, Margaret. *Paris 1919: Six Months that Changed the World*. New York: Random House, 2002.
Nicolson, Harold. *Some People*. London: Constable, 1927, repr. 1931
Roessel, David. "The Significance of Constantinople in *Orlando*." *Papers on Language & Literature* 28.4 (Fall 1992): 398-416.
Sackville-West, Vita. *Collected Poems*. Garden City, New York: Doubleday, 1934.
Woolf, Leonard. *An Autobiography*, vol. 2: 1911-1969. London: Oxford UP, 1980.
Woolf, Virginia. *The Voyage Out* (1915), ed. Jane Wheare. London: Penguin, 1992.
———. *Mrs Dalloway*, intro. Elaine Showalter, ed. Stella McNichol. London: Penguin, 1992.
———. *To the Lighthouse* (1927). intro Hermione Lee, ed. Stella McNichol. London: Penguin, 1992.
———. *Orlando: A Biography* (1928), intro. Sandra Gilbert, ed. Brenda Lyons. London:

Penguin, 1993.
——. *Orlando: The Holograph Draft*, ed. Stuart N. Clarke. London: S. N. Clarke, 1993.
——. *A Room of One's Own and Three Guineas* (1929, 1938), ed. Michèle Barrett. London: Penguin, 1993.
——. *A Passionate Apprentice: The Early Journals 1897-1909*, ed. Mitchell A. Leaska. London: Hogarth Press, 1990.
——. *The Diary of Virginia Woolf*, vols. 1 (1915-19), 2 (1920-24), 3 (1925-30), ed. A. Olivier Bell with Andrew McNeilllie. London: Hogarth Press, 1977, 1978, 1980.
——. *Moments of Being*, ed. Jean Schulkind, 2nd ed. London: Hogarth Press, 1985.
——. "The New Biography," *Collected Essays* 4. London: Hogarth Press, 1967: 229-235.

If Orlando Came to Portugal: Some Fantasies and Considerations
Maria Cândida Zamith Silva

> *Who can say where life ends and literature begins?*
> Virginia Woolf

Portugal is the westernmost country of Europe. Our geographical situation is more marginal still than Russia's, since after us there is no more land, the sea is our horizon. Therefore, we, the Portuguese, may sometimes feel or be seen as outsiders in Europe. Geographically speaking, the wanderer Orlando might easily be appropriated by us, inasmuch as we have always been wanderers ourselves, our aspirations having always been too great to be confined to our tiny European territory. We explored new maritime ways and discovered unknown faraway countries. We mixed with all kinds of exotic peoples, always appropriating something of their cultures and leaving with them something of our own. We went to them as ruthless warriors and conquerors, or else as praising poets and enamored settlers.

This is partly why Orlando might have felt at home in Portugal, be it as a boy in the sixteenth century or as a woman in the twentieth. Being a man or a woman is not, for Orlando, the crucial factor that marks every individual for life. For Orlando is not an individual, he/she is the testament of the generations, reminding us that every human being is as important as any other human being, all of them endowed with seeds of femininity and masculinity, but, at each moment, in different proportions.

As suggested in the text itself, Orlando is made up of thousands of different people—"Some say two thousand and fifty-two" (277), says the narrator; an idea that is also developed, in a more logical way, in *The Waves*, where Woolf makes Bernard say "I am not one person: I am many people" (212). Here, in *Orlando*, the people involved make up centuries of history, and thus the novel/biography, as suggested by Henry Seidel Canby when it was published, resulted perhaps in "the first readable history […], the spiritual history of English literature since the Renaissance" (Canby 417, 420). Knole itself, the Elizabethan mansion of the Sackville-Wests—and of Orlando—is, as Mark Hussey points out, "a repository of English cultural and social history" (202).

Virginia Woolf's single visit to Portugal was not very rewarding. She came by sea in 1905, with her brother Adrian, a long and boring voyage; "something went wrong" with the engines, they had to land in Porto and travel by train to

Zamith Silva

Lisbon. Still on board, she wrote to Violet Dickinson: "I feel as though I had been cut adrift from the world altogether" (*L*1 184). In Lisbon she did visit Henry Fielding's tomb (where she let loose a caged bird in homage to the writer) and she confessed that "Lisbon is a splendid town" (*L*1 185), but she was not given much further opportunity of interest and delight, since they stayed there for less than twenty-four hours before taking the evening train to Spain. Nevertheless, the day was well spent, and Virginia set down in her diary for Friday, 7 April: "A really delightful day—the town is spacious & brilliantly white and clean, every street almost with its swift electric tram, which makes sightseeing a delight" (*PA* 262).

Had Woolf known a little more about Portuguese history, she might have taken advantage of the opportunity and gathered interesting material for future writings. For instance, Orlando's Russian lover Sasha might have been superseded and forgotten through the miracle of a pair of Portuguese dark eyes belonging to a personality as exotic/erotic—from Orlando's point of view—as Sasha herself. Or, later, she might have met a British citizen in the town of Porto, busy in the trade of Port Wine, flourishing since the Methuen Treaty signed by both countries in 1703.

The first Portuguese heroine I would like to suggest for Orlando to fall in love with is Isabel Juliana, the protagonist of *Bichinho de Conta*, a historical novel written by Rocha Martins and published in 1942. This young aristocrat, Isabel, who took her nickname from a little wood-louse that knows how to protect itself, was bold enough to oppose the all-powerful and despotic Prime Minister Marquês de Pombal, the one who reconstructed downtown Lisbon after the terrible earthquake of 1755. Scenes of the devastated town might compete in color and pathos with the episode of the London Great Frost. As to the girl herself, she had the strength of character and the stubbornness that Orlando lacked in his youthful years. In a comparative scrutiny of Sasha's and Isabel's personalities, the latter would prove much worthier of Orlando's love and, on the other hand, would serve Woolf's purpose of emphasizing the importance of feminine assertiveness.

Analyzing both characters, we may conclude that Sasha's sex is ambiguous from the beginning, and this circumstance raises more doubts about Orlando's sexual preferences; Sasha's love for Orlando is superficial, a mere adventure, her inconstancy is undeniable; Sasha easily gives up her English lover, and goes back home as soon as the opportunity arises. On the contrary, Isabel Juliana is one hundred per cent feminine, but endowed with a strength of character seldom ascribed to her sex; her constancy in love makes her endure severe punishment from the patriarchal instances of power: coming from a noble family, she was chosen by Pombal to marry one of his sons, but she loved

If Orlando Came to Portugal

another man; the Minister had the power to force her to marry against her will, but Isabel was never a wife to that imposed husband and as a consequence she had to suffer banishment from family and friends and even imprisonment in a convent; but she did not yield to political or family pressures and did not give up. It may also be added that Isabel was also much worthier of Orlando's love than the equine Roumanian Archduchess Harriet Griselda. Thus, we may guess that a different kind of story would have been told by Woolf if she had looked for Orlando's lovers in Portugal. Or, perhaps, the same kind of story told in a different way. The more so if Sasha is considered, as advertised by Woolf herself in a letter to Vita (*L*3 430), as a representation of Violet Trefusis, with whom Vita had eloped to France in 1920 in a fit of violent passion. A passionate love suits Isabel better than Sasha.

In the nineteenth century, Orlando, now a woman, disliking the antipathetic spirit of the age, wanted somebody to lean upon but could not think of a suitable partner, not even the Roumanian Archduke, formerly Archduchess Harriet Griselda. It might be the ideal moment for her to meet Charles Whitestone, the handsome young Englishman who was born and lived in Porto, a fictional character created by Júlio Dinis in his novel *Uma Família Inglesa* (*An English Family*). Charles (or Carlos, his Portuguese name) was, in a way, the same kind of youth as the Elizabethan Orlando. Belonging to the upper, moneyed class, he had everything, and had not to work for it. And he loved girls. He was very young, but, in the context of Orlando, that is not of great consequence. In the spring of 1855 (exactly the same year Lord Palmerston became Prime Minister and could annul Orlando's Turkish marriage to Pepita) it would be the right moment for the feminine Orlando to try and captivate Charles before he fell in love with a Portuguese girl. In Porto, Orlando would have the possibility to get acquainted with a number of British families who gave their names to renowned centuries-old brands of Port Wine. By the way, Virginia herself, during the few hours she spent in Porto on the 6th of April 1905, was happy "to see over the 'Lodge' of one of the great port wine merchants, which was a cool scented place" (*PA* 261). And Orlando might even have the opportunity to visit the mountain slopes bordering the Douro river, where the grapes for this exquisite and unique quality of wine are grown. The text of *Orlando* reproduces, through the ages, human realities in typical surroundings. The circumstances and the typical surroundings in the Portuguese novel would be a suitable background for such a versatile and immutable personality as Orlando. At the time *Orlando* was written, Woolf could be considered as an innovator in the reshaping of the concept of the historical novel, which emerged, as happens in this work, tinted by subtle irony and ambiguity. This was not immediately recognized, partly due to the confessed purpose of the book and the introductory photographs. Elisabeth Wesseling explains the general situation of this and similar experimental novels:

> Some modernists were already designing alternative modes for adapting historical materials. Within the Anglo-Saxon literary traditions, Virginia Woolf (*Orlando*, 1928, *Between the Acts*, 1941) and William Faulkner (*Absalom, Absalom!*, 1936) have played a particular role in the reshaping of the genre. The fact is, however, that it took some time before these works were consciously read as *historical novels*, that is, before they were placed in a relation of continuity and innovation with preceding literary adaptations of historical materials. (In Marinho 1999, 283).

In Portugal, the fashion of the historical novel was one of the consequences of Romanticism, and the followers of Walter Scott contended that a good historical novel conveyed more instruction than the historians themselves could. By the fourth decade of the twentieth century, Rocha Martins was of the opinion that the historical novel was, in the general consensus of literary criticism, "an outmoded literary genre" (Martins 7). Nevertheless, he justified his choice of the genre on the ground that "in the course of time, men have changed more the form of their clothes than of their souls" (Ibid.), an assertion that could well be ascribed to Orlando.

Naturally, the kind of historical novel Woolf intended to write and *did* write does not particularly aim at describing the continuity of historical events, but rather the continuity of the essence of human nature, be it masculine or feminine. Although *Orlando* has frequently been associated with writings about androgyny, an association that the personality of Vita herself might convey, the implications of the text and the evolution undergone—or not—by the hero/heroine, seem to point to equivalence of identity values rather than to a combination of both sexes' characteristics. Besides, as Kari Elise Lokke stresses, feminist criticism has proven that "androgyny is a problematical concept, particularly because it often comes to mean a union of neatly complementary characteristics that are stereotypically masculine and feminine, an idealized synthesis of opposites that leaves political or power relations essentially unchanged" (235). In Woolf's work, Orlando is a human being capable of acting and reacting in a normal way, either as a man or as a woman according to the situation and to the circumstances, and not a new fantastic type of hermaphrodite phoenix.

Reading *Orlando*, one feels that the relations to "the Other" are always something contingent and fragile, irrespective of historical moment or situation. As is stressed in the text, in spite of the radical physiological change experienced in Constantinople, "Orlando remained precisely as he had been" (127). This is the main point. Throughout the centuries and the changes in for-

If Orlando Came to Portugal

tune and sex, and even considering the many "selves" in which his whole self is divided, Orlando is alone, as every human being is always alone in the universe. The poem to the oak tree that outlives the poet and symbolizes nature's permanence versus human transience, brings forth the importance of the written word, that outlives its creator and keeps him/her alive throughout the generations.

Words have a life of their own, they can change unexpectedly, they have a tremendous capacity to surprise us, to provoke, to move, to open or close horizons. The same can be said of Orlando, in the hundreds of pages of text and hundreds of years of life. And the reader is aware that the sensations triggered by mere words are shared by the protagonist him/herself. The words of the text, same as Orlando as a character, have indeed the ability and the power to surprise us and question our established beliefs and certainties.

The word, as any other artistic achievement, is the only means of defeating death, of being able "to set oneself free from death's law" (in the words of the Portuguese poet Camões), overruling that inexorable decree of nature that thousands of years ago struck the legendary hero Gilgamesh at the end of his arduous quest for his deceased friend Enkidu. Orlando goes through somewhat similar trials and performances, only to reach the equivalent conclusion of perpetual mutation, of irreversible progress to an end. Only the poem, "The Oak Tree," has some possibility of survival, in spite of the artificially positive fulfillment of Orlando's destiny in the twentieth century.

The writer's option in this point did not satisfy the successful film-maker Sally Potter, who chose to bypass the book's conventional problem-solving conclusion, and gave a non-committal, open end to "her" screen-Orlando. The lightness and incompleteness of her beautiful version of the story is partly redeemed by this wise decision. For one can easily feel that the novel should not have been given a conventional conclusion, Orlando should not be destined to settle down in the author's contemporaneity, the book should not have been definitively closed by a "Happy Ending."

Orlando's utopian everlasting life can be seen as the demonstration of the precariousness and nothingness of human existence itself. This ironic, quasi-Socratic method of making a statement or presenting a situation to prove or support the opposite is not unusual in Woolf's work. In several instances in this book, echoes of the sixteenth-century way of viewing life and poetry are apparently used by Woolf only as an ironic means to construct her biographic *divertissement*.

Even when he was experiencing, with Sasha, "the delights of love" (43), Orlando was prone to fall into "one of his moods of melancholy," meditating that "nothing thicker than a knife's blade separates happiness from melancholy," and saying that "all ends in death" (44). This idea accompanies the development of the biography and is recurrent in the text, for instance, when thoughts reminiscent of *Othello* make Orlando consider that "the life of man ends in the grave" (54); this can be understood as: "the life of man dissolves into nothingness." The very interchangeability of the protagonist shows his/her lack of substance, and whatever is built without substance belongs to the realm of the imagination. The author makes Orlando go through this kind of experience near the end of the narrative: to avoid a repulsive sight, "when her eyelids flickered, she was relieved of the pressure of the present [and "present" here means "reality"]. There was something strange in the shadow that the flicker of her eyes cast [...] for it has no body, is as a shadow without substance or quality of its own, yet has the power to change whatever it adds itself to" (289). One might say that it is when one flickers one's eyes, that's to say, when one shuts away the outside reality and stops to think, that one can catch a glimpse of truth behind appearances. The first time one reads *Orlando*, the protagonist seems a lucky person, capable of living several lives and experiencing different opportunities. But when one re-reads the fantasy-biography and takes the time to think it over, the shadow covers the comedy and the fragility of the so-called reality becomes apparent.

Perhaps this is exactly what Virginia felt about Vita and the real existence of their dwindling love affair. By that time Vita was frequently changing her favorite feminine partner: Mary Campbell and other well known names of their circle of friends were some of her more recent "flames," and hardly anything other than an uncompromising routine friendship could be left over for Virginia. This situation led her to write *Orlando*, where the connections to Vita are numerous and ostensible. She said it expressly in a letter: "I try to invent you for myself" (*L3* 204). The very idea of a biography across centuries was suggested in Woolf's diary as early as 1923, when she states: "Snob as I am, I trace her [Vita's] passions 500 years back and they become romantic to me" (*D2* 234). Then, very shrewdly, she had her book preceded by a collection of well selected or expressly composed photographs that introduce the story as honest and acceptable: pictures of Vita's ancestors as characters in the novel, Vita labeled "Orlando," and Virginia's niece Angelica presented as "Princess Sasha as a child" are some examples. Woolf was already familiar with such personality disguises from the time the members of the Bloomsbury Group started, in 1909, the game of letter writing under archaic pseudonyms "in which the disguises served only to embolden the participants" (Rosenbaum 63) to talk freely about their actual lives. This mixing of fiction and non-fiction in pseudo-genuine letters opened the way to more daring incursions in the fantasy/reality combination of worlds created by mere words.

If Orlando Came to Portugal

The strategy of displaying the photographs as a preface to the book can be considered as a predecessor of the technique of *ekphrasis*: the collaboration between visual and verbal languages. Woolf offered the reader, prior to the text, a translation of the words into images, thus orienting the point of view from which the words should be read. In recent reprints, the work has regrettably been deprived of this visual apparatus. It is true that the text has in the meantime acquired a personality of its own, which makes the verbal "translation" less necessary, but, nevertheless, robbed of its ekphrastic preface, the work becomes less rich and meaningful than it was initially prepared by its author.

What strikes the reader of the novel *Orlando* most is the lack of wonder the protagonist Orlando feels each time at finding him/herself in certain new circumstances. Actually, one can consider that Orlando goes through three different sexual states: he begins as a man, then wakes up to be a woman, and finally becomes a *mother*, a condition that can easily be understood as a third sex. Indeed, it is true that "a woman who is a mother and a woman who isn't —that is almost two sexes" (Losa 68n). This unquestionable reality has been too easily overlooked through the ages, even by feminists themselves. Woolf's perception in this case appears innovative and clever.

What is stressed in stereotyped pictures of motherhood is the woman's devotion to the infant in her lap. Men and women alike forget too easily that the one who holds the child is also a human being in her own name, deserving an independent and personal attention—exactly as the child itself, who is not a mere offspring of human being but a human being proper.

The utopia of a pleasant, cooperative partnership of man and woman has not yet come true. Woolf understood this when writing *Orlando*: she makes the protagonist become a woman after having been a man, thus in a position to understand the limitations of both situations—and, finally, she made her "newborn" heroine become a mother—that "third sex"—happily married to a man who is almost permanently absent on the opposite side of the world. Vita Sackville-West, the admitted object of the biography, was also happily married to a man who was frequently away from home, in some distant country.

Virginia admired Vita and her many achievements before falling in love with her, as she heartily stated in her diary in September 1924:

> I like her being honorable, & she is it; a perfect lady, with all the dash & courage of the aristocracy, & less of its childishness than I expected. [...] I rather marvel at her skill, & sensibility; for is she not mother, wife, great lady, hostess, as well as scribbling? How little I do of all that: [...] Vita [...] is like an over ripe grape in features, moustached, pouting, will be a little heavy; meanwhile, she strides on fine legs, in a well cut skirt, & though embarrassing at breakfast, has a manly good sense and simplicity about her which both L[eonard] & I find satisfactory. Oh yes, I like her; could tack her on to my

equipage for all time; & suppose if life allowed, this might be a friendship of a sort. (*D2* 313)

This portrait is surely warm, but one cannot help wondering whether it is actually coincident—apart from the legs—with the essence of Orlando. Vita's fantasized biography is also an inter-sexual biography of the whole humanity. After all, beyond the limelight of the confessed sentimental purpose of the work, how important actually is Vita within the complete, complex meaning/meanings of the text? Deep and sincere as Virginia's feelings for her might be, Vita was but a pretext, a starting point for the unwinding of the historical-social-philosophical considerations that crossed Woolf's mind at the time. In the words of Cecília Meireles, the Brazilian poet who was the first translator of *Orlando* into Portuguese, "alternately man and woman, Orlando represents the experience of the individual in the different situations in which nature has placed him/her in the world; the fluidity of life requires this overlooking of the sex. [...] And when one says 'Orlando'—one might simply mean—human creature" (preface to *Orlando*; my trans.).

One should not forget that *Orlando* and *A Room of One's Own* are quasi-simultaneous writings, and since the ideas displayed in the feminist essay were occupying the writer's mind at the moment, they had forcibly to find an echo in the fantasy-biography. On the other hand, it is true that, as Alex Zwerdling stresses, Woolf "was a feminist, though she did not like the term. And many of her works, both fictional and discursive, are shaped by her desire to contribute to the liberation of women from the constraints of their lives." And he goes on to affirm that "the general problems facing women—their restricted vocational opportunities, their relation to power and money, their rights and duties, their connections with men and with their own sex—are important in almost all her writings" (210). *Orlando* is a good example of this, and confirms how those problems were acutely present in Woolf's thoughts at the time.

Woolf's kind of feminism did not contemplate a reversal of powers, the establishment of women's supremacy over men, but the acknowledgement of the mutual rights, particularly concerning education and opportunities to write and be accepted as an intellectual and political partner in society. This was not considered assertive enough by the radical feminists of the mid-twentieth century, but is being more favorably appreciated in recent years. The vitality of Woolf's discourse in *A Room of One's Own* is undeniable, and many of the adverse circumstances she denounces and stigmatizes are unfortunately still prevailing three quarters of a century later. In the preface to a rather recent translation of *A Room of One's Own*, Maria Isabel Barreno, a Portuguese feminist, stresses the continuity of adverse circumstances for women in today's society: to start with, women still have to have money and space of their own;

to that purpose, they have to enter the world of men, that traditionally masculine exterior world where money and space and knowledge can be obtained. She emphasizes the fact that scantiness has been woman's lot and surplus man's right; and this will continue being so as long as "women perform functions in the domestic world so that men can perform their own in the exterior world" (11). This is exactly the spirit of *A Room of One's Own*, and this is also the lesson taught through the centuries in the text of *Orlando*, with the assistance of the narrator's ironic descriptions and remarks.

These and other writings by Virginia Woolf were soon to influence feminist thought, first in England and North America but subsequently also in the European continent. The feminist cause in Portugal had been slumbering for some two decades, after having known a period of great activity at the turn of the century. The fact is that feminist ideas began to be uttered in Portugal rather early, but were never as aggressively expressed as in England.

Two centuries before Mary Wollstonecraft, and also before the Lisbon earthquake and the despotic masculine rule of Marquês de Pombal, there was in Portugal a man's voice calling attention to the rights of women. In 1557, Ruy Gonçalves, a University professor, wrote *Dos Privilégios e Prerrogativas que o Género Feminino tem por Direito Comum e Ordenações do Reino, mais que o Género Masculino* (Of the Privileges and Prerogatives that the Female Gender has by Common Right and by Regulation of the Kingdom more than the Masculine Gender). Several other theoretical writings by eminent entities followed in the subsequent centuries, but it was only by the end of the nineteenth century that the women had involved themselves in the subject, mostly in a milder way than the English suffragettes. The first feminist magazine, *A Voz Feminina* (*The Feminine Voice*), came into existence in 1868 but did not last for more than two years. Another one followed in 1883, *A Mulher* (*Woman*), but its fate was not much better due to the strong masculine (and also feminine) opposition and persistently rude criticism (cf. Lamas 23-26). The movement, however, did not die. In 1898 Caiel (pseudonym of the writer Alice Pestana) defines feminism under two different angles: the one she names socio-economic feminism, and the other sentimental feminism. She considers the feminist question as the most important of all to ensure the establishment of a new social order. In 1909 another writer, Maria Velleda, expresses the opinion of the group: "To be a feminist is, first of all, to be a protector of woman—of the woman who suffers, of the factory worker, of the dishonored, of the beggar…it is to forget oneself, as an apostle, to bring light to those who are in darkness, to bring instruction to the workshop, to bring words of love and comfort to the victims of seduction, to bring advice and forgiveness to the jail!" (cf. Silva 7-11).

Much in the line of thought that Virginia Woolf would follow, the chief claims of these feminists were for education and dignity, even before civil and political rights. Their fight was mainly carried out through the written text, since most of them were writers and pedagogues. They joined in short-lived Groups or Leagues until some stability was reached in 1914 when the National Council of Portuguese Women was formed and connections established with similar foreign movements and organizations. The First Portuguese Feminist Conference was held in Lisbon in 1924, and the second and most important one in 1928, the year *Orlando* was published.

However, this kind of feminism was doomed to failure at the time, in spite of its less aggressive demands, because the society was dominated by men's laws and power and the political-military movement that would end up in a fascist system of government did not welcome women's ideals of promotion and independence.

The kind of feminism vindicated by the Portuguese women of the first decades of the twentieth century has great affinities to Woolf's ideals stated in *A Room of One's Own* and in other writings. Therefore, when her work, some way or other, reached Portugal, it soon influenced the "daughters of educated men." One of the first to feel and acknowledge this influence was Manuela Porto who, in 1947, addressed a lecture to Portuguese women, which was published as *Virginia Woolf: O Problema da Mulher nas Letras* (Virginia Woolf and the Problem of Woman in Literature). The author explains how she was fascinated by Woolf's novels, which she read avidly, and thereafter by *A Room of One's Own*. Reading this essay made her understand why the bulk of Woolf's writings had given her the impression of a common trait. She says: "one can guess somewhere, very deep, a clearly formulated train of thought, always ready to preside at every achievement" (15). She ascribes to Woolf's capacity of self-analysis her own extraordinary gift for discerning the distance existing between reality itself and whatever was presented to her as such: prior to accepting any premise she had to analyze it herself, free, as much as possible, from other people's prejudices and influences (17). After summarizing the content of the essay, stressing the importance and reach of Woolf's ideas, Manuela Porto tries to convey to her audience the actuality and pertinence of Woolf's lesson, and the responsibility each woman has in the construction of a new better future for all women. With great conviction, she says: "I believe that everything can still be different, and that it will be so, when those that start showing that they have a voice, will finally be allowed to speak" (44; my trans.). I, myself, think that Manuela Porto, as mouthpiece of Virginia Woolf's feminist thought, is absolutely right.

Manuela Porto was also a translator, but she did not translate *Orlando*. However, being one of the first Portuguese intellectuals to be touched by

If Orlando Came to Portugal

Virginia Woolf's talent, she did translate some of her short stories, among them "The Mark on the Wall" and "Lappin and Lapinova," together with the Septimus Warren Smith section of *Mrs. Dalloway*. This anthology was published in 1951.

At present, there are three different translations of *Orlando* available in Portugal. One of them is out of print, but copies can still be bought at second-hand bookshops. A comparative analysis of these translations shows that there are no great discrepancies regarding the solutions adopted by the three translators. And Woolf's thought is never substantially betrayed.

Perhaps because Woolf's novels were not immediately translated, at the time they were *Orlando* was no longer regarded as a light amusement only, but the depth of its meanings was duly taken into consideration and this became visible in the Portuguese versions.

In Portugal, in the course of our long history, we have also had to deal with privileges of the nobility, huge mansions belonging to a single owner, women who could not inherit their ancestors' property, queen's or king's favorites eventually fallen in disgrace, kings that were dethroned and their partisans evicted or killed, artists that almost starved for lack of money and others who were sponsored by prominent patrons. All this belongs to every old country's history. But Woolf had a rare talent to give life to, or merely suggest the possibility of, particular characters acting differently from the expected standards.

In her preface to the translated anthology of Woolf's stories, Manuela Porto says something very pertinent about the reception of this English writer's works in Portugal and the specificity of the Portuguese nature that can explain why *Orlando* took some decades to be translated into Portuguese:

> As a rule, the Portuguese readers prefer that things be presented to them plainly as they are, that a spade be called a spade, they don't like to take the trouble of having to complete what was merely suggested to them or what was left there for them to guess. But it happens that only very rarely does Virginia Woolf tell us her thought, although one can guess at each moment that such a thought exists in a well formulated way in her mind, precise, being however the reader's task to look for it, to guess it, to find it at last, and often to feel it as if it were a product of his/her own mind's creation. (Porto 1951, 8; my trans.)

All the Portuguese Woolfians—and they are many nowadays—are indebted to Manuela Porto for her endeavors to make her contemporaries know better, understand and appreciate the scope of Virginia Woolf's writings and the hidden treasures to be discovered behind the surface value of each one of her words and phrases. I hope to have left it somewhat clearer in what concerns *Orlando*, a very special case offering a multiplicity of possible approaches and interpretations.

Zamith Silva

Works Cited

Canby, Henry Seidel. "*Orlando, a Biography*." 1928. In *Critical Assessments* vol. 2. Ed. Eleanor McNees. Mountfield: Helm Information, 1994: 416-421.
Dinis, Júlio. 1867. *Uma Família Inglesa* [*An English Family*]. Porto: Civilização, 1971.
Hussey, Mark. *Virginia Woolf A to Z*. New York: Oxford UP, 1996.
Lamas, Rosmarie Wank-Nolasco. *Mulheres para Além do Seu Tempo* [*Women Beyond Their Time*]. Vendas Novas: Bertrand, 1995.
Lokke, Kari Elise. "*Orlando* and Incandescence: Virginia Woolf's Comic Sublime." *Modern Fiction Studies* 38.1 (Spring 1992): 235-252.
Losa, Margarida. "Michael Henchard *versus* Elizabeth-Jane and Elaine Showalter: Another Reading of *The Mayor of Casterbridge* in Thomas Hardy." Porto: Afrontamento, 1992.
Marinho, Maria de Fátima. *O Romance Histórico em Portugal* [*The Historical Novel in Portugal*]. Porto: Campo das Letras, 1999.
Martins, Rocha. *O Bichinho de Conta* [*The Wood-louse*]. Lisboa: Inquérito, 1942.
Porto, Manuela. *Virginia Woolf: O Problema da Mulher nas Letras* [*Virginia Woolf and the Problem of Woman in Literature*]. Lisboa: Seara Nova, 1947.
Porto, Manuela (ed. & trans.). *Antologia do Conto Moderno: Virginia Woolf* [*Anthology of the Modern Short Story: Virginia Woolf*]. Coimbra: Atlântida, 1951.
Rosenbaum, S.P. *Aspects of Bloomsbury: Studies in Modern English Literary and Intellectual History*. London: Macmillan, 1998.
Silva, Regina Tavares da. *Feminismo em Portugal na Voz de Mulheres Escritoras do Início do Séc. XX* [*Feminism in Portugal in the Voice of Women Writers of the Early Twentieth Century*]. Lisboa: Edição da Comissão da Condição Feminina, 1982.
Woolf, Virginia. *Orlando, A Biography*. 1928. London: The Hogarth Press, 1970.
——. *Orlando* (trans. Cecília Meireles). Lisbon: Livros do Brasil, n/d.
——. *Orlando* (trans. Lucília Rodrigues). Mem Martins: Publicações Europa-América, 1991.
——. *Orlando—Uma Biografia* (trans. Ana Luísa Faria). Lisboa: Relógio d'Água, 1994.
——.*The Waves*. 1931. London: The Hogarth Press, 1972.
——. *A Room of One's Own*. 1929. London: Granada Publishing, 1981.
——.*Um Quarto Que Seja Seu* [*A Room of One's Own*] (trans. Maria Emília Ferros Moura) (preface Maria Isabel Barreno). Lisboa: Vega 1996.
——. *A Passionate Apprentice: The Early Journals*. Ed. Mitchell A. Leaska. London: The Hogarth Press, 1990.
——. *The Diary of Virginia Woolf*. Ed. Anne Olivier Bell. Vols. 1-3. London: Penguin Books, 1979-1982.
——. *The Letters of Virginia Woolf*. Ed. Nigel Nicolson .Vols. 1-5. London: The Hogarth Press, 1975-1979.
Zwerdling, Alex. *Virginia Woolf and the Real World*. Berkeley: U of California Press, 1986.

A Study of the Concept of the Androgyny in Virginia Woolf's *Orlando*
Bilge Nihal Zileli

The aim of this study is to examine Woolf's treatment of the theme of androgyny in *Orlando*, one of her major works. The main argument is that the theme of androgyny questions gender roles imposed by the patriarchal society, which attempts to reduce the individual to a type; and appears as a means of liberating the individual from the confines of gender roles, so that the individual can preserve his/her autonomy and engage in creative activity.

In 1927 Woolf was the author of five novels and she had an impulse for a very different kind of writing, which would be realized in *Orlando*. As she recorded in her diary, she was bored with all this serious stuff and all she needed was "an escapade after those serious poetic experimental books whose form is so closely considered. I want to kick up my heels and be off" (qtd. in Kemp xii). Thus, she began to write *Orlando* in such a light-hearted attitude.

However, Woolf's desire was not only to have "a writer's holiday," but also to portray Vita Sackville-West, with whom Woolf fell in love passionately around 1925, and to depict her family's history. Thus began *Orlando*, "[the] most charming love letter in literature" in which Woolf "weaves her in and out of the countries, tosses her from one sex to another, plays with her, dresses her in furs, lace, and emeralds,...drops a veil of mist around her, and ends by photographing her in the mud at Long Barn, with dogs, awaiting Virginia's arrival next day" (Nicolson qtd. in Rose 180).

Rose asserts that *Orlando* is "a mock-biography...[which] parodies... unambiguous gender" (179). Parody is a branch of satire and "a kind of satirical mimicry" (Cuddon 682). Woolf also acknowledged that the work would have a satirical tone: "Satire is to be the main note—satire & wildness...My own lyric vein is to be satirised. Everything mocked" (qtd. in Kemp xii), and one of the main things satirized, or mocked, are the gender roles imposed by the patriarchal society and regarded as fixed and unchangeable. Thus, the targets of Woolf's satire are both gender roles and the patriarchal society.

Woolf, in any case, did not believe in the fixity of gender. On the contrary, she always regarded it as something fluid and changeable, which is manifested by Orlando's abrupt sex reversal. According to the conventional belief, which assumes that there are rigid differences between the two sexes, Orlando would have completely changed after the sex reversal; however, the narrator acknowledges that Orlando remains the same after the sex reversal: "Orlando had

203

become a woman—there is no denying it. But in every other respect, Orlando remained precisely as she had been, the change of sex, though it altered their future, did nothing whatever to alter their identity" (98); thus, emphasizing the fact that Orlando remains the same though his/her sex has changed, Woolf mocks the idea that one's sex determines one's character and identity and implies that "sexually defined selves or roles are merely costumes" (Gilbert xix).

There is also an interesting point worth mentioning about the Turkish translation of *Orlando*. Translation is always a challenging job since the translator should both deal with the difficulties emerging from the nature of translation in general and have both the reader and the writer in mind while doing this. One of the biggest problems a Turkish translator of *Orlando* comes across must be the translation of the personal pronouns "he" and "she", and the possessive pronouns "his" and "her" in the sex reversal scene since in Turkish there is only one word corresponding to each couple; that is, "o" for "he" and "she" and "onun" for "his" and "her". For example, in the original form the narrator explains Orlando's situation as follows:

> Orlando had become a woman—there is no denying it. But in every other respect, Orlando remained precisely as he had been. The change of sex, though it altered their future, did nothing whatever to alter their identity. Their faces remained, as their portraits prove, practically the same. His memory—but in future we must, for convention's sake, say 'her' for 'his', and 'she' for 'he'—her memory then, went back through all the events of her past life without encountering any obstacle. (*O* 98)

So, in order to emphasize the sex change the narrator uses "she" instead of "he." In Turkish translation having only one word, the word "o," for "she" and "he" makes Seniha Akar, the translator, replace "she" with "kadin Orlando," meaning "the female Orlando," or "kadin," meaning "woman," and "he" with "erkek Orlando," meaning "the male Orlando" or "erkek," meaning "man." Besides this, she also replaces "her" with "kadinin," meaning "the woman's," and "his" with "erkegin" meaning "the man's":

> Orlando kadin olmustu; bunu yadsimak olanaksiz. Ancak baska her bakimdan eskiden ne idiyse oydu. Cinsiyet degisimi gelecegini degistirse de kimligini hiç degistirmemisti. *Erkek ve kadin Orlando'larin* yüzleri, portrelerinin de kanitladigi gibi hemen tümüyle ayniydi. Erkegin bellegi—ancak bundan sonra adet yerini bulsun diye *erkek* yerine *kadin, erkegin* yerine *kadinin* demeliyiz—yani kadin Orlando'nun bellegi hiçbir engelle karsilasmaksizin geçmis yasaminin tüm olaylarinin ta en basina kadar uzanabiliyordu. (*Orlando* 96; emphasis added)"

A Study of the Concept of Androgyny

On the other hand, in this scene the narrator does not seem to pay much attention to the correct use of pronouns for Orlando since Orlando is still the same person despite the sex reversal in the eye of the narrator. Thus, the narrator's reckless attitude towards such conventions underlines the fact that sex reversal has not changed anything in Orlando. To illustrate, although s/he says "Orlando has become a woman," s/he uses the personal pronoun "he" for the female Orlando, and later on s/he corrects him/herself just "for convention's sake." Thus, the narrator seems to mock very subtly and cleverly the gender roles imposed on sexes. True, Orlando is still the same person, but just because Orlando's sex has changed, her gender and her personality have also changed in the eye of society. Yet, all these are lost in the Turkish translation because of having only one personal pronoun, "o," in Turkish, so the narrator's reckless and mocking attitude towards such conventions cannot be conveyed to the Turkish reader in the translation. For example, in the Turkish translation the narrator uses "o," corresponding to "he," so the narrator's incorrect use of the personal pronoun is inevitably missing in the Turkish text. Then, it seems inevitable for a Turkish translator to come across such problems in such places where the narrator plays with personal or possessive pronouns in order to question the issue of gender.

Although the change of sex did not change Orlando's identity and character, "it altered their future" (98) because what the society expects from the two sexes is completely different and the members of each sex are required to abide by the expectations their gender is associated with. Thus, it is implied that although gender is not innate, but something socially constructed, it determines the way an individual leads his/her life and dictates one's choices, feelings and even tastes, which leads to an artificial distinction between the sexes. Before the question of gender enters the scene, Orlando is not terrified at all when he looks in the mirror and sees that he has become a woman: "Orlando looked himself up and down in a long looking-glass, without showing any sign of discomposure, and went presumably to his bath" (98). Undoubtedly, Woolf deliberately understates Orlando's reaction to his sex change to emphasize that sex is just a detail for Orlando, since society has not yet interfered with the matter. When she lives with the gypsies in Turkey, she is totally free among them, for there is no society which tells her what she is or how she should behave or live her life, and so for Orlando it is not significant whether she is a man or a woman. However, as soon as she buys dresses "appropriate" for a young woman as the society expects her to, she begins to think about her sex, because now the issue of gender enters the scene in the full array of societal characteristics:

Zileli

> It is a strange fact, but a true one, that up to this moment she had scarcely given her sex a thought. Perhaps the Turkish trousers which she had hitherto worn had done something to distract her thoughts; and the gypsy women, except in one or two important particulars, differ very little from the gypsy men. (108)

Consequently, she becomes confused when she reflects how she should change although she is the same. For example, as a woman first of all, she "must be obedient, chaste, scented, and exquisitely apparelled" (110). These are the qualities that are regarded as essential for a woman, and on one of them the narrator makes an ironical remark: "the whole edifice of female government is based on that foundation stone; chastity is their jewel, their centerpiece, which they run mad to protect, and die when ravished of" (108). Orlando is also aware that these qualities are not innate, but are learned. On the other hand, she also knows that she will be obliged to adapt these qualities by the society, assigning rigid gender roles to both sexes:

> "Now I shall have to pay in my own person for those desires" she reflected; "for women are not (judging by my own short experience of the sex) obedient, chaste, scented, and exquisitely apparelled by nature. They can only attain these graces, without which they may enjoy none of the delights of life, by the most tedious discipline." (110)

Then, she asks herself what this "most tedious discipline" by which "women can only attain these graces" is: "'There's the hairdressing,' she thought, 'that alone will take an hour of my morning; there's looking in the looking-glass, another hour; there is staying and lacing; there's washing and powdering; there's changing from silk to lace and from lace to paduasoy; there's being chaste year in year out...'" (110).

It is not different at all for men, since they are exposed to the same restrictive function of gender and made limited and ridiculous like the members of the opposite sex, which Orlando is very well aware of:

> And mincing out the words she was horrified to perceive how low an opinion she was forming of the other sex, the manly, to which it had once been her pride to belong. 'To fall from a mast-head', she thought, 'because you see a woman's ankles; to dress up like a Guy Fawkes and parade the streets, so that women may praise you; to deny a woman teaching lest she may laugh at you; to be the slave of the frailest chit in petticoats, and yet to go about as if you were the Lords of creation—Heavens!' she thought, 'what fools they make of us—what fools we are!' (113)

A Study of the Concept of Androgyny

Woolf seems to be mocking the two sexes; however, actually "Woolf is mocking...these everlasting distinctions between what is masculine and what is feminine" (Rose 184) because gender restrictions form artificial boundaries for both sexes and confine them within these boundaries. Orlando is capable of distancing herself from both sexes and criticizing either, for she is an androgyne: "for the time being, she seemed to vacillate; she was man; she was woman; she knew the secrets, shared the weaknesses of each." So, she "was not sure to which she belonged," for she did not fit in the norms of either sex, but undoubtedly being an outsider, or an androgyne, gave her an insight and she could see how one-sided and "full of the most deplorable infirmities" (113) both sexes were. Furthermore, since Orlando is an androgyne, she has both "male" and "female" characteristics, which shows how ludicrous and man-made, the rigid divisions of gender are. Thus, as Rose argues, "Woolf seems to take the position that...everyone has potentialities for male and female behaviour [; however,] cultural endorsement of one or the other makes us limit our responses" (184). It seems then that not one's sex but "cultural endorsement" influences one's behavior, and this can be illustrated by several examples from the novel. For instance, Orlando feels the impulse to cry, but she cannot cry until she remembers that she is a woman: "Do what she would to restrain them, the tears came to her eyes, until, remembering that it is becoming in a woman to weep, she let them flow" (118-119).

While in *Orlando* Woolf questions the restrictiveness and artificial nature of gender roles, she also criticizes the patriarchal society, which imposes gender roles on the individual. First of all, its evil and hypocrisy are satirized by means of the "ritual masque" (Marder 112) that the narrator presents just before the reader learns that Orlando has become a woman. Before Orlando undergoes the sex reversal, he falls into a deep sleep, which lasts for seven days. Meanwhile, since the narrator is unwilling to announce the fact that Orlando has become a woman, s/he presents this "ritual masque." True, Woolf creates suspense in this scene, but it also exposes the hypocrisy and evil of the patriarchal society hidden under such titles as those of the three sisters. Marder states that if one compares the words of the Lady of Chastity in *Orlando* with Woolf's reflections on the same issue in *Three Guineas*, one can easily understand Woolf's idea about such values. Marder argues:

> [In *Three Guineas* Woolf] protested that chastity is a false ideal, twisting the minds of women, playing havoc with their instincts, an instrument of oppression. Chastity is a masculine invention, traceable to St. Paul. It is a "complex conception",...[Woolf] wrote, founded, "subconsciously, upon a very strong and natural desire that the woman's mind and body shall be reserved for the use of one man and one only." (Marder 14)

Thus, Woolf thinks that such values are only the instruments of the patriarchal society used for the oppression of women. That is the evil of the patriarchal society. It is hypocritical at the same time, for it presents these as desirable and ideal values for women. For instance, while the narrator describes these three sisters, s/he continuously praises them, for what they symbolize seem to be the ideal, desired values for women to attain. However, when the descriptions are read carefully, it is seen that beneath the surface lies their evil and destructive nature. For instance, while the Lady of Purity admits that she covers "vice and poverty" and "on all things frail or dark or doubtful...[her] veil descends," the Lady of Chasity, Woolf's target in *Three Guineas* too as mentioned before, is famous for her touch that "freezes." Not only is her touch but also her "glance" fatal because it "turns [anything] to stone" and "where [her] eyes fall, they kill" (95). Lastly, the Lady of Modesty is famous for her ever-lasting virginity, so she is the symbol of infertility. Therefore, "the fruitful fields and the fertile vineyard" (96) are not the place for her. At the end, when they speak together, their evil and hypocritical nature is further revealed, because they are the values, which belong to:

> those who prohibit; those who deny; those who reverence without knowing why; those who praise without understanding; the still very numerous (Heaven be praised) tribe of the respectable; who prefer to see not; desire to know not; love the darkness; those still worship us, and with reason; for we have given them Wealth, Prosperity, Comfort, Ease. (97)

They are the values providing benefit for the supporters of the system. First of all, such values provide the maintenance of the patriarchal society with all its organizations and institutions, because they supply societal fixity, which is essential for the preservation of the system. Societal fixity is best provided when certain values are injected into the brains of the individuals and so they are cast into certain roles. The most convenient way of assigning roles to individuals is, of course, to classify them according to the sexes. Therefore, the members of both sexes are turned into types, for not only are their roles fixed, but so are their views of each other. In this way, the maintenance and the perfect running of the system are achieved through its members' functioning in the desired and planned manner. That is why the three sisters try to prevent Orlando's awakening, for it is a threat to patriarchy.

While questioning gender roles in *Orlando*, Woolf also presents androgyny as a means of setting the individual free from the confines of gender roles which prevent the individual from developing fully and freely. Therefore, androgynous individuals are able to preserve their autonomy, since they are not slaves to gender roles in contrast to those confined in the borders of their sex and stereotyped by gender roles.

A Study of the Concept of Androgyny

In *Orlando*, especially the female Orlando struggles hard to keep her autonomy, and she achieves this as an androgynous character. For instance, after Orlando becomes a woman, she sees that as a woman she will not be able to do what she pleases. Moreover, she is expected to adapt to a number of roles. However, instead of internalizing those roles imposed on her, she chooses to resist them. For example, in order to be able to live as she likes, not in the way society tells her, she disguises herself as a man. Therefore, she "[recaptures] the freedom and range of experience she had as a man" (Rose 182) and preserves her autonomy through the rejection of conventional roles. However, when the nineteenth century began, Orlando had to struggle hard to preserve her autonomy because of the coercive atmosphere of the Victorian age symbolized by the negatively changing climate:

> The great cloud which hung, not only over London, but over the whole of the British Isles on the first day of the 19th century stayed, or rather did not stay, for it was buffeted about constantly by blustering gales, long enough to have extraordinary consequences upon those who lived beneath its shadow. A change seemed to have come over the climate of England. Rain fell frequently, but only in fitful gusts, which were no sooner over than they began again. The sun shone, of course, but it was so girt about with clouds and the air was so saturated with water, that its beams were discolored and purples, oranges, and reds of a dull sort took the place of the more positive landscapes of the 18th century. (157)

In such an atmosphere it becomes more difficult for Orlando to keep up her androgyny day by day and thus her autonomy. At the beginning she does not seem to be influenced by all these changes and tries to continue with her old, free life style. However, this does not last for a long time since "even she, at length, was forced to acknowledge that times were changed" (159).

Especially after a particular event Orlando has to completely yield to the fact that she cannot go on with her old life style, for the time has changed. One day, while Orlando is passing through St. James's Park in her coach, "a pyramid, hecatomb, or trophy—a conglomeration at any rate of the most heterogeneous and ill-assorted objects, piled higgledy-piggledy in a vast mound where the statue of Queen Victoria now stands" (160) attracts her attention. What Orlando sees terrifies her in the extreme, for "she [has] never, in all her life, seen anything at once so indecent, so hideous and so monumental" (160). However, what is more striking is that "the whole [is] supported like a gigantic coat of arms on the right side by a female figure clothed in flowing white; on the left, by a portly gentleman wearing a frock-coat and sponge-bag trousers" (160). The female and the male figures represent the stereotypes of the Victorian patriarchal family, a microcosm of the patriarchal society, because as observed in the clothes and physical appearance of the figures, the roles imposed on women and attributed to men are so distinctly separated that while the woman in her "flowing white clothes" represents the angel in the house, the rather fat man in his fashionable clothes represents power and authority. Thus, coming across all these, Orlando can no longer pretend that she can run her life as she wishes. On the contrary, she feels the oppressive atmosphere of the Victorian period and "a blush, vivid and singular, overspread her cheeks as she passed Buckingham Palace and her eyes seemed forced by a superior power down upon her knees" (161). The reason why she blushes is that when she looks down upon her knees, "suddenly she [sees] with a start that she [is] wearing black breeches" (161); since she has to accept that it is shameful for a woman to wear breeches, as soon as she arrives home, she puts on a crinoline like all other women of the age, which seems to be "Orlando's fall into conformity" (Burns 354). Burns asserts that "the fabric of the age…drags Orlando down and overwhelms her avowed passion for independence" (354). Thus, Orlando has to live through "the most socially coercive of eras" (Burns 352), which makes her conform to the traditional gender roles. In other words, Orlando faces a "crisis" "as she attempts to resist the 'Spirit of the Age,' which dictates marriage. Not in the least inclined to matrimony, Orlando's 'natural temperament, we are told, is to cry 'Life! A Lover!' not 'Life! A Husband!'" (Burns 353). Since Orlando is forced to do something that she does not want to, she is in danger of being a type like others in society and so losing her autonomy:

> Though the seat of her trouble seemed to be the left hand, she could feel herself poisoned through and through, and was forced at length to consider the most desperate of remedies, which was to yield completely and submissively to the spirit of the age, and take a husband. (167)

Thus, Orlando is in a state of conflict since what she really wants and what the age imposes on her are in superfluous opposition. In other words, "the external world and [Orlando's] inner self are polarized with respect to questions of influence, then…[Orlando] loses control over…her self" (Burns 353). Therefore, as the narrator informs, Orlando has to yield to the demands of the age: "Such is the indomitable nature of the spirit of the age,…that it batters down anyone who tries to make a stand against it more effectually than those who bend its own way" (167).

Burns argues that Orlando falls into conformity "to save her writing" (353). She states that as a result of the conflict caused by the polarization of the external world and her inner self, Orlando "can no longer write" (353). Throughout the novel Orlando works on a poem called "The Oak Tree."

A Study of the Concept of Androgyny

Finally, she manages to complete it in the 20th century and wins the "'Burdett Coutts Prize.'" Orlando has been writing "The Oak Tree" along with many other poems, but this poem is really precious for him, for "the night after reading "Greene's Visit to a Nobleman in the Country" [a satire written on Orlando], he burnt in a great conflagration fifty-seven poetical works, only retaining 'The Oak Tree', which was his boyish dream and very short" (67). Moreover, Orlando keeps the manuscript of "The Oak Tree" in her bosom all the time. It has been kept there for such a long time that it is "sea-stained, blood-stained, travel-stained" (163). So, there is really a strong bond between Orlando and her work as told by the narrator: "The manuscript looked like a piece of darning most conscientiously carried out. She turned back to the first page and read the date, 1586, written in her own boyish hand. She had been working at it for close on three hundred years now" (163).

However, although she has managed to work on her poem under extremely hard conditions, she cannot write any longer in the Victorian period. As Burns states, "she suddenly sees her own hand and pen possessed by 'the spirit of the age'. Spilling out 'the most insipid verse she had ever read in her life,' her pen creates a parody of Victorian period" (Burns 353). To put it differently, she cannot write what she wants but what the age wants her to write. Then, she starts to search for the reason for her not being able to write any more: "What happened to her? Was it the damp, was it Bartholomew, was it Basket, what was it? she demanded" (164). Then, she becomes aware of a strange tingling in her left ring finger, "the first sign of coercion toward marriage" (Burns 353). From then on, she becomes obsessed with wedding rings and the idea of marriage and eventually asks "Whom...can I lean upon?" (169), but as the narrator states, "it was not Orlando who spoke, but the spirit of the age" (169). Orlando understands that she will no longer be able to write unless she yields to the demands of the age. Therefore, "in order to regain control of her writing, Orlando must give up her preferred social position of the single, sexually ambivalent [i.e. androgynous] subject" (Burns 353). For the sake of her writing, she agrees to conform to the convention and marries Marmaduke Bonthrop Shelmerdine. However, this does not show that Orlando completely conforms to the womanly roles because her marriage is not a traditional one at all. First of all, she marries a man who is androgynous like herself, so there are no fixed roles on either side. Therefore, although she is a married woman, she still feels free, which can be observed in her reflection on her marriage: "She was married, true; but if one's husband was always sailing round Cape Horn, was it marriage? If one liked other people, was it marriage? And finally, if one still wished, more than anything in the whole world, to write poetry, was it marriage? She had her doubts" (182). So, it cannot be said that Orlando has been

211

defeated by the oppressive period because although she yields to the marriage institution, she never adapts to womanly roles and therefore once more she succeeds in keeping her autonomy by refusing to be a type. Also, she thinks that her marriage shows enough of conformity, so it is not necessary to keep conforming, and she can go on with her writing:

> She had only escaped by the skin of her teeth. She had just managed by some dexterous deference to the spirit of the age, by putting on a ring and finding a man on a moor, by loving nature and being no satirist, cynic, or psychologist—any of which goods would have been discovered at once—to pass its examination successfully. (182)

Since she has managed to reconcile "the external world and [her] inner self" through her untraditional marriage, she regains control over her writing, too. First, she hesitates to work on "The Oak Tree," for she is afraid of being unable to write. However, she sees that she can write again:

> She plunged her pen neck deep in the ink. To her enormous surprise, there was no explosion. She drew the nib out. It was wet, but not dripping. She wrote. The words were a little long in coming, but come they did. Ah! But did they make sense? she wondered, a panic coming over her lest the pen might have been at some of its involuntary pranks again. (183)

While working on her poem, Orlando stops writing because of the words "Egyptian girls," because using these words may get into conflict with the "spirit of the age." Finally, she decides against it, for she is a married woman. That is, she gains freedom through her conformity: "You have a husband at the Cape, you say? Ah, well, that'll do" (183). Afterwards, she thinks that she has achieved the essential transaction that should take place between a writer and the age:

> And she heaved a deep sigh of relief, as, indeed, well she might, for the transaction between a writer and the spirit of the age is one of infinite delicacy and upon a nice arrangement between the two the whole fortune of his work depends. Orlando had so ordered it that she was in an extremely happy position; she need neither fight her age, nor submit to it; she was of it, yet she remained herself. Now, therefore, she could write, and write she did. She wrote. She wrote. She wrote. (184)

Woolf believed that only an androgynous mind could be truly creative. She said, "perhaps a mind that is purely masculine cannot create any more than a mind that is purely feminine" (*AROO* 89). For her, a fusion between the two parts of the brain is essential for the mind to be able to use all its faculties. As Rado states, "virtually all the scientists themselves agreed that androgynous individuals commonly possessed heightened creative abilities" (150). A person

A Study of the Concept of Androgyny

who is confined within borders of his/her sex has a limited point of view thus tending to be one-sided. This is what Woolf means when she says that a mind "purely masculine" or "purely feminine" "cannot create." On the other hand, an individual with both "feminine" and "masculine" traits of mind has a much broader perspective, for s/he is not restricted by certain roles attributed to his/her sex. In other words, since s/he manages to break down the barriers between the two approaches to reality, s/he can use both of them fully. As a result, such people become many-sided, broad-minded and creative individuals.

The novel leaves us under no doubt that Orlando has a passion for literature. Writing poetry is one of his daily routines that he never ignores: "Orlando slowly drew in his head, sat down at the table, and, with the half-conscious air of one doing what they do every day of their lives at this hour, took out a writing book labelled 'Aethelbert: A Tragedy in Five Acts', dipped an old stained goose quill in the ink" (13). Though he vows at the beginning that he will be like his ancestors and gain glories like them, later on he thinks "they and their deeds were dust and ashes," whereas literature is "immortal" and "standing upright in the solitude of his room, he vowed that he would be the first poet of his race and bring immortal lustre upon his name" (57). Afterwards, since he gets furious with Nick Greene, who has written a satire whose target is Orlando, he burns all of the manuscripts of his poems, except that of "The Oak Tree" and thinks that "literature [is] a farce" (67), but this does not last long. In a short time his passion for writing revives, but this time he is more conscious of his direction in literature:

> Orlando swore one of the most remarkable oaths of his lifetime, for it bound him to a servitude than which none is stricter. "I'll be blasted", he said, "if I ever wrote another word, or try to write another word, to please Nick Greene or the Muse. Bad, good, or indifferent, I'll write, from this day forward, to please myself." (71)

This is "one of the most remarkable oaths of his lifetime" because Orlando will see that it is terribly difficult to write for oneself, especially if one is a woman artist, for society has a great influence on one's writing. It is true that "she had...managed...to pass its examination successfully" (184); yet, this is not the end of her struggle to write as herself, because as long as she writes, she will be involved in constant struggle. As a twentieth-century woman writer, Orlando is aware that it is too difficult for her to do anything creative without imitating men. At this point she has two choices: either to follow men or to write independently. As an androgynous character who would not yield to stereotyping and limiting gender roles, once again she rejects the former and easier way, and chooses to struggle: "Damn it all! she exclaimed, launching a penny streamer so vigorously that the poor little boat almost sank in the bronze-coloured waves" (199). Then, she transforms the toy boat into her husband's brig and the little waves in the Serpentine into the huge waves in the Atlantic:

> Orlando mistook the toy boat for her husband's brig; and the wave she had made with her toe for a mountain of water off Cape Horn; and as she watched the toy boat climb the ripple, she thought, she saw Bonthrop's ship climb up and up a glassy wall; up and up it went, and a white crest with a thousand deaths in it arched over it; and through the thousand deaths it went and disappeared—'It's sunk!' she cried out in an agony—and then, behold, there it was again sailing along safe and sound among the ducks on the other side of the Atlantic. 'Ecstasy!' she cried. 'Ecstasy!' (199)

As Rado asserts, "essentially, Orlando sublimates her terror over the possibility of being inundated, drowned, extinguished by the condemnation of critics like Greene into an imaginative fantasy over which she maintains total control" (160). Then, it can be said that the toy boat, which Orlando imagines among the huge waves of the Atlantic, symbolizes Orlando's struggle to survive in the world of literature among men as an androgynous woman writer. Orlando is determined to be victorious in this fight and to create as an androgyne. Since she is not a stereotype who is programmed to act and think in a certain way with a limited point of view, but a person who keeps her individuality distinct, in the end she will be able to create without imitating men.

Works Cited

Burns, Christy L. "Re-Dressing Feminist Identities: Tensions Between Essential and Constructed Selves in Virginia Woolf's *Orlando*." *Twentieth Century Literature* 40 (1994): 342-364.
Cuddon, J. A. *Dictionary of Literary Terms and Literary Theory*. London: Penguin, 1977.
Gilbert, Sandra M. "Introduction." *Orlando*. London: Penguin: xi-xxxix.
Kemp, Sandra. "Critical Commentary." *To the Lighthouse*. London: Routledge: 197 218.
Marder, Herbert (1968). *Feminism and Art: A Study of Virginia Woolf*. Chicago: U of Chicago P.
Rado, Lisa. "Would the Real Virginia Woolf Please Stand Up? Feminist Criticism, the Androgyny Debates, and *Orlando*." *Women's Studies* 26 (1997): 147-169.
Rose, Phyllis. *Woman of Letters: A Life of Virginia Woolf*. London: Pandora, 1986.
Woolf, Virginia. 1929. *A Room of One's Own*. New York: Harvest, 1957.
——. 1928. *Orlando*. London: Penguin, 1993.
——. *Orlando*. Istanbul: Ayrinti Yayinlari, 1993.

The National and "the Other" as a Biography of the Creative Mind: *Orlando* by Virginia Woolf
Natalia Solovyova

The problem of the creative mind as one that combines temporal and spatial, ethnic, linguistic, and cultural characteristics, has always been at the forefront of English writers' attention, from the Romantic period onwards. But it is the modernists, Virginia Woolf included, who made the dynamic of the creative mind an autonomous structural unit. In my paper I would like to address the interplay of the national and "the Other" as shaping the creative mind of Orlando the protagonist, as well as the biographical aspect of the novel itself.

In *Orlando* the literary and cultural context of the past is projected through the author's creative mind. But its parallel vision is concentrated in the protagonist's creative mind that is not complete, and cannot be completed. The poem "The Oak Tree" that is written over three centuries is a mission which should be fulfilled by Orlando the poet, and it also serves as a sign that the poet must break from illusions and come back to poetry as a real thing.

In *Orlando* Woolf gives us to understand that modern consciousness can almost go without a language, and the simplest phrase will do if there are no expressions at hand. The most common talk often turns out to be poetical, and the most poetical is just what cannot be written down. These speculations about the art of writing belong to Woolf but they are also applicable to the creative process in general. Woolf seems to find language to be not a mere tool for verbal experiments but a fine instrument for combining ideas, defining the notions of "national," "foreign" and "creative," and speculating on the issues of identity and gender.

The tendency of modernist writers to integrate similar trends from other arts dates back to their first response to the exhibitions of Post-impressionist paintings at the Grafton Galleries in 1910 and 1912 arranged by Roger Fry, who saw in the works of Picasso, Braque, and Matisse a clear appeal to society to accept the idea of art's autonomy.[1] A strong Russian influence cultivated in the Bloomsbury Group, and Virginia Woolf's appreciation of the significance of Russian culture and its importance for world civilization, led to a remarkable deviation from the acknowledged national stereotype. The introduction of "the Other" and unfamiliar material always imbues the common and well-known models and patterns with the taste of novelty and charm. The

215

impressionist and post-impressionist landscapes are typical of the biography of the creative mind as they orchestrate shifts and changes in consciousness. They express the poet's irrepressible identity.

"The Other" has its name, clothes and language. The stranger's name is the Princess Marousha Stanilovska Dagmar Natasha Iliana Romanovitch. A strange combination of first names and family names, both familiar (like Natasha) and foreign (like Dagmar), produces a striking effect of the unfamiliar. It sounds exotic and perhaps clumsy. It is difficult to pronounce and it jars on the English ear. The unknown and the foreign, the new and the unusual always bear mystery and provoke curiosity. This effect is emphasized by the Princess's figure and her dress: "The person, whatever the name or sex, was about middle height, very slenderly fashioned, and dressed entirely in oyster-coloured velvet, trimmed with some unfamiliar greenish-coloured fur"(*O* 17). The simplest, most routine things become very poetical and romantic as Orlando the poet tries to understand his feelings and transform impressions into well-shaped forms. The beginning of their conversation in French makes Orlando laugh, and helps him to formulate his state. The creative mind works without intermission, it functions in the silent atmosphere of mutual misunderstanding. Orlando intends to express his emotions in a sonnet. But then he hears her addressing him in English, and pronouncing the only phrase she knows in this language: "Would you have the goodness to pass the salt?" Romance ends with everyday concern, however politely expressed. The national and "the Other" are given at two different levels of thinking and understanding. To the Russian princess, two English lords seem to be bumpkins with the manners of stablemen. To Orlando, her questions about English traditions and customs, which she fires all at once, sound hilarious and provocative. The courtship that follows can be regarded as the answer to all questions. Strange as it may seem, Orlando's bride is very slow to take offence, nor does she pay much attention to his negligence. All that surrounds Orlando is still and silent like frozen waters, but the clouds are gathering. Orlando's creative mind is opposed to Sasha's impressions of the English court as "the Otherness" that is beyond her understanding. Finding himself in love, the hero becomes a complete stranger to her and to himself. His mind burdened with the images that this foreigner inspired in him is as silent as Sasha. His questions about her family background are given through reported speech. The author's voice is subtle and unobtrusive. It does not break the romantic spell or the characters' feelings. Romantic love is associated with the opposition of the national and the familiar. "The Other" is received as something foreign, yet understandable. The crucial point in the protagonist's life comes dressed in the dramatic metaphor of darkness and fireworks as expressing the opposite ends of being:

The National and "the Other"

> As they approached the carnival, they heard a deep note like that struck on a tuning-fork which boomed louder and louder until it became an uproar. Every now and then a great shout followed a rocket into the air. Gradually they could discern little figures breaking off from the vast crowd and spinning hither and thither like gnats on the surface of a river. Above and around this brilliant circle like a bowl of darkness pressed the deep black of a winter's night. And then into this darkness there began to rise with pauses, which kept the expectation alert and the mouth open, flowering rockets; crescents; serpents; a crown. At one moment the woods and distant hills showed green as on a summer's day; the next all was winter and blackness again. (*O* 26)

Flashes in Orlando's mind stimulate his memory and poetic activities; the rhymes prompted by his creative dialogue with "the Other" bring him back from the savage and foreign to the national and civilized.

Russian scenes viewed against the background of the Great Frost are richly intertextual. The description of the Great Frost itself seems to be prompted by Shelley.[2] The winter scenes are somehow associated with the Russian Embassy, and present a specific feature of the Russian landscape. The lovers speak French, a language that is foreign both to Sasha and Orlando. The most important events of national history and culture are evoked when different literary standards, tastes and attitudes clash. The image of Russia is metonymic by definition. The images of other cultures and languages are metaphoric. The relationship between metonymy and metaphor helps us to see a specific character of the language acting as a full-fledged personage at different levels in the novel-biography. The picturesque scenes of childhood, emerging from the secret corners of memory, are orchestrated by the powerful imagination. English spring and autumn, Russian winter, the hot, exhausting Turkish summer are swimming around Orlando, whereas his creative mind stretches itself over three centuries.

The colors are supposed to highlight Orlando's emotional state, his expectations and flight with Sasha. Romantic details accompany the protagonist's walk around the streets of London. The black is characterized as inky blackness. The opposition of the national and "the Other" is enriched by the opposition of the real and possible; the fantastic images of silence and darkness become compassionate to his suffering and violent heart.

In contrast with London, the Constantinople scenes are static and picturesque. They create the atmosphere of intermissions in thought which ultimately bring the protagonist back to his real ambitions and identity. The dreams stimulate the change within the creative mind that sticks to the core of national identity by drawing up from the bottom of the subconscious colorful images bound by time and location. Creative process is extensive, unpredictable and completely autonomous. The metamorphoses of the subconscious become the subject of a specific dialogue within the typically English identity. Metaphors of the most extreme and extravagant kind twine and twist in Orlando's mind: "He called her a melon, a pineapple, an olive tree, an emerald and a fox in the snow" (*O* 17-18). But we note that these unusual combinations come from the secret corners of his childhood. The explanation is given in brackets, as the voice of a modern commentator. In the following episode two versions of the national identity are interwoven—the one that exists in the minds of the English, and the "real" one told by the natives:

> Very little was known of the Muscovites. In their great beards and furred hats they sat almost silent; drinking some black liquid which they spat out now and then upon the ice. None spoke English, and French with which some at least were familiar was then little spoken at the English court. (*O* 8)

The lovers belong to two different cultures. They are involved in a dialogue that can help to see the national and "the Other" as representing their lack of knowledge. "Unfamiliar" is a predominant word that defines the meaning of their strangeness. Orlando describes the extremes of Sasha's personality by means of inventing an extravagant combination of trees, fruit and animals, i.e. "a melon, a pineapple, an olive tree, an emerald and a fox in the snow." The trees and fruit of the above type do not grow in England, and this detail just emphasizes "the Otherness." The same is true of the fox that can be transformed into a Russian white fox, cruel and soft as snow with teeth of steel the memory of which Orlando keeps from his childhood. It is a warning of future developments, and a hint at the real character of the Muscovite (however, it is lost on Orlando). Yet the dominating feature of the Muscovite scene is the dialogue within Orlando's mind that has many allusions to English Romantic poetry—*Darkness* by Byron,[3] *Frost at Midnight* by Coleridge,[4] Shelley's poems, etc. The boy is inexperienced, full of Englishness, and his transformation is sudden and unpredictable: he changes, he throws off his boyish clumsiness, and becomes "a nobleman, full of grace and manly courtesy" (*O* 19).

The lovers' escape from the English is purely symbolic. It is described as a wish to be alone and come to know each other better. But Sasha's stories about Russia again are concoctions of "the Other" mind, a mixture of reality and stereotypes: she describes Russia with "rivers ten miles broad on which one could gallop six horses abreast all day long without meeting a soul"(*O* 20).

Woolf shows where the cultural difference begins and how it brings about the catastrophe. Sasha's wish to see the Tower, the Beefeaters, the Heads on Temple Bar unexpectedly causes Orlando's strange response:

The National and "the Other"

> Then, suddenly Orlando would fall into one of his moods of melancholy...
> "All ends in death," Orlando would say, sitting upright, his face clouded with gloom. (For that was the way his mind worked now, in violent see-saws from life to death, stopping at nothing in between, so that the biographer must not stop either, but must fly as fast as he can and so keep pace with the unthinking passionate foolish actions and sudden extravagant words in which, it is impossible to deny, Orlando at this time of his life indulged.) (*O* 21)

Elizabethan landscape, both physical and mental, is very much different from "the Other." After all, Sasha has no English blood in her; she comes from Russia, a country that has little in common with England: "[there] the sunsets are longer, the dawns less sudden, and sentences often left unfinished from doubt as to how best to end them..." (*O* 21).

The strange character of their communication is heightened by their using French, which notoriously loses its flavor in translation. This comment is very important as it describes the evolution of passion in Orlando and his appreciation of it. He lives in two minds, and his creative poetic activities are a mixture of reality and imagination. The primary character is transformed and blurred and enriched with new impressions:

> ...he forgot the frozen waters or night coming or the old woman or whatever it was, and would try to tell her...what she was like. Snow, cream, marble, cherries, alabaster, golden wire? None of these. She was like a fox, or an olive tree; like the waves of the sea when you look upon them from a height; like an emerald; like the sun on a green hill which is yet clouded—like nothing he had seen or known in England. (*O* 21-22)

Again, the hero uses the familiar images of childhood that quarrel with poetic images, and this dispute within his mind leads him to a very strange conclusion. He is in the midst of the otherness but he deploys the national characteristics for the explanation of Sasha's thoughts and feelings and his own impressions: "[Orlando] wanted another landscape, and another tongue. English was too frank, too candid, too honeyed a speech for Sasha. For in all she said...there was something hidden" (*O* 22). Here we see that the state of mind and feelings is confused. Does Orlando translate her French into English, or does she sometimes speak English: "Would you have the goodness to pass the salt?" He wants to get rid of all his contradictory thoughts: "[he] ran wild in his transports and swept her over the ice, faster, faster, vowing that he would chase the flame..." (*O* 22).

The courtship is progressing, and Sasha tells him about the cruelty of Russian life whereas he tells her about his ancestors. He recalls stories about the Russians, and they are horrible: the women in Muscovy wear beards and the men are covered with fur from the waist down. The conflict is aggravated when he becomes aware of something hidden from him. In his typically civilized manner he thinks that she lives in a barbaric country; he thinks of public opinion—"his friends would deride him for ruining the finest career in the world for a Cossack woman and waste of snow" (*O* 23). Obstacles and hardships exist because of the difference between the national and "the Other." First they seemed to be attractive as they were new and warmed with love. Imagination was dominating, and reality lost the battle. "The Other" is always linked with male characteristics and can be identified with the poetic mind.[5] It works and functions, and then is silent. Reality is done in purely symbolic style, magnificent in splendor and many colors.

"Darkness" and "otherness" are synonymous to a certain degree. They express danger and uncertainty. The passion is also painted in dark colors. The cold as the context of the unfolding events can be interpreted at two levels. On the one hand, it is the gradual subsiding of passion subconsciously felt by the hero. On the other, the cold is a national characteristic of Russia, like the fog in Britain. The dark colors express the state of waiting and potential betrayal. The landscape changes overnight. The cold is replaced by a flood, and the symbolic substitution is orchestrated by Orlando's emotional crisis. Inky darkness and stillness are the key characteristics of the "waiting" episode. The protagonist's state of mind resembles those human beings who had been trapped in the night and now paced their twisting and precarious islands in the utmost agony of spirit. The author insists on it being a biography that she writes, and at the same time she confesses that she is telling a story of Orlando's life. Some private and historical documents are used but this is not actually a story, for the author only states facts "and so let the reader make of them what he may"(*O* 31).

So, the story is also the reader's speculation, and his or her active role in rearranging the facts and episodes is part and parcel of Orlando's biography. Yet nobody but the author can explain how Orlando's creative mind works. The great sleep that follows the great frost and the flood is a metaphor that can be interpreted as a pause in Orlando's creative activities and therefore, the pause in the flood of images that could have risen from the bottom of his memory. And it is also a pretext to speak about another combination of the national and "the Other" within the individual mind. The metaphoric imagery of sleep serves to show the work of the creative mind irrespective of its physical life:

> But if sleep it was, of what nature, we can scarcely refrain from asking, are such sleeps as these? Are they remedial measures—trances in which the most galling memories, events that seem likely to cripple life for ever, are brushed with the dark wing which rubs their harshness off and gilds them, even the ugliest and basest, with a luster, an incandescence? Has the finger of death to be laid on the tumult of life from time to time lest it rend us asunder? Are we

The National and "the Other"

so made that we have to take death in small doses daily or we could not go on with the business of living? And then what strange powers are these that penetrate our most secret ways and change our most treasured possessions without our willing it? Had Orlando, worn out by the extremity of his suffering, died for a week, and then come to life again? And if so, of what nature is death and of what nature life? (*O* 32)

The national dominates the closing part of the story about Orlando the man. It shows that Woolf was very well read in ghost stories and could mock them in her narrative. Anyway, Orlando comes back to his ancestors and examines coffin after coffin and speaks to their noble remains. Imagination prompts another type of national identity, "the Other" with very short-term characteristics—this time from the Romanian territory. An extremely tall woman is taken for an apparition. Orlando follows her and finds that she "resembled nothing so much as a hare. ...This hare, moreover, was six feet high and wore a headdress into the bargain of some antiquated kind which made her look still taller. Thus confronted, she stared at Orlando with a stare in which timidity and audacity were most strangely combined"(*O* 55). The exotic name of the Archduchess Harriet Griselda of Finster-Aarhorn and Scandop-Boom expresses "the Otherness" and strangeness in her behavior. Again, her appearance, her clothes and her manners point at her foreign origin. She knows wines and firearms, and the customs of sportsmen in her country. A born poet and artist, Orlando is fascinated by the unusual figure, but her image is as mysterious as her feelings, and instead of a bird of love he sees a harpy. The transformation of feelings is expressed through some impressive metaphor—the Paradise bird becomes an ugly embodiment of lust.

Oriental episodes show the progress of Orlando's career and the new approaches towards the national and "the Other." He is involved in diplomatic affairs, and this service keeps him busy and indifferent to everyday life determined by routine duties. The narrator's tone becomes livelier when she describes foreign manners and customs. Orlando accepts the oriental lifestyle only to a certain degree, remaining a typical Englishman. The ritual of greetings is presented outside the unknown society, and is interpreted as ridiculous though it parodies English table talk:

> Profound bows and curtseys were exchanged. In the first room, it was permissible only to mention the weather. Having said that it was fine or wet, hot or cold, the Ambassador then passed on to the next chamber, where again, two figures rose to greet him. Here it was only permissible to compare Constantinople as a place of residence with London; and the Ambassador naturally said that he preferred Constantinople, and his hosts naturally said, though they had not seen it, that they preferred London. In the next chamber, King Charles's and the Sultan's healths had to be discussed at some length. In

> the next were discussed the Ambassador's health and that of his host's wife, but more briefly. (*O* 59-60)

The opposition of the national and "the Other" is given through documents that are scanty and burned, so they cannot be verified. The character of the hero is padded with rumors and legends, anecdotes and talks floating about, so this opposition probably exists only in some private papers like John Fenner Brigge's, the naval officer who was present at the ceremony dedicated to the celebration of Dukedom and the Order of the Bath. "The Otherness" is expressed by the Englishman who remembers crowds "so unpleasantly close" that he had to climb "into a Judas tree." The author of the papers believed the British to be superior in demonstration of skills "in the art of pyrotechny" (*O* 62). The disturbances during the ceremony also reveal "the Otherness" in its savage uncivilized manner when one of the ladies dashes the candelabra to the ground.

On the whole, the Constantinople episodes are bizarre in structure: they pile up the diaries full of burns and holes, extracts from newspapers and private papers. "From the Gazette of the time, we gather that 'as the clock struck twelve, the Ambassador appeared on the centre Balcony which was hung with priceless rugs'" (*O* 63). The whole description is done in the documentary manner.

He speaks Turkish. The local population are called "natives" and they expect miracles to happen. The transformation of Orlando in Turkey is sudden and shocking but not for the reader of Woolf as she has already prepared the audience for unexpected things and happenings. She introduces the female as stabilizing, calming, a familiar anodyne.

Virginia Woolf is romantic, and her main point is returning. No matter how much she desires to escape, her escape will only lead her back to her own ruins, history, ancestors, to her addicted self.

This is a biography of the poet's mind that can materialize in real works of art when the artist finds himself or herself in unusual circumstance; the national and "the Other" are disputing, and the national wins. "The Otherness" in *Orlando* is often identified with nations and peoples other than British. The imaginative faculty of the creative mind can transform male into female without any difficulty or dangerous consequences.

The unknown world of gypsies lack things dear to Orlando as a creative person, that is, they lack ink and paper. They do not understand her Englishness. "The English disease, a love of Nature, was inborn in her, and here, where Nature was so much larger and more powerful than in England, she fell into its hands as she had never done before" (*O* 70). "The Otherness" distances her from the gypsies and provokes a strong desire to return to her poem.

The National and "the Other"

This work makes her happy, but it causes hostility among the gypsies. The dialogue with herself started in the blank verse poem initiates a revaluation of the ancestors and her glorious past that means nothing to the gypsies. Different standards of life and different types of mentality widen the gap between the national and "the Other." The national within her creative mind works a long-expected miracle. The sight of the cliffs of England comes as the pivotal point in her life signifying her coming back to familiar activities as a poet. Now she could think only of the glory of poetry. "The Otherness" vanishes as soon as she finds herself in London and wraps herself in the familiar lifestyle. The Enlightenment period and the Victorian Age are very important for the English as the periods of the formation of the British nation and British Empire, as well as the beginnings of modernity. Yet in the case of Orlando, who is propelled through these times, they kick-start her speculations about English history.

The structure of the traditional novel, with its rounded characters, logically articulated plot, and solidly specified setting, gradually melts away in *Orlando*. The culminating points in the plot are consecutively pushed to the margins of the novelistic discourse, in the form of asides and parentheses. The narrator's voice, safe and reliable, fades away as the discourse locates itself in the minds of characters. The unity and coherence dissolve in the repetition of motifs and symbols, while the texture of writing becomes more and more densely embroidered with metaphor and simile. Finally, the metaphorical mode seems to aspire to the condition of lyrical poetry:

> Nothing, he reflected, gazing at the view which was now sparkling in the sun, could well be less like the counties of Surrey and Kent or the towns of London and Tunbridge Wells. To the right and left rose in bald and stony prominence the inhospitable Asian mountains, to which the arid castle of a robber chief or two might hang; but parsonage there was none, nor manor house, nor cottage, nor oak, elm, violet, ivy, or wild eglantine. ...The houses were white as eggshells and as bald. That he, who was English root and fibre, should yet exult to the depths of his heart in this wild panorama, and gaze and gaze at those passes and far heights, planning journeys there alone on foot where only the goat and shepherd had gone before; should feel a passion of affection for the bright, unseasonable flowers, love the unkempt, pariah dogs beyond even his elk hounds at home, and snuff the acrid, sharp smell of the streets eagerly into his nostrils, surprised him. (*O* 58-59)

It is with such fragments as the above that we can make up a picture of Orlando's life and character at the time.

Orlando leaves Constantinople in company of a gypsy who rides a donkey. This comical picture represents circumstances that are absolutely new for the heroine as she joins the gypsy tribe. It is a good chance to face another identity, and compare it to the familiar one. The gypsies do not know the word

Solovyova

"beautiful," they ignore Orlando's hundred and seventy rooms; they wear different clothes and are used to a different lifestyle. But "the Otherness" offers a chance for a dialogue and recollections. The past and present meet together in the creative mind:

> And then Nature, in whom she trusted, either played her a trick or worked a miracle. ...The heat was intense... Suddenly, a shadow, though there was nothing to cast a shadow, appeared on the bald mountain-side opposite. ...She could see oak trees... the deer stepping delicately from shade to shade, and could even hear the hum of insects and the gentle sighs and shivers of a summer's day in England....snow began falling; soon the whole landscape was covered and marked with violet shades instead of yellow sunlight... [And] she [came to the gypsies and] told them that she must sail for England... (*O* 73-74)

Writing "The Oak Tree" is the central theme of the novel, for it is a biography of the poet's mind, its growth and functions. It often reads like Wordsworth,[6] a name often mentioned in the novel.

The most impressive figure in Orlando's life, though, is Marmaduke Bonthrop Shelmerdine. He is a soldier, sailor and an adventurer. Also, he is "the Other," and his "Otherness" is expressed in quite a different manner from the way it happened before: "they would go on talking or rather, understanding, which has become the main art of speech in an age when words are growing daily so scanty in comparison with ideas that 'the biscuits ran out' has to stand for kissing a negress in the dark when one has just read Bishop Berkeley's philosophy for the tenth time" (*O* 127-128).

So the fragments of memory and imagery combine in the creative mind. The process of writing and composing poetry is complicated, since it involves the national and "the Other," as they reflect the diversity of mentalities, cultures, and languages. The language of poetry as such is inherently diverse, for the philosophical content expresses itself in concrete images. Sometimes it takes much time to understand the capacities of mind and its intricate turns and ways to manifest the progress of imagination. Many other selves live within Orlando's creative mind, which has no sex, knows no age. It is deeply rooted in English history, its traditions and intertextuality that help to plunge into the deep waters of the past. Woolf's modernist novel contains a strong dash of postmodernity. In fact there are two minds, that of Woolf and that of Orlando. Though the two exist independently of each other, they sometimes come together and make a dialogue, then they collide and take their different ways. They comment on each other, and both are equally important. There is also a guide in this poetic world, who travels through centuries and analyzes the changing situation. I mean Nicholas Greene, the poet and critic, who symbolizes the essential in a given context. He speaks about the decay of literature and the end of the age of heroes and individuals.

The interplay of the national and "the Other," therefore, has a very significant function in *Orlando*. It allows us to understand the real value of close links with culture and history to win the cause of art and humanity.

Notes

[1] Cf. "As interpreted by Roger Fry this exhibition, showing work by Picasso, Matisse, Braque and Derain, signaled not so much a new direct address to the modern world as an assertion of artistic autonomy"(Brooker 6).

[2] Cf. Shelley's *Lines*: "The cold earth slept below, / Above the cold sky shone, / And all around, with a chilling sound, / From caves of ice and fields of snow, / The breath of night like death did flow / Beneath the sinking moon" (523).

[3] Cf. the following lines: "I had a dream, which was not at all a dream..." (Byron 93).

[4] Cf. Coleridge, 240.

[5] On the difference between male and female texts in connection with the opposition of realism–anti-realism see Jean Radford's "Coming to terms: Dorothy Richardson, Modernism and Women." Cf. "Realism, in this kind of argument, is identified as 'masculine', and disruptions or departures from it are, in terms of this binary logic, equated with the feminine—the feminine is taken as an instance of the subversive or dissident, the return of what is repressed from the dominant culture" (In Brooker 96).

[6] Cf. *The Prelude* in Wordsworth.

Works Cited

Brooker, Peter, Ed. *Modernism/Postmodernism*. London and New York: Longman, 1992.

Byron, George Gordon. *The Collected Poems*. Wordsworth Poetry Library. Chatham, Kent: Mackays of Chatham, 1994.

Coleridge, Samuel Taylor. *The Poems of Samuel Taylor Coleridge*. Ed. Ernest Hartley Coleridge, Henry Frowde. London, New York, Toronto, Melbourne and Bombay: Oxford UP, 1912.

Shelley, P. B. *Complete Works*. Ed. Thomas Hutcherson, Henry Frowde. London, New York, Toronto, Melbourne: Oxford UP, 1909.

Woolf, Virginia. *Orlando*. London: Wordsworth Classics, 1995.

Wordsworth, William. *Selected Poetry and Prose*. A Signet Classic. Ed. Geoffrey Hartman, 1970.

Androgyny, Writing, and Place in Woolf's *Orlando* and *A Room of One's Own*
Deborah Epstein Nord

> What a phantasmagoria the mind is and meeting-place of dissemblables. At one moment we deplore our birth and state and aspire to ascetic exaltation; the next we are overcome by the smell of some old garden path and weep to hear the thrushes sing
> (Orlando 176).

In this passage from chapter four of Virginia Woolf's 1928 novel-cum-fictional biography *Orlando*, the protagonist, now a woman, has returned to her home in Blackfriars after her momentous sojourn in Turkey. She marvels at the nearly contradictory feelings that have possessed her and at the unexpected pleasure she now takes in leaning out into the damp winter air from her window. Having left England willingly, anxious to abandon her homeland to escape the "harpy" Love and desirous of "ascetic exaltation" in the court of Constantinople, Orlando is now besotted with the sights, smells, and sounds of home. The passage comments not only on the changeability of human desires and attachments but on the mind as a "phantasmagoria," in which "*dissemblables*"—unlike things—meet and converge. It is Woolf's belief in this quality of mind as an indispensable aspect of artistic creation, of the writer's craft, that I want to explore in this essay, and I will do so by focusing on both androgyny and the disintegration of geographic boundaries as types of mind-travel. I argue here that Woolf's interest as a writer in ridding herself of the kind of subjectivity constituted by sex, place, nation, even history, forms the core of her notion of androgyny and gives shape to the setting of Orlando's sex-change in chapter three of the novel.

I begin by looking at Woolf's most explicit elaboration of androgyny in *A Room of One's Own*, published a year after *Orlando* but based, as we know, on lectures that Woolf had given at Newnham and Girton during the previous year. In some respects other than the merely temporal, the essay on women and writing and the "biography" of Orlando are companion pieces: both focus on the needs of the writer, both address directly the matter of gender (or sex), and both, in the words of Hermione Lee, "set their women free from histories of repression" and "work playfully through literary periods and come out with an idea of a new, modern freedom" (520). Readers and critics of *A Room of One's Own* have often looked at Woolf's discussion of androgyny with an emphasis on the author's apparent—and to some, disturbing—reification of gender characteristics. She appears to depend on certain essentialist notions of masculinity and femininity, some believe, in her effort to imagine the fusion of the two sexes, to associate the masculine mind with logic, hard thinking, and egotism, feminine thought with "suggestive power" and the knack of fertilization. Woolf employs these categories of mind in her estimation of the potential for androgynous creation in a number of writers past and present. The emotions that permeate the works of Galsworthy and Kipling, for instance, seem "incomprehensible" to a woman reader; indeed, on these grounds the works of these "virile" writers bear some resemblance, she ventures, to the fascist experiment in Italy. Keats, Sterne, Cowper, Lamb, and Coleridge were androgynous, and so was Shakespeare; Milton, Ben Jonson, Wordsworth, and Tolstoy were a bit too male; Proust was, strangely enough, "wholly androgynous" and yet "perhaps a little too much of a woman" (*AROO* 102-3).

It is not the game of who succeeds and who fails at androgyny that interests me here. Nor do I want to engage in a critique or endorsement of Woolf's essentialist tendencies. Rather, I am struck by the image that launches Woolf's meditation on androgyny in chapter six of *A Room of One's Own* and by the feeling of relief this image seems to afford her at this point in the text. The sight, glimpsed through her window, of a man and a woman, separately "coming down the street and meeting at the corner" and then getting into a taxi together, she writes, "seems to ease the mind of some strain" (*AROO* 96). Two unlike things—"dissemblables," to use her word in *Orlando*—meet, converge, and co-exist within the frame of the car. But what is this strain that needs to be eased? Why does the writer welcome relief after expatiating on a woman writer's need for financial independence and a private place to write? And why does the sight of a man and woman getting into a taxi together provide a reprieve? She tells us pretty directly: she is tired of thinking about one sex as distinct from the other and especially about the differences between the sexes that are the result of their differential treatment, both historically and in contemporary life. The man and woman bring her back to a contemplation of the world as it is lived in the moment but, more importantly, they free her of the focus on discrimination and grievance that her contemplation of woman's lot inevitably entails. The couple becomes, then, an image of union both in the world and in the mind of the writer, a revivifying object of the writer's attention and an emollient for her agitated spirit. Put differently, the moment she glimpses the couple getting into the taxi is the moment when fiction writing takes over.

In the course of explaining the restorative power of this image, Woolf seems to imply that the woman who writes critically about woman's place in culture and the mind of the woman who writes fiction are separable; indeed, they are sometimes at odds. The former—the narrator of *A Room of One's Own* up to this point—places herself "outside of [civilization]" and emerges as "alien and critical" (*AROO* 97). The latter—an unsexed entity, not a sexed person, as Woolf suggests by referring to the mind as "it"—can travel anywhere and take any perspective, think back through both mothers and fathers, be separate from people it sees or join with them and enter their very beings. The writer's mind cannot dwell in grievance or it will lose its unity, its integrity, and it will cease, to use Woolf's word, to "fertilise." What a surprise for the reader to learn that the very enterprise in which the author has been engaged in this essay requires repression, the repression that makes it possible to write truly, as a creative and fecund mind rather than as a critical or angry sensibility. Woolf blames the emergence of the "woman question" itself for the aridity of the hyper-masculine writer who must now defend himself against a feminist onslaught and for the nearly crippling strain and self-consciousness that inhibits, indeed is "fatal" to, the feminist writer herself. Her apparent nostalgia, ironically expressed, for the days before political sex-consciousness ("the happy age, before Miss Davies and Miss Clough were born") sends her back to writers, for the most part male, who predate current controversies over exactly the issues she has been contemplating over five chapters of her book. Some of these are the androgynous ones.

From this perspective, androgyny seems less interesting as some amalgam of sex characteristics or mental tendencies one might label masculine and feminine and more significant as a type of disembodiedness or disentanglement from the social circumstances that foster resentment. In her essay "Women and Fiction," which appeared in the same year as *A Room of One's Own*, Woolf puts this more crudely. In works like Charlotte Brontë's *Jane Eyre* and George Eliot's *Middlemarch*, she writes, we are

> conscious not merely of the writer's character, as we are conscious of the character of Charles Dickens, but we are conscious of a woman's presence—of someone resenting the treatment of her sex and pleading for its rights. This brings into women's writing an element that is entirely absent from a man's, unless, indeed, he happens to be a working-man, a Negro, or one who for some other reason is conscious of a disability....The desire to plead some personal cause...has a distressing effect, as if the spot at which the reader's attention is directed were suddenly two-fold instead of one ("Women and Fiction" 47).

This kind of subjectivity, one that will not allow the writer to separate him- or herself from disabling circumstance, has a way of dividing both the reader's and the writer's attention. Although it is disconcerting that Woolf appears only to recognize the self-alienation or social embeddedness of women, working-class people, "Negroes," and the like (as if the imaginations of hale, middle-class, white Englishmen are not also partly determined by social conditions), we find here nonetheless a gloss on her idea of androgyny. The androgynous mind, which can enter into the most disparate of characters and circumstances, allows the writer an escape from "disabling," distorting, and fracturing subjectivity. Androgyny, as Woolf understands it, can separate the mind, which can be whole, from the being, which is socially circumscribed and, as a result, split off from itself. The wholeness of the writer's mind is what Woolf calls androgyny, not simply or, perhaps, even primarily because it partakes of masculine and feminine qualities, but because it is "resonant and porous," free and at peace, because it unites disparate things (in this case, male and female) and is unfettered by the bonds of social circumstance or disadvantage.

The intensity of Woolf's focus on the disadvantage of sex in *A Room of One's Own* makes her desperate for the relief she imagines in that couple entering the taxi. And, although the concentration of her energies on women's grievances in this text was presumably greater than that which she experienced while writing fiction, sex-consciousness surely plagued her in her novel writing as well. As Woolf would no doubt have conceded, the mind that creates fiction is never wholly free of the self—the woman—whose subjectivity is constituted by social circumstance. Lily Briscoe's rejection of marriage in *To the Lighthouse*, Elizabeth Dalloway's sense of possibility and promise as she walks down the Strand in *Mrs. Dalloway*, the Pargiter sisters' struggles with convention and historical change over a period of fifty years in *The Years*—all of these are, needless to say, informed by their creator's keen political sense of what it meant to be a woman in the late decades of Victoria's reign and in the transition to what Hermione Lee calls "modern freedom." Is it in *Orlando*, then, that Woolf allows herself a full holiday from the "alien and critical" stance of the aggrieved woman—by traveling from one sex to the other, one period in history to another, one place or nation to another, and yet by refusing to leave any of her points of origin behind, by keeping all "*dissemblables*" current and conjoined?

The third chapter of the "biography" contains the pivotal episode of Orlando's sex change, but it places the change in a setting outside of England—in Turkey—and thereby introduces other unstable aspects of his/her identity as well. Clothes play a crucial role here and throughout *Orlando*, as does the perverse idea that bodily change can follow a change in sensibility, rather than the other way around. Mind makes the man—or woman—and affinity makes the Englishman/woman—or, in the case of Orlando in Turkey, the Gypsy. "It was *a change in Orlando herself*," we read, "that dictated her choice of a woman's dress and of a woman's sex" (*O* 188; emphasis added). Clothes can, in a

Androgyny, Writing, and Place

Carlylean vein, be symbolic of "something hid deep beneath," but they can also advertise one sex to the public while another sex lurks below ("underneath the sex is the very opposite of what it is above"). The latter occurs when Orlando decides to wear men's clothing to navigate the streets of eighteenth-century London, even after she has become a woman. The alternation between petticoats and breeches, even when the body does not change, affords her multiple pleasures and useful protections. But clothes can also, if they appear sufficiently sexually ambiguous, allow for and perhaps even encourage a change of body to suit a change of mind. This is what happens in Constantinople.

The sojourn in Turkey calls into question not only Orlando's sexual identity but his Englishness—his national identity and what might be called his ethnic origins. Even before the question of sex comes up, in fact, Orlando finds himself unexpectedly smitten with the Asian landscape and the atmosphere, not always salubrious, of the Turkish streets:

> That he, who was English root and fibre, should yet exult to the depths of his heart in this wild panorama, and gaze and gaze at those passes and far heights, planning journeys there alone on foot where only the goat and shepherd had gone before; should feel a passion of affection for the bright, unreasonable flowers, love the unkempt, pariah dogs beyond even his elk hounds at home, and snuff the acrid, sharp smell of the streets eagerly into his nostrils, *surprised him. He wondered if, in the season of the Crusades, one of his ancestors had taken up with a Circassian peasant woman; thought it possible; fancied a certain darkness in his complexion*, and, going indoors again, withdrew to his bath. (*O* 121; emphasis added)

His Englishness ought to have dictated that he miss the English countryside and feel alien amidst the arid mountains and odor-filled bazaar, but instead his delight in the strange sights and smells seems to make him aware of another identity altogether and even to darken his complexion. What transpires inside of him is expressed bodily, and he invents for himself a Circassian ancestress to account for the darkening skin and unexpected affinities. Orlando's story rejects the kind of subjectivity Woolf tires of in *A Room of One's Own* and "Women and Fiction," a subjectivity based upon conditions of birth—upon sex, nationality, citizenship, social class, and even race. This novel, because of its anti-realist assumptions and comic bravado, allows Woolf to turn the usual patterns of identity around. The imagined ancestress, she implies, is just that: a creation of the shifting mind that looks for the origins of temperament and taste in birth, biology, and body.

Like Orlando's darkening skin, his body follows his affections, though not in any straightforward way. A week before Orlando awakens with a new sex, an episode occurs that is the subject of tales and rumors but remains uncertain ("nobody has ever known exactly what took place...that night"). Observers claim that, after a ceremonial occasion, a mysterious peasant woman was drawn up to Orlando's balcony by a rope, that the two then embraced and entered his rooms. The appearance and identity of both forms are murky: the figure, assumed to be male, that comes out onto the balcony is cloaked and obscured; the woman's shape is "much muffled." No one sees Orlando awake for seven days (the length of the Biblical creation), the peasant woman is never seen again, and a deed of marriage joining Orlando and Rosina Pepita, a dancer and perhaps a Gypsy, is discovered.[1] As in *A Room of One's Own*, the writer conjures a man and woman who are united and then disappear from view. Clearly this is a potent, a fertile, image for Woolf. But here the aftermath of union is unclear: did love make Orlando a woman? Or did two people become one, Pepita absorbed into Orlando, changing his sex? In this creation story, is Eve formed out of Adam's body through fusion rather than splitting?

The capes, cloaks, and mufflings that hide Orlando's and Pepita's forms on the night in question share with other elements of the "eastern" wardrobe the power to obscure the body's sex. While western clothing advertises and fixes sexual identity, the seemingly androgynous garb of "the east" makes sex change an easy matter—or at least this seems the case in the westerner's imagination. In Turkey, we learn, coats and trousers could be "worn indifferently by either sex" (*O* 139). The billowing Turkish trousers that Orlando wears after becoming a woman and running off with the Gypsies distract her even from thinking about her sex: to her mind they do not signify one sex or the other. And the Gypsy women, she thinks, "differ very little from the gipsy men," except in a couple of particulars (*O* 153). It is only dressed once again in western clothing, now a "coil of skirts about her legs," that she becomes acutely conscious of her sex, of both its privileges and its disadvantages. Turkish garb, in other words, had allowed for that release from the strain of sex consciousness for which Woolf longs towards the end of *A Room of One's Own*. A return to England and to voluminous western skirts summons back the need to think again of one sex as distinct from the other, of herself as distinct from men, because of bodily form and social circumstance. Why, then, does she go back?

The answer, in part, lies in her sojourn with the Gypsy tribe she joins outside of Broussa after fleeing Constantinople as a woman on the back of an old Gypsy's donkey. Familiar to readers of Bildungsroman and nineteenth-century fiction generally, this running away story links Orlando to other heroines—and heroes—who find the constraints of social and sexual convention stifling and seek refuge with their own kind among peripatetic Gypsies. We think of Maggie Tulliver's escape from certain punishment at the hands of her family to a sanctuary she imagines to contain her truer kin—the Gypsy tribe on Dunlow

Androgyny, Writing, and Place

Common. Woolf draws on a second element of the Gypsy plot when she notes that the Gypsies regarded Orlando "as one of themselves....her dark hair and dark complexion bore out the belief that she was, by birth, one of them and had been snatched by an English Duke from a nut tree when she was a baby and taken to that barbarous land [i.e. England] where people live in houses because they are too feeble and diseased to stand the open air" (*O* 141-2). Here the customary novelistic patterns of kidnapping, hidden identity, and the fantasy of noble birth are reversed in a kind of inverted Freudian family romance, so that Orlando turns out to be a Gypsy, as well as a woman, her true identity ennobling her only in the eyes of the Gypsies. But given Woolf's interest in *Orlando* in playing with, and reversing, the ordinary influence of birth on identity, she also makes the Gypsies guilty of crude biological determinism. If Orlando acts and looks like a Gypsy, they seem to believe, she must have been born one (just as anyone seeing her now would assume, falsely, that she had been born a woman). But, as we know from previous speculations that one of Orlando's ancestors had "taken up with a Circassian peasant woman," birth—what we would call heredity—has little to do with it.

The Gypsies expect that Orlando's ostensible Gypsy origins will make her exactly like them: that she will regard Nature as a cruel god, do a thing only for the sake of doing it, and believe in the sheep-skin and the basket. Instead, they discover that she adores, even worships, Nature (they begin to suspect that this is an "English disease") and that she is, furthermore, someone "who doubts" and who sees, not the everyday objects before her (sheep-skins and baskets), but "something else." She is, in short, a writer, and her mind floats free, beyond the limitations of body, place, and birth, finding meanings hidden from view, reading the camp-fire flames, losing her adeptness at milking and cheese-making, and generally disdaining the realm of the literal. The Gypsies' literal-mindedness makes them unable to tolerate difference, and one wonders if here Woolf is mocking English xenophobia by means of the Gypsies. Orlando, visited by a vision of a summer's day in England, knows she must go home. She is homesick and her throat in danger of being slit by the Gypsies but, more than that, Woolf seems to signal England as the place of literary creation, to which the writer must inevitably return.

Still, to leave Turkey behind and to revert to pure Englishness seems like a relinquishing of foreignness, of multiple identities, and of a place where, for Orlando at least, androgyny is possible. This might be the case if Orlando's identity were ever fixed by sex, history, chronology, or even emotion. Her/his identity is, rather, cumulative: it accrues, gathers, and absorbs all aspects of time and experience into itself. So that at the end of the narrative, when Orlando has almost reached "the present" and contemplates the landscape of her home, the whole of England and Scotland, the past of Drake and then of Nelson, her former castle, the church towers and vast fields, suddenly the "bare mountains of Turkey" appear to her in her mind's eye. She hears her old Gypsy friend's voice challenging her to explain why her lineage and race would be superior to the sun, goats, and hills of Turkey. The experience of Turkey is indelibly marked and rooted in her consciousness—her imagination—and erases the borders of time and place. In another moment, though, the eastern landscape falls away again and other memories, places, times flood in. Orlando's identity is composed of all that she has savored, of "the great variety of selves" she has been, of all the landscapes, nations, homes, historical epochs, and bodies she has occupied.

Orlando allows Woolf the ubiquity and integrity of consciousness she imagines through the metaphor of androgyny in *A Room of One's Own*. Orlando him/herself is something of a metaphor for the same thing: a being who combines disparate, even contradictory, phenomena and floats free of earthly bonds, who unites past and present, male and female, east and west, without losing wholeness of purpose and intensity of focus. Escaping both the spirit of social grievance of the woman's lot and the egotism—the arid "I"—of man's subjectivity, the writer longs to enter deeply into experience and hold nothing back. The writer's mind, like the couple in the taxi and like Orlando, is a phantasmagoria of rapidly changing images and a "meeting place of dissemblables."

Note

[1] The obscure Pepita is a reference to Vita Sackville-West's Spanish grandmother, reputed to be the descendant of Gypsies, who bore five illegitimate children to Lionel Sackville-West. If Orlando is Vita, he is also Vita's grandfather, and perhaps grandmother too. See Nicolson 47-8.

Works Cited

Lee, Hermione. *Virginia Woolf*. New York: Vintage, 1999 (1996).
Nicolson, Nigel. *Portrait of a Marriage*. New York: Bantam, 1974.
Woolf, Virginia. *A Room of One's Own*. 1929. New York: Harcourt Brace, 1981.
——. *Orlando: A Biography*. 1928. New York: Harcourt Brace, 1956.
——. "Women and Writing." *Women and Writing*. Ed. Michèle Barrett. New York and London: Harcourt Brace, 1979.

IV

Reading Russian—Russian Readings

"A railway accident": Virginia Woolf Translates Tolstoy
Natalya Reinhold

As is known, Woolf compared her reading of books by Russian writers in translation to reading texts stripped of their style. We find this observation in "The Russian Point of View," which came out in 1925 as part of the first series of *The Common Reader*.[1] Interestingly, Woolf made this disturbing statement after having been engaged in co-translating three books from the Russian in 1922 and 1923.[2]

We certainly remember that Woolf read Russian works first in French and then, in English translations.[3] Knowing her view of 1925 we can assume that she undertook the co-translation from the Russian out of her dissatisfaction with reading the works by Dostoevsky, Tolstoy, and Chekhov in translated form. However, her experience as a translator seems to have changed her attitude to translation very little. On the contrary, Woolf emphasizes the irreparable losses a Russian text, and, for that matter, any source text undergoes in translation.

Was Virginia Woolf then an adherent of the "untranslatability" approach to literary texts? It was not uncommon with the modernists. For example, T. S. Eliot had similar doubts about the translatability of prose and still more of poetry. Basing his ideas on the difference between thinking and feeling, the conscious and the unconscious as they get expressed in a language, Eliot asserts the resistance of poetry to traveling across cultures because of its irreducible national idiom: "It is true...that prose writings have significance in their own language which is lost in translation; but we all feel that we lose much less in reading a novel in translation than in reading a poem...It is easier to think in a foreign language than it is to feel in it. Therefore no art is more stubbornly national than poetry" (18-19).

In the case of Woolf, the "untranslatability" view seems also to embrace cultural specificity. In fact, she begins her essay by drawing a parallel between the English audience being as much baffled in their reading of Russian literature as in their reception of the work of Henry James, who, despite his becoming a British subject, nevertheless belongs to a culture other than English:

> Could any one believe that the novels of Henry James were written by a man who had grown up in the society which he describes, or that his criticism of English writers was written by a man who had read Shakespeare without any

sense of the Atlantic Ocean and two or three hundred years on the far side of it separating his civilization from ours? A special acuteness and detachment, a sharp angle of vision the foreigner will often achieve; but not that absence of self-consciousness, that ease and fellowship and sense of common values which make for intimacy, and sanity, and the quick give and take of familiar intercourse. (*CR*1 219)

Yet what seems to be obvious at first glance, that is, Woolf's sharing the view of the untranslatability of literary works, together with the impenetrability of cultures, is best taken with a pinch of salt. And not only because of the observation she makes further on in the essay, in a way correcting her opening judgment: "What remains is, as the English have proved by the fanaticism of their admiration, something very powerful and very impressive..." (*CR*1 220). The very idea of style as a coat or dress that literature can be easily stripped of in translation reads as an intentionally simplified one when taken literally, with a view to Woolf's own sophisticated writing practice.

Another argument for it being a more complicated case with Woolf is the irony which invariably accompanies the discussion of the dichotomy of style versus meaning in her works. A rhetorical question the speaker asks and leaves unanswered in *A Room of One's Own* serves as a canonical example: "But then one would have to decide what is style and what is meaning, a question which—but here I was actually at the door which leads into the library itself" (*AROO* 11).

If not for the style, then what was Woolf looking for as a translator and reader of Russian works?

I have already written about my view of the reasons for Woolf's turning to reading and reviewing Russian books,[4] and I still believe that nothing but her interest in further stretching the possibilities of English prose is responsible for her critical reading of Russian literature. Yet the long-term Russian-related activities of Woolf are diverse enough for us not to grow complacent in making a few general observations about her owing this or that device to this or that Russian writer. Similarly, we should not take the image of the great Russian writers as deprived by a railway accident of their clothes, manners, and idiosyncrasies of character as a figure of speech alone. There is something suggestive in it. The analysis of its implications will take us first to look at some of Woolf's co-translations from the Russian.

Of the diversity of directions in which Woolf's work on Russian material takes us, I would like to focus on those which suggest her identity as a world writer. We get a glimpse of one of these from an analysis of the choice of Russian works she agreed to assist Koteliansky with translating. This will take us to the archive materials found among the Hogarth Press papers at the library of Reading University. I assume that the study of extra-literary sources can help us map the milieu Woolf was interested in as a translator and reader of Russian literature.

The Hogarth Press papers No. 493 and No. 595 give us an insight into the background story of Woolf's collaborating with S. S. Koteliansky in translating and publishing two works of and about Leo Tolstoy. They are Tolstoy's early letters to Valeriya Vladimirovna Arsenyeva (1836 - 1909), dated 1856-1857, and Aleksandr Borisovich Goldenveiser's two-volume diary, *Vblizi Tolstogo* [Near Tolstoy] (1922 - 1923).[5] The letters were selected and translated by S. S. Koteliansky and Virginia Woolf, and published by the Hogarth Press in 1923 as *Tolstoi's Love Letters*. The diary appeared in the same year as *Talks with Tolstoi*, with the same translators' names on the title page.

The list can hardly be called exhaustive,[6] yet for the purpose of this article I will have to limit myself to only one of the above mentioned sources, that is *Talks with Tolstoi*. So far it has been on the periphery of scholars' attention. Yet I claim that it gives an insight into the shaping of Woolf's idiom as a world writer.

I proceed from the assumption that by the early 1920s, Woolf's conviction that English translations from the Russian were inadequate or crude and lacking in vividness and depth was already strong enough. It was the result of her more than a decade-long reading of Russian books in translation (mostly by Constance Garnett). So, it is probably with a view to making up for the above lacunae wrought by translations that Woolf undertook the co-translation of Goldenveiser's diary and Tolstoy's letters to Arsenyeva. She may have needed the "texture" of Tolstoy's views, the daily observations, his spontaneous responses, etc. Note how practically Woolf went about the whole matter of unsatisfactory translations. I mean she used translation as a tool to get information about "[Tolstoy's] manners, the idiosyncrasies of...[his] character[ ]" (*CR* I 220).

Taking up the central issue of a broad cross-cultural agenda behind Woolf's work as a co-translator and reader of Russian literature, I would like to address the point about the selection of passages from Goldenveiser's diary *Vblizi Tolstogo*, which went into the English edition. By comparing the extracts published in Woolf-cum-Koteliansky's translation with the Russian source text, i.e. the two-volume edition of Goldenveiser's diary, we can get a clearer view of what particular aspects of Tolstoy's personality and lifestyle she was presumably interested in.

Judging by the correspondence of 1923 between Leonard Woolf and S. S. Koteliansky found in the sections No. 38, 493 and 595 of the Hogarth Press archives, Koteliansky and Virginia Woolf worked on translating both Tolstoy's letters and the book by Goldenveiser in spring 1923. The first mention of Koteliansky's suggestion that the Hogarth Press should publish the translation of Goldenveiser's "diary" as he referred to it occurs in his letters to Leonard Woolf of 14 and 16 February 1923. (Initially they had discussed the project of translating the book about Tolstoy together.) By the end of April 1923 the proofs were ready. It is at that final stage that the English target text got a new title, *Talks with Tolstoi*. It could well be that a selection of chapters from the Russian source text received this title thanks to the obvious analogy with *Gespräche mit Goethe in den letzten Jahren Seines Lebens* by Johann Peter Eckermann (1823-1832).[7]

In August 1923 Leonard Woolf and Koteliansky resumed their correspondence about the copyright for the American publication. In October 1923 the English translation of Goldenveiser's book came out in the Hogarth Press in London. There seems to be no trace left of the translators' discussion of the principles of selecting the fragments from the book for the English edition of A. B. Goldenveiser's memoirs, except for the following remark, somewhat ruffled in tone, made by Koteliansky in his letter to Leonard Woolf of 23 February 1923:

> If you, the Hogarth Press, agree to publish the book, I cannot accept the principle that you "have the right to make the selections of what is to be included." The right must belong to the translators—on their mutual agreement what to include. *Not that I doubt Virginia's taste, not a bit of it.* I simply cannot put myself in a position of being dictated in such matters. Especially when I dont claim that everything I translate should be included. The selections of what is to be included should be done by the translators, by mutual agreement.[8] (emphasis added)

The above emphasized hint at Virginia Woolf as the principal adviser gives us good grounds on which to reconstruct the logic which the co-translators, or, to be more exact, one of them, that is, Virginia Woolf pursued in selecting the passages for the translation, by relating the English edition of Goldenveiser's book to the background view of Virginia Woolf's literary interests. I assume that the comparison of the Russian source text to the English target text will allow us to interpret certain fragments included in the Hogarth Press edition as prompted by Woolf's writerly and critical interests.

The comparison leaves the reader under the impression that Woolf thought it very important to get straight from the horse's mouth what Tolstoy thought about arts, and modern art in particular. She must have found interesting the sensory approach the Russian writer chose to apply to contemporary art:

Virginia Woolf Translates Tolstoy

> Among the sensations experienced by our senses of touch, sight, hearing, etc., there are some, which are unpleasant and painful—for instance, a violent knock, a deafening noise, a bitter taste, etc. Now modern art often works upon us not so much by means of its content, as by irritating our organs of sensation, painfully. As regards taste, an unhealthy taste needs mustard, whilst it produces an unpleasant impression upon a pure taste. So it is in the arts. (Goldenveiser 83)

She would have certainly paid attention to Tolstoy's critical view of contemporary literature as oriented to "the last word":

> Tolstoi[9] went on to say: "Now books are written by people who have nothing to say. You read but you do not see the writer. They always try to give 'the last word'. They reject the real writers and say that they have become obsolete. Modern books are read just because one can get to know 'the last word' from them, and this is easier than to read and know the real writers. These purveyors of 'the last word' do enormous harm, they make people unused to thinking independently." (Goldenveiser 150-1)

Woolf could not help highlighting Tolstoy's 1905 view of the future of fiction which, in his opinion, will be less taken up with the fictional:

> "It seems to me that in time works of art will cease to be invented. It will be a shame to invent a story about a fictitious Ivan Ivanovich or Marie Petrovna. Writers, if such there be, will not invent, but will only describe the significant or interesting things which they have happened to observe in life." (Goldenveiser 152)

A Woolf scholar can find it rewarding to relate Tolstoy's remark to Woolf's (or rather, her speaker's) speculation in *A Room of One's Own* about the possible directions contemporary women's writing could take in the near future. There seems to be some link between the Russian and the English writers' estimations of the state of the novel:

> Mary Carmichael, I thought, still hovering at a little distance above the page, will have her work cut out for her merely as an observer. I am afraid indeed that she will be tempted to become, what I think the less interesting branch of the species—the naturalist-novelist, and not the contemplative. There are so many new facts for her to observe. (*AROO* 153)

Virginia Woolf must have been interested in comparing her own judgment of the work of art *per se* to Tolstoy's view of the same subject: "At the basis of a true work of art there must lie some perfectly original idea or feeling, but it must be expressed with slavish adherence to the smallest details of life" (Goldenveiser 161).

Woolf, who shaped new novelistic modes in English writing, could not have missed Leo Tolstoy's judgments about the significance of artistic form:

> Then Tolstoi turned the conversation to the importance and province of form in art: "I think that every great artist necessarily creates his own form also. If the content of works of art can be infinitely varied, so also can their form. Once Turgenev and I came back from the theatre in Paris and discussed this. He completely agreed with me. We recalled all that is best in Russian literature and it seemed that in these works the form was perfectly original. Omitting Pushkin, let us take Gogol's *Dead Souls*. What is it? Neither a novel nor a story. It is something perfectly original. Then there is the *Memoirs of a Sportsman*, the best book Turgenev ever wrote; then Dostoevsky's *House of the Dead*, and then, sinner, that I am, my *Childhood*[10]; Hertzen's *Past and Thoughts*; Lermontov's *Hero of Our Time*..." (Goldenveiser 81-2)

Taking into account Woolf's ideas of the fullness of being and life experience as expressed in the novel[11] we can imagine how glad she would be to come across similar judgments in the talks of Tolstoy who, in his turn, referred to Goethe. Cf. "A real writer, as Goethe justly observed, must be able to describe everything. And I must say that, although I am not very fond of Goethe, he could do it" (Goldenveiser 80-1).

Sometimes the reader of Koteliansky-cum-Woolf's translation of Tolstoy's "diary" would think that Woolf reveals herself, so to speak, in those passages where Tolstoy expresses his liberal and skeptical views on contemporary University education. It seems that Woolf, as an enthusiastic supporter of women's creative activities, would have necessarily spotted these bits.[12]

Also, Tolstoy's speculations about brain work and madness must have caught the eye of Virginia Woolf as one who shaped the English modernist novel. The writer whose observations were later collected in *A Writer's Diary*[13] would have certainly become interested in the minutest details of Tolstoy's description of the way he worked on a new book. But what I find to be particularly striking is Tolstoy's remark about the significance of the moment in the work of a writer—"the moment of being," I am tempted to say: it was duly selected and included in the English version of the book:

> Tolstoi said further:
> "Brain work often tires the head, and when tired, you can't work as fruitfully as with a fresh head. Generally speaking, in brain work the moment is very important. There are moments when your thoughts come out as if molded in bronze; at other moments nothing happens." (Goldenveiser 151)

Another meaningful parallel to Woolf's priorities in the arts is found in Tolstoy's numerous observations about the art of music, which were repro-

Virginia Woolf Translates Tolstoy

duced in the English translation of Goldenveiser's book. See the note made on 28 July 1905:

> Today Tolstoi was enthusiastic about Mozart's operas, particularly about *Don Juan*. Together with the extraordinary richness of its melody, he rates very high its power to give in music the reflection of characters and situations. Tolstoi recalled the statue of the commander, the village scene, and particularly the duel. (Goldenveiser 81)

On the whole, the fact that Woolf took part in translating Goldenveiser's book about Tolstoy testifies to her great interest in the Russian writer's personality, and her intention to have a full scope of his views of art and social life, the issues of war and peace, men and women. It could well be that, infected with Gorky's sharp essay on Leo Tolstoy,[14] Woolf took a chance to feed on the facts of Tolstoy's life by co-translating Goldenveiser's diary. Obviously, our knowledge of "the Russian theme" in Virginia Woolf's work shall not be complete without a comparative study of the Russian source texts and her co-translations.

Going back to the Hogarth Press archives, let me add that a passage from Goldenveiser's *Talks with Tolstoi* in Woolf-cum-Koteliansky's translation was read on the BBC on 30 September 1947.[15]

Parallel to the translation and editing of the book by A. B. Goldenveiser, there took shape the project of editing Tolstoy's letters to Valeriya Arsenyeva. A fragment from Virginia Woolf-cum-Koteliansky's translation of *Tolstoi's Love Letters* was first published in *John o' London Weekly* in March 1923.[16] The full collection of letters to Mme Arsenyeva was published by the Hogarth Press in May-June 1923. Till 1976, when there came out a two-volume edition of Tolstoy's letters selected and translated by R. F. Christian, it had remained the only publication in English of Leo Tolstoy's letters to Valeriya Arsenyeva,[17] and since then it has become a rarity.

Thus what the Russian section of the Hogarth Press archives makes clear about Woolf's taking part in the translation and publishing of the materials related to Tolstoy in the shaping years of 1922-1923 is that, interested as she was in a broader agenda of the Russian writer's views, she went about the matter in a practical, cross-cultural and comparative way.

To sum up, the Hogarth Press papers and Virginia Woolf-cum-Koteliansky's translations give us an insight into a broader social-cultural and literary-biographical agenda behind Woolf's work with Russian materials. The study of these sources being inevitably of a secondary order in relation to writing *per se*, it nonetheless makes us aware of a clash of Woolf's agnostic position (cultures and languages are impenetrable) with her epistemological search, accompanied by her practical approach to arts (what information does the text convey; what were the conditions of life then? etc.). Let me take up the quotation from "The Russian Point of View" I referred to at the beginning of this article, and re-address it:

> ...we have judged a whole literature stripped of its style....Thus treated, the great Russian writers are like men deprived by an earthquake or a railway accident not only of all their clothes, but also of something subtler and more important—their manners, the idiosyncrasies of their characters....
> They have lost their clothes, we say, in some terrible catastrophe...
> (*CRI* 220)

When we come back to Woolf's view enriched with the knowledge of her huge critical and co-translation work done on Russian literature, we get at a denser meaning of her striking image of "[Russian] literature stripped of its style...deprived by...a railway accident...of...manners, the idiosyncrasies of ...characters." Besides the obvious reading of it as the losses a source text undergoes in translation, it allows for other interpretations. The potent metaphor she uses points at her social-political interest in current developments in the world, for the image of "men deprived by an earthquake or a railway accident not only of all their clothes, but also of...their manners, the idiosyncrasies of their characters" hints at the post-revolutionary refugees from Soviet Russia, stripped of their property and incomes. Cf. the description of the Russians, fleeing from their homeland in 1919, in Vladimir Nabokov's novel *Glory* (1931-1932):

> From that year on Martin developed a passion for trains, travels, distant lights, the heartrending wails of locomotives in the dark of night, and the waxworks vividness of local stations flashing by, with people never to be seen again. The slow heaving off, the grating of the rudder chain, the internal tremor of the Canadian freighter on which he and his mother left Crimea in April 1919, the stormy sea and the driving rain were not as conducive to viatic excitement as an express train, and only gradually did Martin get penetrated with this new enchantment....Despite the abundant luggage—lumpy, hastily gathered, fastened with rope instead of straps—all these people somehow gave the impression of traveling light, of sailing as if by chance; the formula of distant journeys could not accommodate their bewilderment and melancholy. (24-25)

There is more, however, to the railway metaphor than just an allusion to the political turmoil of the time, for it also expresses Woolf's view of Russian literature as focused on the most fundamental issues of being. The image of a person deprived of his/her belongings can stir up in the reader's subconscious the memories of Leo Tolstoy's famous parable "How Much Land Does a Man Need?"[18] with its emphatically existential dimension. Yet I would like to stretch the point about the suggestiveness of the image even further and say that

Virginia Woolf Translates Tolstoy

what is striking about it is not so much the intertextual halo (after all, it differs with every reader) as its intrinsically cross-cultural idiom.

Being aware of how often Woolf played around with Carlyle's comparison of people's position in society to the clothes they wear, and of her strategy of investing her own "I" in the clothes of a definite social type,[19] we cannot miss her rapid short-cut to the modernist image of twentieth-century prose writers as being like those who have "lost their clothes...in some terrible catastrophe," and thus face a radically new situation in writing. By describing "the great Russian writers" as "deprived by...a railway accident...of all their clothes," Woolf echoes (if not foreshadows) Osip Mandelstam's definition of the then contemporary Russian prose as "railroad prose" which he gave in his autobiographical essay "The Egyptian Stamp" (1928):

> The railroad has changed the whole course, the whole structure, the whole rhythm of our prose. It has delivered it over to the senseless muttering of the French *moujik* out of *Anna Karenina*. Railroad prose, like the woman's purse of that ominous *moujik*...is divorced from any concern with beauty and that which is beautifully rounded.
>
> Yes, it is there where the beefy levers of locomotives are covered in hot oil that this dear little prose breathes, stretches out at its full length...[20]

The image of Russian writers standing on the railway platform "deprived of their clothes" (Woolf), "divorced from any concern with beauty and that which is beautifully rounded" (Mandelstam), "penetrated with this new excitement" of "an express train" (Nabokov) brings up, in a suggestive and cross-cultural way, an essentially modernist background for Virginia Woolf as a world writer.

Notes

[1] Cf. "Not only have we all this to separate us from Russian literature, but a much more serious barrier—the difference of language. Of all those who feasted upon Tolstoi, Dostoevsky, and Tchekov during the past twenty years, not more than one or two perhaps have been able to read them in Russian. Our estimate of their qualities has been formed by critics who have never read a word of Russian, or seen Russia, or even heard the language spoken by natives; who have had to depend, blindly and implicitly, upon the work of translators. What we are saying amounts to this, then, that we have judged a whole literature stripped of its style" (*CR*1 219-220).

[2] See F. M. Dostoevsky, *Stavrogin's Confession and the Plan of the Life of a Great Sinner*. With Introductory and Explanatory Notes. Trans. from the Russian by Virginia Woolf and S. S. Koteliansky. Richmond: The Hogarth Press, 1922; *Tolstoi's Love Letters*. With a Study on the Biographical Elements in Tolstoi's Work by Paul Biriukov.

Reinhold

Trans. from the Russian by S. S. Koteliansky and Virginia Woolf. Richmond: The Hogarth Press, 1923; A. B. Goldenveiser, *Talks with Tolstoi*. Trans. by S. S. Koteliansky and Virginia Woolf. Richmond: The Hogarth Press, 1923.

[3] Woolf refers to Dostoevsky's *Le Crime et le Châtiment* and *Un Adolescent* in her letters to Lytton Strachey of 1 September 1912 (Woolf and Strachey 41; *L2* 5), and 1 December 1912 (Woolf and Strachey 47). *The Eternal Husband and Other Stories* and *An Honest Thief and Other Stories* by Dostoevsky, as well as *The Bishop and Other Stories* by Anton Chekhov, and *The Two Friends and Other Stories* by Ivan Turgenev were read in Constance Garnett's translation in 1917, 1919, and 1921, respectively (*BP* 116, 120, 123, 106). Woolf read *A Russian Schoolboy* by Sergey Aksakoff in the translation of J. D. Duff (*BP* 101), and *The Stories of E. Militsina and M. Saltikov* in Beatrix L. Follemache's translation (*E2* 341-44): the latter two are the rare exceptions to the rule!

[4] See "Virginia Woolf's Russian Voyage Out" in *Woolf Studies Annual* 9 (2003): 19-20.

[5] Aleksandr Borisovich Goldenveiser (1875 - 1961), a Russian pianist and composer, got acquainted with Leo Nikolaevich Tolstoy in 1896. He became a frequent visitor in the Tolstoys' home in Moscow, and he often played music to Tolstoy in Yasnaya Polyana. Almost immediately after meeting Tolstoy for the first time Aleksandr Goldenveiser began taking notes of his regular talks with Tolstoy. He was very careful in recording the writer's judgments, opinions, and remarks, however casual they might be. So it came about that the last fifteen years of Tolstoy's life were thoroughly described by a person who became his close and devoted friend. The two-volume memoirs, *Vblizi Tolstogo* [Near Tolstoy] that were first published in Russian in 1922-1923 bear the sub-title, "Notes of the last fifteen years of Tolstoy's life."

[6] The Hogarth Press papers include other Russian-related materials, namely No. 7 (Avvakum); No. 38 (Bunin, Ivan. *The Gentleman from San Francisco*. 1922-1951); No. 39 (Bunin, Ivan. *The Grammar of Love*. 1934-1939); No. 590 (Bunin, Ivan. *The Elaghin Affair*. 1935); No. 40 (Bunin, Ivan. *The Well of Days*. 1931-1945); No. 130 (Gorky, Maxim. *Reminiscences of Leo Nicolayevitch Tolstoi*. 1928-1953); No. 327 (Olyesha, Yuri. *Envy*. 1936-1958); No. 483 (Tchekhov, Anton. *Notebooks*. 1944-1948); No. 492 (Tolstoy, Leo N. *On Socialism*. 1935-1945). The Hogarth Press archives also provide us with the background story of Woolf's collaboration with Koteliansky in translating a chapter of F. M. Dostoevsky's novel *The Possessed* (No. 72). The chapter was published in 1922 as *Stavrogin's Confession and The Plan of the Life of a Great Sinner*. Also, see the publication "F. M. Dostoevsky: Plan of the Novel 'The Life of a Great Sinner'," *The Criterion* (October 1922: vol.1: No.1), 16-34; trans. by Virginia Woolf and S. S. Koteliansky, with the editor's note: This plan will appear in a volume to be published very shortly by the Hogarth Press, containing also Stavrogin's 'Confession' ."

[7] Johann Peter Eckermann, *Gespräche mit Goethe in den letzten Jahren seines Lebens* (1823-1832). Berlin, Weimar: Aufbau-Verlag, 1982.

[8] See The Hogarth Press papers, No. 595.

[9] Note the alternative use of two variants of transliterating Tolstoy's name. One corresponds to the norm, which existed in the 1920s, and the other is current usage.

[10] L. N. Tolstoy, *Childhood, Boyhood and Youth*. (1852) With an Introduction by W. L. Phelps. London: Oxford UP, 1928.

Virginia Woolf Translates Tolstoy

[11] Cf. "...a real life is wonderfully prolific; it passes through such strange places and draws along with it a train of adventure that no novelist can better them, if only he can deal with them as with his own inventions." "Sterne" (1909) (*GR* 168).

[12] Cf. "...the true object of teaching—to answer the questions which arise in the minds of the students" (Goldenveiser 122); "Sergey Lvovich asked Tolstoi why he did not go in for his examinations at Petersburg University. Tolstoi said: 'I began to work hard, passed two examinations, was awarded two marks of distinction, but then it was spring; it drew me to the country; well, I gave it up and went away." (Goldenveiser 123).

[13] Virginia Woolf, *A Writer's Diary* (1953). London: The Hogarth Press, 1969.

[14] See "Gorky on Tolstoi," review of *Reminiscences of Leo Nicolayevitch Tolstoi* by Maxim Gorky. Unsigned. In *The New Statesman* (1920:7 August), 506-506; rpt. *E3* 252-55; also, see the Hogarth Press papers No. 130 (Gorky, Maxim. *Reminiscences. 1928-1953*).

[15] The Hogarth Press papers No. 595.

[16] See the letter of 1 March 1923 of the weekly Editor-in-chief to Leonard Woolf in the Hogarth Press archive No. 493; also, Leonard Woolf's letter of 22 March 1923 to S. S. Koteliansky, No 493.

[17] See R. F. Christian (ed). "Preface" to *Tolstoy's Letters*. 2 vols. University of London: The Athlone Press, v. 1, 1978: v.

[18] Lev Nikolaevich Tolstoy. *Mnogo li cheloveku zemli nado* (1886). See L. N Tolstoy. *How Much Land Does a Man Need*. London: Daniel, n.d. Cf. Woolf's speculation on the existential dimension of Tolstoy's work in "The Russian Point of View": "Life dominates Tolstoi as the soul dominates Dostoevsky. There is always at the centre of all the brilliant and flashing petals of the flower this scorpion, 'Why live?' There is always at the centre of the book some Olenin, or Pierre, or Levin who gathers into himself all experience, turns the world round between his fingers, and never ceases to ask, even as he enjoys it, what is the meaning of it, and what should be our aims" (*CR1* 231).

[19] I assume that taking a fake or an exotic identity, which would serve her as a disguise of a definite socio-cultural type, became one of Woolf's strategies in her essay-writing. It is in the essays that she would, metaphorically speaking, put on different fine clothes, investing herself each time with "a certain social demeanour." Curiously, she would underestimate the mode of disguising oneself with socially fashionable clothes in writing, thinking it to be secondary to the authentic art. She is quite straightforward about it in her early essay "Modes and Manners of the Nineteenth Century" (1910): "For this reason a history of modes and manners must use phrases which are as empty as any in the language, and the history is not a history of ourselves, but of our disguises. The poets and the novelists are the only people from whom we cannot hide" (*BP* 27). This is a statement made in essentialist terms about high art as creating a meaningful and unique language of its own as opposed to a writing mode which requires fashionable disguises and the common language of the time. Woolf is very straightforward in thinking the first one to be authentic, the other secondary and trite. Not only is she critical about writing which follows the current social disguises and patterns, but she is also well aware of the origins of the comparison of people's positions with the clothes they wear. They are found in Carlyle's *Sartor Resartus* (1833-1834), which in its turn goes back in time to the Christian metonymy of a dress for belonging to a particular denomination (cf. Swift's "A Tale of a Tub"). Both sources are explicated by Woolf in the same essay (*BP* 23).

Reinhold

[20] Osip Mandelstam, "Egipetskaia marka" (1928). See Osip Mandelstam, "The Egyptian Stamp." In Mandelstam: 188.

Works Cited

Eliot, T. S. "The Social Function of Poetry." (1943) In *On Poetry and Poets*. London: Faber and Faber, 1986.
Goldenveiser, A. B. *Talks with Tolstoi*. Trans. by S. S. Koteliansky and Virginia Woolf. Richmond: The Hogarth Press, 1923.
Mandelstam, O. E. *The Prose of Osip Mandelstam*. Trans., with a critical essay, by Clarence Brown. Princeton: Princeton UP, 1967.
Nabokov, Vladimir. *Glory*. [Podvig] Trans. from the Russian by Dmitri Nabokov in collaboration with the author. New York, Toronto: McGraw-Hill Book Company, 1971:24-25.
/Reviews/Tchekov on Pope. The Rape of the Lock. M121 - Typescript, with the author's MS corrections, unsigned and undated. In *Virginia Woolf Manuscripts*. From the Henry W. and Albert A. Berg Collection at the New York Public Library. Woodbridge, CT: Research Publications, 1993.
Tolstoy's Letters. Ed. with Preface by R. F. Christian. 2 vols. University of London: The Athlone Press, 1978.
Virginia Woolf and Lytton Strachey: Letters. Ed. Leonard Woolf and James Strachey. London: The Hogarth Press, Chatto and Windus, 1956.
Woolf, Virginia. *Books and Portraits*. Ed. Mary Lyons. London: The Hogarth Press, 1977.
——. *The Common Reader*. Second edition. London: The Hogarth Press, 1925.
——. *Granite and Rainbow*. London: The Hogarth Press, 1958.
——. *A Room of One's Own*. New York: Harcourt, Brace and Company, 1929.

Tolstoy and the World of English Literature: A Survey of Leo Tolstoy's Book Collection in Foreign Languages in the Estate Museum, Yasnaya Polyana
Galina Alekseeva

> *Galina Alekseeva's article is an extended version of her paper read at the symposium's closing panel at Yasnaya Polyana on "Virginia Woolf and Russian Literature." Though it does not mention Virginia Woolf or in fact any of the Bloomsbury names, it adds contextually to the cross-cultural discussion of the Russian theme in the work of Virginia Woolf, Tolstoy in particular. This detailed survey of Tolstoy's immediate responses to English literature as a reader, writer and thinker makes it a two-way street for the reader: there is "The Russian Point of View" on one side, and Tolstoy's comment on English books and writers, on the other. (Ed.)*

Leo Tolstoy's Book Collection in Yasnaya Polyana[1] contains about 22,000 books and periodicals in Russian and foreign languages, including approximately 2,200 volumes in English. Of these around 1,500 books are by British writers, and many of them had been on Tolstoy's reading list since his childhood. In this article I am going to make a brief survey of some of the abovementioned books in English, to see what criteria Tolstoy went by as a reader, writer and thinker.

In the 1850s-1870s Tolstoy read many works by English writers. This interest continued in the last decades of his life, though it took a somewhat different direction. In his interviews with English and American journalists Tolstoy always emphasized his special regard for nineteenth-century literature, and such English writers as Dickens, Trollope, and Thackeray. In his letter of 12 March 1860 to Ye. P. Kovalevsky, the first chairman of the Literary Foundation (Literaturnyi Fond), he referred to England as "the most educated country" (*PSS* 60, 330). In spring 1861 Tolstoy spent sixteen days in London and visited such places as Parliament and St. James Hall, where he attended a talk by Dickens. Tolstoy noted in his letter of 17 March 1876 to his friend P. D. Golokhvastov: "It seems to me that of all European countries I could have lived only in England" (*PSS* 62, 260). He said to the English journalist R. E. Long: "There is much I like in England, but what I know about its people I have drawn, for the most part, from English literature" (*Tolstoy i Zarubezhnyi Mir* 112-113).

Alekseeva

One of the first English writers to enrich the aesthetic experience of young Tolstoy was Laurence Sterne, a copy of whose *Sentimental Journey Through France and Italy* (Sterne) is in the Yasnaya Polyana library. While in the Caucasus in 1851 Tolstoy worked on a translation of *A Sentimental Journey*, of which three fragments have survived.[2] No doubt Tolstoy was influenced by the style of Sterne, as is obvious from his early works of the 1850s.[3]

There is a strong likelihood that Tolstoy read Walter Scott in the 1850s, though only one of the Scottish novelist's books in English, *Ivanhoe*, remains in the library. At the time of his involvement in a debate on art, alongside V. P. Botkin and I. S. Turgenev in 1857, Tolstoy emotionally noted in his letter of 21 October - 1 November 1857 to both of them: "One should not, as Walter Scott very likely said, make a crutch, or a stick, of literature" (*PSS* 60, 234). As is suggested by the authors of the first volume of *Correspondence with Russian Writers*, Tolstoy knew this statement of Scott through A. V. Druzhinin's article, "The War Stories of Count Tolstoy and the Provincial Sketches of N. Shchedrin" (*Perepiska s Russkimi Pisateliami* 227).

In his letter of 9/21 July 1857 to V. P. Botkin, Tolstoy wrote with obvious delight about Charlotte Brontë, who in many respects may be considered a successor of Walter Scott. Tolstoy read Brontë's *Jane Eyre* in the second half of the 1850s, at the time when he was greatly interested in problems of education. Tolstoy highly appreciated the novel, which raised such timely issues as the education of the lower classes.

In 1885 Tolstoy wrote to his wife: "I am reading Eliot's *Felix Holt*. It is an outstanding piece of work. I had read it previously, but at a time when I was very stupid, and now I see I have completely forgotten it. It is something that should be translated, if it hasn't been already" (*PSS* 83, 477). The book, published in 1867, bears Tolstoy's *marginalia* which were most likely made in 1885. Among the underlined passages there are several with philosophical connotations which Tolstoy undoubtedly approved of. Earlier, in 1859, Tolstoy wrote to A. A. Tolstaya referring to *Scenes of Clerical Life*, and the story *Janet's Repentance* in particular: "Fortunate are the people, who, like the English, imbibe Christian teaching with their mother's milk, and in such an elevated, purified form as evangelical Protestantism" (*PSS* 60, 300). In his essay *What is Art?* (1897-1898), Tolstoy defined Eliot's novel *Adam Bede* as a model of "highest art," in contrast to Turgenev who considered *The Mill on the Floss* to be her best work. According to his diary, Tolstoy turned to reread Eliot in 1900 (*PSS* 54, 35) and indeed, there are found five works by Eliot published under the *Collection of British Authors* series in the Yasnaya Polyana library. Tolstoy's book collection also possesses the works of Eliot's companion George Henry Lewes.

Tolstoy and the World of English Literature

In his mature years Tolstoy enjoyed rereading the works he had first come to know as a young man. One example is Jonathan Swift's *Gulliver's Travels*, to which he made several references in his diary entries dating from 1896 to 1897. The library has two books by Swift in French. The first one, published in the eighteenth century, has dog-eared pages and was no doubt acquired by Tolstoy's parents, while the second one was printed in 1841. Another example is Defoe. According to V. F. Bulgakov, Tolstoy's secretary, in September 1910 Tolstoy "wanted to reread *Robinson* [*Crusoe*]" (Bulgakov 333). There are many books in Tolstoy's library that belonged to his parents and N. S. Volkonsky, his maternal grandfather, who is considered to be one of the founders of the Yasnaya Polyana library of L. N. Tolstoy. Among the books, which originally belonged to Volkonsky and to Tolstoy's parents, is the second oldest book in the library, *The Humbled Sinner* by Obadiah Sedwick (1656), as well as works by Byron, Richardson, and A. Smith (six volumes in French with the pages uncut). There is also an eight-volume edition of the works of Thomas Macaulay, as well as four-volume and twenty-one volume editions of the writings of David Hume, published in the late eighteenth and early nineteeth century. From April to June 1852, Tolstoy read Hume's *Histoire d'Angleterre* "with pleasure," and he included one of Hume's aphorisms in his weekly *Circle of Reading* (*PSS* 41, 384).

Describing the list of English authors in the Yasnaya Polyana book collection one cannot help mentioning William Shakespeare. There are several separate editions of Shakespeare's works, including a seven-volume set published by Bernhard Tauchnitz as part of the *Collection of British Authors* series. Volumes three to six bear numerous traces of Tolstoy's reading, a fact that contradicts the observation made by the English journalist Robert Long that the writer was not familiar enough with Shakespeare's plays (*Tolstoy i Zarubezhnyi Mir* 115). Tolstoy made many pencilled notes in the margins of *Romeo and Juliet*, *Hamlet*, and *Othello* in volumes five and six. Among the positive remarks left by Tolstoy, the letters "NB" appear in the pages of *King Henry IV* and *Julius Caesar*. We also come across numerous negative judgments like "bad taste," "nonsense," "stupid," "rubbish," "banal," "what for," "remarkably artificial," etc. Most likely, Tolstoy made these marginal notes just before writing his critical essay "On Shakespeare and Drama." It opened with the following remark: "Now, I've made a special point of re-reading the whole of Shakespeare in my seventy-fifth year, to verify my opinions, before getting down to write this article" (*PSS* 35, 217). Despite the less than positive nature of "On Shakespeare and Drama," Tolstoy received sympathetic responses from John G. Sinclair, E. W. Ellis, and George Bernard Shaw.

Alekseeva

The name of George Gordon Byron appears in the materials for the novel *The Decembrists*. Interestingly, Tolstoy specified that "Byron arrived in Missolonghi in 1824" (*PSS* 17, 462). Byron's name is also mentioned in the variants to the second volume of *War and Peace* among Tolstoy's speculations about Nikolai Rostov (*PSS* 12, 368). Byron appears again in the treatise *What is Art?* as one of the "exceptional personalities," such as Leopardi and Heine, who expressed in their art "a feeling of the melancholy of life" (*PSS* 30, 88). In his introduction to F. von Polenz's novel, *The Peasant* [*Der Buttnerbauer*], Tolstoy wrote: "In England after [Byron], Dickens, Thackeray, and George Eliot there is a poor imitation of art mixed up with pseudo-Christian idea" (*PSS* 34, 526). And yet in his letter of 11 February 1856 to the writer F. Tishchenko about his story "The Sinner," Tolstoy sternly observed: "You've spoiled your story with Byronic note of indolence" (*PSS* 63, 326).

At one time the Yasnaya Polyana library possessed books by Henry Fielding.[4] In his note of 16 October 1906, Tolstoy's doctor D. P. Makovitsky recorded Tolstoy's intention to read *Tom Jones* for the first time. In another of his entries for the same year, Makovitsky reproduces Tolstoy's comment: "As if anew I am rereading the 'newest' writers—Goldsmith, Fielding, and Swift" (*U Tolstogo* 2, 273).

In his list of books that made an impression on him in the 1860s-1870s, Tolstoy noted "Miss Wood. Novels. Very large." He also read Trollope, whom he praised a lot. Tolstoy first mentioned this English novelist on 29 September 1865: "I am reading Trollope. It would be good if it weren't for diffuseness" (*PSS* 48, 63). In his diary the following day there is a remarkable discourse on Trollope's "poetry." On 2 October, Tolstoy is still reading Trollope: "Trollope kills me with his skill. I console myself with the knowledge that he has his own and I have mine" (*PSS* 48, 64). According to the diary entry of 3 October, Tolstoy finished reading *The Bertrams* (the book is no longer in the library) and came to the conclusion that "too much of it is conventional" (Ibid.). Tolstoy's next reference to this English novelist did not appear until January 1877, when, in a letter to his brother Sergei, he stated, "*The Prime Minister* [the last book in Trollope's trilogy of political novels] is excellent" (*PSS* 62, 302).

In the 1860s a four-volume collection of the letters and speeches of Oliver Cromwell found its way onto the library shelves. At that time the book collection also included works by Walter Besant, Hall Caine (with a dedicatory inscription), Dinah Craik, Sarah Grand, Charlotte Yonge (who wrote one hundred and twenty novels), Scottish novelist Edmund Yates, Florence Marryat (a prolific author of eighty volumes), and the novelist Henry Kingsley.

In 1877 Tolstoy received a copy of Thomas Carlyle's *Sartor Resartus* from N. N. Strakhov, still to be found in the library. The book collection also con-

Tolstoy and the World of English Literature

tains *The Work of Life: Thoughts from Carlyle* (London, 1908) with notes by Makovitsky. In 1900 the library received *The Prophets of the Nineteenth Century* by May Alden-Ward (in I. S. Durnovo's translation), which contained the biographies of Thomas Carlyle, John Ruskin, and Leo Tolstoy.

The library has nine books by William Morris whose utopian ideas made an important contribution to the philosophy of Socialism; it also contains his biography written by John Mackail, an Oxford University professor.

All his life Tolstoy admired Dickens, though we do not know for sure when he began to read him. We know that in the early 1850s he read *David Copperfield*, as indicated in his diary entry of 2 September 1852 (*PSS* 46, 140). In his letter of 21 January - 3 February 1904 to James Ley, he wrote: "I think that Charles Dickens is the greatest novelist of the nineteenth century, and that his works impressed me with the true Christian spirit. They have done, and will continue to do a great deal of good to mankind" (*PSS* 75, 24). The library has thirty-three books by Dickens published mostly in the Tauchnitz series. Several of the volumes bear traces of having been read by Tolstoy. In 1886 he wrote to V. G. Chertkov: "Dickens interests me more and more" (*PSS* 85, 324). Tolstoy called Dickens "a world genius," and "a genius, the likes of which are born once in a hundred years." In *What is Art?* Tolstoy names Dickens's works among the few examples of what he refers to as "the highest art."

On 26 May 1856 Tolstoy wrote in his notebook: "Dickens's characters are the common friends of the entire world, they serve as a connection between a person in America and the one in St. Petersburg. To compare, the characters of Thackeray and Gogol are faithful, malevolent, and aesthetically satisfying, but they are not loved" (*PSS* 47, 178). There are seven editions of the works by Thackeray in the Yasnaya Polyana library, most of which were published in the *Collection of British Authors* series. In his notebook of 9 June 1856, Tolstoy observed: "Thackeray is so objective that his characters defend their false, opposing views with terribly intelligent irony" (*PSS* 47, 184). Tolstoy referred to Thackeray at various times throughout his life. In June 1855 he read *The History of Henry Esmond, Esq.* and *Vanity Fair*, and then *The Newcomes* a year later. It was apparently owing to Thackeray's representation of contemporary English society as a "fair of worldly vanities" that Tolstoy wrote in his story "Sevastopol in May": "Why did the Homers and the Shakespeares speak of love, glory, and suffering, while the literature of our era is only an endless story of 'snobbery' and 'vanity'?" (*PSS* 4, 24). In his letter of 19 October 1856 to V. V. Arsenieva, Tolstoy recommends that she read *Vanity Fair* in the French translation. Tolstoy included Thackeray's aphorism, "Sow a deed, and you'll reap a habit; sow a habit, and you'll reap a character; sow a character and you'll reap a destiny" (*PSS* 40, 202) in the collection *Daily Wisdom* written at the end of his life.

When Tolstoy's publishing house *Posrednik* [*Mediator*] was set up, he recommended the historical novels of Edward Lytton for translation. One of his books, *Kenelm Chillingly: His Adventures and Opinions*, is still in the library and was mostly likely read by Tolstoy some time in the 1870s. Tolstoy also chose for translation a collection of stories by Mary Braddon (Mary Maxwell). One of the books preserved in the library, *Only a Clod*, bears Tolstoy's handwritten remark. There are also novels by Mrs. Humphry Ward (Mary A. Ward), whom Tolstoy highly praised and of whom he wrote to S. A. Tolstaya in 1892: "I am reading a very good book by the author of *Robert Elsmere*. The author's goal is to reveal the deceptiveness and appeal of feminine beauty. It is handled very subtly and intelligently" (*PSS* 84, 174; also *PSS* 50, 19). Probably Tolstoy also read *Miss Bretherton*, a copy of which is found in the library. In all her works Mrs. Humphry Ward touches on themes of moral purification and personal renewal, concepts that were very much in keeping with Tolstoy's ideas.

In his famous letter to Mikhail Lederle of 25 October 1891 Tolstoy mentions that the sermons of the theologian Frederick William Robertson made a "great" impression on him when he was between fifty and sixty-three years old (*PSS* 66, 68). The library has two editions of Robertson's sermons.

The library also contains Oscar Wilde's last poem, *The Ballad of Reading Gaol* (New York, 1889). Tolstoy's aesthetic and psychological views were far from either Wilde's objections to realism in art, or his credo of "art for art's sake," as proclaimed in the lecture, "The Renaissance of English Art." Tolstoy was sharply critical of "decadents and aesthetes such as Oscar Wilde" in his treatise *What is Art?* (*PSS* 30, 172).

Tolstoy not only read the works of George Bernard Shaw, but he also corresponded with him. The library has three books by Shaw, *John Bull's Other Island* (London, 1907), *Man and Superman* (London, 1906) (with the author's inscription), and *The Shewing-up of Blanco Posnet* (London, 1909) (also inscribed by the author). Tolstoy's numerous remarks can be found in the margins of the first two books. Tolstoy first became acquainted with Shaw's works in January 1907 when he read *Man and Superman*. Tolstoy held a rather negative opinion of this play, considering it to be "artificial" and "vulgar," and he wrote in his notebook on 12 January 1907: "Finished Shaw. He has more brains than is good for him" (*PSS* 56, 179). In his witty remark Tolstoy paraphrased the words addressed to Don Juan by the statue of the Commander in the third act of *Man and Superman*. Tolstoy had underlined and marked the words "you have more brains than is good for you" in page 120 of the book and had put "NB" beside them. Tolstoy's copy of the play, which he had received from

Tolstoy and the World of English Literature

Shaw through the translator Aylmer Maude, is covered with his notes and comments. The inscription in the book reads: "The interlude in the third act, pp 86-137 contains the author's conclusions as to religion, theology, and evolution, and is founded on his personal experience. Tolstoy's own experience will enable him to distinguish easily between the art and fantasy of the scene and its reality as a confession and creed" (*Biblioteka L. N. Tolstogo* 2, 349). In actual fact, a great number of Tolstoy's annotations, including the letters "NB," are found in pages 106 to 135. It is fully evident that Tolstoy had high regard for the negative attitude of the play's characters toward bourgeois civilization. At the time of the play's composition, Shaw agreed with Tolstoy that moral perfection should precede social reforms. On 9 March 1908 Tolstoy read Shaw's article "The Impossibility of Anarchism," sent to him by Maude, and noted: "Very interesting. Everything of his (including plays) is very talented" (*PSS* 78, 111). Shaw did not welcome anarchism, regarding it as an aspiration to transform the existing order by revolutionary means, that is to say by violence. Maude made every effort to entice Tolstoy to read Bernard Shaw. Every one of Shaw's books in the Yasnaya Polyana library was sent there by Maude. At one point, while inquiring whether or not Tolstoy was acquainted with Shaw's article on anarchism, Maude asked: "Are you not interested in the works of our leading playwright?" (*PSS* 77, 277). For his eightieth birthday Tolstoy received a special address from a number of English writers, and those who signed it included Shaw, E. Carpenter, G. Meredith, and R. Kipling. On 17 August 1908 Tolstoy wrote a long letter to Bernard Shaw about his play *Man and Superman*, in which he emphasized the differences in their perception of the world. In 1910 Shaw sent Tolstoy *The Shewing-up of Blanco Posnet*, and in the accompanying letter commented on Tolstoy's own play, *The Power of Darkness*, saying that among all the plays he knew, he could not recall a scene that so enraptured him as the one with the old soldier in the *The Power of Darkness* (*PSS* 81, 255). Tolstoy replied: "I read your play with pleasure. I am in full sympathy with its subject" (*PSS* 81, 254). On the envelope with Shaw's letter there is a note in Tolstoy's handwriting: "From Shaw, smart-silly" (*PSS* 58, 361).

The Yasnaya Polyana collection contains six books by H. G. Wells. One of these, *The Future of America*, has an inscription by the author and another, *New Worlds for Old*, is heavily underlined by Tolstoy. The books were sent by Wells himself. On 21 November 1906, Wells wrote to Tolstoy: "My friend Aylmer Maude has informed me that you would be interested in taking a look at two or three of my books. I have never sent you my books because I imagine you are submerged under a stream of books that have been presented to you by every young writer from Europe and America...From the bottom of my heart I hope that this torrent of books does not bore you in the slightest. I think that I have read around eighty of your works, everything that is possible to acquire in English" (*PSS* 76, 253). Tolstoy expressed his gratitude in his reply: "I expect great pleasure in reading them" (*PSS* 76, 252). It seems likely Tolstoy subsequently became interested in *New Worlds for Old*, in which he underlined numerous passages. On 17 October 1906 Makovitsky noted: "Maude recommended Herbert Wells to Tolstoy: 'He is read by people of advanced views.' L. N.: 'It does not interest me'" (*U Tolstogo* 2, 272). On 5 December 1906 Makovitsky records Tolstoy as having said: "I do not like this English refinement. This Wells, all these allusions, the need to know everything, such words...It is so banal! Supermen don't exist, all people are ordinary. I read three chapters of *The Future of America*, it is uninteresting, and I won't read any further" (*U Tolstogo* 2, 322).

There are two books by John Galsworthy sent to Yasnaya Polyana by the author. One of them, *Justice* (London, 1910) has Galsworthy's inscription. As was described by Makovitsky, Tolstoy read this play on 23 March 1910. Makovitsky noted that Tolstoy had initially refused to read Galsworthy's play commenting, "Drama is not my favourite" (*U Tolstogo* 4, 189). There is no mention of Tolstoy reading Galsworthy's earlier plays, *The Silver Box*, *Joy*, and *Strife*, of which the 1909 edition is in the library.

In 1904, shortly after the visit of the Irish patriot Michael Davitt to Yasnaya Polyana, Tolstoy received a book from him with an inscription. The library also contains a number of books by the Irish feminist Frances Cobbe and one of these, *An Essay on Intuitive Morals*, has Tolstoy's approving remarks. William Booth, the founder of the Salvation Army, also sent Tolstoy his writings.

In the 1890s Tolstoy read the works of the English philosopher and social reformer John Stuart Mill. *The Principles of Political Economy* shows signs of having been read by Tolstoy. In his diary and in letters to N. N. Strakhov, Tolstoy argues with Mill over his theory of the relation of the common good to the individual. In August of 1895, Tolstoy read *Social Evolution* by the philosopher and idealist Benjamin Kidd, and left numerous remarks.

During the years of his work on *What is Art?* Tolstoy thoroughly studied the works of English philosophers and historians of art. However, no such books remain on the shelves in Yasnaya Polyana, and it is clear from his correspondence that the bulk of them were sent by N. I. Storozhenko from the Rumyantsev Library in Moscow for reference. A copy of Herbert Spencer's *An Autobiography* (published in 1908) was sent by Charles Wright, who translated several works of Tolstoy. In thanking Wright for the book, Tolstoy wrote: "...I am not an admirer of Spencer, but I will read his autobiography

Tolstoy and the World of English Literature

...Important psychological facts appear to a greater extent in autobiographies often quite independently of their author's will. Such facts, I recall, struck me in Mill's autobiography" (*PSS* 75, 82). Commenting on *Machiavelli* by John Morley (with the notes by an unidentified person), Tolstoy wrote: "I haven't read *Machiavelli*, but I know in advance that J. Morley must be good" (*PSS* 88, 49).

John M. Davidson, a Christian socialist, sent six books of his writings. On Tolstoy's initiative, Davidson's books were published in Russian by *Posrednik*. Tolstoy and Davidson corresponded, and in 1894 Tolstoy wrote to him: "It is the greatest joy of my life to know persons such as you, and to see that the ideas, which I live for, are likewise the mainspring in the life of others" (*PSS* 67, 178).

There are thirteen books by John Kenworthy[5] in the library, many of them inscribed by the author, and Tolstoy himself the subject of several of them. Tolstoy wrote about Kenworthy that "in terms of convictions he is one of the closest people to me" (*PSS* 68, 130). Tolstoy granted Kenworthy's Brotherhood Publishing Company the rights to the first English translations of his works.

There are four books by Edward Carpenter, a former priest, poet and socialist who lived on a small farm in Sheffield. One of his books, kept in the Yasnaya Polyana library, *Prisons, Police, and Punishment*, contains Tolstoy's reading notes, such as "NB," which were probably made in 1909. In 1905 Tolstoy read Carpenter's *Civilization: Its Cause and Cure* and included an excerpt from it in his *Circle of Reading*. Tolstoy remarked in one of his letters after reading this book: "In my opinion he is a worthy successor to Carlyle and Ruskin" (*PSS* 75, 214). There are five English editions of John Ruskin's works in the library, but in distinction from the Russian editions, they show no signs of having been read by Tolstoy, who first became acquainted with the writings of Ruskin in the 1880s. Tolstoy read Ruskin with delight and also translated his works and wrote a foreword to a collection of his thoughts. He called Ruskin "one of the most remarkable people not only of England and of our time, but of all countries and all times" (*PSS* 31, 96).

There are two books sent to Yasnaya Polyana by Albert Blake. One of his books, *Modern Pharisaism*, carries Tolstoy's notes, and there is a letter from Blake inserted between the pages. In 1888 Tolstoy wrote to Blake: "Thank you for the books you sent me. I read them at once and was pleased to find in *Modern Pharisaism*, in particular, an adequate understanding of Christ's teaching, and indignation against those who would try to hide the latter" (*PSS* 64, 195). Blake's religious writings arrived when Tolstoy was working intensively on a series of religious-cum-philosophical works.

Alekseeva

Tolstoy included an excerpt from the works of the religious writer and doctor Anna Kingsford in his *Circle of Reading*, and her book, *The Perfect Way*, which is also found in the library shows evidence of having been read by Tolstoy.

In the 1900s the library received the books of James William Petavel, and according to Makovitsky, Tolstoy remarked upon reading one of them, *Christianity and Progress*: "It is evident from his book that his attitude toward Christianity is ill-defined—half Christian, half clerical" (*PSS* 76, 141).

The library has a large number of polemical treatises by John George Tollemache Sinclair, translator of works in English into French; some of his books in Tolstoy's library are in English, some in French. Nearly all of them contain the author's inscription.

V. G. Chertkov sent Tolstoy Robert Young's *Analytical Concordance to the Bible* (Edinburgh, 1880), and the book still rests on the shelf in the writer's study.

The library also possesses a small book by the religious writer Frederic Farrar who interpreted Tolstoy's religious doctrine with great subtlety and understanding. The name of the English theologian appeared in the diary for the years 1879 and 1880. Tolstoy responded negatively to Farrar's article about him in *Forum* (October 1888, No. 2): "...a press-clipping from *Forum* with Farrar's article—utterly shallow. An objection to Christ in the name of Christ. Terrible. Replied via Tanya" (*PSS* 50, 13). Tolstoy also criticized this article in his treatise *The Kingdom of God is Within You*. In reply to N. N. Strakhov, who had offered to send him *The Life of Christ* by Farrar, Tolstoy wrote that he "cannot stand" Farrar and referred to him as an "hypocritical writer" (*PSS* 65, 176). In the 1900s, however, Tolstoy included his maxims in the *Circle of Reading* and *Daily Wisdom*.

Books on pacifism are part of the collection, and the one devoted to the World Congress on Peace of 1890 in London has numerous notes made by Tolstoy. The library also has a large number of works on the Quakers. Of these, *War: Its Causes, Consequences, Lawfulness, Etc.* (Manchester, 1889) by Jonathon Dymond, may have been sent to Tolstoy by Chertkov. In his letter of 9 - 10 June 1885 to Chertkov, Tolstoy made the following remark about Quaker beliefs: "I have always been sympathetic to their teaching" (*PSS* 85, 225). A book of selections from the writings of William Penn is also found in the library.

There is a whole set of books on vegetarianism. One of these, *The Ethics of Diet* (London, 1883) by Howard Williams, was published by *Posrednik* in Russian. Eleven books by Alexander Haig on the ethics of nutrition are also in the library. Tolstoy noted in his letter of 7/20 March 1905 to Haig that among the materials the doctor had sent him he liked best *Truth, Strength and Freedom,* or *Mental and Spiritual Evolution,* and *The Parting of the Ways and Some Fragments.* Tolstoy was also surprised to encounter a man with religious views among scientists and doctors (*PSS* 75, 232).

There were no hard and fast rules or fixed artistic standards for Tolstoy the reader. He possessed a wide spectrum of writings in English, from "high art" to religious homilies, polemical treatises, pamphlets, and essays on efficient nutrition and healthy lifestyle. His numerous *marginalia* in the books of English authors in the Yasnaya Polyana library offer an insight into how the writer interpreted what he read. By researching the books from his personal collection, and analyzing the *marginalia*, we can see how Tolstoy arranged a dialogue with his contemporaries and also, the writers of the past. This communication via reading and letters inspired him in his creative activities, as a writer of fiction and books of wisdom.

Notes

[1] *Biblioteka L. N. Tolstogo v Yasnoi Polyane: Bibliographicheskoe opisanie: Knigi na inostrannykh iazykakh.* [Leo Tolstoy's Book Collection in Yasnaya Polyana: Bibliography. Books in Foreign Languages]. 3 Vols. In 2 parts. Tula: Izdatel'skii Dom Yasnaya Polyana, 1999.

[2] State Museum of L. N. Tolstoy in Moscow (GMT), Manuscript Division.

[3] *Istoriia Vcherashnego Dnia* [Yesterday's Chronicle], *Detstvo* [Childhood], *Metel'* [Snowstorm].

[4] According to Sergei Tolstoy, the eldest son of Leo Tolstoy, many books were lost at different periods of the history of the Yasnaya Polyana library. See S. L. Tolstoy, *Mat' i Ded L. N. Tolstogo.* [L. N. Tolstoy's Grandparents] Moskva: Federatsiia, 1928, 33-36.

[5] John Coleman Kenworthy (b. 1860), English writer and journalist, follower of Leo Tolstoy's religious teaching.

Works Cited

Alekseeva, Galina. "Describing Tolstoy's Private Library: English Books at Yasnaya Polyana," in *Tolstoy Studies Journal* 13 (2001): 98-107.

Biblioteka L. N. Tolstogo v Yasnoi Polyane: Bibliographicheskoe opisanie [Leo Tolstoy's Book Collection in Yasnaya Polyana: Bibliography]. 3 vols. 2 parts. "Knigi na inostrannykh yazykakh" [Books in Foreign Languages]. Tula: Izdatel'skii Dom Yanaya Polyana, 1999.

Bulgakov, V. F. *Tolstoy v Poslednii God Ego Zhizni* [Tolstoy in the Year 1910]. Moskva: Pravda, 1989.

Alekseeva

Eikhenbaum, B. M. *Lev Tolstoy: Semidesiatye Gody* [Leo Tolstoy: The 1870s]. Leningrad: Khudozhestvennaia literatura, 1974.

L. N. Tolstoy: *Perepiska s Russkimi Pisateliami* [Correspondence with Russian Writers]. Vol. 1. Moskva: Khudozhestvennaia literatura, 1978.

(*PSS*) *Polnoe Sobranie Sochinenii* [Complete Works by Leo Nikolaevich Tolstoy]. Moskva: Khudozhestvennaia literatura, 1928-1958.

Sterne, Laurence. *A Sentimental Journey through France and Italy*. Paris: French Library, 1835.

Tolstoy i Zarubezhnyi Mir. Literaturnoe Nasledstvo [Tolstoy and the World: Literary Heritage]. Vol. 75 (2). Moskva: Nauka, 1965.

Tolstoy, S. L. *Mat' i Ded L. N. Tolstogo*. [L. N. Tolstoy's Grandparents] Moskva: Federatsiia, 1928, 33-36.

U Tolstogo: Yasnopolyanskie Zapiski D. P. Makovitskogo. *Literaturnoe nasledstvo* [*At Tolstoy:* Yasnaya Polyana Diary by D. P. Makovetsky. *Literary Heritage*]. Vols. 90. Moskva: Nauka, 1979.

The Cultural and Poetic Synthesis in Virginia Woolf's Texts
Natalia Morzhenkova

The development of Woolf's poetics seems to move in the direction of generating experimental patterns and techniques adequate to representing not just the flux of subjective inner life but a model of universal synthesis. The search for this universal correspondence defines the evolution of Woolf's novel form.

Although the novels exhibit different styles, trends and periods of the writer's work, they together make up a complete image of Woolf's universe. Every novel contains its own model of the world and consciousness. In *Jacob's Room, To the Lighthouse, Orlando*—novels of three different periods and of three different poetics—those models are "empty room"; "house-home" (neglected and restored); "oak-tree" (Orlando's poem, an attempt at universal, cultural and sexual synthesis).

The sequence of the novels has not only a dialectical value, but also a philological one. The whole macro-text is constructed on the basis of anadiplosis.[1] The final chronotopical "revelation" of each novel becomes the generative space of the next.

For example, Jacob's room, that is the quintessence of the hero, presupposes Mrs. Ramsay's house, which becomes not only a building but a container of memory— biographical, cultural and mythological.

The images of room and house in Woolf's writings seem to have a double essence. With their practically endless metaphoric possibilities they belong to two different spheres—visible/invisible, historical/horizontal, and mythological/vertical. Woolf developed the image of the enclosed room within which the culture's poetic text is fabricated from historical and mythological, individual and universal, eternal and temporary signs. Room and house as the central chronotopos of the writer's poetic world can be characterized by constant semantic increase, tending toward universal mytho-ontological wholeness and completeness. The enclosed room is a metaphor of the walled-in individual consciousness. At the same time it appears to be the container where the culture's fabric is being woven, where the cosmos is separated from the chaos. The room of cultural memory begets a special dynamic hero—Orlando, a traveler, trickster, poet, alter ego of claustrophobic Virginia Woolf who seeks for her adequate dimension and chronotopos. The haunted house, Jacob's room, the Ramsays' house, Orlando's vast mansion, Orlando as a dynamic cultural hero all function as variants of the same polysemantic constant image of the writer's

261

universe. The "catch up" technique is also seen at the lexical level. Certain sets of words and motives break the boundaries of separate novels and form a universal epistemological reality, where wind-window-widow-willow mean emptiness, absence and death; light-lamp-lantern-lighthouse mean life and frail hope; triangle-three-oak tree mean mythological wholeness and correspondence. The chains of words are made in accordance with the same catch up principle of paronymic attraction.[2] By means of phonetic repetition the semantic links between different images are established. The correlation between phonetic form and meaning functions as the main structural principle of Woolf's texts and arranges the images of her writings in what is from a semantic point of view an elaborate net. These lexical paronymic sets on the syntagmatic level "inspire" the stream of consciousness, while on the paradigmatic level they fabricate a vertical "cord," an *axis mundi* that unifies the writer's text with the whole macro-text, Woolf's universe. In the terms of Woolf's poetics this technique of repeated structural elements can be defined as a vehicle that molds the female text.

Another vehicle that generates the mythological, literary and biographical memory of Woolf's texts is the range of number-symbols (3, 6, 7) woven into the narrative patterns. Their symbolism evokes the Pythagorean mystical meaning of numbers. In *To the Lighthouse* the idea of mythological triplicity, universal trinity, works as the main constructive principle realized at different levels of the novel: three parts, three periods of life, three deaths, three times of the novel (subjective inner time, eternity, chronometric time) combined in the polytemporal structure. The number three often occurs in the narrative pattern of the novel adding symbolic meaning and bringing an element of universal order into the text (the composition of Lily's picture has a "triangular purple shape," Lily's vision of Mrs. Ramsay is a "triangular shadow over the step").

In *Orlando* the idea of triplicity is expressed first of all in the image of the oak tree which evokes several meanings. The oak tree is Orlando's poem, cultural synthesis, mythological universal tree unifying three worlds (underworld - middle world - heaven), and three times (past - present - future). The image of the universal tree with its three parts is "enciphered" in the correlation of other structural elements of the novel. The fragments of textual reality line up the mythological cord:

>moon
>rooks
>wood
>root

The Cultural and Poetic Synthesis

The graphic parallelism and phonetic repetition establish semantic connection between these words/images arranging them in the mythological three-part universe where moon belongs to the upper sphere, wood to the middle one, root to the underworld, and rooks can be regarded as tricksters (like Orlando) traveling from one universal sphere to another. The motif of the dream also has some phonetic-semantic correlation with the number three (three - tree - dream).

The poetics of numbers in Woolf's novels is realized by means of the symbols six and seven as well. The six chapters of *Orlando* can be regarded as corresponding with the mythological image of the universe as God's six day creation. The Great Frost finishes with the blows of the rain—"six drops became sixty; then six hundred; then ran themselves together in a steady spout of water"—and with the sixth stroke, Orlando understands that the Russian Princess will not come. After six hundred drops The Great Frost seems to turn into The Great Flood; the sixth stroke brings the feeling of disaster. So six works as the cultural symbol of some sacred measure of universal completeness; the overcoming of this measure means catastrophe and collapse.

The number seven also introduces some mythological implications to the text. Joined with the motif of dream (Orlando sleeps and does not show any sign of life for seven days; at the end of his second trance he wakes up on the seventh day), the number seven intensifies the transcendental meaning of this motif connecting it with the idea of mythological miracle. In a way these episodes of the novel can be read as an allusion to the Christian legend about seven youths who slept more than 300 years and eluded the pursuit of the emperor Decius. On the 7th of January (the day of Russian Christmas) Orlando meets the Russian Princess. It seems that the events marked in Woolf's writings by the numbers six and seven acquire some mystical meanings. Creating different implications and allusions, numbers in her texts prove to be containers of cultural memory.

Numbers play a very important role in Woolf's poetic world, perhaps more important than names which are for the most part conventional, playful or decorative. Names either form an allusive aspect of the character (Orlando's and Jacob Flanders' names have obvious connotations, biblical and literary), or make the story sound (pseudo) realistic, factographical (a lot of minor, secondary characters have full names). I suggest that names (together with facts) in Woolf's texts represent the objective, outward and so "male" and "wrong" type of world. Names seem uncomfortable for her (as for her character Rosalind in "Lappin and Lappinova" who thinks that "Ernest," her husband's name, is difficult to get used to). Numbers, together with sounds and colors, reveal a more intimate, essential, female, "true" dimension of reality.

263

Morzhenkova

The tendency of Woolf's texts to dissolve the borders between separate writings and merge with the intertext of European culture is a distinguishing feature of the writer's macro-text. The idea of cultural synthesis seems to define the key techniques of her poetics, revealed in the different types of citation. In this context, allusions to and quotations from European art appear to be significant features of Woolf's texts.

The comparison of her works with certain paintings by European artists may help to reveal the techniques of interaction between different languages and cultural codes combined by Woolf in her works. "Translation" of non-verbal precedent texts into verbal forms works as a specific version of the catch up technique of repeated elements which constitute the spine linking different texts to the intertext of European culture. I think that the picturesque nature of her metaphorical consciousness is rather literal and it is possible to draw certain parallels between the structural patterns of her texts and some paintings of European modernism. For example, the architectonics of Woolf's novels are often based on the montage insertion of poetic interludes into the narrative fabric of the texts. The function of these poetically marked fragments protruding from the less poetic textual environment may be compared with the functions of ornament as one of the main expressive elements of the modernist style in painting. Ornament in the "art nouveau" style works not only as a decorative detail or background, but molds composition and has significant symbolic meaning. The combination of decorative ornamental backgrounds and realistically represented details is typical of "art nouveau" paintings. The works of Austrian artist Gustav Klimt are quite illustrative in this context. Klimt combined realistic portraits and elaborate design of decorative surfaces.

A similar compositional arrangement is typical of Woolf's novels. The chains of episodes depicting the everyday, routine, ordinary life of the characters are often interrupted by poetically marked, usually uninhabited, descriptive interludes, very decorative fragments of the text. This blurring of the boundaries between poetry and prose, decorative elements and realistic details, can be defined as a common trend of modernistic poetics in general. As a peculiarity of Woolf's macro-text it can be also defined as the combination of two different discourses—poetic female and prosaic male, descriptive and narrative, imaginary and factual.

It is especially interesting to draw parallels between certain episodes in *Orlando* and certain paintings functioning in this context as non-verbal source texts. In *Orlando*, playing with cultural memory and tradition, deconstructing them and joining their elements together, Woolf created a kind of artistic remake of European culture. The text of the novel is constructed as an elaborate dialogue among different discourses typical of various periods and trends.

The Cultural and Poetic Synthesis

The technique of quoting and adopting various cultural codes works as the main constructive principle.

Playful juxtaposition of discourses of different cultural periods (the Elizabethan, baroque, Victorian, romanticism, impressionism, etc.) and their interaction in the heterogeneous textual pattern generate ironical and theatrical aspects of the novel. The adapted, borrowed nature of all major images, motives and plot lines is evident. The very name of the main hero-heroine, Orlando, revives different cultural epochs and justifies the so long life of Orlando, who turns out to be some kind of cultural matrix, the container of cultural memory. The plot of the novel is constructed as the juxtaposition of variations of known themes and plotlines. The events in *Orlando* seem to be the writer's adaptations from source texts of Shakespeare, Sterne, Austen, and Carroll. The plot of the novel reminds us of a patchwork. It is made of well-known or at least recognizable micro-plots enclosed in their cultural chronotopos and connected with each other as different acts of the same play. The main hero-heroine is depicted playing different cultural roles, trying on various cultural masks. The narrative pattern of the novel is fabricated as a kind of potpourri, a pageant of English literary tradition and history. The worldviews, ideology, and spirit of different cultural periods are conveyed by means of "ready-made" borrowed cultural codes and styles. And *Orlando* can be defined as a postmodernist biography of European culture, as a female reception of the culture's intertext.

The text of the novel tends to break verbal borders and include other aspects of a cultural matrix. The comparison of some episodes of *Orlando* with paintings (non-verbal texts) might help to specify the peculiar intertextual essence of this novel. As Hermione Lee has remarked, the Elizabethan episodes of the novel are reminiscent of Breughel paintings. The parallels might be drawn at the levels of composition and theme. As I have said, the chronotopos of the Great Frost is closely connected with the biblical image of the Great Flood. The symbolic essence of this episode is evident. This borrowing of the biblical theme in the novel can be regarded as an intricate simultaneous double quotation from the sacred text and the Dutch painting tradition. The symbolic flood in the novel happens in England in the 16th century. Similar transplantation of biblical plots to the local environment is very typical of Dutch painting of the 16th century. For example, Peter Breughel represented a well known bible episode in his painting "The Numbering at Bethlehem" happening in a Dutch village in the 16th century. The people are depicted in the costumes of that time against the background of a typical Dutch landscape. The episode of the flood as the culmination of the Great Frost in *Orlando* can be also compared with the paintings of another Flemish artist of the 16th century, Hieronymus Bosch.

At the theme level, the connection is rather clear: the description of the flood and of dying people in Woolf's novel evokes Bosch's favorite subject, tortures of sinners in the underworld. It is also possible to draw certain structural similarities at the composition level. The narrative pattern of this episode consists of several scenes taking place on different fragments of ice: "...but what was the most awful and inspiring of terror was the sight of the human creatures who had been trapped in the night and now paced their twisting ...islands in the utmost agony of spirit...Sometimes quite a cluster of these poor creatures would come down together, some on their knees, others suckling their babies. One old man seemed to be reading from a holy book....One crew of young watermen or post-boys....roared and shouted the lewdest tavern songs ...Among other strange sights was to be seen a cat suckling its young; a table laid sumptuously for a supper of twenty; a couple in bed" (*O* 61-62). The everyday scenes are plunged into the dreadful context. The juxtaposition of realistic details combined by means of montage in a grotesque way is similar to the poetics of Bosch's paintings (see, for example, "The Last Judgment").

In this context it is possible to regard the picture of a snowy landscape, looking at which Orlando starts crying, as a verbal quotation of Peter Brueghel's work "Winter Landscape with a Bird Trap" (1565). A group of people skating on the frozen river is represented in this canvas. Certain parallels between the subject of the picture and the Elizabethan episodes are evident. The fragmentariness and montage as constructive principles work in both texts, verbal and non-verbal. It is very likely that Woolf saw this famous painting as copies are available in museums in Vienna, Toledo, Rome, Paris, and London.

The Turkish episodes of *Orlando* evoke the concept of escape from the European chronotopos to a wild, barbaric one. The development of this leitmotif goes back as far as the epoch of Romanticism and remains very attractive to modernists. In some way, Orlando's escape can be read as a variation (though with a hint of irony) of Rimbaud's, Matisse's, and Gauguin's nostalgia for barbaric chronotopes. The city landscape Orlando contemplates from the balcony is reminiscent of Asian city landscapes by Henri Matisse ("The Entrance into Kazba" 1912-1913; "The View out of the Window. Tangier" 1912, for example). The very point of view of the observer looking at objects top-down determines the composition in many canvases by Matisse, the typical features of which are flat, decorative arrangement of details without clear contrast of foregrounds and backgrounds.

The certain merging of foregrounds and backgrounds, and smoothed perspectives characterize Constantinople's landscape in the novel. Orlando's eyes

The Cultural and Poetic Synthesis

seem to move not from nearer details to further but to slide in two-dimensional space. The details s/he observes are depicted as if they were stuck on the same flatness. The syntactic pattern of complex sentences with asyndeton,[3] homogeneous parts and repeated elements accentuate this impression of decorative flatness ("turbaned pilgrims without eyes or noses; there women, there the innumerable donkeys; there the pariah dogs picking up offal; there the shawled horses carrying long poles" [120]).

Revealing certain cultural and poetic similarities between Woolf's texts and non-verbal texts from European art can be interesting not only from a theoretical point of view, but may also encourage some ideas in the sphere of the design and publishing of the writer's works. I suggest that *Orlando* could be designed in the form of an art album with different discourses (Elizabethan, Baroque etc.) combined with corresponding paintings belonging to the same cultural matrix. The first chapter of *Orlando* is constructed as an elaborate stylization in the manner of Elizabethan poetics. The carnival unreality of descriptions, poetically accented narration, and the fabulous and unworldly nature of images turn the depicted world into a kind of performance of the Elizabethan theatre. The episodes, in which the love of the old Queen Elizabeth for young Orlando is described, might be illustrated with paintings by Lucas Cranach the Older, "The Old Woman in Love and the Youth" (1520-1522) and "Misallied Couple" (1522), representing obviously unsuitable matches. The image of Orlando suffocating in the old Queen's embrace is created in a similar grotesque comic manner.

The vivid decorative essence of the Queen's image, its theatrical aspect and similarity to a mannequin could be accented by comparing Woolf's Elizabeth with the portrait of Queen Anna (1540s) in the Arts Museum, Budapest, created by an unknown artist who worked in the style of Jacob Zaizingger.

The Baroque fragments of the novel might be compared with aristocratic portraits created by A.Van Dyck, who was a court painter at the time of Karl I. Such works of the English period as the pair portrait of George Digby and William Rassel (1637), or the portrait of James Stuart with his favorite hound (c. 1634-35) could be chosen to illustrate the development of Baroque esthetics with its focus on theatrical and metaphorical interpretation of portrait images.

The design of *Orlando* in the form of an art album might be regarded as an interpretation and development of the writer's idea to illustrate the text of the novel with photos of Vita Sackville-West and Angelica Bell in costumes and to use photos of ancient family portraits from Sackville-West's estate. These images included in the text emphasize the theatrical aspect of the novel, its "constructed" nature, the very essence of the characters, which appear to be polysemantic cultural masks and mythological symbols.

The combination of verbal and non-verbal texts should be based rather on structural parallels than on thematic ones. This would help to trace some generic peculiarities of different cultural languages. Such a design seems to be adequate to the very essence of the novel as it underlines its intertextual basis and correspondence with the broad context of European culture. I believe another direction in the search for adequate forms for Woolf's texts is connected with the idea of design art books, especially with handmade artist's books as they seem to be a perfect visual representation of female discourse. The idea of a book as a cultural synthesis can be regarded as the attempt to dissolve the borders between separate cultural texts and merge them into the vertical dialogical context.

Notes

[1] The term "anadiplosis"—rhetorical repetition of the last element from the previous segment of text at the beginning of the next—is used here to underline the research approach according to which separate novels are regarded as elements of the writer's macrotext.

[2] The phenomenon of paronymic attraction typical of modernist texts is realized in the correlation between phonetic proximity and semantic links. In a modernist text (poetic and prosaic) phonetic similarity often marks complex semantic connections between different elements of the text.

[3] Asyndeton refers to the omission of conjunctions between clauses, resulting in a hurried rhythm or vehement effect.

Works Cited

Lee, Hermione. *Virginia Woolf*. NY: Knopf, 1996.
Woolf, Virginia. *Orlando, A Biography*. 1928. NY: Harcourt, 1973.

The Issue of Self-Identification in Woolf's *Mrs. Dalloway* and Cunningham's *The Hours*
Natalia Povalyaeva

It is difficult to find a period as radical in changing the criteria and strategies of self-identification as the past century. Old values once considered to be vitally important and central to being were quickly dismantled, and new ones rushed to take their place. In spite of undoubted achievements in the field of societal democratization and the unprecedented broadening of possibilities for self-identification, it is exactly in the late twentieth century that there appeared the notion of *identity crisis*. This reflects one of the socio-cultural paradoxes of the postmodern age—with all the rights and licenses gained, the individual's perception of him/herself as an auto-identical personality is being questioned at every step in contemporary society.

I assume that one of the most complicated and controversial problems in contemporary arts are the ways and options of a personality's self-identification. Postmodernist fiction seems to be breaking new ground in the all-round consideration of this issue. To quote just one example, identity crisis lies at the narrative core of the novel *The Hours* (1998) by the American writer Michael Cunningham. The novel leaves no doubt that it is a postmodernist interpretation of Virginia Woolf's novel *Mrs. Dalloway*. In this article I am going to analyze and compare the strategies Woolf and Cunningham deploy in addressing the self-identification issue in their respective works.

There are three narrative lines developing simultaneously in *The Hours*. Line one comes down to the following: in New York, at the end of the 1990s, a successful editor, Clarissa Vaughan, is preparing a reception in honor of her old friend Richard who has been awarded a prestigious literary prize. Line two takes us to the suburbs of Los Angeles, 1949, when a young housewife, Laura Brown, is getting ready to celebrate the birthday of her husband, Dan. And line three shows Virginia Woolf who is in "health imprisonment" in Richmond under her husband's supervision and is writing in torment her new novel. All three lines are in one way or another connected with the plot of Woolf's novel or with the facts of the writer's biography. As is known, postmodernist narrative deploys conceptual distance from a source text. Cunningham, however, does not seem to differ much from Woolf in the treatment of the problem of self-identification. What looks common to both writers is, first of all, their understanding of the ways and methods of self-identification of a personality in the world: communication with other people, love, family, career, art. Furthermore, the shaping of a set of characters for Woolf is a most important means of revealing this problem. Much has been said about the double characters in her works, yet I must say that there are some examples of inverse interrelation which we can provisionally define as *mirror relationship*. In the case of such interrelation one character serves as a mirror for the other, and this mirror is a critical one: it lays bare the shortcomings of the one who looks into it. Cunningham uses a similar method of self-identification in his novel.

Let us focus on the mirror interrelations in *Mrs. Dalloway*.

There is a mirror-like connection between Clarissa and Peter. To Peter, Clarissa is a reminder that he is a failure both in his career and in his private life. He is far from respectable Richard, he is not invited to fashionable routs and business parties, he has to look for happiness in the colonies, and finally his manners are not refined, and the memory that Clarissa turned him down and preferred Richard gives him no peace; his love affair with a married woman looks vulgar and absurd when compared to the blameless family background of the Dalloways. These thoughts haunt Peter Walsh persistently on his visit to Mrs. Dalloway: "And she would think me a failure, which I am in their sense, he thought; in the Dalloways sense" (*MD* 67).

The offence narrows Peter's mind very much and the world narrows in his perception down to the cycle of the Dalloways and the Whitbreads. Walsh is in a mad rush bitterly realizing that he is a failure and trying to make his dream—to gain his foothold—come true:

> He was not old, or set, or dried in the least. As for caring what they said of him—the Dalloways, the Whitbreads, and their set, he cared not a straw—not a straw… He had been sent down from Oxford—true. He had been a Socialist, in some sense a failure—true. Still the future of civilization lies, he thought, in the hands of young men like that; of young men such as he was, thirty years ago…(77)

However, it is not an easy ordeal for Clarissa to meet with Peter, and even when she does not see him she has ceaseless violent inner arguments with him. The stumbling-block in their relations is Clarissa's respectability, her status as a wife of Her Majesty's high-ranking official. She constantly recollects the hints which he made in Bourton many years ago that her calling is to become the wife of a man with "status" and to dissolve entirely in this role: "How he scolded her! How they argued! She would marry a Prime Minister and stand at the top of a staircase; the perfect hostess he called her (she had cried over it in her bedroom)" (13).

The Issue of Self-Identification

In Peter's presence Clarissa begins to see herself and everything in a different light: everything that seemed to her important and sincere turns into something useless and artificial under Peter's critical glance. So at her party one glimpse of Peter was quite enough for Clarissa to feel the vanity of this social affair:

> It was extraordinary how Peter put her into these states just by coming and standing in a corner. He made her see herself; exaggerate. It was idiotic. But why did he come, then, merely to criticize? Why always take, never give? Why not risk one's one little point of view?...Life was that—humiliation, renunciation. (252-3)

Peter is not able to understand that Clarissa's parties ("*offerings*," as she herself calls them) are the most important elements of her identification. But Clarissa is sure that "her only gift was knowing people almost by instinct" (15), which is why she considers her parties as opposed to life's chaos, separating people. But this feature of Mrs. Dalloway's character is hidden in equal degree both from Peter and Richard:

> They thought, or Peter at any rate thought, that she enjoyed imposing herself; liked to have famous people about her; great names; was simply a snob in short. Well, Peter might think so. Richard merely thought it foolish of her to like excitement when she knew it was bad for her heart. It was childish, he thought. And both were quite wrong. What she liked was simply life. (183)

The main thing that distinguishes Clarissa from Peter is the chosen strategy of self-identification. Communication and intimacy with people and the surrounding world seem quite true and correct to Mrs. Dalloway. She is the only one among all the characters in the novel who can sense herself, though for a moment, as part of an internal and continuous life stream. Peter, on the contrary, chooses the way of confrontation with the whole world. This basic difference in apprehension of their own part in life and the methods of achieving it becomes the reason for the "failure of communication" between Clarissa and Peter.

Similar mirror relations link Mrs. Dalloway and Miss Kilman. Miss Kilman tries to construct her personality according to the pattern of Christian saints—self-denial in the name of other people who need help. However, her bitterness against the whole world, which rejected her gifted personality, becomes a serious obstacle on this way. And Clarissa Dalloway, who, in Miss Kilman's opinion, is stuck in vain and empty aspirations, becomes for her the embodiment of this world. Miss Kilman dreams of the "ideological subjection" of Clarissa: "But it was not the body; it was the soul and its mockery that she wished to subdue; make feel her mastery. If only she could make her weep;

could ruin her; humiliate her; bring her to her knees crying, You are right!" (189).

On the other hand, Miss Kilman realizes that her condemnation of Clarissa comes from her envy of Clarissa's high social status and well-being. Thus her displeasure with Clarissa flies at Miss Kilman as a boomerang and makes their relations a real torture. In her turn Mrs. Dalloway, who tries with all her might to forbid herself to condemn other people, cannot agree with Miss Kilman's "double standards" in her relations with surroundings:

> it being her experience that the religious ecstasy made people callous (so did causes); dulled their feelings, for Miss Kilman would do anything for the Russians, starved herself for the Austrians, but in private inflicted positive torture, so insensitive was she, dressed in a green mackintosh coat. (20)

Lack of understanding becomes a serious obstacle in the way of gaining auto-identity by both characters.

In Woolf's opinion the categories that are directly related to the process of self-identification are love and marriage. Love for Clarissa is evidently an ambivalent term, bearing both a positive as well as negative meaning. She is sure that love is good for people only in cases where it is synonymous with freedom. In Peter's love there prevailed the wish to absorb the object entirely, to make it part of himself, which is why Clarissa turns Peter down:

> So she would still find herself arguing in St. James's Park, still making out that she had been right—and she had too—not to marry him. For in marriage a little license, a little independence there must be between people living together day in day out in the same house; which Richard gave her, and she him. (13-4)

In the true sense of the word, the love between Clarissa and Sally Seton was ideal; however, by virtue of different objective and subjective reasons this love was not to be followed-up.

Finally, it is worth noting in connection with the problem of self-identification that Woolf was occupied with the issue of correlation between such terms as *illness* and *norm*. Illness (and the writer knew it from her own experience) becomes a fatal obstacle on the way of self-identification in the society where the norm, or the *sense of proportion*, using the word of Dr. Bradshaw, dominates. Septimus Smith is mentally ill and in his opinion this is the punishment for his inability to feel. The black hole between the character and his surroundings is the result of a lack of coincidence of perception and communication codes: that what Septimus sees the surroundings do not see; that what delights or excites him makes other people indifferent. The illness destroys the

The Issue of Self-Identification

personality of Septimus, but the treatment of Dr. Bradshaw can only increase this process; that's exactly why the character chooses suicide.

Michael Cunningham sends his characters in search of self-identification along the same paths as Virginia Woolf sends hers. In the narrative line "Mrs. Dalloway," Clarissa Vaughan thinks (not unlike Woolf's character) that her main calling is simply to live enjoying every moment:

> What a thrill, what a shock, to be alive on a morning in June, prosperous, almost scandalously privileged, with a simple errand to run. She, Clarissa Vaughan, an ordinary person (at this age, why bother trying to deny it?), has flowers to buy and a party to give. (*Hours* 16)

But this joyful feeling of harmony with the surroundings and herself is darkened every time the character associates with Richard in thoughts or in reality. Constructing the interrelations between these characters Cunningham uses the same scheme as Woolf does in the case of Peter and Mrs. Dalloway: "Richard has always been Clarissa's most rigorous, infuriating companion" (*Hours* 27).

However, the image of Richard essentially differs from that of Peter Walsh. Richard is a writer, and in his mind the reality and the text are mingled. He perceives life as a narration whose author he is himself. People and situations for Richard are only raw material, which needs serious treatment:

> It is only after knowing him for some time that you begin to realize you are, to him, an essentially fictional character, one he has invested with nearly limitless capacities for tragedy and comedy not because that is your true nature but because he, Richard, needs to live in a world peopled by extreme and commanding figures. (*Hours* 69)

Clarissa clearly understands that by giving her the nickname "Mrs. Dalloway" thirty years ago Richard imposed a self-indulgent strategy on her. It was obvious to him that "she, Clarissa, was clearly not destined to make a disastrous marriage or fall under the wheels of a train. She was destined to charm, to prosper. So Mrs. Dalloway it was and would be" (*Hours* 17).

But Clarissa preferred to break the given role and Richard cannot forgive her for this. He considers her to be an ordinary philistine and he cannot palate either her successful career (though as an editor Clarissa does not only publish commercially successful books but also supports unprofitable independent projects), nor her marriage to Sally (Clarissa undoubtedly challenged society, most of whose representatives consider marriage to be only heterosexual even at the end of the twentieth century). Richard's final attempt to bring Clarissa back to the role planned for her was his book. But his book was not a success, it didn't change the world, and Clarissa broke free from his power. As in the case of Peter Walsh and Mrs. Dalloway, self-identification strategies chosen by

Richard and Clarissa Vaughan distinguish them. Richard chooses the way of "correcting reality," using his own discretion. Perhaps the fact that his beloved mother left Richard in his childhood played its part in it: as reality once deceived him rudely he decides to oppose his imaginary world to reality. But Clarissa tries to feel this "real reality":

> Tonight she will give her party. She will fill the rooms of her apartment with food and flowers, with people of wit and influence. She will shepherd Richard through it, see that he doesn't overtire, and then she will escort him uptown to receive his prize. (*Hours* 24)

It is just this position that allows Clarissa to live in spite of everything, whereas Richard, having come to a failure in creating his epic "life" and destroyed by incurable disease, voluntarily ends his earthly existence.

Mary Crowell is the second character who acts as Clarissa's mirror reflection. Like Miss Kilman in Woolf's novel, Mary hates Clarissa for the things she herself for the most part would not mind having—high social status and well being. Mary hides all her numerous complexes behind the mask of aggressiveness, and as Clarissa understands this Mary hates her even more.

Similar to Woolf, Michael Cunningham pays much attention to love. Clarissa was truly in love with Richard and in some way she continues to love him even thirty years later. However, at some stage she understood that her intimacy with Richard could threaten her with the loss of her ego. Richard's love didn't give her a free hand. Sally's love is a phenomenon of another kind. To her great surprise Clarissa realizes that having lived with Sally for eighteen years they have never quarreled, and that this is not an indicator of habit but shows that the most important point of this marriage is the respect of the partner's right to personal freedom. Freedom can't be an obstacle to true intimacy. Both Clarissa and Sally feel that some parts of their personalities do not belong to them but are properties of their common soul.

In the narrative line "Mrs. Brown" the mirror which makes the heroine doubt the rightness of her life choice is Virginia Woolf's novel *Mrs. Dalloway*. Reading the book, Laura Brown feels "as if she is standing in the wings, about to go onstage and perform in a play for which she is not appropriately dressed, and for which she has not adequately rehearsed" (42).

From the point of view of the people who surround Laura she had her chance of luck: she married a war hero, has a lovely son and a beautiful house where she is a housewife. Laura keeps reminding herself that it is a shame for her to dream of something more. So Laura, a happy wife and mother, is getting ready to bake a cake for her husband's birthday. At that moment she is fully satisfied with her part:

The Issue of Self-Identification

> She is herself and she is the perfect picture of herself; there is no difference. She is going to produce a birthday cake—only a cake—but in her mind at this moment the cake is glossy and resplendent as any photograph in any magazine; it is better, even, than the photograph of cakes in magazines. She imagines making, out of the humblest materials, a cake with all the balance and authority of an urn or a house. The cake will speak of bounty and delight the way a good house speaks of comfort and safety. This, she thinks, is how artists or architects must feel (it's an awfully grand comparison, she knows, maybe even a little foolish, but still), faced with canvas, with stone, with oil or wet cement. Wasn't a book like *Mrs. Dalloway* once just empty paper and a pot of ink? (84)

However the joy of the achieved harmony does not last long. That day everything seems to go wrong to make Laura lose her balance: little Richie's mood-swings from overwhelming joy to inconsolable grief discourage her; the visit of Laura's neighbor Kitty and the news of her forthcoming test at the oncologist's cause gloomy thoughts about mortality; and finally, to her great surprise, Laura realizes that despite being a faithful wife to her husband she is at the same time in love with Kitty. On top of it all the cake turned out to be far from delicious. And so Laura Brown, to use her own words, makes an "escape from the cake." She goes to town, takes a room in a hotel, reads Woolf's novel, thinks about suicide, and then returns home. It may be possible to say that she is on the way back to perform her former familiar part of a happy housewife, but it is not so. Her identity balance is disturbed forever:

> She is herself and not herself. She is a woman in London, an aristocrat, pale and charming, a little false; she is Virginia Woolf; and she is this other, the inchoate, tumbling thing known as herself... (200)

That day Laura will indeed play her part to the end, yet at the end of the novel we learn that after the birth of her second child she left her family and went to live in Canada, where she outlived her husband and children who never forgave her. Laura found herself in a tragic situation of "identity crisis," and there was no positive way out of this situation for her.

Neither was there a positive way out for Woolf, a character of the third narrative line in *The Hours*. Here Cunningham puts in the first place two categories—art and illness. Art is the only sphere in which Virginia Woolf would like to dissolve, but she is never sure of her creative ability. The moments of satisfaction are superseded by moments of despair: "She herself has failed. She is not a writer at all, really; she is merely a gifted eccentric" (*Hours* 9). Illness aggravates this situation; it makes the writer constantly check her behavior with what is considered to be "a norm." "Normal behavior" for Virginia is a pass to freedom, to London. Her illness, however, is implacable, and the writer feels that very soon it will become the basis of her personality: "The voices are back and the headache is approaching as surely as rain, the headache that will crush whatever is she and replace her with itself." Freedom is dearer, Woolf thinks, and commits suicide (*Hours* 10).

Thus the characters of Woolf's and Cunningham's novels experience an "identity crisis" and find themselves in a situation where the choice made before is now found somewhat flawed. The situation as interpreted both in *Mrs. Dalloway* and *The Hours* is dramatic, and at times tragic. Under these conditions hope is the only thing that offers the possibility of survival. Virginia Woolf and Michael Cunningham are unanimous in this. Both Mrs. Dalloway and Clarissa Vaughan are certain about it—one should live enjoying the moments of brightness which are granted to us by fate as a reward for sufferings and lost dreams:

> There's just this for consolation: an hour here or there when our lives seem, against all odds and expectations, to burst open and give us everything we've ever imagined... Still, we cherish the city, the morning; we hope, more than anything, for more. (*Hours* 230)

Works Cited

Cunningham, Michael. *The Hours*. New York: Picador, 2002.
Woolf, Virginia. *Mrs. Dalloway*. 2nd edition. London: The Hogarth Press, 1925.

The Play in the Sky of the Mind: Dialogue, "the Tchekov method," and *Between the Acts*
Christine Froula

> *Thinking is my fighting.*
> Diary, *15 May 1940*

> *Dear John, I'd decided, before your letter came,*
> *that I cant publish that novel as it stands. Its too silly & trivial.*
> Letters, *27? March 1941*

In *Between the Acts* the inhabitants of an English village stage their annual pageant on a June day in 1939, just weeks before Hitler's invasion of Poland. The narrative poses La Trobe's daringly experimental play against the coming war to explore relations between the characters' everyday lives and their festival roles as director, actors, audience, and hosts; between "real" life and art; history and spectatorship; insular nationalism and Europe's fate and future; embodied community and (in Auerbach's phrase) the political "orders over which men fight and despair" (552-53). My talk today explores Woolf's free elaboration of what she called "the Tchekov method" in the virtuosic interplay of utterance, conversation, silent reflection and communication, reported speech, citation, the written word in books and newspapers, talking objects and rooms, script, and performance—the animate web of spoken and unspoken words from all across the bandwidths that is *Between the Acts* ("An Essay in Criticism" 90). Embodying the "very latest notion" that "nothing's solid," as a departing spectator says, Woolf's last novel dissolves plot, story, event, and character into these myriad voices, seemingly random yet orchestrated, as if ordinary language were throwing off mundane functionality and aspiring to the condition of music (*BTA* 199). Capturing ephemeral thought, speech, and performance on the wing, *Between the Acts* is a tour de force of listening to the words for the sake of a music that plays through and between them, beyond the reach of sound.

The affinity of *Between the Acts* with Chekhov that I wish to highlight comes into view in Woolf's remarks on voice and dialogue in her 1927 "Essay in Criticism," on Hemingway's stories.[1] Contrasting the French and Russian masters of the short story, Woolf writes that "The great French masters, Mérimée and Maupassant," made the story "self-conscious and compact," with a final sentence that "flares up" to illumine the "whole circumference and significance" ("Essay in Criticism" 90). "The Tchekov method" creates "the very opposite" effect: "Everything is cloudy and vague, loosely trailing rather than tightly furled. The stories move slowly out of sight like clouds in the summer air, leaving a wake of meaning in our minds which gradually fades away." Of these two methods, "Who shall say which is the better?"; any choice is mere personal preference, not an aesthetic judgment (90). Hemingway follows the French masters "with considerable success," and where he falters, it is not because of his method but because "he is modern in manner but not in vision" (90, 92). Whereas "the moderns make us aware of what we feel subconsciously" and "even anticipate" our experience, "giv[ing] us a particular excitement," Hemingway's characters "are people one may have seen showing off at some café" who are "terribly afraid of being themselves, or they would say things simply in their natural voices" (86, 89). Beside Maupassant's "they are crude as a photograph"; beside Chekhov's, "flat as cardboard," "bare, abrupt, outspoken," their dialogue "excessive" (89, 87, 91). For, Woolf writes, "when fictitious people are allowed to speak it must be because they have something...important to say"; they must not say "what the author could say much more economically for them" (91). Whereas the "true writer stands close up to the bull and lets the...truth...pass him close each time," the "brilliantly and enormously skilful" Hemingway "lets his dexterity, like the bullfighter's cloak, get between him and the fact" (91-92). Instead of revealing unconscious feeling, he "fake[s]," until "At last we are inclined to cry out with the little girl in 'Hills Like White Elephants': 'Would you please please please please please please stop talking?'" (91).

Woolf begins and ends the "Essay in Criticism" by insisting on the critic's "prejudices," "instincts," and "fallacies," and her own alliance with a peculiarly Chekhovian modernity is felt from *Jacob's Room* forward (92). Reviewing the 1920 Arts Theatre production of *The Cherry Orchard*, she had described Chekhov's power to give voice to "the human soul set free from all trappings and crossed incessantly by thoughts and emotions which wing their way from here, from there, from the furthest horizons": There is "no conflict of individual wills"; the characters speak suddenly and vaguely, "as if thinking aloud," so that "one thought scarcely grazed, let alone struck sparks from, another," yet "though the leap from one thought to another was so wide as to produce a sense of dangerous dislocation, all the separate speeches and characters combined to create a single impression of an overwhelming kind" ("*The Cherry Orchard*" 198).[2] Chekhov "shed[s] over us a luminous vapour in which life appears as it is, without veils, transparent and visible to the depths....[W]e seemed to have sunk below the surface of things and to be feeling our way among submerged

The Play in the Sky of the Mind

but recognisable emotions...[H]ow the words go sounding on in one's mind—how the whole play resonates with such sentences, which reverberate, melt into each other, and pass far away out beyond everything" (199).

"There is nothing in English literature the least like *The Cherry Orchard*," Woolf observed, and before long had herself created something a bit like it in *Jacob's Room* ("*The Cherry Orchard*" 197). Her review cites Charlotte's "strange speech in the beginning of the second act. 'I have no proper passport. I don't know how old I am; I always feel I am still young....When I grew up I became a governess. But where I come from and who I am, I haven't a notion. Who my parents were—*very likely they weren't married*—I don't know'" (198-99, emphasis in original). In *Jacob's Room* Chekhov's Charlotte resonates in the prostitute Florinda, with her uncertain parentage, and in Charlotte Wilding, a dinner guest at the Durrants' country house who in her whimsical wit and rootlessness might almost have sauntered out of *The Cherry Orchard* and into Woolf's first novel (tellingly) "in my own voice."[3] The shotgun and magic tricks of Chekhov's Charlotte metamorphose into Charlotte Wilding's little bets on eating flowers with fish and on how many sounds can be heard on a summer's night. Both Charlottes distill the human voice in its immitigable solitude, its solitary flutesong of being behind the words not more tragic than comic, as Chekhov insisted to Stanislawski. The Charlottes' nonchalant loneliness is the matrix of Chekhovian dialogue, wherein the characters' speeches glance across and ricochet off one another, and the feeling in their words, missing its human mark, hangs in the air. What the characters do utter is almost as unheard by them as what they cannot speak, and what they cannot speak sounds almost more distinctly to the spectator than what they do say. To let characters talk too much, Woolf suggests, is to muffle this real drama, the unuttered speech beneath the words that play and narrative exist to make heard.

In *Between the Acts* the narrator's figure of the "play...in the sky of the mind—moving, diminishing, but still there" affiliates the village pageant with "the Tchekov method" where all is "cloudy and vague, loosely trailing," drifting like clouds and leaving "a wake of meaning" that "gradually fades away" (212, cf. 23, 213). La Trobe herself, with her exotic name, is not "presumably pure English"; her "eyes and something about her" remind one matron of "the Tartars" (57-58). Her possible "Russian blood" aside, her Russian soul is suggested when she transfigures the Pointz Hall terrace into an "open-air cathedral," its trees "columns...in a church without a roof...where swallows...danc[e], like the Russians,...to the unheard rhythm of their own wild hearts" (58, 64-65). This quasi-Russian Englishwoman sets the stage for a modern English pageant re-formed in the image of the outsider's patriotism described in *Three Guineas*: a love of England that serves her "to give to

England first what she desires of peace and freedom for the whole world" (109). "The play...in the sky of the mind" locates pageant and narrative at once in an English village and in the "whole world"—that deterritorialized country of the mind, the unbounded regions of thought and feeling that are the outsider's dwellingplace—and gestures with Chekhovian tenderness and inconclusion toward the possible consequence of this art of seeming inconsequence for a world at war.[4]

In 1939, Woolf was negotiating between her philosophical and practical Outsiderhood on the one hand, and on the other her fierce ambition, which surfaced in rivalries with such longtime friends as T. S. Eliot. With *Pointz Hall* underway, she felt "selfishly relieved" when Eliot's *Family Reunion* failed and wondered "why? Had it been a success would it have somehow sealed—my ideas? does this failure confirm a new idea of mine—that I'm evolving in P[ointz] H[all] about the drama?" She thought his characters "stiff as pokers....And the chief poker is Tom: but cant speak out. A cold upright poker. And the Fates behind the drawing room curtain. A clever beginning, & some ideas; but they spin out: & nothing grips: all mist—a failure: a proof hes not a dramatist. A monologist. This is stated very politely by the papers this morning."[5] Having thus raised the question of dialogue in formally specific terms, Woolf covertly replies to Eliot's blank-verse drama with her own "play-poem" (a generic hybrid as apt for *Between the Acts* as for *The Waves*): against the monologist who "wont speak out," the dialogist La Trobe, who (no less paradoxically) hides in the bushes to harangue her audience through a megaphone, along with a dialogist narrator, who writes this poetics large on the plane of the narrative (*D3* 139, 18 June 1927).

Bodying forth "the death of the author," La Trobe's avant-garde theatrical practice casts the spectators as the play's co-creators.[6] As Bart informs his guests, "Our part...is to be the audience. And a very important part too" (*BTA* 58). La Trobe does not invent this dialogic drama out of nothing. "One year we wrote the play ourselves," Lucy Swithin recalls at the family luncheon on which Mrs. Manresa and William Dodge have intruded with their picnic hamper. The blacksmith's son "had the loveliest voice" and "Elsie at the Crossways," a born mimic, "[t]ook us all off," she remembers. "People are gifted—very. The question is—how to bring it out? That's where she's so clever—Miss La Trobe" (59). In line with this job description, La Trobe (a. k. a. "Miss Whatshername") strives to bring out the community's voices, both hidden and potential (197). And the villagers need her, for we glimpse the sort of thing they come up with when they write the play themselves when Colonel Mayhew wonders, "Why leave out the British Army? What's history without the Army, eh?" and his wife soothes him by looking forward to what

The Play in the Sky of the Mind

La Trobe has probably planned for a finale: "a Grand Ensemble. Army; Navy; Union Jack; and behind them perhaps—Mrs. Mayhew sketched what she would have done had it been her pageant—the Church. In cardboard. One window looking east, brilliantly illuminated to symbolize—she could work that out when the time came."[7] La Trobe's part is not to execute their conventional visions—which arguably resemble them far less closely than does her mirror play at the end—but (like the "moderns" in the "Essay in Criticism") to "anticipate" their mute thoughts and feelings. Her part is to be their "Bossy" leader ("Someone must lead. Then too they could put the blame on her") and equally their "slave" ("O to write a play without an audience—*the* play") in the effort to call out voice, speech, and feeling they do not yet know they have (63, 94, 180).

The narrator of *Between the Acts* both depicts La Trobe's dialogism and practices it herself. As La Trobe opens the pageant's borders to chance, letting nature shimmer through art's illusion, the narrator records every event and voice with stenographic fidelity so that the pageant becomes but one voice among many, its first scene nearly lost amid other sounds and voices:

> [1] "What luck!" [2]Mrs. Carter was saying. [1] "Last year..." [2]Then the play began. Was it, or was it not, the play? [3]Chuff, chuff, chuff [2]sounded from the bushes. It was the noise a machine makes when something has gone wrong. Some sat down hastily; others stopped talking guiltily. All looked at the bushes. For the stage was empty.... While they looked apprehensively and some finished their sentences, a small girl, like a rosebud in pink, advanced; took her stand...and piped:
>
> [4] *Gentles and simples, I address you all...*
> [2] So it was the play then. Or was it the prologue?
> [4] *Come hither for our festival* [2](she continued)
> [4] *This is a pageant, all may see*
>   *Drawn from our island history.*
>   *England am I...*
> [5+] "She's England," [2]they whispered. [5+] "It's begun." "The prologue," [2] they added, looking down at the programme.
>
> [4] "*England am I*," [2]she piped again; and stopped.
> [2] She had forgotten her lines.
> [6] "Hear! Hear!" [2]said an old man in a white waistcoat briskly. [6] "Bravo! Bravo!"
> [7a] "Blast 'em!" [2]cursed Miss La Trobe, hidden behind the tree....
> [7b] "Music!" she signalled.... [2]But the machine continued: [3]Chuff, chuff, chuff.
> [7c] "*A child new born* . . ." [2]she prompted. (76-77)

Before the play has progressed six lines we hear at least seven voices: Mrs. Carter, the narrator, the gramophone ("chuff"—the voice of the thing itself,

281

mediating nothing), little Phyllis, whispering spectators, the kind old man, and the director—first sotto voce ("Blast 'em!"), then calling for music, then prompting from the script, a sort of eighth voice. Like Mr. Erskine, who tells Charlotte Wilding that he can count "twenty different sounds on a night like this" in *Jacob's Room* (60), the narrative records each one moment by moment, as if it were a rolling camera pointed at the scene: "'Sorry I'm so late,' said Mrs. Swithin...'What's it all about? I've missed the prologue. England? That little girl? Now she's gone....And who's this?'...It was Hilda, the carpenter's daughter....'A cushion? Thank you so much'"; "'O,' Miss La Trobe growled behind her tree, 'the torture of these interruptions!'" (*BTA* 79-80).

Who speaks? Together the spectators' unscripted comments, the faltering little actor, the exasperated director, the gramophone's scraping needle, the script, and the observant narrator create the rustling, glancing voice of the play in performance—and something more: a voice beyond all these voices, a meta-voice that belongs to no one, not even the narrator, whose gaze and reportage more nearly resemble a documentary cinematographic apparatus than an omniscient, moralizing storyteller. Yet there is nothing mechanical about the quality of the narrator's attention, which suffuses this Chekhovian human comedy with aesthetic feeling. It is as if she at once attends to every moment for its own sake and listens, watches, for designs and refrains to appear; for that ephemeral "something" that *Orlando* calls "beauty" to transform the documentary field of human speech—marked out by the novel's first sentence, "they were talking," and its last, "They spoke"—into the play-poem (*O* 322, *BTA* 3, 219). Or, it is as if, behind the narrative's quasi-documentary mode, a meta-voice (the artist? the author? We'll come back to this question) were weaving everything, from the not so privileged script to the most trivial interruption, into an encompassing intention or design, a whole that requires each element as a tapestry requires each thread or an orchestral composition every note, motif, and instrumental voice. Recalling Woolf's caution that fictitious people must not say what the narrator can say more economically for them, we begin to see that it is the very triviality of the characters' utterances that makes them transparent to this meta-voice behind the voices. Triviality is indispensable to the aesthetic effect that lifts what they say "simply in their natural voices" out of the mundane and exceeds, yet does not violate, the director's plan ("Essay in Criticism" 89). This poetics parallels on the narrative plane La Trobe's effects—at once fortuitous and astonishing—with cows, rain, "real swallows," mirrors in her daring experiment "try ten mins. of present time" (*BTA* 164, 179). The pageant provides an occasion and a temporal frame to hang the human voices on, a canvas for the narrator's pointillist art. Its mere existence is drama enough: anticipation, preparations, acts, intervals, performance, and

The Play in the Sky of the Mind

aftermath on this festival day engender the subtly eventful social panoply by which the solid pageant sublimes into a play-poem in the sky of the mind.

The question, then, is less Who speaks than How, although thinking about How they speak leads to a different understanding of Who. *Between the Acts* dissolves any notion of a divide between functional and poetic language. Like a stone chip in a mosaic, the most ordinary utterance brushes against, calls out, becomes suffused with poetry through context and contiguity, as when, at tea in the Barn, a voice says, "A bit too strong? Let me add water," and Isa thinks, "That's what I wished…when I dropped my pin. Water, water" (104). On this afternoon when words "cease[] to lie flat in the sentence," rise, shake menacing "fists at you," speech is never naked (59). As Lucy Swithin "increas[es] the bounds of the moment by flights into past or future; or sidelong down corridors and alleys," the narrator's kaleidoscopic juxtapositions leave every utterance richly laden, nuanced, made strange by spatial and temporal harmonics, reverberating with and against others like the strings of a piano (9).

As in *Jacob's Room*, the narrator notes epistemological limits only to exceed them in practice. No one knows "what it meant to Mrs. Sands" to have to wait by the oven keeping meat hot for people who miss trains, though Isa's, Giles's, William's, Bart's, thoughts are rendered without anxiety (*BTA* 39). The narrator is not a conventional moralizing imagination. Rather, she's after the moment-by-moment "truth" not just of the characters' actual and inward voices but of rooms and things: "Paint my dog," says the ancestor in the portrait; "Empty, empty, empty," sings the dining-room (49, 36). No wavelength eludes her antennae. So punctiliously does she document what people say—Mrs. Haines on the cesspool: "What a subject to talk about on a night like this!" and, a few moments later, "What a subject to talk about on a night like this!"—that we trust her on what they don't, as when, in reply to Bart's complaint that little George is "a coward," Isa "frowned. He was not a coward, her boy wasn't. And she loathed the domestic, the possessive; the maternal. And he knew it and did it on purpose to tease her, the old brute, her father-in-law. She looked away" (3-4, 19).

Between the Acts is, of course, a novel about "the things people don't say" such as Terence Hewet imagines in *The Voyage Out* (216). Virtuosic transcriptions of unspoken talk turn Chekhovian dialogue inside out: if Chekhov's characters talk past each other, Woolf's talk silently, in subliminal or somatic speech. Not only does the narrator hear their unspoken thoughts; they overhear each other's and soundlessly converse in a hyperreal form of free indirect discourse. Isa, for example, overhears Giles launching stealth missiles at William Dodge:

> A toady; a lickspittle;...a teaser and twitcher, a fingerer of sensations; picking and choosing; dillying and dallying; not a man to have straightforward love for a woman...but simply a—At this word, which he could not speak in public [though Giles isn't in fact speaking], he pursed his lips; and the signet-ring on his little finger looked redder, for the flesh next it whitened as he gripped the arm of his chair. (60)

Isa "guesse[s] the word" Giles suppresses and voicelessly counters, "Well, was it wrong if he was that word?" (61). Deducing that Mrs. Manresa "preferred men obviously," Isa (her silence making its "unmistakable contribution to talk") mocks, "Or what are your rings for, and your nails, and that really adorable little straw hat?" (39). Mrs. Manresa defies this unspoken though not unheard appraisal; she too is fluent in speech without words: "She gave [Bart] an arch roguish twinkle, as if to say—but the end of that sentence was cut short," as if this moment needs a gloss (202). Giles hears Isa intimate "as plainly as words could say it, 'No,...I don't admire you....Silly little boy with blood on his boots'" (in quotation marks, as if her feeling is so palpable that she seems to have spoken) (111). He silently wonders: "Whom then did she admire?...Some man, he was sure, in the Barn. Which man? He looked round him" (111). The air throbs with silent, wireless talk: "Well, if the thought gave [Lucy] comfort, William and Isa smiled across her, let her think it" (175). William asks half-aloud, "'Isn't that enough?' Beauty—isn't that enough? But here Isa fidgeted....'No, not for us, who've the future,' she seemed to say. The future disturbing our present" (82). Yet, for all this voiced and soundless speech, Woolf's fictitious people do not say "what the narrator can say more economically for them." As (Lucy notes) the Chinese "put a dagger on the table and that's a battle," Isa and William, with the "doom of sudden death" hanging over them, talk in the greenhouse "as if they had known each other all their lives"—and we hear not a word (142, 114). Undistracted by a "superfluity of dialogue," we can hear Giles say clearly "(without words), 'I'm damnably unhappy,'" and Dodge echo "'So am I,'" and Isa "'And I too'" ("Essay in Criticism" 91, *BTA* 176).

Recorded with the sharpness and clarity of actual talk, these ethereal conversations anticipate the pageant's most breathtaking sound effect at the moment the actors ("Children? Imps—elves—demons") skip and leap out of the bushes, flashing mirrors, tins, candlesticks, "Anything that's bright enough to reflect, presumably, ourselves," so that the spectators glimpse their own faces onstage by the broken wall (183). "What's more," as the narrator says, they hear themselves—and even see their thoughts embodied—as each actor "declaim[s] some phrase or fragment from their parts"—not least, that very important part, the audience (185). Earlier in the day, Giles mutters, "I fear I

The Play in the Sky of the Mind

am not in my perfect mind" watching Great Eliza come apart onstage (85); during the Victorian scene Mrs. Lynn Jones reflects on "something—not impure, that wasn't the word—but perhaps 'unhygienic' about the home" (174); Isa broods on the Whitehall rape, picks Old Man's Beard, and improvises a melodramatic apostrophe to a dagger ("'Plunge blade!'") for William in the greenhouse (113). Now, in the play's last scene, the actors echo, mime, and embody these unscripted moments in a sound-collage as mysterious as Chekhov's breaking string: "*I am not* (said one) *in my perfect mind....Home? Where the miner sweats, and the maiden faith is rudely strumpeted....Is that a dagger that I see before me?*" they chant, echoing the echoes of Shakespeare's *King Lear*, Sonnet 66, and *Macbeth* that have flitted through various characters' minds this afternoon, while "the girl in the Mall" and "the old man with a beard" dance out from the bushes with the rest (185).

How is this done? Has La Trobe, busy in the bushes during the Intervals, transcribed those "stray voices, voices without bodies, symbolical voices they seemed to her, half hearing, seeing nothing, but still, over the bushes, feeling invisible threads connect the bodiless voices" (151)? Does she direct her actors to catch the spectators' utterances and freely repeat them in this scene—to make their secret voices sound in this final chorus of aural mirrors? Or—since "She felt everything they felt"—does she somehow divine and give speech to her audience's inward voices, just as she hears "the first words" of next year's play the moment that Isa and Giles speak them (180, 212)?

Whatever her method, it is writ large by the narrator, for whom it is a small step from silent conversation to a collective voice; from the characters' inner voices to the audience's and even the pageant's. After the mirrors splinter the audience's longing for heroic spectacle ("a Grand Ensemble. Army; Navy; Union Jack;...the Church") while the braying megaphone urges them to rebuild civilization's broken wall, La Trobe's cacophony of voices culminates in music (179). As "Bach, Handel, Beethoven, Mozart or...merely a traditional tune?" rises from the gramophone in the outdoor theater, they wonder, "Was that voice ourselves? Scraps, orts, and fragments, are we, also, that?" (188-89). And when the gramophone asserts, "*Dispersed are we; who have come together. But...let us retain whatever made that harmony,*" "O let us, the audience echoe[s]..., keep together. For there is joy, sweet joy, in company" (196). As "ourselves," the music bodies forth Woolf's "philosophy" in her 1939-40 memoir "A Sketch of the Past" that "Hamlet or a Beethoven quartet is the truth about this vast mass that we call the world. But there is no Shakespeare, there is no Beethoven; certainly and emphatically there is no God; we are the words; we are the music; we are the thing itself" (*MOB* 72). Who speaks?—no "thick little ego" (in Clive Bell's phrase), no solitary, bounded mind, but the "we"

285

who are the words, the music, the thing itself (*Proust* 85). The gramophone gestures toward a greater music of the human voice and of the world, a music not merely heard but felt and imagined as that great unfathomable pattern or design to which the narrative attunes us.

In this voice too harmony and discord contend. As, instead of the hoped-for Grand Ensemble of Army, Navy, flag, and Church, the music bodies forth "the whole population of the mind's immeasurable profundity," the community, with the doom of sudden death hanging over them, affirms itself not in its univocality but in the inexhaustible differences without which no pattern, music, or "we" can exist (189). The music's inner voices now "strain[] asunder," now are "solved; united," made "whole"; now sound "On different levels ourselves" going "forward; flower gathering some on the surface," or "descending to wrestle with the meaning; but all comprehending; all enlisted" (189). Against the enforced univocality of totalitarianism, parodied and deconstructed by the megaphone, the music gathers up in its aural mirror a dialogic community, to which real differences, as Hannah Arendt says, are so much less dangerous than indifference; a community of spectators who enact a public "form of being together" where "no one rules and no one obeys," where people seek to "persuade each other" (113, 141). It is almost as if the pageant gives voice to the "we" Churchill vowed would "fight in the fields" against the Nazis' scapegoating perversion of community, at the same time that it bodies forth the outsider's wish to "give to England first what she desires of peace and freedom for the whole world."[8] Ephemeral as a cloud or play, perpetually moving between unity and dispersal, pageant and novel together listen for the meta-voice of that "rambling capricious but somehow unified whole," that "we" whose "hidden...pattern" embraces "all life, all art, all waifs & strays" (*D5* 135, 26 April 1938, *MOB* 72).

"What's more" (to borrow the narrator's phrase), even as the narrative voices silent speech beneath the sounds, it also, like Reverend Streatfield, "speak[s]...in another capacity," to which the "distant music" of twelve warplanes in formation that cuts his word in two draws attention (193). The "opp...portunity" (broken but mended with three ps) to "illuminat[e]...our dear old church" recalls the opp portunity to rebuild civilization's broken wall, staged in the last scene and urged by the megaphonic voice (193). As the warplanes cut through a word that a merely human voice ("I speak only as one of the audience, one of ourselves") completes around them, the question voiced at the end of the pageant reverberates: How rebuild the wall, a world laid ruin by war (192)? That question lingers and floats with the play in the sky of the mind, as when Lucy wonders whether civilization's fragile "blue thread," if broken here, might flourish elsewhere (205). Meanwhile, Isa, the privileged spectator

The Play in the Sky of the Mind

of this year's pageant, becomes the unwitting protagonist of next year's. As La Trobe listens in the pub (looking at a picture of a cow, but in fact standing close to the bull to let the truth pass her close once again), Isa and Giles speak the first words. And now we are the audience, that very important part; collaborators in the play. Will their speech, which is to say ours, be, as some readers think, mere repetition ("What a subject to talk about on a night like this!")? Or might it be the new speech to whose infinite possibilities the myriad speech acts—voiced and unvoiced, actual and potential—captured in the narrative attest? Woolf's last ending beckons her readers over the edge of the page toward an opp portunity that the violence of modern history continually interrupts yet can never completely foreclose.

Notes

[1] Woolf's 1925 short story "Together and Apart" also associates dialogue and conversation with the sky/meaning/mind metaphor: "The conversation began some minutes before anything was said, for both Mr Serle and Miss Anning looked at the sky and in both of their minds the sky went on pouring its meaning[,] though very differently[,] until the presence of Mr Serle by her side became so distinct to Miss Anning that she could not see the sky, simply, itself, any more, but the sky shored up by...Roderick Serle, and knowing how foolish it was, she yet felt impelled to say: 'What a beautiful night!' Foolish! Idiotically foolish" (*CSF* 189).

[2] When citing Woolf on Chekhov I keep her then-standard transliteration ("Tchekov"). See also Leonard Woolf's 1917 review of the short stories in Constance Garnett's translation, in *Chekhov: The Critical Heritage*, ed. Emeljanow, 162-64.

[3] *D2* 186, 26 July 1922. "[L]ooking very beautiful, tragic, and exalted," Sandra Wentworth Williams holds "a little book convenient for traveling—stories by Tchekov" (*JR* 141). Much later, Woolf noted in her diary that John Maynard Keynes (married to the Russian ballerina Lydia Lopokova) judged *The Years* her "best book," "very moving[;] more tender than any of my books," and thought that "one scene, E[leanor]. & Crosby, beats Tchekov's Cherry Orchard" (*D5* 77-78, 4 April 1937). The Woolfs had seen recent productions of *Uncle Vanya* and *The Three Sisters* and would dine with the director, Michel Saint-Denis, at Vanessa's the following year (*D5* 57 &n7, 128, 129n1; 18 February 1937, 10 March 1938).

[4] Cf. Woolf's 1940 essay "The Leaning Tower": "Literature is no one's private ground; literature is common ground. It is not cut up into nations; there are no wars there. Let us trespass freely and fearlessly and find our own way for ourselves. It is thus that literature will survive this war and cross the gulf—if commoners and outsiders like ourselves make that country our own country, if we teach ourselves how to read and to write, how to preserve and how to create" (*M* 154).

[5] *D5* 210, 22 March 1939. Woolf had missed Eliot's religious pageant play *The Rock* at Sadler's Wells (28 May-9 June 1934) because of flu, but she read it and—noting her "anti-religious bias"—was "disappointed" by its "cheap farce and Cockney dialogue and dogmatism" (*L5* 315, 10 July 1934).

⁶ As Woolf puts it in "The Leaning Tower," "We have got to teach ourselves to understand literature. Money is no longer going to do our thinking for us. Wealth will no longer decide who shall be taught.... [W]e must become critics because in future we are not going to leave writing to be done for us by a small class of well-to-do young men.... We are going to add our own experience, to make our own contribution. That is even more difficult. For that too we need to be critics" (*M* 152).

⁷ *BTA* 157, 179. *Pointz Hall* reads: "Mrs. Mayhew had sketched her own version of what was to be the conclusion. If she had written the words, she would have a splendid finale. The Army; the Navy; the King and Queen. Very likely that was what Miss La Trobe had planned" (Later Typescript, 401)—as if parodying the spirit promulgated by the modern English pageant master Anthony Parker: "on to the Finale. The Arena is a blaze of light as the Choir sings the Triumph Song in praise of the Pageant town and all its people. Group by group, the entire casts of all the Episodes enter, forming a great semi-circle of colour right across the Arena, with all their horsemen and all their flags and banners. Then there appear one or more symbolic figures, perhaps representing the Spirit of the Pageant Town, or perhaps the central figures of the Pageant itself. They speak some short verses in praise of the Past and looking with hope towards the Future, and leading up to the National Anthem, which is sung by all the players and the audience. Then, to the stirring music of the March Past, the whole of the performers pass in review before the stands, and our Pageant is over" (Parker 44-45).

⁸ Speech to the House of Commons, 4 June 1940, following the massive evacuation of Allied troops from Dunkirk (Churchill 713); Woolf, *Three Guineas* 109. J. H. Plumb cites British historian G. M. Trevelyan: "'Winston Churchill in his great war speeches made us all conscious of our past, as never before'" (32).

Works Cited

Arendt, Hannah. *Lectures on Kant's Political Philosophy*. Ed. with an interpretive essay by Ronald Beiner. Chicago: U of Chicago P, 1982.

Auerbach, Erich. *Mimesis: The Representation of Reality in Western Literature*. Trans. Willard R. Trask. 1946. Princeton: Princeton UP, 1953.

Bell, Clive. *Proust*. New York: Harcourt Brace Jovanovich, 1929.

Churchill, Winston. "We Shall Never Surrender (Speech to the House of Commons, 4 June 1940)," in *Churchill Speaks 1897-1963: Collected Speeches in Peace and War*, ed. Robert Rhodes James. New York: Barnes and Noble, 1998: 708-713.

Emeljanow, Victor, ed. *Chekhov: The Critical Heritage*. London: Routledge & Kegan Paul, 1981.

Parker, Anthony. *The Pageant*. London: Bodley Head, 1954.

Plumb, J. H. *G. M. Trevelyan*. London: Longman's, Green, 1951.

Woolf, Virginia. *Between the Acts*. 1941. New York: Harcourt Brace Jovanovich, 1969.

——. "The Cherry Orchard" (review). In *Chekhov: The Critical Heritage*, ed. Emeljanow. Reprinted from the *New Statesman*, 14 July 1920: 446.

——. *Complete Shorter Fiction*. 2nd ed. Edited by Susan Dick. New York: Harcourt Brace Jovanovich, 1989.

——. *Diary*. 5 vols. Edited by Anne Olivier Bell. New York: Harcourt Brace Jovanovich, 1977-84.

The Play in the Sky of the Mind

———. "An Essay in Criticism." Review of Ernest Hemingway's short stories *Men Without Women*. In *Granite and Rainbow: Essays*. New York: Harcourt Brace Jovanovich, 1958. Reprinted from the New York *Herald Tribune*, Sunday book section, 9 October 1927.
———. *Jacob's Room*. 1922. New York: Harcourt Brace Jovanovich, 1950.
———. "The Leaning Tower." 1940. *The Moment and Other Essays*. New York: Harcourt Brace Jovanovich, 1948.
———. *Letters*. 6 vols. Edited by Nigel Nicolson and Joanne Trautmann. New York: Harcourt Brace Jovanovich, 1975-1980.
———. *Moments of Being: Unpublished Autobiographical Writings*. 2nd ed. Edited by Jeanne Schulkind. New York: Harcourt Brace Jovanovich, 1985.
———. *Orlando*. 1928. New York: Harcourt Brace Jovanovich, 1956.
———. *Pointz Hall: The Earlier and Later Typescripts of Between the Acts*. Edited by Mitchell A. Leaska. New York: University Publications, 1983.
———. *Three Guineas*. 1938. New York: Harcourt Brace Jovanovich, 1966.
———. *The Voyage Out*. 1915. New York: Harcourt Brace Jovanovich, 1948.

Notes on Contributors

Galina Alekseeva (Candidate of Philology, Institute of World Literature, Russian Academy of Sciences, Moscow; Kennan Institute graduate, 1998, Washington DC; Fulbright Scholar, 2002-2003, New York U. S. A.), has authored a number of publications on Tolstoy and American writers, and on Tolstoy and English writers; she is editor and compiler of Volume 3 (in 2 books) of *The Annotated Bibliography of Tolstoy's Library at Yasnaya Polyana*, and Head of the Academic Research Department at the State Museum-Estate of Leo Tolstoy at Yasnaya Polyana (Tula).

AnneMarie Bantzinger is an independent scholar in The Netherlands who has been reading and studying Woolf since 1970. She is currently working on a study about the reception of Woolf's work in her country, and also trying to trace Leonard Woolf's ancestry and the Woolfs' footsteps in The Netherlands. Bantzinger has been a Montessori teacher since 1968, working in Hilversum, Amsterdam and Bilthoven, and from 1970-1972 at the Near North Montessori School in Chicago.

Julia Briggs is Professor of English Literature at De Montfort University, Leicester and an Emeritus Fellow of Hertford College, Oxford University. She is the author of a history of the ghost story, *Night Visitors* (1977), a study of renaissance literature in its historical context, *This Stage-Play World* (1983, revised 1997), and a biography of the children's writer *E. Nesbit : A Woman of Passion* (1987). She acted as general editor for thirteen volumes of Virginia Woolf reprinted in Penguin Classics, and is currently completing a major new study of Woolf, provisionally entitled, "A Life in Books," focused upon Woolf's writing process, to be published by Penguin in March 2005.

Myunghee Chung is Professor of English at Kookmin University in Seoul, Korea. As president of the Virginia Woolf Society of Korea she helped publish the first cooperative work, *The Complete Short Stories of Virginia Woolf*, and translated several short stories. She has also translated *Mrs. Dalloway* (1996), *Between the Acts* (2004), and Hermione Lee's *Virginia Woolf* (2001). Her written work is mostly focused on Woolf, but she has also written about Freud and feminism for journals in Korea such as *Feminist Studies in English Literature*, *Studies in Modern Fiction* and *James Joyce Journal*.

Woolf Across Cultures

Maria DiBattista is Professor of English and Comparative Literature at Princeton University. Her books include *The Fables of Anon: Virginia Woolf's Major Fiction, First Love: The Affections of Modern Fiction*, and, as co-editor and contributor, *High and Low Moderns: British Literature and Culture 1889-1939*. Her latest book is *Fast Talking Dames*, a study of American film comedy of the thirties and forties.

Deborah Epstein Nord is Professor of English at Princeton University, where she also teaches in the Program for the Study of Women and Gender. She is the author of *The Apprenticeship of Beatrice Webb* (1985), *Walking the Victorian Streets: Women, Representation, and the City* (1995), and numerous articles on Victorian literature, culture, and history. Most recently, she has edited a volume of John Ruskin's *Sesame and Lilies* as part of the "Rethinking the Western Tradition" series at Yale University Press. She is currently at work on a book about the Gypsy in the nineteenth-century imagination.

Peter Faulkner is an Honorary Fellow of the University of Exeter, having retired from the School of English there in 1998. He read English at Cambridge, and taught at the University of Durham before moving to Exeter. His publications include *William Morris, The Critical Heritage*, 1973; *Humanism in the English Novel*, 1976; *Modernism*, 1977; *Robert Bage*, 1979; *Angus Wilson, Mimic and Moralist*, 1980; *Against the Age: An Introduction to William Morris*, 1980; he edited *A Modernist Reader* in 1986, and, with Dr. Christopher Brooks, *The White Man's Burdens: An Anthology of British Poetry of the Empire* in 1996. He is the Honorary Secretary of the William Morris Society.

Christine Froula is Professor of English, Comparative Literature, and Gender Studies at Northwestern University. She is the author of *Virginia Woolf: War, Civilization and the Bloomsbury Avant-Garde* (Columbia University Press, forthcoming), *Modernism's Body: Sex, Culture, and Joyce* (Columbia, 1996), *To Write Paradise: Style and Error in Pound's Cantos* (Yale, 1984), *A Guide to Ezra Pound's Selected Poems* (New Directions, 1983), and other writings on interdisciplinary modernism, contemporary theory, and textual scholarship.

Mark Hussey is Professor of English, Women's & Gender Studies at Pace University in New York. Among his publications on Woolf are *The Singing of The Real World: The Philosophy of Virginia Woolf's Fiction*,

Notes on Contributors

Virginia Woolf and War, and *Virginia Woolf A to Z*. He is an editor of *Virginia Woolf Miscellany* and founding editor of *Woolf Studies Annual*.

Noriko Kubota is Professor of English literature at Tsuru University, Japan. She has published numerous articles and books on Jane Austen, George Eliot, and Virginia Woolf in Japan. She is a co-editor of *Igirisu Josei Sakka no Han-Seiki* (*Contemporary English Women Writers*), a series in five volumes (Tokyo: Keiso Shobo, 1999-2000). In this series, she wrote articles on Margaret Drabble, Barbara Pym, Jeanette Winterson, and A. S. Byatt. She is a co-translator of Elaine Showalter's *A Literature of Their Own* into Japanese (Tokyo: Misuzu Shobo, 1993). Currently she is engaged in editing a book on *Mrs. Dalloway*, which will be published in 2005 by Minerva Shobo in Japan.

Hogara Matsumoto is Senior Lecturer of English at Sophia University, Japan, where she teaches courses in Modernist literature, Women's Literature, and Post-Colonial Literature. She is working on a book based on her dissertation, "The Rhetoric of Otherness: Race, Gender, and Modernism in Virginia Woolf's Novels." Her current research interests center on the problems of intertextuality between the works of Virginia Woolf and her contemporaries, especially lesbian writers.

Makiko Minow-Pinkney is a senior lecturer in English at The Bolton Institute of Higher Education, UK, where she teaches courses on critical theory, feminist theory and women's writing and runs the MA course in English: Literary Modernism. She is author of *Virginia Woolf and the Problem of the Subject* (1987) as well as many articles and book chapters on Woolf, feminist theory, and modernism, including "Virginia Woolf and the Age of Motor Cars" (in *Virginia Woolf in the Age of Mechanical Reproduction*, 2000) and "Psychoanalytic Approaches" (in *Palgrave Advances in Virginia Woolf Studies*, forthcoming). Her current book project examines the construction of modernist subjectivity by investigating the intersections between Western modernism and Japanese modernization.

Natalya Morzhenkova (Kandidatskaya degree in philology [Ph.D], Russia) specializes in twentieth-century English literature. The main focus of her research and published essays is English modernist literature, particularly the writings of Virginia Woolf. She is currently a professor of the English language at Nizhny Novgorod State University of Architecture and Civil Engineering.

Woolf Across Cultures

Hee Jin Park is Professor Emeritus of Seoul National University and received her PhD from Indiana University (USA). She wrote a book on Virginia Woolf in 1994 and translated *To the Lighthouse* (1996) and *The Waves* (2004). She is now translating *Orlando*. She acts as advisor to the Virginia Woolf Society of Korea.

Natalia S. Povalyaeva (Candidate of Philology, Minsk, Republic of Belarus) has authored eight publications on twentieth-century English women's prose. Among them is *Polyphonic Prose of Virginia Woolf*. She is currently a teacher of English literature of the Victorian Age and twentieth century, and foreign literature of the turn of the nineteenth and twentieth centuries at the Foreign Literature Department, Belarusian State University. Her primary interest is English women's modern and contemporary prose and feminist criticism.

Natalya Reinhold (PhD in English, Exeter University, UK; Dr. of Philology, Moscow, Russia) has authored numerous publications on twentieth-century English literature, Comparative Studies, and Translation. Among them are *English Modernism: Psychological Prose*, published essays-cum-interviews with Iris Murdoch, Piers Paul Read, John Fowles and Martin Amis, translations of Virginia Woolf's essays on Russian writers and *A Room of One's Own*, literary criticism of T. S. Eliot, *The Good Soldier* by Ford Madox Ford, et al. She is currently head and professor of the Department for Translation Studies at the Russian State University of the Humanities in Moscow.

Marilyn Schwinn Smith is an independent scholar affiliated with Five Colleges, Inc. in Amherst, MA, where she is an occasional instructor and lecturer. She has presented papers internationally on Russian poet Marina Tsvetaeva and British novelist, Virginia Woolf. Most recently, Dr. Smith has served as coordinator of the Northampton Silk Project and as program coordinator of the 13th Annual Conference on Virginia Woolf, held at Smith College in June 2003. Her current research concerns the impact of imagination and reading on lives of achievement, focused primarily on Anne Morrow Lindbergh and Dr. Ruth Gruber.

Natalia Solovyova (Doctor of Philology, Lomonosov State University of Moscow, Russia) has numerous publications on twentieth-century English literature, Comparative studies, Pre-Romanticism and Romanticism to her name. Among them are *Traveling to the Country of Masterpieces*, *The Origin*

Notes on Contributors

of the English Romanticism, *English Preromanticism and the Rise of Romanticism*; she has also published essays on Virginia Woolf, A. S. Byatt, John Fowles, and Peter Ackroyd. She is a professor in the World Literature Department, Philological faculty, Lomonosov State University of Moscow.

Galina Yanovskaya (PhD in Philology, Kaliningrad State University, Russia) has authored numerous publications on twentieth-century English and Russian literature including articles on the problems of artistic consciousness of V. Nabokov, M. Tsvetaeva, and A. Tarkovskiy. Her most important publications are devoted to V. Woolf's works: the problems of organization of real communicative space and the communicative space of memory. She has also published on such phenomena as parenthesis, segmentation of narrative flow and structure of narration in Mrs. Dalloway. She is currently assistant professor in the Department for Foreign Literature and Journalism of Kaliningrad State University, Russia.

Maria Cândida Zamith Silva is a Research Member in the Institute of English Studies at the Faculdade de Letras da Universidade do Porto (Portugal), where she collaborates with a group of scholars who have undertaken to translate into Portuguese the complete dramatic works of Shakespeare, and where she taught, amongst other subjects, English Culture of the sixteenth to nineteenth centuries. Her main interest in literature concerns Virginia Woolf and the Bloomsbury Group. Her PhD thesis deals with Virginia Woolf and her attitude toward life.

Bilge Nihal Zileli was graduated from the department of Foreign Language Education at Middle East Technical University in 1997. She has been working in the same department at Middle East Technical University as a research assistant, and teaching several courses at the department for six years. She wrote her MA thesis on the concept of androgyny in Virginia Woolf's *Orlando*, *Mrs. Dalloway*, and *To the Lighthouse*, graduating in 2000. She is presently writing a PhD dissertation on the absurdity of the human condition in novels by Samuel Beckett and Albert Camus and expects to finish by the end of 2004.

Index

Adorno, Theodor 34
Aeschylus 88, 90
Aimone, Laura 59n
Akhmatova, Ann 11n
Albee, Edward 55, 99
Alden-Ward, May 253
Aldington, Richard 38, 40
Alekseeva, Galina xiii
Algemeen Dagblad 139
Alice in Wonderland 6
Allen, Walter 54
America: reception of Woolf in: 48-51, 100; Leslie Stephen and: 47; Woolf's attitude to: 47-48; women in: 63-4, 68-74
Amsterdam University Library 133
anadiplosis 261
androgyny [*see also A Room*] xiii, 39, 227f.; and *Orlando*: 194, 203f., 230f.
Annan, Noel 47
Arendt, Hannah 286
Aristophanes 27
Arsenyeva, Valeriya Vladimirovna 239, 243, 253
"Artist and Politics, The" 11n
Asso, Paulo 30n
asyndeton 267
Ataturk, Kemal 186-87
Atkins, Eileen 55
Attridge, Derek 43
Atwood, Margaret 57
Auden, W. H. 52
Auerbach, Erich 19-20, 23, 26, 33, 277
Austen, Jane 184, 265
Avery, Todd 42-43
Ayuso, Mónica 59n

Babel 83, 89
Baroque 267
Barreno, Maria Isabel 198
Barrett, Eileen 59n
Barrett, Michèle 55
Baudelaire, Charles 36, 82
Baudrillard, Jean 34
BBC 243
Beckett, Samuel 8, 33, 35
Beer, Gillian 107, 108
Begemann, Nienke 137, 138, 139
Bell, Angelica 267
Bell, Clive 53, 54, 59n, 184, 285
Bell, Michael 36
Bell, Quentin 49, 133, 137, 145n, 149, 150, 157
Bell, Vanessa 132, 179, 184, 287n
Benjamin, Walter xii, 34, 79f.,
Bennett, Arnold 66
Berg Collection *see* New York Public Library
Bergonzi, Bernard 33
Berman, Marshall 34
Besant, Walter 252
Between the Acts xiii, 48, 277f.; community in: 107; critics on: 95; doubleness in: 28-29; Englishness of: 98; LaTrobe's play in: 277, 279, 280-82, 285, 286-87; Mrs. Manresa in: 18, 284; narrative style of: 102; translations of: 99, 103, 114; and war: 106, 277, 286
Bhabha, Homi 154
Bible 82, 117
Black, Naomi 74n, 75n
Blake, Albert 257
Bloem, J. C. 133
Bloomsbury Group 2, 4, 42, 53-4, 99, 100, 154, 155, 156, 196, 215
Boebel, Charles 74n

297

Index

Booth, William 256
Bosch, Hieronymus 266
Botkin, V. P. 250
Braak, Menno ter 131, 132, 144n
Braddon, Mary (Mary Maxwell) 254
Bradshaw, David 40-41, 43
Bradshaw, Sir William 160, 272-73
Brantlinger, Patrick 42-43
Braque, Georges 215
Brecht, Bertholdt 35
Breughel, Peter 265, 266
Briggs, Julia ix, xiii, 48, 55, 106
Briscoe, Lily *see To the Lighthouse*
Brockney, James 134, 136
Brontë, Emily 88, 229, 250
Brooker, Peter 34, 35
Brookner, Anita 57
Brouwers, Marja 139
Browne, Sir Thomas 17
Brunt, Nini 134, 140
Bulgakov, V. F. 251
Buñuel, Luis 38
Burns, Christy L. 210-11
Byron, George Gordon 218, 251, 252

Caine, Hall 252
Campbell, Mary 196
Campos, Julieta 57
Canby, Henry Seidel 191
Cantor, Norman 37
Captain's Death Bed and Other Essays, The 5
Caramagno, Thomas C. 158
Carey, John 41
Carlyle, Thomas 245, 247n, 252-53, 257
Carpenter, Edward 255, 257
Carroll, J. B. 113
Case, Janet 185
censorship 2-3, 4

Cézanne, Paul 84
Chekhov, Anton ix, xiii, 3, 4, 85, 237; and *Between the Acts*: 277f.; "The Cherry Orchard": 21-23, 25, 278-79, 287n; short stories of: 277-78
"Cherry Orchard, The" *see* Chekhov, Anton
Chertkov, V. G. 253, 258
Childers, Mary 53
Childs, Donald 40
Childs, Peter 37-39, 43
Christ, Carol 70
Christian, Barbara 59n
Churchill, Winston 286, 288n
Cixous, Hélène 37
Clemençeau, Georges 186
Cobbe, Frances 256
Coleridge, Samuel Taylor 218, 228
Common Reader, The 67
Communist Manifesto, The 34
Conquest, Robert 10n
Conrad, Joseph 18, 38, 40, 43-44, 99
Constantinople xiii, 179f., 194, 217, 222, 231, 266-67
Constantinople (Sackville-West) 182
Coombes, B. L. 52
Cowley, Malcolm 19, 95
Cowper, William 228
Craik, Dinah 252
Cranach, Lucas 267
Critische Bulletin II 131
Cromwell, Oliver 252
Cuddy-Keane, Melba 43
Cunningham, Michael xiii, 54-6, 59n, 103, 111, 140, 269-70, 273-76
Curzon, Lord George 187

Daily Worker 52
Dalloway, Clarissa *see Mrs. Dalloway*
Dalloway, Elizabeth 230

Index

Daly, Mary 49
Darwin, Charles 37
Daugherty, Beth Rigel 59n
Davidson, John M. 257
Davitt, Michael 256
Davies, Margaret Llewelyn 47, 75n
Defoe, Daniel 251
De Groene Amsterdammer 139
DeKoven, Marianne 150-51, 161, 162
De Nieuwe 139
De Nieuwe Linie 136
Derrida, Jacques 81, 83, 84, 89, 92-3, 155, 161
Dettmar, Kevin 43
De Volkskrant 137
De Vrije Bladen 131
Dial 67
DiBattista, Maria ix, xii, xiv
Dickens, Charles 229, 249, 253
Dickinson, Emily 69
Dickinson, Violet 179, 192
différance 84, 155
Dinis, Júlio 193
Dos Passos, John 11n
Dostoevsky, Fyodor 3, 10n, 27, 88, 237, 245n, 246n
Druzhinin, A. V. 250
Dryden, John 117
Dubino, Jeanne ix,
Dubliners 1
Dubois, Pierre 136
DuPlessis, Rachel Blau 37
Durnovo, I. S. 253
Dworkin, Andrea 49
Dyck, A. van 267
Dymond, Jonathon 258

Eckerman, Johann Peter 240, 246n
Eco, Umberto 34
Edwards, Lee 73

Einstein, Albert 37
Eisenstein, Sergei 38
ekphrasis 197
Ellis, E. W. 251
Eliot, George 229, 250
Eliot, T. S. 33, 35, 36, 38, 39, 40, 42, 44, 54, 237, 280, 287n
Elizabethans 17-18, 28, 183-84, 219, 265, 266, 267
Empson, William 96, 102
Engels, Friedrich 52
"Essay in Criticism" 277-78, 282
eugenics 40-41
Euripides 29
Eyck, P. N. van 133

Farrar, Frederic 258
Faulkner, Peter ix, xii
Faulkner, William 36, 111
Feminine Mystique, The see Friedan, Betty
feminism 63-5, 68-74, 95, 98, 102-03, 156, 198-200
Fenollosa, Ernest 155, 163n
Fernald, Anne 59n
Ferrer, Daniel 50
Fielding, Henry 192, 252
Fitzgerald, F. Scott 36
Fleishman, Avrom 96, 97, 99, 102, 103, 105
Flush 7, 137, 167
Folios of New Writing 52
Ford, Ford Madox 36, 38
Forster, E. M. 1, 38, 44, 95-6, 97, 108n, 155
Forum (Netherlands) 131
Forum (England) 258
Fothergill, Anthony 33
Foucault, Michel 149, 157
Four Quartets 39

299

Index

Franken, Gerardine 139, 140, 141, 142
Freshwater 167
Freud, Sigmund 28, 37, 97, 108n, 233
Friedan, Betty xii, 63-4, 68-9, 70-4
Friedlender, Georgii 5, 11n
Friedman, Susan Stanford 57
Froula, Christine x, xiii
Fry, Roger 53, 184, 215
Fuentes, Carlos 34
Fujioka, Sakutaro 176

Galsworthy, John 228, 256
Garnett, Constance 239
Garnett, David 1, 10n
Gauguin, Paul 266
genbun itchi 94
Genieva, Ekaterina 5-6, 7-8
Genjii, Tale of 155-56, 163n, 170, 176n; influence on *Orlando* of: 156
Gilgamesh 195
Gilman, Charlotte Perkins 161
Girton College 227
Goethe, J. W. 242
Gogol, Nikolai V. 253
Goldenveiser, Aleksandr Borisovich 239-43, 246n, 247n
Goldsmith, Oliver 252
Golokhastov, P. D. 249
Gonçalves, Ruy 199
Gordon, Lyndall 179
Gorodetskii, Sergey 11n
Grand, Sarah 252
Greshnykh, V. I. 130n
Grootenboer, Doris 139
Gumiliov, Nikolai 11n

Haan, Jacques den 137
Habermas, Jürgen 34

Haggard, H. Rider 43
Haig, Alexander 258-59
Handley, William 53
Hardy, Thomas 38, 40, 88
Haunted House, A 138
Haywood, Eliza 108n
H. D. 35, 36, 38-39
Heady, Chene 66, 73
Heilbrun, Carolyn 57
Heine, Heinrich 252
Hemingway, Ernest 36, 277-78
Hengel, Mirjam va 138
Hensher, Philip 54
Het Finaciële Dagblad 138
Het Vaderland 134, 136
Hibberd, Dominic 40
Hirata, Hosea 80
Hite, Molly 55
Hitler, Adolf 72, 277
Hobson, J. A. 43
Hogarth Press 239, 240
Holmes, Oliver Wendell 47
Holst, A. Roland 133
Homer 27
Horowitz, Daniel 69, 72, 75n
Hours, The see Cunningham, Michael
"How Should One Read a Book?" 7, 42
Howard, Maureen 56
Hume, David 251
Hussey, Mark ix, xii, xiv, 30n, 191
Huyssens, Andreas 37
Huxley, Aldous 1, 10n,
Hydriotaphia 17

Index op Nederlandsche Periodieken van Algemeene Inhoud 131, 143
"Intellectual Status of Women, The" 66, 73, 74n

Index

International Virginia Woolf Society ix
Irigaray, Luce 161

Jacob's Room 8, 103, 261, 282, 283; and Chekhov: 278, 279; translations of: 139
Jakobson, Roman 91-2
James, Henry 18, 35, 38, 237
Jameson, Fredric 34
Japan 79-80, 93, 149, 151-53, 155-57, 162, 167f.
Jardine, Alice 37
Johnson, Barbara 81, 82
Johnson, Samuel 26, 228
Jonson, Ben 183-84
Joplin, Patricia 49
Joyce, James 1, 2, 7, 8, 10n, 18, 33, 36, 38, 44, 75n, 97, 98-9, 111, 130, 144n, 156
Juliana, Isabel 192

Kabuki 169
Kafka, Franz 7, 36
Kamiya, Miyeko xii, 149f.
Kamuf, Peggy 49, 50
Kaplan, Cora 52
Karatani, Kojin 93
Kawabata, Yasunari 176
Keats, John 228
Kenworthy, John 257, 259n
Keynes, J. M. 53, 287n
KGB 3
Kidd, Benjamin 256
Kidman, Nicole 55, 56
Kilman, Doris 271-72
Kingsford, Anna 258
Kingsley, Henry 252
Kipling, Rudyard 43, 228, 254
Klimt, Gustav 264

Korea: attitudes to feminism in: 98; graduate schools in: 98, 111; publishing in: 105, 114; reception of Woolf in: 98f.
Kosugi, Sei 157, 161
Koteliansky, S. S. 238-40, 246n
Kovtunova, I. I. 123
Kozlova Zaseka x
Kratkaia literaturnaia entisklopediia 5
Kristeva, Julia 34, 37, 90, 91
Kubota, Noriko xii
Kuin, J. 137
Kuzmin, Mikhail 11n

Lacan, Jacques 79, 89, 91
Lamb, Charles 228
LaTrobe, Miss *see Between the Acts*
Lawrence, D. H. 1, 2, 7, 33, 36, 38, 40, 99
Lawrence, T. E. 44
"Leaning Tower, The" 52, 58, 287n, 288n
Leavis, F. R. 33, 35, 47, 95, 98, 106
Leavis, Q. D. 52
Lederle, Mikhail 254
Lee, Hermione 50, 53, 55, 100, 107, 227, 230, 265
Lehmann, John 51, 277
Lemoine-Luccioni, Eugenie 174
Lenin State Library 5
Leopardi, Giacomo 252
"Letter to a Young Poet, A" 7
Levenson, Michael 36
Lewes, George Henry 250
"Lewis Carroll" 7
Lewis, Wyndham 36
Ley, James 253
Lindsay, Jack 4, 11n
Literaturnaia Rosiia 7

Index

Lloyd George, David 186
logocentrism 81
Lokke, Kari Elise 194
London, Bette 49
London Scene, The 139-40
Long, R. E. 249, 251
Lowell, Amy 156
Lowell, James Russell 47
Loy, Mina 36, 37
Lukács, Georg 5, 11n, 34, 86, 98
Lyotard, J.-F. 34
Lytton, Edward 254

Macaulay, Rose 38
Macaulay, Thomas 251
MacCarthy, Desmond 42, 66
Mackail, John 253
macro-text 261-62, 264
Madwoman in the Attic, The 153
Makovitsky, D. P. 252, 253, 256, 258
Mallarmé, Stephane 36, 123
Malraux, André 44
Mandela, Nelson 57
Mandelstam, Osip 6, 11n, 245, 248n
Mann, Thomas 44, 75n
Mansfield, Katherine 37, 38
Marcus, Jane 48, 51, 56
Marder, Herbert 207
Marinetti, Filippo 36
Marryat, Florence 252
Marshall, Paule 57
Martins, Rocha 192, 194
Marx, Karl 37, 52
Matisse, Henri 84, 215, 266
Maude, Aylmer 254
Maupassant, Guy de 277-78
Maurer, Alfy 84
Mayer, H. 132
McNeillie, Andrew xiv, 47
McNett, Jeanne 59n

McVicker, Jeanette 145n
Meireles, Cecília 198
Meisel, Perry 108n
Melville, Herman 88
Mendelsohn, Daniel 55-6
Meredith, George 27, 255
Mérimée, Prosper 277
Messer-Davidow, Ellen 51
Mew, Charlotte 37, 38
Meyer, Maaike 138
Mill, John Stuart 256
Millett, Kate 49
Milton, John 183, 228
Minow-Pinkney, Makiko xii, 154, 155
Mirsky, Dmitri 2-4, 6, 10n, 11n
Missis Dalloway 7
Mitz 132
"Modern Fiction" 27
modernism: 33-44, 91-2; criticism of: 84, 86; in England 80, 156; historical context of: 43, 44, 194, 215; incompleteness of form of: 87-8; in Japan: 79-80, 93, 151; poetics of: 264; Russian: 10n; Soviet view of, 5-6, 10n; subjectivity and: 151; translation and: 79, 85, 121f.,; and war: 39-40
"Modes and Manners of the Nineteenth Century" 247n
Moments of Being 139, 167
Monro, Harold 40
Moore, Marianne 36, 54
Morley College 52, 53
Morley, John 257
Morris, William 253
Morrison, Toni 57
Moscow ix, 19; publishing industry in, 2, 7-9
Moscow Arts Theater ix
"Mr. Bennett and Mrs. Brown" 92

Index

Mrs. Dalloway 7, 9, 39, 101, 144n; Clarissa in: 39, 64-6, 67-8, 185-86, 270-72; Constantinople in: 181; and *Feminine Mystique*: 63f.; film technique in: 38; and *The Hours*: 269-76.; Sally Set on in: 18, 272; Septimus Warren Smith in: 39, 74, 134, 272-73; translations of: 103, 114, 121f., 133-35, 167, 168; and war 39;
"Mrs. Dalloway in Bond Street" 66, 67; thoughts on death in: 73
Mrs. Dalloway's Party 138
Munro, Alice 57
Murasaki Shikibu *see Tale of Genji*
Murphy, Ann 59n
Mussolini, Benito 187

Nabokov, Vladimir 10n, 244
Nakamura, Shinichiro 156
Naremore, James 96-7, 103, 105, 141
"Narrow Bridge of Art, The" 88
National Literary Museum (The Hague) 134
Neefjes, Annemiek 139
Nelson-McDermott, Catherine 156
New Bearings in English Poetry 33
"New Biography, The" 188
Newnham College 227
New York Public Library 49
Nicholls, Peter 36
Nicolson, Ben 53, 182
Nicolson, Harold 181, 186-88
Nietzsche, Friedrich 37
Night and Day 103, 139
No Man's Land 38, 49, 175
Norton, Charles Eliot 47
novel 85-6, 87, 179, 223
Novyi Mir 7, 8

NRC-Handelsblad 134, 135, 136, 138, 139

Olsen, Tillie 52
"On Not Knowing Greek" 21, 23-24, 26-28, 88
Oorschot, G. A. van 134, 135
Oort, Dorinde van 134, 137
Open Society Institute xiv, 5, 8
Orlando [*see also* androgyny; Vita Sackville-West] xi, xii-xiii, ; and Constantinople 179, 217, 222-23, 266-67; English culture in: 138, 215-27, 233-34; European culture in: 264-66, 267-68; genesis of: 181, 188, 196; number symbolism in: 263and *A Room*: 198; translations of: 8, 9, 103, 135-36, 167-69, 198, 201, 204-05 ; triplicity in: 262-63; and Woolf as world writer: 17, 215
Orlando: in Constantinople: 179f., 217, 222-23, 227, 231, 266-67; credulity of: 22; as cultural hero: 261; and gypsies: 184, 205, 222-24, 230, 232-33; as poet 17-18, 195, 212-13, 215, 224; as trickster: 261; Vita Sackville-West and: 188, 203
Ormerod, Eleanor 67
Orwell, George 113
Osgood, C. E. 114-15
Othello 183, 196
ottepel 6, 11n

palimpsest technique 121, 123
Pargiters, The 70
Park, In-whan 111
Paris Peace Conference 182, 186
paronymic attraction 262

303

Index

Penn, William 258
Pepita, Rosina 182, 232, 234n
perestroika 1, 7, 8
Perron, Edgar du 131, 132, 144n
Pestana, Alice 199
Petavel, James William 258
phonocentrism 81
Picasso, Pablo 35, 215
Pilnyak, Boris 10n
poetry 88-9, 93
Poincaré, Raymond 187
Plenz, F. von 252
Porto, Manuela 200-01
Portrait of a Marriage 136
Post-Impressionism 84
Postma, Hannamieke 135
poststructuralism 81
Potter, Sally 195
Pound, Ezra 33, 35, 40, 44, 54, 155
"Professions for Women" 154
Proust, Marcel 44, 156, 228

Quiller-Couch, Arthur 183

Redford, Jean 35, 225n
Rado, Lisa 214
Roomful, Mamphela 57-8
Raverat, Jacques 90
reception *see* Woolf, Virginia
Reception of Virginia Woolf in Europe xi, 59n
Reinhold, Natalya xi, xiii, 10n, 143, 156
Return of the Soldier, The 39
Rhys, Jean 37
Rich, Adrienne 63, 74n
Richardson, Dorothy 35-36, 37
Richardson, Samuel 251
Rimbaud, Arthur 36, 266
Robberechts, Daniël 136, 137

Robertson, Frederick William 254
Robinson, Roxana 55
Roessel, David 181
Romanov, Panteleimon 10n
Rogat, Ellen Hawkes 49
Room of One's Own, A xii, 5, 8, 9, 18, 35, 39, 42, 44, 48, 49, 54, 72, 97, 102-03, 154, 179, 198, 238, 240; androgyny in: 212, 227-30; and feminism: 102-03, 198-200; translations of: 104, 114, 135, 167, 198
Roos, Elisabeth de 131, 132
Rose, Jacqueline 50
Rose, Phyllis 203, 207
Rostov, Nikolai 252
Ruotolo, Lucio 97
Ruskin, John 253, 257
Russ, Joanna 49
"Russian Point of View, The" 7, 21, 22, 24-25, 30n, 79, 85, 237, 244, 247n, 249

Sackville-West, Vita 133, 136, 181-82, 188, 193, 194, 196, 197-98, 203, 234n, 267
Said, Edward 43, 44
Santa Sofia 179-80, 181
Sapir, Edward 112
Sartre, Jean-Paul 7
Sasha (*Orlando*) 192-93, 195, 216-20, 263
Saussure, Ferdinand de 37
Schouten, Diny 138
Scott, Bonnie Kime 38
Scott, Walter 194, 250
Sedwick, Obadiah 251
"Sentimental Journey, The" 7
Shakespeare, Judith 97

304

Index

Shakespeare, William 27, 88, 183, 228, 251, 265, 285
Shaw, G. B. 40, 251, 254-55
shell-shock 39
Shelley, P. B. 182, 217, 218, 225n
Shklovsky, Viktor 91, 92
Silman, Tatiana 123
Silver, Brenda 48, 54, 97, 99-100, 105, 108
Simons, Wim 134, 136
Sinclair, John G. 251, 258
Sinclair, May 38
Sitwell, Edith 38
"Sketch of the Past, A" 89, 150, 158, 285
Smith, A. 251
Smith, Agnes 53, 59n
Smith, Marilyn Schwinn xii, 74n
Smith College 55, 63, 68-9, 70, 72, 74n, 75n
Smith, Septimus Warren *see Mrs. Dalloway*
Snaith, Anna 43, 59n,
Society of Outsiders 59n
Solzhenitsyn, A. I. 12n
Sontag, Susan 58
Spalding, Frances 55
Spanish Civil War 58
Spencer, Herbert 256
Spender, Stephen 19, 33, 34
Spivak, Gayatri 80, 91, 92, 93
Staley, Thomas F. 138
Stalinism 2-3, 4, 10n
Stanislawski, Constantin 279
Stassaert, Lucienne 139
Stein, Gertrude 36, 39, 84-5,
Stenich, Valentin Osipovich 11n
Stephen, J. K. ("Jim") 160
Stephen, Leslie xii, 47, 160, 182
Stephen, Thoby 158-59

Sterne, Laurence 27, 88, 228, 250, 265
Stevens, Wallace 36
Stimpson, Catherine 98
Storozhenko, N. I. 256
Strachey, Lytton 65, 66, 158, 184
Strakhov, N. N. 256, 258
Streep, Meryl 55
Supheert, Roselinde 132-33, 143
Suzuki, Yukio 168
Swift, Jonathan 247n, 251, 252
Sydney-Turner, Saxon 158

Talks with Tolstoi 239, 240
Tanabe, Seiko 176
Tawney, R. H. 52
Tchehov, Anton *see* Chekhov
Thackeray, William Makepeace 249, 253
Three Guineas xii, 18, 26, 44, 47, 50, 52, 53, 54, 57-8, 63, 69, 71, 73, 74, 107, 154, 207, 279 80; translations of: 104, 114, 138
Three Lives 84
Three Sisters 3, 287n
Times, The 47
Tischenko, F. 252
"Together and Apart" 287
Tolstaya, A. A. 250, 254
Tolstoi's Love Letters 239, 243
Tolstoy, Leo: 237; *Anna Karenin* 86 7; in *A Room*: 228; book collection of, xiii, 249f.; Lukács on: 86; theme in Woolf's work ix, 85, 88; translated by Woolf: 239f.
Tolstoy, Sergei 259n
To the Lighthouse xiii, 7, 8, 9, 57, 101, 179, 261; Constantinople in: 179-80; Lily Briscoe in: 89, 179, 230, 262; number symbolism in: 262;

Index

structure of: 180; translations of: 103, 114, 138, 167, 168;
Translation: goal of: 83, 156; limitations and problems of: 106-07, 114, 115, 121, 134f., 150, 155, 162, 204-05; studies xi, 10n, 113; theories of: 80-83, 114, 131; and translatability: 81-2, 92, 237-38; of Woolf in Japan: 79, 149, 155-57, 167-68; of Woolf in Korea: 103-05, 106, 113-18; of Woolf in The Netherlands: 133f.; of Woolf in Russia: 121f.
Trefusis, Violet 193
Trinh T. Minh-ha 49
Trollope, Anthony 249, 252
Trotter, Michael 36
Turgenev, I. S. 250
Turkey xiii, 172, 204-05, 222, 227, 230

Uncle Vanya 287n
United States *see* America
Usui, Masami 157-58, 160-61
Utrecht, University of 133, 143
Utrechts Dagblad 134
Utrechts Nieuwsblad 136

Veblen, Thorstein 52
Velleda, Maria 199
Venizelos, Eleutherios 186
Vestdijk Circle 132, 144n
Vestidjk, Simon 132
Vinrace, Rachel 56, 65, 70, 161, 183
"Virginia Woolf's Autobiography" *see* Kamiya, Miyeko
Virginia Woolf Out of Bounds x-xi,
Virginia Woolf Studies see Kamiya, Miyeko

Virginia Woolf Society of Korea 102, 103, 104-06, 107, 118
Vogelaar, J. F. 139
Vogue 156
Volkonsky, N. S. 251
Voprosy Literatury 5, 10n
Voyage Out, The 9, 65, 91, 139, 161, 167, 183, 283
Vrij Nederland 138, 139
Vygotskyi, L. S. 123

Waals-Nachenius, C. E. 135, 141
Waldrop, Rosemary 118
Waley, Arthur 155-56, 170, 176n
Walker, Alice 57
Walsh, Peter 270-71
Wang, Ban 154
Ward, Mary A. (Mrs. Humphry) 254
Warner, Sylvia Townsend 38
Waste Land, The 39
Watanabe, Shin-ichiro 176
Waves, The 9, 39, 42, 88, 90, 92, 101, 191, 280; translations of: 103, 114, 115-16, 139, 167, 168
Wells, H. G. 40, 41, 255-56
Welty, Eudora 56
Werk & Criterium 131
Wesseling, Elizabeth 194
West, Rebecca 38
Wheare, Jane 66
Whitman, Walt 58
Whitworth, Michael 41
Whorf, Benjamin Lee 112-13
"Why Art Today Follows Politics" 11n
Wickham, Anna 38
Wilde, Oscar 254
Wilkinson, Sarah 44
Williams, Howard 258
Williams, Raymond 34, 35, 53

Index

Williams, William Carlos 36
Wolff, Janet 38
Wollstonecraft, Mary 37, 199
women: [see also America] education of: 69-70, 71, 152-53; fear of intellect in: 99-100, 151; and modernism: 161
Women and Writing 138
Women's Co-Operative Guild 53
Woolf Across Cultures Symposium ix-x, xiv, 1, 17, 56, 131
Woolf, Leonard 48, 53, 105, 132, 158 59, 185, 239, 240, 247n, 287n
Woolf, Philip 48
Woolf, Virginia: attitude to strangeness of, 18, 162, 216; and class: 52-4; fear of: 99, 111; English reaction against: 47, 51-2, ; and European painting: 264; and Greek culture: 20-21, 27; and historical novel: 194; in Holland: 132; house image in works of: 261; on humor 22-23, 27, 28; as icon: 100-01, 102; mental illness of: 100, 152, 157, 159-60, 161; names in fiction of: 263; as outsider: 18, 279-80; poetics of: 261, 262-63, 267, 282; in Portugal: 191-2, 193; reception of ix, x, xi, xii, 1-9, 48, 95-108, 131f.; room image in works of: 261; Russian theme and influences in: xiii, 20-21, 80, 85, 215-17, 237f., 249; short fiction of: 104, 114; style of: 121f., 131, 154, 155, 162, 167, 238, 264; suicide of: 100, 111; translations of works of: xi, xii, 1-2, 7-9, 79, 103-04, 113-14, 198, 201; as translator: 237f.; traumatic experience of: 150, 157; and

women's movement: 50-51, 63-4; as world writer xi, 17-29, 108, 227
Wordsworth, William 226, 228
Workers Education Association 52
World War I 185
World War II 133, 140
Wright, Charles 256-57
Writer's Diary, A 53, 105, 136, 137, 149, 150, 157, 160, 242
Writing for Their Lives 38
Wycherly, William 27

Yasnaya Polyana ix, x, xiii, 249f.
Yates, Edmund 252
Years, The 47, 101, 111, 230, 287n
Yeats, W. B. 35, 38, 40, 44, 133, 155
Yonge, Charlotte 252
Young, Robert 258
Young, Robert J. C. 154
Yourcenar, Marguerite 115-16

Zaizingger, Jacob 267
Zamiatin, Yevgenii 10n,
Zhantieva, D. G. 11n
Zonneveld, Peter van 137
Zwerdling, Alex 52, 66, 73, 97, 107, 198
Zytaruk, George J. 11n

www.ingramcontent.com/pod-product-compliance
Lightning Source LLC
Chambersburg PA
CBHW021819300426
44114CB00009BA/240